Without Justice for All

Without Justice for All

The New Liberalism and Our Retreat from Racial Equality

edited by
Adolph Reed Jr.

Westview Press
A Member of the Perseus Books Group

Published in 1999 in the United States of America by Westview Press, 5500 Central Avenue, Boulder, Colorado 80301-2877, and in the United Kingdom by Westview Press, 12 Hid's Copse Road, Cumnor Hill, Oxford OX2 9JJ

Without justice for all : the new liberalism and our retreat from racial equality / edited by Adolph Reed Jr.
p. cm.
Includes bibliographical references and index.
ISBN 0-8133-2050-X (hc)
1. United States—Race relations. 2. United States—Politics and government—1993- . 3. United States—Social policy—1993- . 4. Racism—Political aspects—United States —History—20th century. 5. Afro-Americans—Civil rights—History—20th century. 6. Liberalism—United States—History—20th century. I. Reed, Aldolph L., 1947- .
E185.615.W57 1999
305.8'00973—dc21 98-49324
CIP

The paper used in this publication meets the requirements of the American National Standard for Permanence of Paper for Printed Library Materials Z39.48-1984.

10 9 8 7 6 5 4 3 2 1

To my comrades in the Chicago labor movement
and activist community, in gratitude
for all you've done for me and
all we've done together

Contents

Figures and Tables

Figures

Tables

Without Justice for All

Introduction: The New Liberal Orthodoxy on Race and Inequality

Adolph Reed Jr.

THIS BOOK COMES TOGETHER as a direct challenge to a rightward-tacking narrative that has gained currency in American liberal politics in general and the Democratic Party in particular. Partly spurred by Reaganism's success in the 1980s, this narrative has become an orthodoxy—if not a hegemonic ideology—in the 1990s. In this New Liberal orthodoxy, liberals and leftists have lost favor with the American electorate because they have moved away from the American people and have become too closely identified with "special interests." These special interests typically are held to include the labor movement, feminists, gays, secularists, civil libertarians, poor people, and nonwhite minorities, especially blacks. The punch line in this narrative is that restoring liberal, or Democratic, credibility requires establishing distance from these supposedly "marginal" constituencies and appealing to a "mainstream" American voter. In this context, mainstream means relatively well-off, white, and male, in some combination or another. Militant devotion to this mainstream is a symbolic meeting ground for several tendencies that rest uneasily within a Democratic Party that has become the institutional home of left-liberal politics since the decline of the activist movements of the 1960s.

From one direction, a neoliberal element would recast liberal politics along lines that break with the Keynesian pragmatism and pluralist public budgeting that has defined the liberal-progressive axis in American politics since the New Deal. This neoliberalism either trumpets the triumph of the market as the ultimate basis of social rationality or insists that challenging the market's hegemony is futilely impolitic, which amounts to the same thing. This strain therefore advocates reducing and privatizing public functions—or, in the Orwellian euphemism coined by David Osborne and operationalized by Vice President Al Gore, "reinventing government"—in service to a narrowly market-oriented notion of efficiency and an ideal of fiscal responsibility. Although this neoliberalism often includes support, or at least acceptance, of conventionally liberal stances on such "social issues" as abortion rights, gay rights, environmental protection, or even drug legalization, it retreats from downwardly redistributive social welfare policy, a disposition characteristically justified with a rhetoric stressing fiscal constraint, realpolitik, and the need to direct public policy toward encouraging personal responsibility or "choice."

From a second direction, a communitarian tendency similarly draws on the rhetoric of responsibility, though in service to a more actively coercive social vision. This vision is propelled by a commitment that public policy should enforce, or at least reinforce, putatively majoritarian values. Though it is less self-consciously technocratic than neoliberal critiques, the communitarian tendency is hardly averse to social engineering. Indeed, communitarians may exhibit a firmer faith than even the conventional left-liberals they denigrate that government action can produce specifically virtuous outcomes. Thus, communitarians see public policy as a vehicle for inculcating desired individual values and behavior and therefore often argue for such interventions as limiting income support for impoverished single parents and denying it to single teenaged parents, restricting access to abortion, and toughening divorce laws as mechanisms for strengthening families. The communitarian critique maintains that left-liberal politics has erred in not honoring majoritarian notions of virtue and desert and has alienated its natural base by coddling and rewarding those who fail to honor dominant norms. From this perspective, the draconian turn in criminal justice policy—for example, capital punishment, three-strikes provisions, mandatory sentencing, suspension of the Bill of Rights for residents of low-income public housing—and punitive social policy appeal both as deterrents and as signals of good faith to the heretofore affronted majority's sentiments.

From a third direction, a more familiar cohort of conservative, mainly southern Democrats has bristled at the left-egalitarian, socially liberal presence in the party all along. This source of tension goes back to the New Deal. Although the black electoral empowerment ensuing from the 1965 Voting Rights Act effectively bolstered the relatively moderate wing of the Democratic Party in the South by driving its most right-wing elements to the GOP, white southern Democratic elites have remained the party's most consistently conservative force. (In this context, after all, "relatively moderate" is defined in relation to reactionaries such as U.S. senators John Stennis and James Eastland in Mississippi, U.S. representative John Rarick and Governor John McKeithen in Louisiana, Georgia's governor Lester Maddox, and South Carolina's senator Strom Thurmond.)

In addition to concerns about black prominence, many conservative southern Democrats are disturbed by the rise of environmentalist, civil libertarian, gay rights, abortion rights, and other feminist constituencies within the party. Even "moderates"—a category mainly including those white Democrats who have adapted the familiar style of biracial brokerage politics to the new environment—express discomfiture that the Democrats command electoral support of only a minority among whites. (That this formulation does not beg questions as to why an electoral majority of *whites*, rather than a majority of the general electorate, should be seen as the standard of political health is a revealing aspect of the current discourse.)

This element of the Democratic coalition asserted itself conspicuously first in Jimmy Carter's candidacy, as Carter went on to become the most conservative Democratic president since Woodrow Wilson, at least up until then. Instructively, this was also the segment of the party from which the Democratic Leadership Council, the organizational and ideological center of the New Liberalism, sprang after Walter Mondale's defeat in the 1984 presidential campaign.

These three tendencies overlap programmatically, certainly, but they also differ significantly. Neoliberals are not necessarily concerned with directing public policy to inculcate virtue; their objectives run more toward greasing markets, and they are as likely as not to be libertarian on social issues that have no direct economic or budgetary consequences. Communitarians' notions of social compact at least leave space for assertions of corporations' obligations to the communities in which they operate, notions that appeal to neither neoliberals nor southern conservatives. And the latter's associations with a politics that is overtly antiegalitarian and authoritarian, and at least borderline racist, sexist, nativist, and homophobic, do not comport well with either neoliberals' or communitarians' intimations of progressive sensibilities.

Not unlike the Republican right's ostensibly unstable coalition of fiscal, social, and religious conservatives, the rather disparate tendencies that make up the New Liberalism cohere around a set of affectively resonant but fluid symbols and clearly identified common adversaries. A unifying programmatic rhetoric emphasizes the need for political flexibility based on pragmatic adjustment to the requirements of global economic competition and a changed national mood, criticizes the social movements of the 1960s for allegedly turning toward narrow identity politics, and calls for an agenda that supposedly reconnects with a traditional social base anchored among working-class and middle-class whites, who are depicted as social conservatives concerned with "bread-and-butter" or economic issues. The claim is that such a focus would facilitate re-creation of a broad, majoritarian coalition by deemphasizing potentially divisive, "hot-button" social issues associated with identity politics.

Of course, what neoliberals, southern conservatives, and communitarians mean by economic bread-and-butter issues often differs, particularly as the communitarian camp also extends to association with an at least nominal populism that sometimes approaches a class politics. In part, these differences are muted through nostalgic evocations of the "traditional" Democratic coalition that emerged around the New Deal as the model of a successfully majoritarian politics. They also are obscured by artifacts of that model: a presumptive elision of the distinction between economic growth and redistribution, the related presumption that stimulating private-sector growth contributes by definition to general social well-being, and a corollary that the benefits of such growth automatically filter equitably through the population, the shopworn faith that a "rising tide lifts all boats." Significantly, however, this nostalgia for the New Deal coalition overlooks its central commitment to the principle that government has an obligation to mobilize public resources to sustain the general welfare and to curb the excesses of private wealth and the injustices and irrationalities of the market.

The language of responsibility is central to resolving the New Liberalism's centrifugal tendencies. Communitarian and conservative briefs against conventional left-liberalism's "permissiveness" equally meld into calls to restore the balance between rights and responsibilities. Neoliberalism's market-based openness on social issues equally comports with the language of responsibility: The line on abortion rights is to be held for those who can afford to pay for them, out-of-wedlock childbearing should be tolerated only for women who can support the children on their own, and commitment to racial integration presumes class homogeneity.

What makes this language of responsibility so effective a rallying cry for the different strains of the New Liberalism, however, is that it is a subtly coded proxy for a more familiar racial discourse that centers on rejection of the pursuit of racial equality. Much as in the late nineteenth century, exhortations to retreat from the struggle against racial injustice have become both objective and pretext for a rightward shift in the ideological and programmatic consensus of liberal politics.

A century ago, in the wake of Reconstruction, liberal Republicans' defection from the cause of black freedpeople anchored a broader reaction against egalitarian political agendas. A proliferation of new scientistic theories justifying racial, gender, and class inequalities reflected and legitimized that shift. A consensus formed among elites that government did not have the capacity to secure blacks' civil rights, though it obviously did have the capacity to support railroad development and "pacify" the Native American population in the West. A discourse glorifying self-reliance and disparaging "dependence" spread through political debate and popular culture. Horatio Alger's stories of moral rectitude and character development exemplify that discourse most familiarly to us; it was also in that context and largely through that discourse that Booker T. Washington rose to prominence as an advocate of black self-help, which was a counsel of political quietism and acceptance of white supremacy.

A conciliationist wing of the Republican Party successfully agitated for a view that the party needed to shed its identification with the intrinsically divisive race issue and build a majoritarian consensus around an economic program. (As a formulation, the neutral-sounding "race issue" already marked a concession; it—then, as now—leaves space for an equivalence between the interests of advocates and foes of racial equality.) That strategy, proponents maintained, would serve blacks even better because removing their status from the limelight of political debate would make it possible to improve their condition without inflaming white opposition.

The U.S. Supreme Court undercut the legal apparatus of civil rights enforcement, arguing that such measures—for example, the 1875

Civil Rights Law—granted blacks unfair special advantages, and the Court shaped these arguments mainly through a formalistic rhetoric that was insistently abstracted from the specific facts of racial oppression in American politics either in general or at that historical moment. That is to say, the Court justified the proceeding attack on black Americans' civil rights by willfully overlooking social and political realities and appealing to what was in effect an abstract standard of color-blind justice. Moreover, white supremacist southern legislatures typically took care to craft their strategies of disfranchisement on similarly color-blind bases.

If this sounds eerily familiar, it should. Indeed, the parallels between racial reaction at this century's end and the last's grow steadily more striking and should give us pause as we are swept along with the New Liberalism's momentum. It has frequently been remarked that black Americans are the mine canaries for this society's social problems—first to be afflicted, as well as hardest hit, by structural change and inegalitarian initiatives and harbinger of the fate of others. To some extent, that unfortunate role is a function simply of blacks being one of the nation's poorest and most vulnerable populations, though black Americans' persistence in that status requires explanation. (The relentless recurrences of scientific racism are impelled by the will to explain that persisting inequality as a consequence of blacks' essential defectiveness.) To a greater extent, this role is the result of racial targeting, whether strategic or otherwise.

Using race—more specifically, opposition to blacks—as a foundation for political solidarity among whites who on that basis support policies and programs that might otherwise disadvantage them is a motif in American politics that can be traced back through the white supremacist consolidation in the South at the end of the nineteenth century, to the formation of the antebellum Jacksonian coalition, and all the way to Bacon's Rebellion in the 1670s. This history by itself should suffice to fuel skepticism regarding the New Liberalism's interpretation of the American realpolitik and the strategic and programmatic responses it proposes. That is certainly the perspective around which this book coheres.

The authors whose work makes up this book share the view that the New Liberalism is part of an emergent orthodoxy on race and inequality that is wrongheaded and intellectually inadequate, as well as dangerous and politically retrograde. The chapters that follow challenge the new orthodoxy's general features and provide an alternative account of the ways that racial stratification is built into the texture of American political life and public policy, including the New Deal coalition romanticized by many proponents of the New Liberalism as a race-transcendent, harmonious formation. The authors propose policy and strategic directions consistent with that account and argue concretely and forcefully for the need to maintain and expand the struggle against racial inequality as an element of a larger struggle against social injustice and for a more humane world.

Philip Klinkner examines Bill Clinton's career as an expression of the New Liberalism's emergence and concrete substance, demonstrating how the Clinton presidency exemplifies the mind-set and program of the New Liberalism in power. Indeed, an element of Clinton's political genius is that he has variously and simultaneously embodied each of the main strains—neoliberal, communitarian, and southern conservative—that constitute the New Liberalism's base. Micaela di Leonardo and Brett Williams, respectively, dissect two of the principal ideological mystifications that undergird the New Liberalism's prelapsarian narrative of political decline: the morality tale of racial/ethnic succession and the ideological use of the notion of family. Williams and di Leonardo debunk the culturalist premises on which those mystifications—which are by and large racialist arguments by proxy—rest. These authors present alternative interpretations grounded in a sophisticated examination of the empirical realities of contemporary American patterns of household and kinship organization and racial/ethnic stratification and their foundations in the dynamics of political economy and public policy.

Michael K. Brown lays out a critical overview of the racialized origins and basis of the segmented welfare state that emerged from the New Deal, and Dennis Judd provides a similarly fine-grained argument regarding the history of federal urban policy. Chapters by Mimi Abramovitz and Ann Withorn, and Larry Bennett and Adolph Reed Jr. examine instances of the New Liberalism's current approaches to social welfare and urban policy—the obscene debacle of the 1996 welfare reform and contemporary initiatives in urban redevelopment policy. Each of these chapters grounds analysis of the substance of the specific policy initiatives in a critique of its ideological and political foundations.

Stephen Steinberg rebuts those who argue that affirmative action is divisive or superfluous or that it does more harm than good. He demystifies the discussion around affirmative action policies to focus on the real problems they are designed to address. Alex Willingham similarly clarifies the terms of debate around voting rights enforcement and reaffirms the need for continued efforts to preserve and expand political participation.

Preston Smith and Willie Legette examine two of the most prominent manifestations of the current ideological environment within black politics. Smith dissects the rhetoric of self-help that has gained standing in black American political discourse and lays bare its conservative and quietistic roots and implications. Legette turns a critical lens toward the currently pervasive imagery of a special crisis among black males; he concludes, based on careful examination of the arguments of its proponents and assessment of socioeconomic conditions among black men and women, that the notion of a special *male* crisis is without justification except as a rationale for male priority in black political life and gender relations.

Finally, Rogers M. Smith presents a synoptic account of the recurring pattern of partial victories over racial inequality and reaction against that progress from the 1790s to the present, noting similarities between current arguments for turning away from the goal of equality and those evinced in earlier periods of reaction. He proposes a way to reformulate the warrants of liberal egalitarian politics on more positive theoretical and programmatic grounds that focus on guaranteeing all members of society access to the requirements for effective participation in its life and institutions.

As a group, these chapters take the New Liberalism apart, examine and expose its racialist underpinnings, content, and objectives, and they suggest ways to reorient the terms of political debate on grounds that both more accurately represent the dynamics shaping American life and presume an unambiguous commitment to egalitarian goals and values. The authors are united in the belief that this is an important and necessary intervention into a political discourse that takes an increasing human toll as it slides ever more to the right.

PART ONE

The New Orthodoxy on Race and Inequality

I

Bill Clinton and the Politics of the New Liberalism

Philip A. Klinkner

On May 2, 1997, President Bill Clinton spoke at the opening of the new memorial to Franklin D. Roosevelt. At this ceremony, Clinton praised FDR as "the greatest President" of this century for his belief in "the duty we owe to ourselves, to one another, to our beloved nation, and increasingly to our fellow travelers on this small planet."[1]

Yet only hours earlier, rather than honoring these very same duties, Bill Clinton had ignored them by agreeing to a balanced budget compromise with congressional Republicans. This agreement rested largely upon cuts in Medicare and Medicaid and included significant tax cuts, the bulk of which accrued to the richest Americans. The agreement built upon and extended the budget developed by Clinton and the Republicans the previous year, the most important aspect of which was the abolition of the federal guarantee of assistance to poor Americans under Aid to Families with Dependent Children, one of the central accomplishments of Roosevelt's New Deal. Together, these agreements almost exactly inverted the programmatic legacy of Roosevelt's New Deal by cutting programs for the poor and working class and providing tax cuts for the wealthy.[2] Thus, in one day Bill Clinton neatly symbolized the Democratic

I want to thank Rogers Smith for his assistance with this chapter.

Party's abandonment of the liberal legacy first forged by Franklin Roosevelt.[3]

This abandonment represented the culmination of the Democratic Party's "New Liberalism." Though presented in many different forms by many different voices, the central tenets of the New Liberalism claimed that the traditional liberalism espoused by the Democratic Party from the 1930s to the 1960s was no longer relevant or politically practical. Not only were traditional liberalism's economic policies unsuited for the market über alles ethos of the 1980s and 1990s, the New Liberals argued, but also liberalism's emphasis on equality and justice for all was increasingly unpopular and an affront to "traditional" values.

Although historically myopic and laced with selective biases both overt and covert, the New Liberalism had come to dominate Democratic Party politics and discourse by the late 1980s. Consequently, the advocates of the New Liberalism believed that the only way for the Democrats to win at the presidential level and to govern effectively was to shed their traditional support for and identification with the poor, the working class, and minorities and to reach out to disaffected whites and economic elites by moving to the right on issues such as crime, affirmative action, welfare, and economic justice.

In many ways, the ascent of the New Liberalism parallels the career of Bill Clinton. As governor of Arkansas, chair of the Democratic Leadership Council (DLC), presidential candidate, and president, Bill Clinton openly declared his belief in the New Liberalism and structured many of his political decisions and policy proposals around its basic precepts. In fact, Clinton's rise to the White House and his experience as president present a textbook example of the New Liberalism in practice. This chapter examines the association between Bill Clinton and the New Liberalism and in doing so analyzes the fundamental flaws in the ideology and political strategy of the New Liberalism.

Bill Clinton's association with the principles expounded by the New Liberalism stretches back to his 1980 defeat for reelection after one term as governor of Arkansas. By all accounts, the defeat was one of the most painful and important events in Clinton's political life, and from it he drew the lesson that he could not actively push a liberal agenda in the face of a dominantly conservative and racially polarized state. After returning to the governor's mansion in 1982,

Clinton recast himself into the moderate, "New South" image that has characterized him since. With his policies and governing style, he sought to walk a fine line among the state's various racial and economic groups. While pushing a limited number of ostensibly progressive programs, such as school reform (financed with a regressive sales tax), Clinton avidly supported the state's use of capital punishment, gave only lukewarm support to a failed effort at a state civil rights bill, and made sure that his tax and environmental policies were acceptable to Arkansas's business interests. All of this seemed designed to reassure Arkansas's whites that he was unwilling to challenge the state's economic and racial status quo.[4]

Clinton's strategy of racial and economic moderation proved successful in Arkansas and allowed him to move into the national political arena through the DLC. The DLC first began in the aftermath of Walter Mondale's loss in 1984, as several Democratic elected officials sought to create a conservative Democratic organization that not only would inoculate them from accusations that they were too liberal for their constituents, but also would serve as a vehicle to shift the party rightward. Although the DLC criticized traditional liberal Democrats on a range of issues, the topic of race was never far below the surface of its discussions. Few were as open as former LBJ aide Harry McPherson, who declared after Mondale's loss: "Blacks own the Democratic Party. . . . White Protestant male Democrats are an endangered species."[5] Nevertheless, many of those associated with the DLC believed that the Democrats had become beholden to various "special interests," usually perceived as blacks and other minorities, women, and gays and lesbians. These were precisely the terms the Reagan Republicans used to attack the Democratic Party.[6]

Criticizing the Democrats for their connection to special interests was rather ironic for the DLC, given its financial reliance on corporate lobbyists and political action committees. According to John Hale:

> The annual budget of the DLC's early years was around $500,000, much of it raised in large contributions from executives, lawyer, lobbyists, and other Democratic financial patrons supportive of the DLC's goals, and/or its early stalwarts. . . . The annual budget of the post-1988 institutionalized DLC pushed the $2 million mark, with corporate sponsorships bringing in substantial portions. Of 100 DLC "Sustaining Members" in 1991–92, 57 were corporations and another 12 were

professional or trade associations. The energy, health care, insurance, pharmaceutical, retail, and tobacco industries were all represented.[7]

The efforts of the DLC to back away from the Democrats' traditional concern for racial equality and economic justice are evident in its policy statements. Though ostensibly a rejection of both traditional liberalism and Reagan-Bush conservatism, the statements of the DLC often steered closer to the latter. According to one DLC missive, as a result of the Democrats' failings, "since the late 1960s, the public has come to associate liberalism with tax and spend policies that contradict the interests of average families; with welfare policies that foster dependence rather than self-reliance; with softness toward perpetrators of crime and indifference toward its victims; with ambivalence toward the assertion of American values and interests abroad; and with an adversarial stance toward mainstream moral and cultural values."[8] Moreover, the DLC often echoed conservative Republicans by emphasizing such code words as "law and order," "traditional values," and "personal responsibility."[9]

Much like the Republicans, the DLC also used white fears of racial equality to drum up support for its conservative economic policies. This was most evident during Clinton's tenure as DLC chair from 1990 to 1991. At their 1991 convention in Cleveland, DLC delegates, who included "lobbyists for several major corporations that helped underwrite the three-day gathering,"[10] took a page from George Bush's and David Duke's playbook and approved a platform plank opposing racial "quotas." Clinton claimed disingenuously that the statement was a "reaffirmation of civil rights and affirmative action."[11] To those who saw the statement as an effort to roll back the Democrats' commitment to racial equality, he offered the wan promise that as the DLC grew larger, their voices would ultimately be heard.

The relationship between Bill Clinton and the DLC was a symbiotic one. Clinton gained not only a national platform but also an alternative party structure and a corps of political and financial supporters from which to launch his eventual presidential bid. The DLC gained a political leader who could help to package and popularize its neoliberal policy positions. According to Al From, the DLC's executive director, "This guy [Clinton] understood the importance of values politics better than anybody else."[12] Most importantly, the

DLC gained a potential presidential candidate, someone who could serve as a vehicle for the DLC's message in the 1992 primaries and, hopefully, into the general election and the White House.[13]

Along with the DLC, Clinton sought to identify himself with several of the journalists-cum-analysts who during the late 1980s and early 1990s worked to lead the Democratic Party away from its traditional support for racial equality. Clinton often cited the work of E. J. Dionne and Thomas and Mary Edsall in his speeches.[14] Both Dionne and the Edsalls argued that the plight of the Democrats stemmed from their identification with special-interest politics and abandonment of white working class concerns.[15] Throughout the campaign, Clinton attempted unsuccessfully to solicit Dionne for political advice, and at one point early in the 1992 campaign Clinton characterized himself as the candidate best able to overcome the racial divide described by the Edsalls.[16] Clinton even went so far as to provide several supportive quotes and a book jacket blurb for journalist Peter Brown's *Minority Party,* a book whose racism is matched only by its astoundingly faulty analysis. According to Bill Clinton: "In *Minority Party,* Peter Brown argues that most middle class Americans who believe we Democrats care more about minorities and the poor than about them, are not racists, but are acting out of perceived self-interest. He offers a challenge to Americans that is worth listening to, and Democrats should listen."[17]

And listen Clinton did, structuring his presidential campaign along the pattern suggested by Brown and others who advocated that the Democrats retreat from their commitment to racial equality and comply with the fears and prejudices of conservative whites. Presenting himself as a "New Democrat," Clinton picked up on many of the terms used so effectively by the Republicans. His "New Covenant" offered government support in return for greater "personal responsibility." In particular, he promised to "end welfare as we know it." To those on welfare who "refuse" to work, Clinton warned, "we will do with you. We will not do for you."[18] The Clinton campaign, however, did little to combat the misperception that the major problems with welfare were chiefly those of irresponsible minority recipients, nor did it provide many suggestions as to how the country would "do with" those who lost public aid.

Furthermore, Clinton's policy appeals to conservative whites did not speak as loudly as the symbolism of his actions. In January

1992, in the crucial days before the New Hampshire primary and in the midst of the Gennifer Flowers contretemps, Clinton departed from the campaign trail to return to Arkansas for the execution of Rickey Ray Rector, a brain-damaged and mentally incapacitated black man. Clinton's return to Arkansas was not necessary, and the execution seemed charged with political calculation. It sent an unmistakable message to conservative whites that a President Clinton would have little sympathy for black criminals—even if, like Rector, they had the mental capacity of a child and no ability to understand their fate. (When asked if he wanted to finish his dessert at his last meal, Rector said he would save it for later.) As Democratic consultant David Garth described Clinton: "He put someone to death who had only part of a brain. You can't find them any tougher than that."[19]

During the Los Angeles riots, Clinton sent a similar signal by failing to make a strong statement. Instead, he merely echoed George Bush's law-and-order line. When Clinton did finally speak out about the riots, he denounced racism and racial divisions, but he also suggested that such divisions stemmed, in part, from "the culture of poverty" and dependency in the inner cities. That position was strikingly similar to the Bush administration's assertion that the riots resulted from "failed" Great Society programs.[20] Moreover, Clinton also expressed his understanding of the "fears" of whites who "have been scared for so long that they have fled to the suburbs of America to places like Simi Valley."[21] In so doing, he communicated not only his understanding but also his receptivity to the desires of whites to preserve many of the traditional racial arrangements they found comfortable.

All of this was but prologue to one of the defining moments of the Clinton campaign: his public feud with Jesse Jackson over the remarks of rap singer and activist Sister Souljah. In June 1992, Clinton used his address before Jackson's Rainbow Coalition to criticize the group for earlier giving a forum to Sister Souljah. In a newspaper interview after the Los Angeles riots, she had purportedly stated her belief that the violence was "wise" and that it was justified for blacks to kill whites.

Despite the claims of the Clinton campaign, the incident was not a spontaneous comment triggered by Clinton's conscience and revulsion at racial violence. Instead, it was part of a planned and deliberate strategy to reassure white voters of Clinton's toughness by attacking black extremism and alienating Jesse Jackson. Several points reinforce this assessment. First, Sister Souljah's claim that her effort to convey the views of black gang members was misquoted (which was met with great skepticism by the media) seems at least plausible, as the following transcript of the relevant part of her interview indicates:

> Q: *But even the people themselves who were perpetrating the violence, did they think it was wise? Was that wise reasoned action?*
>
> Sister Souljah: Yeah, it was wise. I mean, if black people kill black people every day, why not have a week and kill white people? You understand what I'm saying? In other words, white people, this government and that mayor were well aware of the fact that black people were dying every day in Los Angeles under gang violence. *So if you're a gang member and you would normally be killing somebody, why not kill a white person? Do you think that somebody thinks that white people are better, or above and beyond dying, when they would kill their own kind?* (Emphasis added)[22]

Here Sister Souljah appears to be putting herself in the mind of a gang member and contending not that she personally believed killing whites was wise, but that for those blacks who wrongly engage in killing, it makes at least as much sense for them to kill whites as blacks. Nevertheless, the opportunity in Sister Souljah's words appears to have been too good for the Clinton campaign to pass up through a charitable (or even accurate) reading.

Second, many of Clinton's advisers had been encouraging him to confront Jackson publicly in order to reassure white voters of his toughness with Democratic Party special interests. According to Bob Woodward, after the speech "Clinton told [campaign advisers Paul] Begala and [George] Stephanopoulos tersely, 'Well, you got your story.'"[23] Third, Clinton aides made sure to tip off several reporters that Clinton would use the occasion to distance himself from Jackson. Finally, Clinton originally intended to give a similar speech immediately after the Los Angeles riots but decided to wait for a more appropriate event.[24]

The response to his criticism of Sister Souljah and, implicitly, Jesse Jackson, was all that Clinton could have hoped. Republican polls indicated that 68 percent of the electorate were aware of the incident—twice the number who were aware of Clinton's economic plan. Moreover, whites approved of Clinton's statement by a three-to-one margin, whereas blacks disapproved by the same margin.[25] As one blue-collar white explained, "The day he told off that fucking Jackson is the day he got my vote."[26]

Clinton's attack also received prominent play from those journalists who were publicly calling for the Democrats to distance themselves from blacks. The day after Clinton's comments to the Rainbow Coalition, a *Washington Post* article by Tom Edsall, "Clinton Stuns Rainbow Coalition," appeared on the front page and covered twenty-five column-inches.[27] In contrast, a *New York Times* article by Gwen Ifill appeared on page thirty and received only sixteen column-inches under the less dramatic title of "Clinton at Jackson Meeting: Warmth, and Some Friction."[28] Follow-up articles and editorial commentaries on the incident tended to reflect the same biases by misinterpreting Sister Souljah's remarks, attacking Jesse Jackson's petulance, and reporting "biracial" support for Clinton's statement.[29] More broadly, Joe Klein, of *New York* magazine and *Newsweek,* praised Clinton's concern about, among other things, "the debilitating consequences of racial preference."[30] Sidney Blumenthal of the *New Republic* extolled Clinton as being at the center of the rethinking of liberalism that he dubbed the "Conversation."[31] Candidates, such as Iowa senator Tom Harkin, who advocated reinvigorating the Democrats' labor-left coalition were treated as anachronisms by the dominantly neoliberal press corps.

Though less dramatically than during the Sister Souljah incident, Bill Clinton spent the rest of the campaign reassuring conservative whites. By selecting Senator Albert Gore Jr. of Tennessee as his running mate, Clinton formed one of the most conservative Democratic tickets in living memory. As Andrew Hacker pointed out, the Democratic platform in 1992 was the first in a half century to make "no mention of redressing racial injustice."[32] In his campaign manifesto *Putting People First,* Clinton scarcely mentioned the word "race," other than opposing racial quotas.[33] The book devotes specific chapters to the interests of farmers, persons with AIDS, artists, children, the disabled, the elderly, veterans, and women, but none to blacks. And as Hacker points out, the "Civil Rights" chapter "devotes more space to biases based on physical disabilities and sexual preference than it does to race."[34] Campaign ads reinforced these policy positions. Clinton's second ad of the general election campaign touted his welfare reform plan. Another described Clinton and Gore as "a new generation of Democrats. . . . They don't think the way the old Democratic party did. They've called for an end to welfare as we know it. . . . They've sent a strong signal to criminals by supporting the death penalty."[35]

Clinton's strategy of ignoring or obscuring issues of racial equality appears to have had the desired effect. The Bush campaign was unable to use racial issues against Clinton in the same way that it had used Willie Horton against Michael Dukakis in 1988. Though Clinton's weak position on civil rights caused black turnout to drop, increased white support for the Democratic ticket more than offset black abstentions. Nevertheless, Clinton's increased competitiveness among whites seems to have resulted from Ross Perot's draining of white support from George Bush rather than from a surge in support for the Democrats. In 1988, Dukakis received 40 percent of the white vote. Four years later, Bill Clinton managed only 39 percent.[36] Overall, Clinton's 43 percent of the popular vote was 3 percentage points less than Dukakis's 46 percent. In the end, the best one can say of Clinton's gamble of offsetting lower black turnout with increased support among whites was that it worked only in the context of a three-way race. Furthermore, the 1992 results indicated that braver strategies might have succeeded with the right candidate. Clinton did not try to be that candidate.

After his election, he expressed a desire for a cabinet that "looks like America," but the key was "looks." Clinton's actual choices were a careful blend of women, minorities, and white men, few of whom (especially those in important cabinet positions) had the inclination or political stature to call for a strong liberal agenda. In fact, when women's groups called for the appointment of more women in his initial cabinet picks, he lashed out, calling them "bean counters" who were "playing quota games."[37]

Clinton reacted similarly when conservatives scurrilously attacked Lani Guinier, his first choice to head the Justice Department's Civil Rights Division. Conservatives pinned her with the racially charged label of "quota queen" for her views on voting rights, even though she actually proposed innovative ways to represent the interests of most blacks without race-conscious districting. Rather than answer these distorted caricatures of his old friend's views, Clinton unceremoniously withdrew her nomination. The position then sat empty for over a year, hindering the work of civil rights enforcement. Clinton's eventual appointee, Deval Patrick, did not find his boss any more supportive of that work. Patrick declined to appear with the president at Martin Luther King's Atlanta birthplace in January 1995 after finding out that Clinton would make no mention of civil rights.[38]

Though Clinton and other proponents of the New Liberalism had claimed that deemphasizing race was necessary for the Democrats to achieve more liberal economic policies, his first year's agenda offered little of the sort. Even though subsequent conventional wisdom claimed Clinton foolishly lurched to the left during that period, this assessment was mostly based on his quickly retracted endorsement of gays in the military. Clinton did propose a relatively small economic stimulus package, a portion of which was directed at inner cities, but he made only a halfhearted effort to cut off a successful Senate Republican filibuster of the package. He also reneged on his campaign promise of a middle-class tax cut in favor of deficit reduction, including a regressive hike in the gasoline tax. This strategy met with the approval of Federal Reserve chair Alan Greenspan and the bond market, but it did little to aid the Democratic Party's traditional constituencies. Though Clinton advocated health care reform, he rejected a progressive single-payer system and offered a "centrist" proposal that simultaneously confused the public, provided ammunition for Republican critics, disappointed liberals, and offered maximum influence and profits for large insurance companies. In November 1993, the administration pulled out all the stops to push the North American Free Trade Agreement (NAFTA) through a reluctant Congress, against the opposition of organized labor and most Democrats. Ironically, the same skill and effort had been nowhere seen during the filibuster of the economic stimulus package.

When liberals began to criticize him for these policy stands, Clinton once again responded angrily. During the NAFTA debate, he blasted the "real roughshod, muscle-bound tactics" of organized labor.[39] Later, an enraged Clinton told journalist William Greider, "I have fought more damn battles here for more things than any president has in 20 years, with the possible exception of Reagan's first budget, and not gotten one damn bit of credit from the knee-jerk liberal press, and I am sick and tired of it and you can put that in your damn article."[40] The fact that these battles were rarely on behalf of liberal measures, and none were efforts to promote racial equality, did not seem relevant to the president.

At the end of his first year in office, President Clinton visited Memphis to address a gathering of black ministers at the same church where Martin Luther King had given his last sermon. Though purporting to honor the memory of King, Clinton abandoned his spirit. King, who had come to Memphis in 1968 to help organize black sanitation workers, saw the crucial role of economic injustice in the plight of black Americans, but no mention of this appeared in the president's speech. Instead, Clinton used the event to stress that there was little the government could or should do to help reduce inequality. The problem resulted not so much from racism or economic injustice as from a lack of personal "responsibility" and violent behavior on the part of many blacks and poor people. Furthermore, the president made the curious assertion that such matters as broken families, illegitimacy, teen births, and crime by blacks were fundamentally an "abuse" of the freedom won by King and the civil rights movement.[41] In doing so, the president sounded less like King than like the opponents of Reconstruction who had claimed that blacks were unable to handle their new freedom.

In 1994, Clinton, burdened by more in a career-long series of allegations regarding his own lack of "personal responsibility" (both personal and financial), seemed strangely inactive as his health care reform proposal sank on Capitol Hill. A combination of special-interest demagoguery and Republican opposition destroyed his most progressive policy proposal. In contrast, Clinton was not passive in the fight over the 1994 crime bill. Among other things, this legislation funded extensive construction of new prisons and expanded the death penalty without providing a mechanism to make sure that it would not be used in a racially discriminatory fashion.

After losing a close procedural vote in the House, the president quickly hit the hustings. In one of a series of speeches, he asked a group of black ministers (seemingly Clinton's audience of choice when seeking to revive his political fortunes) to pray for passage of the bill—something he had not suggested for economic aid to inner cities.[42] In another speech, again to black ministers, he argued that the crime bill was necessary because "there's a disproportionate number of black kids in those pine boxes."[43] Clinton's logic suggested a gruesome trade-off—save the lives of some blacks by passing a bill that would likely put more blacks to death. Eventually, the bill passed, but only after the president compromised with Republicans by shifting it even more from crime prevention to expanded policing and incarceration.

Clinton's conservative posturing proved to no avail. Unable or unwilling to offer a progressive program that would constructively address voters' economic anxieties, their disgust with corrupt campaign finances, or their worries about racial change, Clinton and the Democrats were repudiated in the 1994 election. They lost fifty-four seats in the House, eight in the Senate, and control of Congress for the first time since 1952. In fact, Clinton's various moves to the middle may have hurt more than helped in 1994. Between 1990 and 1994, voter turnout among those making $50,000 a year or more rose from 59.2 percent to 60.1 percent, but turnout among those making under $5,000 fell from 32.2 percent to 19.9 percent, and from 30.9 percent to 23.3 percent for those making between $5,000 and $10,000. In addition, whereas white turnout rose slightly, from 46.7 percent in 1990 to 46.9 percent in 1994, black turnout fell from 39.2 percent to 37 percent and Hispanic turnout from 23.1 percent to 19.1 percent.[44]

Following the 1994 election, those calling for the Democrats to further distance themselves from civil rights and anything that might be associated in the public mind with racial minorities were in full cry. Soon after the election, the December 5, 1994, *New Republic* ran the following cover:

> THEY BLEW IT
>
> The fundamental STRATEGIC MISTAKE of the CLINTON PRESIDENCY is now clear. If President Clinton had pushed for WELFARE REFORM rather than HEALTH CARE REFORM in 1994, we would now be talking about a great DEMOCRATIC REALIGNMENT, rather than a great REPUBLICAN REALIGNMENT.

In the follow-up article, journalist Mickey Kaus fantasized: "Imagine how the midterm election might have looked if Clinton had spent 1994 pushing his tough, popular proposal—standing up to the Congressional Black Caucus, fighting off paleoliberals and neoconservatives, overcoming gridlock, in general showing he is the forceful leader voters have now concluded he's not. Imagine . . . oh, it's too depressing."[45] Strikingly, Kaus chose the Congressional Black Caucus as the principal target for a presidential display of toughness, insisting that this path would make Clinton more "popular." In *Newsweek,* Joe Klein tried to out-Gingrich Newt Gingrich by suggesting that "liberalism" could survive only if it buried the "counterculture McGovernickism" that consisted of an "alliance" between "left-wing elitists" and the dreaded "black underclass."[46]

Clinton took these warnings to heart. Under the advice of Republican consultant Dick Morris, whose previous clients included Jesse Helms, Clinton followed a policy of "triangulation" in 1995–1996 by attempting to distance himself from both the Republicans and traditional liberal Democrats. The ensuing triangle was not an equilateral one, as Clinton positioned himself much more closely to Gingrich and the Republicans than to liberal Democrats. After all the months of political posturing and government shutdowns, Clinton and the Republican leadership in Congress agreed to settle their differences on the budget—largely on the backs of the poor, minorities, and immigrants. A report by the Center on Budget and Policy Priorities found that programs for the poor made up only 23 percent of the nondefense budget but accounted for over 50 percent of the reductions enacted during the 104th Congress (1995–1996).[47]

The most significant piece of legislation passed during the 104th Congress was the Welfare Reform Act of 1996. The most important feature of this legislation was its abandonment of the federal government's guarantee of assistance to poor families, first tendered six decades earlier during Franklin Roosevelt's New Deal. Welfare is now left to the state governments, assisted—for the time being—with block grants from the federal government. By shifting this responsibility to the states, the legislation ignored the history of abusive and racist welfare policies in many states. Furthermore, the new system raises the possibility of a "race to the bottom" as states compete with one another to cut welfare benefits as a way of reducing caseloads and demands on public funds. Finally, the legislation installs work requirements for recipients but does little to provide adequate resources for the job training, transportation, and child care necessary for those on welfare to find meaningful work while raising their children.

Though the Welfare Reform Act was largely the creation of a Republican Congress, Bill Clinton nonetheless rightly claims much of the responsibility for this legislation, making his efforts to distance himself from some of its features debatable. Seeking in 1992 to inoculate himself from charges that he was too much of a traditional liberal, Clinton famously set the agenda by declaring that he would "end welfare as we know it." As a Democrat attacking welfare, Clinton succeeded only in shifting the welfare policy debate even further to the right. Not surprisingly, Republicans quickly responded by coming up with their own even more Dickensian welfare overhaul plans. As the 1996 election loomed, Clinton was forced to sign a bill that even he acknowledged was excessively punitive, lest he be seen as too liberal on the issue, even though he was then leading Bob Dole by large margins in nearly every poll. Nor is the record of the congressional Democrats any better, since a majority of them supported the legislation. Among Democratic senators running for reelection in 1996, only Paul Wellstone of Minnesota had the courage to oppose the bill. He won handily that November.[48]

Since the passage of this legislation, supporters have pointed to a sharp drop in welfare caseloads. Such declines have indeed been impressive in some areas, but the number of people on welfare had been declining even before the passage of the law. Additionally, this drop in welfare cases comes during what is perhaps the best job market in over twenty years. The true test of a safety net comes when people are falling. Therefore, the verdict remains out on the new legislation until the next economic downturn. Even with a booming economy, recent reports by several private charities noted a sharp upturn in those seeking assistance from food kitchens and homeless shelters. Furthermore, the new law's two-year time limit for assistance has yet to expire, leaving open the question of what will happen to those who are unable to find work once their support is cut off.[49]

Clinton proved almost equally impotent when it came to protecting affirmative action from conservative attacks in Congress, the courts, and the states. Though his policy of "Mend it; don't end it" upheld the basic goals of affirmative action, Clinton agreed there were serious problems with some existing policies and vowed to eliminate any program that "creates a quota, creates preferences for unqualified individuals, creates reverse discrimination or continues even after its equal opportunity purposes have been achieved."[50] Since, rightly or wrongly, critics were making those charges against virtually every form of affirmative action, it was not clear what forms the president actually supported.

During the 1996 election campaign, Clinton sounded an even more defensive note. In his election year tract, he focused more on the failures and abuses of affirmative action than on its strengths.[51] The same was true during one of the presidential debates. When asked about affirmative action, Clinton proudly asserted: "I've done more to eliminate programs—affirmative action programs—I didn't think were fair. And to tighten others up than my predecessors have since affirmative action's been around."[52] He also referred only to affirmative action efforts to aid women without explicitly mentioning racial minorities. In addition, despite the fact that he was running well ahead of Dole in the state, Clinton refused to take a strong stand against the perversely named California Civil Rights Initiative, which called for an end to all state-sponsored affirmative action programs. He criticized it sharply only after the election.

Though he won reelection, Clinton's victory was hardly a triumph for the New Liberalism. In an analysis of the election results, Ruy Teixeira demonstrates that the increase in Democratic support from 1994 to 1996 came not from upper-income and highly educated suburban voters long targeted by the New Liberals, but rather from traditional Democrats at the lower ends of the class scale concerned with those issues identified with traditional liberalism—jobs, Social Security, Medicare, and education.[53]

Whatever the reasons for Clinton's victory, it was a rather hollow triumph. Modeled directly on Ronald Reagan's 1984 "Morning in America" campaign, Clinton's reelection effort set out hardly any second term agenda and certainly not a liberal one. Eschewing any major programmatic initiatives in his second term, he seems to have settled on a strategy of emphasizing small and mostly symbolic mini-issues, such as school uniforms, youth curfews, and ad campaigns against teen smoking and drug use. Although a few of these initiatives contain some merit, such as ensuring a minimum forty-eight-hour hospital stay for women giving birth, they do little, if anything, to meet the challenges of racism, growing economic inequality, and the increasing powerlessness of the poor and working classes. Even if Clinton had the willingness to push a more liberal agenda, his ability to do so has been gravely weakened by the scandals that have plagued his second term.

These scandals are not unrelated to Clinton's New Liberalism. By abandoning its traditional bases of support in party organizations, labor unions, community groups, and civil rights organizations, Clinton and other proponents of the New Liberalism have been forced to look elsewhere for the resources necessary to contest elections. Increasingly, this has meant corporate and other special-interest donations. In turn, the reliance on these donations has made it even easier, if not downright necessary, for the Democrats to jettison their traditional liberalism. Thus, Clinton and the Democratic Party's unseemly and perhaps even illegal fund-raising efforts in 1996 can be viewed as a direct outgrowth of the their embrace of the New Liberalism. Even, oddly enough, the Monica Lewinsky scandal reflects on Clinton's New Liberalism. Amid all of the salacious details of the scandal, few have noticed the rank hypocrisy involved. After all, a central theme of Bill Clinton's national political career and of the New Liberalism more generally has been to preach the necessity of exercising "personal responsibility." This, of course, suggests that such statements were not principled credos but only so much political posturing.

Despite a rather unimpressive record on civil rights, brightened only by the fact that he is more liberal than the now thoroughly southernized Republicans, Bill Clinton maintains an image of himself as a racial healer. As he began his second term, President Clinton sought to use the issue of race as a way to burnish for the history books the thus far less-than-awe-inspiring accomplishments of his presidency.

To this end, in June 1997 Bill Clinton announced his Presidential Initiative on Race. The key aspect of this initiative was the appointment of a presidential commission on race relations. Though the president selected several thoughtful and respected individuals to form the commission, most notably his choice of the eminent historian John Hope Franklin as chair, the effort has amounted to little. When the committee submitted its report in September 1998, it was conspicuously lacking in substantive proposals, as seems to have been the intention of the Clinton White House. "There is timidity on this question," commented Thomas Kean, a member of the panel and a former Republican governor of New Jersey. "Race is very divisive. As the year wore on, people became—not the board, but people in the Administration—became concerned. We were not encouraged to be bold. My recommendation was much bolder than anything contained in this report."[54] At best, the initiative provided an ineffective but benign way for Clinton to play the role of therapist in chief. Rather than attempting the more controversial and expensive effort of putting forth substantive policies to deal with the continuing impact of racial exclusion and discrimination, the initiative allowed Clinton a low-cost way to create the impression of concern and action.

Yet the costs may not be so low. At worst, the president's race initiative offered a distraction from the fact that he, the Democratic Party, and the nation in general have sounded an end to the modern era of civil rights reform. In his speeches on the subject, President Clinton has repeatedly stressed that the answer to the nation's racial problems requires not positive governmental action, but a change in the hearts and habits of individual Americans. "We have torn down the barriers in our laws," proclaims Clinton. "Now we must break down the barriers in our lives, our minds and our hearts."[55]

These words have an eerily familiar ring. In the late nineteenth and early twentieth centuries, Republican presidents, then representing the liberal party on race, maintained a rhetorical sympathy for equal rights but disparaged any effort by the government to achieve them. Such views were also espoused by "progressive" Democrats of the era. As the limited scope of his race initiative has become clear, Clinton has expressed admiration for these very leaders. He has suggested that Rutherford B. Hayes and Grover Cleveland were progressive reformers who are today underappreciated; they were, he believes, combating bigotry and economic injustices as much as was possible in their circumstances.[56]

Perhaps Bill Clinton is right that we live in a time of conservative ascendancy. But by tailoring the politics of his administration and of the Democratic Party to this conservatism, Clinton has not so much fought it as he has legitimated and perpetuated it. Furthermore, by advancing such a minimalist and conservative agenda, Clinton and other advocates of the New Liberalism are ignoring the best traditions of the Democratic Party and the needs of its potential coalition.

Throughout much of the history of the Democratic Party, especially from the 1930s to the 1960s, it has, albeit imperfectly, represented the interests of those disadvantaged by the status quo. Thus, the party's reason for being was to advocate programs and policies that challenged, rather than accommodated, the status quo. Not all of these efforts succeeded, but even when they did not, the party still managed to offer a distinctive vision for itself and to hope for future successes.

Such visionary leadership is the reason that Franklin Roosevelt is now honored with a monument, whereas such presidents as Benjamin Harrison and Grover Cleveland are remembered only as mediocrities who failed to challenge the status quo and thus did nothing to advance the nation's welfare. Though only time will tell, it seems likely that Bill Clinton's presidency will be remembered among the latter.

2

"Why Can't They Be Like Our Grandparents?" and Other Racial Fairy Tales

Micaela di Leonardo

THE CITY ON THE HILL has always willfully confused race with righteousness. Since the Puritans' arrival, dominant American political narratives have emphasized the differential moral worth of racial/ethnic populations: whites versus Native Americans, Yankees versus Irish, planters versus slaves, native-born whites versus "the refuse of Europe," and, on the West Coast, whites versus Mexicans and Asians. During the 1970s, the dominant morality play claimed to represent the United States with three characters—well-off WASPs, working-class white ethnics, and poor blacks (dealing Latinos, Asians, and Native Americans out of the game). In this version of "Goldilocks and the Three Bears," Goldilocks (the zeitgeist) rejects the first chair and porridge (WASPs) as too hard, cold, and sexless and the second (blacks) as too hot, irresponsible, and oversexed. The golden mean, Baby Bear's choice, is white ethnics—warmer, more family and community oriented than WASPs, but not "disorganized" and "savage" like blacks.

Portions of this chapter have appeared as "Habits of the Cumbered Heart: White Ethnic Community and Women's Culture as Invented Traditions," in William Roseberry and Jay O'Brien, eds., *Golden Ages, Dark Ages: Imagining the Past in Anthropology and History* (Berkeley and Los Angeles: University of California Press, 1992), 234–252.

This Puritanical inheritance has been transformed, however, in the current climate of center-right convergence in national politics and in the process has lost its overtly racist character. But the raced narrative still lurks, pentimento-fashion, beneath the new platitudes of the "era of limits," of communitarianism, of the need for a rebirth of values, of the "politics of meaning." In what follows, I illuminate both new and old paint and trace their historical and political interrelations. I first lay out the "impulse to cumber" in contemporary political discourse, then return to the Three Bears to consider the actual political-economic ground from which notions of white ethnicity arose. As we see, engaging in some detail with the politics of the 1970s gives us the prehistory of the politics of meaning, a sense of the genealogy of the contemporary usage of "community," "rights," and "responsibility." And this genealogy is key to the rise of communitarianism and thus to the ideological knot at the center of the Democratic Leadership Council, Bill Clinton's original electoral springboard and the source of the contemporary convergence between the Republican and Democratic Parties. To clarify this overpainting, I briefly spotlight two related contemporary political constructions, "women's culture" and the "urban underclass," and lay out their relation to the larger canvas.

Recent writing on the American temperament portrays contemporary U.S. citizens as a people without traditions, except perhaps the tradition of invented and individualizing social orders. Thus, Frances Fitzgerald chooses recently established communities with narrow membership criteria—an affluent white retirement development, a Christian cult, San Francisco's gay neighborhoods—as exemplars of a broad-scale and continuous American turn against both the past and the larger society in attempts to establish utopian orders for a narrow elect.[1] Allan Bloom excoriates American popular culture, and thus America's young, as vulgar, traditionless, and not uncoincidentally subject to the illogical and unnatural "fads" of leftist and feminist thought and action.[2] On the other end of the political spectrum, Russell Jacoby deplores the dying off of an early-to-mid-twentieth-century tradition of American public intellectual life and the retreat of radical intellectuals into an arid and hermetic scholasticism.[3] Finally, and most instructively, Robert Bellah and his coauthors in their multiple-interview study *Habits of the Heart,* and in the subsequent *The Good Society,* determine that Americans primarily conceive the self as unencumbered by dependent others, by community obligations, by institutions, by history.[4] These authors' analysis underscores current images of protean American individualism, and the Bellah group has endorsed a new communitarian political movement calling for mandated "encumbering"(about which more follows).

Habits typifies recent evaluations of American cultural perceptions in other ways as well. The unencumbered selves—such as those making use of "therapeutic" or "managerial" modes of apprehending reality with which the authors find their informants struggling and which the authors wish to adjure us to discard—significantly are white, male, and middle class. This narrow conception of American selfhood is unsurprising when we consider both the authors' demographically skewed choice of interviewees and the prototypically elite primary historical "American Studies" texts to which they turn to flesh out their interviewees' hesitant statements—John Winthrop, Thomas Jefferson, Benjamin Franklin, Alexis de Tocqueville.

Indeed, if we shift the focus to include all Americans, both as agents and as objects of the cultural construction of the self, we perceive instead an American landscape littered with images of very cumbered selves. Although the myth of the nineteenth-century pioneer or frontiersman lives on, it has been joined by those of rebellious black slaves, the planners and sojourners on the Underground Railroad, and the cooperative and contentious struggles of the suffragists. And present-day images reflected in mass media treatment include more than the unencumbered (white, middle-class, and largely male) urban and economic "pioneers"—gentrifiers in inner cities and entrepreneurs in new industries. These images also include the cumbered poor, mixed-sex groups of recent Latin, Caribbean, and Asian migrants to the United States who are financed by and arrive as kinspeople, gain jobs through and work with kin and compatriots, and live doubled and tripled up in apartments and homes throughout urban America. Even those migrants who travel to the United States alone and work in isolation from their kin and compatriots, such as the many thousands of Caribbean and Latin American women working as child-minders and domestic servants, find themselves very cumbered with their largely live-in status and the emotionally intense nature of child care and household labor for others.

The "American temper" or "ethos" is continually reinvented, constructed, and reconstructed in unadmitted relation to changing demographics and political economy. And in configuring America from the Progressive Era to the present, "non-Other" Americans have added to notions of primitiveness and civilization the righteous theological language of morality plays and the Gradgrind terminology of neoclassical economics. What is useful is good and what is good is useful—but the calculus of utility and goodness is applied only to Others, never to "ourselves." Again and again, when Others have attempted to wrest free the right to inclusion, to find an America that allows them equal citizenship, they (we) are driven to justify the claim with reference to the utility calculus. We raise your moral tone. We make contributions. Let us in.

Despite the fact that the very notion of an unencumbered self is, as Bellah et al. point out, a traditional American invention, scholars and popular cultural commentators associate "tradition" in the United States with gemeinschaft, groupness, interdependence, responsibility—with the state of cumberedness.[5] Two American groups have popular cultural "traditions" in this sense: foreign peasantry and their descendants and all women. The Bellah group and other contemporary commentators on the American temper, interestingly, ignore both these Americans and the historical symbolic load they carry. Let us enter into the world that these commentators do not acknowledge, but that nevertheless shapes their interpretations, through an in medias res consideration of the "discovery" of white ethnicity.

White Ethnic Community

Even though certain popular works (such as *Streetcorner Society* [1943] and *The Urban Villagers* [1962]) foreshadowed the American concept of the white ethnic community, it coalesced in the early 1970s, the period in which the term "white ethnic" itself gained currency.[6] A white ethnic, of course, exists in contradistinction to those ethnics defined as nonwhite, and thus white ethnics came into existence as a labeled group in response to the civil rights/Black Power movements and the allied organizing of Latinos, Asians, and Native Americans.

Populations we now label white ethnic—those whose antecedents arrived from (largely southeastern) Europe beginning in the 1840s and increasingly after the 1880s—were subject to intensive, largely deprecating, or patronizing public scrutiny, particularly through the Reform and Depression eras. Popular representations of Irish, Italians, Poles, Russians and other Slavs, Jews from many states, and others as mentally deficient, dirty, diseased, and/or innately criminal were widespread. As knowledge of those representations—and the discrimination that underlay and arose from them—has fallen down the national memory hole, it may be useful to review the record here.

The *New York Tribune* commented in 1882 on the uncouth nature of Jewish immigrants in language strongly parallel to contemporary white New Yorkers' characterization of the minority poor:

> Numerous complaints have been made in regard to the Hebrew immigrants who lounge about Battery Park, obstructing the walks and sitting on the chains. Their filthy condition has caused many of the people who are accustomed to go to the park to seek a little recreation and fresh air to give up this practice. The immigrants also greatly annoy the persons who cross the park to take the boats to Coney Island, Staten Island and Brooklyn. The police have had many battles with these newcomers, who seem determined to have their own way.[7]

IQ testing was actually institutionalized as an effort to evaluate various immigrant populations' fitness for World War I military service and thus their right to remain in the United States, and Jews, despite subsequent popular representations, were frequently defined with other southeastern Europeans as mentally inferior. In 1913, Henry Goddard applied mental tests to newly arrived immigrants and reported that 83 percent of the Jews (but only 79 percent of the Italians!) were feebleminded.

Stanford University president David Star Jordan, in 1922 Senate testimony, distinguished northern from southern Italians on eugenic grounds. The southerners displayed "the incapacity of those hereditarily weak."[8] The sixty-first Congress's Dillingham Commission's official *Dictionary of Races or Peoples* described the southern Italian as "excitable, impulsive, highly imaginative, impractible; an individualist having little adaptability to highly organized society"; and Slavs as representing "fanaticism in religion, carelessness as to the business virtues of punctuality and often honesty, periods of besotted drunkenness among the peasantry, unexpected ferocity and cruelty in a generally placid and kind-hearted individual."[9]

As to crime, University of Wisconsin sociologist Edward A. Ross, countermanding Henry Goddard's findings, wrote in 1914 that "the fewness of Hebrews in prison has been used to spread the impression that they are uncommonly law-abiding. The fact is that it is harder to catch and convict criminals of cunning than criminals of violence. The chief of police of any large city will bear emphatic testimony as to the trouble Hebrew lawbreakers cause him. Most alarming is the great increase of criminality among Jewish young men and the growth of prostitution among Jewish girls."[10]

And this assessment is extremely mild compared to his treatment of Italians and Slavs. Ross went on to quote from "the Jewish press" to the effect that Jews *had* been protesting Gentiles' exaggeration of their crimes but now found themselves forced to admit the "nests of theft, robbery, murder, and lawlessness that have multiplied in our midst."[11] Sounding hauntingly like contemporary black sociologist William Julius Wilson's commentary on the contemporary "black underclass," this Yiddish text laments: "But when we hear of the murders, hold-ups and burglaries committed in the Jewish section by Jewish criminals, we must, with heartache, justify [our critics]."[12]

Ross's estimate of the Irish, whose great period of immigration was three to four generations past on the eve of World War I, was relatively benign: "'Tonio or Ivan now wields the shovel while Michael's boy escapes competition with him by running nimbly up the ladder of occupations."[13] Nevertheless, "the children of the immigrant from Ireland often become infected with the parental slackness, unthrift, and irresponsibility."[14]

All of these representations, and the more positive but equally condescending liberal appraisals of the time, share several interrelated elements. They assume that southern and eastern European migrants and their descendants are "outside the circle of the we," in David Hollinger's apt phrasing; that therefore well-off white professionals have the right to speak for and about the character of those less well-off; and that there is an inextricable connection between cultural Otherness and (self-caused) poverty.[15] Where commentators differ—then and now—is in their evaluation of that cultural difference. Eugenicists presumed it was genetically determined, whereas others used more or less plastic notions of culture, leaving the door open for "assimilation" to erase unpleasant traits.

Feminist theorists, following Simone de Beauvoir (who herself appropriated the immanence/transcendence distinction from Jean-

Paul Sartre's existentialism), have commented on western political theory's pervasive functionalist orientation in interpreting women's lives. Susan Okin notes succinctly that "philosophers, in laying the foundation for their political theories, have asked 'What are men like?' 'What is man's potential?' have frequently, turning to the female sex, asked 'What are women *for*?'"[16]

We can see an analogous orientation in Gilded Age/Progressive Era discourse on "strangers in the land"—the title of John Higham's classic study of American nativism.[17] "We" Wasps simply *are* Americans; there is no need to interrogate our utility to the nation. But "they" may or may not be of use. And for many Americans of (non-Irish) northwest European origin, the meaning of "use" was nakedly obvious. The vast immigrant influx was an economic bonanza for transportation interests—particularly steamship and railroad companies; for tenement owners; for manufacturing, mining, and agricultural firms; and for many other employers of unskilled labor. It was a recurrent nightmare for union organizers and a wide variety of already resident workers whose wages employers could beat down with the specter of immigrant competition. Nativist sentiments were thus filtered (as they are now) through sets of interests—labor under threat and elements of capital that either profited little from new immigration or for which profit could not override racist repugnance.

In 1930, Madison Grant and other racist eugenicists published an anti-immigration compendium whose title, *The Alien in Our Midst, or, Selling Our Birthright for a Mess of Industrial Pottage,* clearly comments on the contemporary tension between perceived economic self-interest and eugenics theory.[18] Of the 1911 Dillingham Commission's forty-one volumes of reports, fully twenty-three deal with immigrant representation, skills, and pay in a wide variety of American industries. A color chart produced by the Central Tube Company in Pittsburgh in 1925 grades thirty-six groups on their "racial adaptibility to various types of plant work," including such categories as "smoke and fumes" and "night shift."[19] Ross himself was fired from Stanford University by Jane Stanford, widow of the university's founder and sole trustee, for his racist speeches against Chinese immigration. Stanford's motives, however, were not antiracist but self-interested: As Rosalind Rosenberg notes, "Stanford's fortune had been built on the backs of Oriental labor and she did not wish to see this diligent labor supply cut short."[20]

It is important to note as well that the populations that would come to be called white ethnics were the first American groups classically defined as "urban poor," both by the nascent reform movement and by the developing field of urban sociology in the 1920s and 1930s.[21] As such, these domestic exotics were heirs to a profound Enlightenment ambivalence about the nature of communities. Since at least the time of Jean-Jacques Rousseau and his critics, "community" has explicitly or implicitly contained the images of both equality, order, civility, and of ignorance, hidebound tradition, narrowness.

This dichotomy was first inscribed as a country/city contrast and was transposed in the urban American context into a contradictory vision of the functioning of newly arrived European peasantry in U.S. cities. Thus, the work of the Chicago School sociologists and anthropologists could describe migrants to the city both as the inheritors of gemeinschaft—the simple, humanly satisfying, face-to-face, traditional rural world that was giving way to the complex, anomic, modern urban world of strangers—and as rude, uncivilized peasants who must modernize, assimilate, Americanize in order to rise to the level of work and social life in the new industrial city. And these urbanizing peasants, as the first populations of impoverished Americans *studied by social scientists,* would inevitably be used as templates against which to compare other groups, especially black Americans, despite the fact that blacks were also present, and subject to even worse treatment than European migrants, in Progressive Era northern cities. The noble versus nasty peasant construct is, of course, directly connected to that of the noble/nasty savage.

Robert Park, a founding Chicago School sociologist, and Herbert Miller reflected this ambivalence well in their 1921 volume *Old World Traits Transplanted:* "At home the immigrant was almost completely controlled by the community; in America this lifelong control is relaxed. . . . All the old habits of the immigrant consequently tend to break down."[22] They argued for assimilation, but in orderly stages, because "a too rapid Americanization is usually disastrous."[23] Immigrant crime, in their vision, is due to culture loss: "There is among [Jews], indeed, a great variety of disorder and personal demoralization—gambling, extortion, vagabondage, family desertion, white slavery, ordinary and extraordinary crime—as a consequence of the rapid decay on America of the Jewish traditions and attitudes."[24]

But crime also arises from imperfectly comprehended American customs, a "misapprehension of the motives of the American models they [immigrants] think they are imitating":

> On October 20, 1911, Walter Shiblawski, Frank Shiblawski, Philip Suchomski, Thomas Schultz, Philip Sommerling, and Frank Keta (all boys) held up and killed Fred Guelzow, a farmer, who was bringing a load of vegetables to Chicago. They had two revolvers, a bread knife, a pocketknife, and a large club. They had been reading novels and planned a hold-up. When Guelzow was ordered to hold up his hands he promptly did so. They took his silver watch and chain, then killed him, mutilated him horribly with bullets and knives, and cut off a piece of his leg and put it in his mouth.[25]

Despite such often harrowing details—no less harrowing than current accounts of underclass crimes—Park and Miller ended in a credo to then-contemporary immigrant populations. They affirmed the assimilability of these populations: "If the immigrant possesses already an apperception mass corresponding in some degree to our own, his participation in our life will, of course, follow more easily."[26] And, unlike Ross and other eugenicists, Park and Miller—and with them the Chicago School in general—announced that the southeastern European "does not differ from us profoundly."[27]

But other Others *are* unassimilable, fated to remain outside the circle of the we. In an uncanny foreshadowing of Pat Buchanan's racist diatribes against (largely nonexistent) African immigration in the 1990s, Park and Miller warned that "if we should receive, say, a million Congo blacks and a million Chinese coolies annually, and if they should propagate faster than the white Americans, it is certain that our educational system would break down."[28] They used a free-floating list of unattributed grotesqueries to define the truly Other:

> If the immigrants practiced cannibalism and incest; if they burned their widows and broke the necks of their wayward daughters, customarily; if (as in a North African tribe) a girl were not eligible for marriage until she had given her older brother a child born out of wedlock, to be reared as a slave; if immigrant families limited their children by law to one boy and one girl, killing the others . . . if immigrant army recruits declined target practice because the bullet would go straight anyway if

> Allah willed it—then the problem of immigration would be immensely complicated.[29]

Finally, in the clinching argument for "our" contingent acceptance of white ethnics into probationary citizenship, Park and Miller asserted their ancestral temporal distance: "In comparison with these examples immigrant heritages usually differ but little from ours, probably not more than ours differ from those of our more conservative grandfathers. Slavery, duelling, burning of witches, contempt of soil analysis[!], condemnation of the view that plants and animals have been developed slowly, not suddenly created, are comparatively recent values and attitudes."[30]

Invocation of the grandparent has become a widespread and revealing trope in American race/ethnic discourse. But first we need to follow that discourse into the present. From the coming of World War II through the 1960s, there was a general hiatus in both scholarly and popular attention to the non-American origins of this large segment of the American population. This hiatus was, in part, an epiphenomenon of restrictive immigration legislation in 1924; by the end of World War II most immigrants had been resident in the United States at least twenty years and had children and often grandchildren. (Some Irish, of course, were at that point marking nearly a century of U.S. residence.) It was also, in part, a result of the conscious efforts (assisted, of course, by capital and state) of migrants and their children to "modernize" and "Americanize." And it was the partial result of social scientists' interests in the changing physical features of the postwar American landscape, such as increasing suburbanization (*The Levittowners* [1967]), and in emerging social types and characteristic social relations related to the maturation of corporate capitalism (*The Lonely Crowd* [1950], *The Organization Man* [1956], *Workingman's Wife* [1959], *Blue-Collar Marriage* [1962]).[31] Even research specifically concerned with ethnic and racial life in the United States during this period (such as Milton Gordon's 1964 *Assimilation in American Life*) continued to use the Progressive Era melting pot metaphor and was more concerned with negative than with positive aspects of "unmelted" populations.[32]

This era of public and scholarly quiescence ended abruptly in the early 1970s as white ethnicity suddenly became a topic of key national concern. Across the nation, moribund ethnic voluntary associations revived and countless new ones were formed; popular books celebrating white ethnic experience, such as Nathan Glazer and Daniel Patrick Moynihan's (second edition of) *Beyond the Melting Pot,* Michael Novak's *The Rise of the Unmeltable Ethnics,* Andrew Greeley's *Why Can't They Be like Us?,* and Richard Gambino's *Blood of My Blood,* became best-sellers; and a stream of scholarly books and articles began to flow from the academy.[33] Werner Sollors has noted that "ethnicity truly was in vogue in the 1970s."[34] Journalistic and scholarly accounts alike parlayed the notions that white ethnics were an unjustly (repressed, maligned, ignored—take your pick) segment of the American population, were just beginning to rediscover their own histories and cultures, and deserved respect and attention in the public arena. Michael Novak, among many others, threw down the white ethnic gauntlet:

> In the country clubs, as city executives, established families, industrialists, owners, lawyers, masters of etiquette, college presidents, dominators of the military, fund raisers, members of blue ribbon communities, realtors, brokers, deans, sheriffs—it is the cumulative power and distinctive styles of WASPS that the rest of us have had to learn in order to survive. WASPS have never had to celebrate Columbus Day or march down Fifth Avenue wearing green. Every day has been their day in America. No more.[35]

Tied to these notions of the nature of white ethnic Americans was the construct of the white ethnic community, which journalists, academics, and individual white ethnics themselves proclaimed as an endangered but surviving inner-city institution. White ethnic communities past and present were characterized in terms reminiscent of Chicago School interpretations of interwar immigrant populations—with the negative end of the pole removed.

> Social life in white ethnic neighborhoods is largely rooted in the family. . . . Most people know or at least recognize one another. There is a sense of community integrity and group identity.[36]

> The pattern of Italian-American life is continuous with that of their ancestors. Its verities continue to demonstrate that family, community and work mean survival and that outsiders are threats to neighborhood

stability which is necessary to the close-knit life and culture of the people.[37]

Within the geographic boundaries of the Italian Quarters the *connazionali* gave life to a closely woven community within which the Italian way of life flourished.[38]

What the [New York Jewish] East Side lacked in sophistication, it made up in sincerity. It responded to primal experiences with candor and directness. It cut through to the essentials of life: the imperative to do right and the comfort of social bonds.[39]

As Stephen Steinberg and I have argued, these claims concerning white ethnic communities rest upon unexamined presuppositions that there *were* in fact such discrete phenomena: long-term, self-reproducing, ethnically homogeneous, inner-city neighborhoods.[40] In reality, American white ethnic populations throughout the nineteenth and twentieth centuries, no matter how abused or discriminated against by majority society, lived in ethnically heterogeneous and shifting urban and suburban neighborhoods—and moved often. Indices of residential segregation for European populations in the United States fell steadily *from 1910 on.* They also took flight to the suburbs in concert with their urban WASP neighbors. Thus, for example, by the mid-1970s, in the height of white ethnic renaissance publicity, California's prototypical Italian-American "community," San Francisco's North Beach, had more than 90 percent Chinese residents and California's Italian-American population was in reality scattered far and wide across the state's urban, suburban, and rural areas.[41]

If such popular claims about white ethnic communities were untrue, were, in fact, a newly invented tradition, what were the purpose and meaning of this ideological construct? Clearly, the assertion of self-worth had psychological benefits for individual white ethnics, but why did these assertions arise at that particular historical moment, and why were they so attentively heeded? In other words, how did the rise of white ethnic community ideology intersect with other contemporary political, economic, and cultural forces? Why did the various social actors who made use of it find it salient?

The late 1960s–early 1970s period in the United States was characterized by continuing economic expansion, the ongoing war in Vietnam, and a linked set of social movements directly related to these two key political-economic realities: civil rights/Black Power, the antiwar movement, the student/youth movement, and the second-wave feminist movement.[42] The connections among these social movements and their links to larger political-economic realities have been exhaustively documented, but in brief: The prospect of partaking in the benefits of postwar economic expansion, protests against being victimized by urban renewal displacement, and anger at the disproportionate induction of black youths for war service helped to fuel Black Power activism. The antiwar and feminist movements drew inspiration and personnel from contemporary black movements. Economic expansion and the demographic bulge of a 1960s college-age cohort laid the material basis for college- and then high-school-located youth rebellion—including civil rights, antiwar, and feminist protests as well as demands for increased autonomy and sexual freedom. Finally, postwar economic expansion led to American capital's greatly increased demands for labor and thus to American women's rising labor force participation rate. The very possibility of supporting themselves without reliance on father or husband allowed many women to challenge male societal dominance, while the low pay, low status, and minimal prospects for advancement that characterized most "women's jobs" in that era stimulated feminist reaction.

These multiple movements for reform and liberation challenged both the federal, state, and institutional structures—such as those of colleges and universities—and individuals who perceived themselves to be threatened by particular demands for social change. The Nixon administration in particular sought to exploit and enhance these social divisions through the use of the polarizing discourse of the Silent Majority—as opposed to the protesting anti-administration "minority." Between administration rhetoric and media response, an image grew of this stipulated entity: the Silent Majority were white—implicitly white ethnic—largely male, blue-collar workers. They were held to be "patriotic" and to live in "traditional" families—ones in which males ruled, women did not work outside the home for pay, and parents controlled their children.

This media image, of course, did not reflect an aggregate social reality. This was the era, after all, in which married working-class women were entering the labor force at record rates and in which their additions to family income maintained working-class living standards in the face of declining real incomes. White labor support for the Democrats actually peaked in 1948—the party's loss of the white working-class had begun long before Watts, Woodstock, and Gloria Steinem. And sexual adventurism and drug use in the late 1960s–early 1970s were the property of working-class no less than middle-class youths. Nevertheless, as a media construct, as a symbol of the hemorrhaging of Democratic voters to the Republican Party, the conservative white ethnic blue-collar worker gained salience in this period. This salience was much enhanced by the shifting populations and power relations in American cities.[43]

In the 1960s, poor black Americans became newly visible and newly defined as a social problem in northern cities. The two great waves of black migration from the South, during World War I and II, had each resulted in cohorts of permanent northern black urban residents. These men and women had come north (often through employer recruitment) both to take advantage of lucrative war jobs and to flee Jim Crow and the effects of the mechanization of southern agriculture, had then often been laid off, and had largely become part of a permanent army of reserve labor. Urban renewal projects in the 1950s and 1960s—an employment boondoggle for white ethnic blue-collar workers—destroyed countless urban black neighborhoods, replaced them with office blocks and sports complexes, and shifted and concentrated the poor black population in areas dominated by inhospitable, poorly built, and badly maintained government housing projects. Ninety percent of the housing destroyed by urban renewal was never replaced, and two-thirds of those displaced were black or Puerto Rican. The Federal Housing Authority deliberately fostered segregated white housing and refused loans to blacks until the passage of the Fair Housing Act in 1968. Douglas Massey and Nancy Denton have noted that the "highest [residential] isolation index ever recorded for any ethnic group in any American city was 56% (for Milwaukee Italians in 1910), but by 1970 the l*owest* level of spatial isolation observed for blacks anywhere, North or South, was 56% (in San Francisco)."[44] Big-city governments refused to shift budgetary resources to basic services for these impoverished areas.

Northern white populations, contra contemporary received wisdom, discriminated against, refused to patronize public establishments with, rioted against, attacked, and killed blacks in the North from the World War I era on. There was no "era of Northern amity" prior to the civil rights movement and Black Power. Neighborhood deterioration, increased crime, and urban uprisings—combined with intensive political organizing—stimulated the establishment of highly visible federal Great Society programs. (But ironically, the late-1960s explosion of welfare rolls was of almost exclusive benefit to poor *whites.*)[45] At the same time, a small cohort of socially mobile blacks, emboldened by the civil rights movement, attempted to buy homes in formerly white urban and suburban neighborhoods. The resulting "white flight" greatly enriched the real estate speculators who fanned its flames and exacerbated inner-city white racism. Black (and Latino) struggles for higher-quality public education, neighborhood services, and civil service and union jobs led to increased friction between white, often white ethnic, and minority citizens in northern urban environments, friction only furthered by the newly oppositional rhetorical style of Black Power advocacy. The first scattered fringe of desuburbanizing bourgeois whites entered into this polarized and often dangerous environment, benefiting, of course, from its resulting low real estate values.

Thus, the white ethnic community construct arose from an extraordinarily complex historical ground, and this complexity was reflected in its multiple expressions and political uses. Key to all expressions and uses, however, was a reliance upon the basic ideological tropes of the civil rights and black cultural nationalist movements as structural templates and thus the construct's posture of competition through emulation. This ideology posited that blacks were a unitary, identifiable group that had experienced and was experiencing extreme forms of discrimination and that therefore was entitled not only to cessation of discriminatory laws and behaviors but also to financial and other sorts of recompense (affirmative action, Head Start, the Comprehensive Employment and Training Act, etc.). Thus, ironically, key expressions of white ethnic resentment were couched in language consciously and unconsciously copied from blacks themselves. (Werner Sollors comments on this mimicry, but as a cultural, not fundamentally political, phenomenon.)[46] Notions, for example, of the strength and richness of white ethnic cultures and their repression by WASPS mimicked black cultural nationalist (and white scholars'—see work by Carol Stack, Herbert Gutman, and Lawrence Levine) celebrations of black culture's endurance despite white domination.[47] Even Andrew Greeley admitted that "what the blacks have done is to legitimate ethnic self-consciousness."[48] When I was doing fieldwork among

California Italian Americans in the mid-1970s, many individuals identified my documentation of their and their antecedents' life histories as "our *Roots*," after the book and television film series based on Alex Haley's southern black family history.

Deliberate denigration of blacks vis-à-vis white ethnics relied as well on the ideological frame of entitlement used by black Americans. Both popular journalistic accounts and grassroots white ethnic discourse, for example, focused on the strength and unity of white ethnic families as opposed to those of black Americans—whose popular image had been shaped in the early 1960s as a "tangle of pathology" by the Moynihan Report. (Readers imagining the accuracy of these claims need only consult Linda Gordon's study of family violence among Boston's poor Irish, Italians, Jews, and others for an unremitting narrative of drunkenness, wife battery, child abuse, desertion, incest, and prostitution.)[49] In my own study, many Italian Americans' racist expressions against blacks focused on inferior black family behavior as both explaining and justifying widespread black poverty—thus the argument that, as the undeserving poor, blacks were not entitled to the largesse of Great Society programs and the approval of elite sponsors, which should instead flow to "deserving" white ethnics:

> The ethnics believe that they chose one route to moderate success in America: namely, loyalty, hard work, family discipline, and gradual self-development. They tend to believe that some blacks, admittedly more deeply injured and penalized in America, want to jump, via revolutionary militance, from a largely rural base of skills and habits over the heads of lower-class whites, instead of forming a coalition of the black and white lower classes, black militants seem to prefer coalition with intellectual elites. Campus and urban disorders witness a similarity of violence, disorder, rhetoric, ideology and style.[50]

This relative entitlement frame is attached, as I argue in *The Varieties of Ethnic Experience,* to a "report card mentality": a model of shifting American class divisions as caused by proper and improper ethnic/racial family and economic behavior rather than by the differential incorporation of immigrant and resident populations in American capitalism's evolving class structure.[51] And proper and improper behaviors are related to notions of cumbered and unencumbered selfhood and to "provisions of temporal distance." The cumberedness that Chicago School social scientists saw southeastern European immigrants as inevitably losing in the gesellschaft of modernizing urban America was rediscovered in the 1970s as a surviving feature of white ethnic selfhood. Scholarship, journalism, and grassroots expressions celebrated white ethnics for their family loyalties and neighborhood ties. In fact, advertising in this period began to exploit "cute" white ethnic imagery: the pizza-baking grandmother, the extended family at the laden dinner table—in order to invest frozen and canned foods with the cachet of the gemeinschaft.

This gemeinschaft, this cumberedness—this community—was delineated as an urban phenomenon existing alongside of and in opposition to urban black populations. Stephen Steinberg has sardonically pointed out that "the Poles and Slavs in Chicago, like the Irish in Boston and the Jews in Forest Hills, rarely experience their ethnicity so acutely as when threatened with racial integration."[52] And here we return to the Three Bears and can see the historical political-economic ground from which the fairy tale at the start of this chapter arose. With this contextualization, it is easy to see how, for a hot minute in the 1970s, American white ethnics commandeered Baby Bear's chair.

This new vision of white ethnics as the proper urban residents, those who maintain stable neighborhoods that nevertheless have "character"—ethnic restaurants, delicatessens, and other small businesses—was a major ideological component of growing gentrification. Ironically, of course, the more that urban professionals were attracted to inner-city neighborhoods, the more real estate prices rose and the less could *any* working-class urban residents and shopkeepers, white ethnic, black, or other, continue to afford to live or to do business in those neighborhoods. Thus, the economic logic of Third World tourism—the more successful one is in commodifying oneself, the less one is able to reproduce the self that has been commodified—came to characterize many American inner-city neighborhoods.

Central to the new construction of white ethnic community has been the Madonna-like (in the older sense) image of the white ethnic woman. Early 1970s popular writers extolled her devotion to home and family, and many of the more conservative Italian Americans in my late 1970s study echoed this fusion of ethnic chauvinism and antifeminism. Clelia Cipolla, a middle-aged civil servant, said, in describing her elaborate cooking for family holidays: "I've always thought of Thanksgiving as the only holiday the American wife really cooks for. . . . Maybe that's a wrong idea of it, but that's the way my feelings are."[53]

Part of this construction's appeal to women and men was the notion that white ethnic mothers, unlike "selfish" WASP and "lazy" black mothers, could control their children and thus were exempt from blame for then-current youth protests. Clelia Cipolla exclaimed to me in response to my narration of a recent Thanksgiving holiday's activities: "You mean Mommy and Daddy *allowed* you to have Thanksgiving away from home?"[54]

But in fact, white ethnic women were no less subject to the pressures and opportunities of the shifting American political economy of the 1970s, and many more of the Italian-American women with whom I worked actively altered or rejected the popular image of the self-sacrificing, kitchen-bound, ethnic mother. What is important to note is not whether white ethnic women fit the model—by and large, they did and do not—but that the model has been so hegemonic as to command belief and to influence the construction of identity. Linda Mornese, for example, judged her own immigrant grandmother as insufficiently ethnic because she did not conform to the nurturant peasant model: "I remember my aunt's mother, she was really the old Italian: white hair, never any makeup, the old dresses, wine barrels in the basement. I always thought: there's a *real* Italian lady. I don't see an Italian lady as one with her hair done. My grandmother's always kept herself, she's always dressed very well, she puts her jewelry on—she's better at it than I am!"[55]

In an era of rising feminist activism, the sudden celebration of a group of women who had been theretofore socially labeled as backward, stolid, and possessive wives and mothers functioned very clearly as antifeminist—particularly anti–women's workforce participation—rhetoric. In addition, in focusing on women's "duties" to husband and children, this rhetoric worked against prevalent civil rights imagery of heroic black movement women whose perceived duties lay in the public sphere. But like all symbols, the white ethnic woman is polyvalent and was and is subject to feminist and progressive interpretation:

> As Barbara Mikulski of Baltimore points out, the white ethnic woman in America is not a dingbat, however warm and humanistic may be the character of Edith Bunker, nor is she limited to "tacky clothes," "plastic flowers," *True Confessions,* and an "IQ of 47." Rather, she is

> Maria Fava and Ann Giordano, who travelled to Albany to express parent and community concern over limitations on day care. She is Rosemarie Reed, who attended a Washington conference on community organizing. She is Marie Anastasi, who is working with senior citizens as well as a "mothers' morning out" group. She is one of dozens of women who have joined with Monsignor Gino Baroni of the National Center for Urban Ethnic Affairs to deal with housing, redlining by banks, and neighborhood preservation.[56]

Many feminist scholars have attempted to celebrate the strength and endurance of "traditional" ethnic women and to use, for example, narratives of past union and strike activities, or consumer protests, to suggest a vision of innately progressive, rebellious, ethnic womanhood.[57] This attempt to wrest the white ethnic woman from the antifeminist right overlapped with another prominent invented tradition of the same period: the notion of women's culture.

Women's Culture and Its Discontents

"Women's culture," a locution in increasing use over the 1970s, evokes both the American feminist shift in emphasis from male-female to female-female relations and what historian Alice Echols has labeled the decline from radical to cultural feminism over the course of the late 1960s to early 1970s.[58] That is, both popular and scholarly feminism during this period moved away from analyses of male dominance to considerations of women's worlds; this move coincided with the blunting of feminism's early radical edge, its explicit demands for change by individual men and the state. Women's culture, as a protean set of claims concerning women's Ur-nature, enabled and rationalized that shift. According to these claims, there is a universal women's nature, which is characterized by moral superiority to men; cooperative, rather than competitive, social relations; selfless maternality; and benevolent sexuality.[59] Many academic expressions of these claims centered on "women's culture":

> Women's culture forms a collective experience within the cultural whole, an experience that binds women writers to each other over time and space.[60]

> There is always a women's culture within every culture.[61]

> The bedrock of women's consciousness is the obligation to preserve life. Now as in the past, women judge themselves and one another on how well they do work associated with being female.[62]

> Women's culture is the ground upon which women stand in their resistance to patriarchal domination and their assertion of their own creativity in sharing society.[63]

> Women not only define themselves in a context of human relationship but also judge themselves in terms of their ability to care.[64]

Three elements are common to all scholarly deployments of women's culture. First, there is the aforementioned "among women" emphasis. Second, women's culture writers plump resolutely for "difference" in what historian Nancy Cott has analyzed as the "two logically opposing poles"—sameness versus difference from men—that have animated feminist political argument since the nineteenth century.[65] Third, all scholars' usages "cumber" women with some combination of home, children, community—what historian Temma Kaplan labels a "shared sense of obligation to preserve life"[66]—or what is now often labeled "women's ethic of care."

This cultural feminist shift is equally visible in feminist activism from the 1970s forward, particularly in peace and environmental politics. Consider, for example, the popular feminist antimilitarist slogan "Take the toys away from the boys." The implicit meaning is that morally superior, maternal women will discipline male warriors who are responsible for world militarism. Or consider the popular T-shirt and bumper sticker slogan "When God created man, He was only practicing." Posters sternly ordering us to "Love your mother"(a photo of the earth) have been staples for years in ecology-minded circles. Popular 1980s feminist slogans such as "Stop raping, stop warring" and "Mothers save your children" make use of women's culture presumptions.

Perhaps more important to the growing hegemony of feminist women's culture tropes, given the progressive demobilization of peace and environmental activism through the 1980s and 1990s, has been the continuous stream of matriarchy/Great Goddess writing from the 1970s on. These popular works are based on old, often Victorian anthropology—although one woman archaeologist of European prehistory, Marija Gimbutas, turned, late in her career, to discerning prior matriarchies in potsherds and claiming their defeat at the hands of violent invaders: "We are still living under the sway of that aggressive male invasion and only beginning to discover our long alienation from our authentic European heritage—gylanic, nonviolent, earth-centered culture."[67]

Such claims of the existence of prior matriarchies always identify them as benevolent, humane states, often associated with the worship of female supernatural beings. Early second-wave works such as Merlin Stone's *When God Was a Woman* and Elizabeth Gould Davis's *The First Sex* have been superseded by a veritable flood of texts.[68] Contemporary writers have produced feminist utopias incorporating women's culture claims, such as Sally Gearheart's *The Wanderground,* and older texts, such as Charlotte Perkins Gilman's *Herland,* were reprinted and became staples of the women's studies classroom.[69] The institutionalization of medieval Europe–inspired feminist witchcraft (or Wicca, or neopaganism) further underlines women's culture themes. Cultural feminist magazines, such as *Chrysalis* and *Womanspirit,* served these overlapping audiences and also provided a bridge to the New Age/Great Goddess texts and commodities.

These widespread feminist constructions of prior perfect women's states are strikingly parallel to the pristine ethnic community of the white ethnic renaissance's imagination and the superior precolonial societies of Africa invoked by black cultural nationalism. In fact, Adolph Reed in 1979 labeled the historical relation of cultural feminism to black cultural nationalism the "feminist photocopy of the black journey on the road to nowhere."[70]

This "feminist photocopy," like its black nationalist original, has also appeared in forms more academically respectable than the Great Goddess genre. Throughout the 1980s and into the 1990s, two major waves of respectable women's culture lapped through major media from the Ivory Tower. The first was the enormous hoopla surrounding the publication of Carol Gilligan's *In a Different Voice.* Gilligan's feminist purpose, in narrow academic terms, was exemplary: to discredit cognitive psychologist Lawrence Kohlberg's claim that women's moral/ethical development over the life course lagged behind men's. But in so doing, Gilligan replicated Kohlberg's epistemological and methodological frames—she assumed that a small population of elite heterosexual whites could stand as a synecdoche for all Americans, that stories told in response to hypothetical problems could stand for lifetime patterns of behavior, and that there is such a thing as gender-universal moral/ethical growth culminating in adulthood. Gilligan hedged some—but by no means all—of her universalizing, generalizing statements: Witness the previous "judging themselves on ability to care" quotation. Despite extensive critiques of her work from academic feminists, she was widely apprehended as the scholar who had provided definitive proof of women's moral superiority, their relational "caringness" when compared to individualistic, rule-governed, rational men.[71] Gilligan was read and allowed herself to be used as a psychological vindicator of women's culture ideology. Her subsequent, more oppositional, collaborative research on girls and schooling has been much less attended.[72] To use Jane Addams's metaphor: When women's culture is deployed for "social housekeeping" claims—when we are urged to let women walk a few steps into the public sphere because of their nurturant interiority—it is relatively successful. But when women's culture is used to demand that men and boys accede to the moral mother's demand that *they* pick up the broom and sweep, all bets are off.

And, indeed, the bulk of women's culture emanations in popular discourse are not at all feminist. Most everyday American expressions incorporating a sense of women's innate difference from men, their superior, benevolent maternality, in fact accept and defend the status quo. Cetta Longhinotti, a middle-aged, working-class woman in my first ethnographic study, to explain her martyred familial role unself-consciously avowed: " I think women are superior. . . . I think God helps us.[73]"

Less pietistic but equally fatalistic assessments infuse American popular culture. Middlebrow entertainment often simply assumes a world of caring women—if not always separate women's worlds. The ubiquitous "Cathy" cartoons gently satirize intimate mother-daughter ties and women's worlds of shopping and food consumption. Popular women's magazines, from the working-class *Family Circle* and *Women's Day* to the higher-register *Victoria* and *Martha Stewart's Living,* cater to notions of women's innately warm interior worlds, their loving ties with other women and children, their heroic self-sacrifices for others. (And media hysteria over obvious counterexamples—"bad women"—only serves to underline happy-face women's culture images.)

Even the Great Goddess trope is easily stripped of all oppositional content and infused with self-help ideology, as in best-selling New Age author Marianne Williamson's appalling *A Woman's Worth*. Williamson, battening on women readers' needs to think well of themselves, bathetically suggests that we are all goddesses: "'What?' you say. 'Me, a goddess?' Yes, I say, and don't act so surprised."[74] Williamson assures us that "we have a job to do reclaiming our glory," but that glory is a 1990s version of women's pedestal. Apparently, we are to approve other women's (Williamson's, obviously) speeches at dinner parties but to eschew any effort to gain more social and political power: "As long as we focus on the outer world, which is not our home base, and try to wield power of the kind only known there (power so crude, by the way, the angels can't help but laugh), we will remain in the weaker, slightly confused position."[75]

Whether women are told to "run with the wolves" by "returning to their instinctive lives, their deepest knowing," or lectured that "men are from Mars, while women are from Venus," the non- (really anti) feminist New Age message is the same: Women are indeed superior goddesses, more connected and caring than men.[76] That's the way it is. Double day? Violence against women? Feminization of poverty? Glass ceiling? Let us avert our eyes, look within, accept, and celebrate. No struggle in the real world, no political change, is needed.

Political commentator Katha Pollitt, following Nancy Cott's historical analysis, has labeled feminist women's culture interpretations "difference feminism." In the witty tour-de-force piece "Are Women Morally Superior to Men? Marooned on Gilligan's Island," Pollitt sends up academic and popular denials of women's equal personhood with men and false claims of mothers' superior morality. She understands the functionalism operating within women's culture discourse: "It asks that women be admitted into public life and public discourse not because they have a right to be there but because they will improve things."[77] Pollitt goes on to claim that "no other oppressed group thinks it must make such a claim in order to be accommodated fully and across the board by society. For blacks and other racial minorities, it is enough to want to earn a living, exercise one's talents, get a fair hearing in the public forum. Only for women is simple justice an insufficient argument."[78] We have seen, however, that in fact functionalist arguments are the staple of historical American discourse on *all*

Others, not just women. They have, if anything, become more central in the era of underclass ideology, part of the entwined rhetorics of identity politics and of the new right.

Women's culture ideology, then, whether feminist or nonfeminist, is like white ethnic community ideology in that it makes claims that are simply false. Women, like men, are members of the human species, and nothing human is alien to them. Women's culture denies many women's closer allegiances to men than to women (what 1970s radical feminists scored as "male identification"). It denies various forms of female cruelty—the reality of female participation in theft, torture, murder, in the abuse, sale, and/or abandonment of children—activities that have been carried on by at least some women in most past and present societies and that are not necessarily explained away by prevalent male domination. It denies what is even more prevalent: female apathy and laziness. And it denies the realities of women's self-seeking strategizing *within* their "nurturant," "unselfish" activities of caring for home and children. Children, after all, until very recently in the industrialized west, labored for their parents and as adults owed them—often especially their mothers—loyalty, labor, and cash.

Clearly, the women's culture concept exists in complex relation to recent political-economic shifts and the ideological constructions of contemporary political movements. Women's culture, in its feminist incarnation, responds to antifeminist accusations that feminists are selfish—that they do not, in other words, accept their proper load of cumberedness—through embracing an a priori functionalist moral high ground. All women are innately morally superior to all men because they are naturally cooperative and nurturant. They are automatically cumbered, but by responsibility for other women and children, not necessarily for men. This feminist essentialist stance, as Janet Sayers labels it, by appeal to biological or near-biological differences between the sexes, neatly preempts accusations that feminists and/or lesbians have lost their femininity.[79] They cannot lose what is innately theirs, which is ascribed, not achieved. In this vision, all women are goddesses and goddesses automatically sit in Baby Bear's chair.

The women's culture construct, then, is structurally related to the white ethnic community construct in two ways. First, it attempts to take over a prior-existing polarized notion of its subjects (warm and orderly versus primitive and insular European migrants, Madonnas versus harridans and sluts) by chopping off and denying the existence of the negative pole. This operation has been relatively successful for the white ethnic community construct. The historical version of the negative pole—the stolid, backward, crime-ridden, socially immobile ethnic community, Harvard historian Stephan Thernstrom's "subculture that directs energies away from work"[80]—has been superseded in the public mind by the black and brown poor, whose segregation, poverty, and high crime rates are presumed to be self-caused. The more recent historically negative vision, that of the racist, conservative white ethnic community, has not been revived, despite, for example, the Irish-led racist antibusing movement in Boston; despite the prevalence of Italian surnames among the Howard Beach and Bensonhurst adolescents and others guilty of recent unprovoked and murderous attacks against blacks and Latinos in New York City; despite the fact that white ethnic leaders in Yonkers risked bankrupting the city in 1988 to continue their four decades-long segregationist tradition; and despite the 1993 white racist vote in ethnic Staten Island to secede from New York City.

The negative pole of women's culture, in contrast, is alive and kicking in popular culture. Recent journalistic coverage—not to mention the behavior of courts and police—of reproductive issues such as surrogate motherhood and prenatal care have tended toward automatic blame of women caught in difficult circumstances. Thus, women who agree to be surrogates are deemed selfish, as was the woman who agreed and then wished to back out of her agreement. And pregnant women who do not follow doctors' orders have been arrested and charged. Negative stereotypes of women abound in popular culture, from the psychotic rejected woman in *Fatal Attraction,* to the evil upper-class boss in *Working Girl,* to the selfish, unmaternal, bourgeois witches of John Updike's recent fiction. American popular press coverage of "rich bitches" such as Ivana Trump, Imelda Marcos, and Leona Helmsley—the consuming wives of far richer and/or more directly evil men—is characterized by a populist venom not aimed at wealthy or powerful men since Richard Nixon and Watergate.

There are a number of obvious reasons for the relative failure of explicitly feminist women's culture ideology. The first is that it transmutes so easily into its much more prevalent antifeminist form. "Revaluing the female sphere" can be, and is, a contemporary argument for backlash against gender equity. Second, it is easier to maintain a counterfactual vision of an elusive ephemeral community—particular neighborhoods and individuals can be labeled inauthentic—than of half the human race. Third, the social base for antiwhite ethnic community sentiment is small. The Nixon era is long over, Ronald Reagan and George Bush's three electoral victories cannot be ascribed to crossover white ethnics alone, and Bill Clinton won the 1992 election with Rustbelt and Eastern Seaboard white ethnic votes while largely losing the good old boy South the Democratic Leadership Council was convinced he had sewn up. In contrast, the key mainstream feminist goal of the 1980s—ratification of the Equal Rights Amendment—failed, and antifeminist ideologies have been strongly represented since the 1980s from the White House down. It is in the current interests of a large number of politically active groups to blame some population of American women—those seeking abortions, those who have children without "men to support them," those who do not have children, those who leave husbands, those who attempt to be attractive to men, those who do not, those attracted to women, those on welfare, those in the labor force, those who protest sexual harassment, those who put their children in day care—for all social ills.

The second relation between women's culture and white ethnic community is not emulation but annexation. In the 1970s context of rising feminism and the first antifeminist construct of the white ethnic woman, feminists responded, as I have noted, by claiming the white ethnic woman for themselves and their discourse. But the feminist women's culture construct also emulates the white ethnic community's annexation of the symbolic structures of the civil rights movement, "swallowing" not only the beleaguered white ethnic Madonna but also the oppressed, heroic woman of color.

It is in this context that the linked phenomena of feminist academic work and popular feminist cultural production have taken on a distinctive shape and thrust. American universities, by default, as Jacoby has noted, have become in the recent conservative era important havens for progressive social thought. Faculty in explicitly new, interdisciplinary programs, such as women's and Afro-American studies, have often evolved a beleaguered circle-the-wagons perspective. This defensiveness is often justified, given the stalled feminist and civil rights agendas in the larger society and recent eruptions of racist, sexist, and homophobic behavior on American campuses. Such a beleaguered sensibility, combined with evidences of aggregate male danger and irresponsibility (high rates of violence against women, little change in indices of occupational segregation by sex, aggregate male failure to pay child support), enhances essentializing cultural feminist interpretations of women's common lot irrespective of their differences and also encourages the presumption of female moral superiority upon which the construction of women's culture rests. This explains the tendency of women's culture writers to annex the construct of the heroic "triply oppressed" woman of color—which is, of course, the obverse of the hegemonic popular cultural vision of the feckless, welfare-dependent, drug-taking, black or Latina teenage mother.

American culture, then, contrary to the assumptions of many observers, has historically abounded in visions of cumbered selves. Two of these, the white ethnic woman and women's culture, have salience and sufficient institutional impedimenta—books, journals, festivals, associations—to constitute full-blown invented traditions. How do these cultural constructs function today in the contested space of the national political arena?

Since the late 1970s, white ethnic community is no longer a hot topic for academic papers and popular cultural accounts. Festivals and meetings of ethnic historical associations and social groups do not receive the public attention they once did. In Andy Warhol's phrase, white ethnicity had its fifteen minutes of fame in the mid-1970s, and other social groups and issues have since captured the public stage.

Nevertheless, the transformed construction of white ethnic community remains "on hold"—Bellah and his colleagues, for example, pay it lip service before hurrying on to their (presumably nonethnic) interviewees. To switch the metaphor back, white ethnic community stands backstage, ready to reenter stage left or right at a given cue. Recently, for example, a series of Democratic politicians attempted to make use of notions of family, stability, and tradition now associated with white ethnicity to bolster their appeal to the electorate. This strategy backfired for Geraldine Ferraro, of course, when both her husband and son fell foul of the law; and it was ultimately useless in insulating the originally progressive Jim Florio from full-scale right-wing attack in New Jersey. But it was quite successful for both Mario Cuomo and Rudolph Giuliani and was one of the few winning elements of Michael Dukakis's ill-fated presidential campaign.

The relative weakness of white ethnic community ideology since the 1980s is also, I contend, related to Reagan era script revisions in the national ethnic/racial morality play. As Debora Silverman compellingly argues in *Selling Culture,* the Reagan White House, the Metropolitan Museum, *Vogue* magazine, and a number of clothing designers formed a sinister interlocking directorate that simultaneously flattered the administration, lauded wealth and aristocracy, and used museum resources to flout any art-historical considerations while shamelessly advertising the work of those designers who pandered most openly to wealth.[81] I would add that, paralleling the rise of colonial chic in popular culture, we saw a renascence of positive images of the wealthy west at home. Public television fare shifted significantly to reruns of BBC productions most nostalgic for the Edwardian upper classes—*Upstairs, Downstairs; Brideshead Revisited*; *The Treasure Houses of Britain. Good Housekeeping* began its "New Traditionalist" advertising campaign featuring obviously affluent, nonworking, blond women and their well-groomed children on the spacious grounds of their suburban or country estates: "She knows what she values—home and family." And her Rolex watch. Wealthy whites took back Baby Bear's chair with a vengeance, and a new romantic halo was constructed over the image—embodied by Nancy Reagan—of the elegant, dignified, adorned, and (publicly at least) devoted wife and mother, the curator of the proper WASP bourgeois home and children.

Meanwhile, popular representations of white ethnics, which in the 1970s had teetered between pious "world we have lost" images of authentically warm, close families and communities and an *All in the Family* condescension, tipped over in the 1980s into permanent condescension and even minstrelsy. Take Italian Americans as an example. In popular film, the ambiguous *Godfather* phenomenon—which lent glamour and gravitas to an organized crime family—gave way to *Moonstruck, Married to the Mob, True Love, Working Girl*—all films that represented working-class and better-off Italian Americans as philistines, tasteless boobs, Guidos and Big Hair girls, the kind of people who would have mashed potatoes dyed blue to match the bridesmaids' dresses. White ethnicity, in some venues at some times, came to mean the inelegant, disorganized enactment of others' life dramas for our condescending amusement—minstrelsy. The media hoopla surrounding the Amy Fisher/Joey Buttafuoco case denied the tragic realities of the emotionally disturbed young girl and the betrayed and wounded wife in sniggering references to the "Long Island Lolita," the auto parts store, and vulgar-sounding Italian names.

The apotheosis of the new Italian-American minstrelsy, however, is the long-running (in New York, Los Angeles, San Francisco, Philadelphia, Chicago) environmental theater piece *Tony 'n' Tina's Wedding,* in which the audience is encouraged to interact with the low-rent wedding party. The usually racially sensitive women's magazine *Glamour* threw all self-consciousness to the winds in its reaction to the production:

> Off-Broadway's most innovative play satirizes a garish New York Italian wedding, and it's all the more fun when the audience joins in: Pin a dollar on the groom (to fund their Poconos honeymoon) and he'll dance with you to Donny Dolce and Fusion's rendition of "We Are the World." Chow down baked ziti and elaborately tiered wedding cake. Watch acqua-eye-shadowed Tina and her tarty, gum-chewing bridesmaids (dressed in red) break into an interpretation of Michael Jackson's "BAD," complete with crotch-grabs. Kissing our way through the reception line, Tina said she had a cute cousin she wanted to fix us up with. Tony whispered, "Don't call me at home no more!"[82]

The Rise of Underclass Ideology

With the economic recovery of the middle and late 1980s, unemployment shrank to early 1970s levels, then rose again with the Bush/Clinton recession, but it shrank less for minority Americans, and of those successively reemployed, many work part-time or at jobs with lower status and pay. As a combination of these shifts and regressive tax legislation, over the Reagan/Bush years the numbers of both the very poor and the very rich rose. We now have the most poor and the smallest middle class, proportionately, in the First World.[83] Despite local grassroots organizing against obvious inequities such as plant shutdowns, toxic waste dumping and other environmental disasters, farm foreclosures, and continuously increasing homeless populations—and despite the 1993 replacement of a

Republican with a conservative Democratic administration—popular political discourse has shifted significantly rightward since the 1970s. Keynesian economic apprehensions of the utility and ease of deficit financing, of deficits as subject to state planning and manipulation, have eroded; neoclassical terror of "handing down debt to our grandchildren" rules the day. In this shrunken universe of kindergarten economics, all social claimants except already well-off whites and the military are derided for "demanding entitlements instead of accepting social responsibility." Civil rights, women's, gay, and labor groups are labeled "special interests." But most crucially, public discourse on the poor, particularly poor blacks and Latinos, has turned nearly hegemonically to automatic deprecation and "blame-the-victim" rhetoric.

This rhetoric, as historian Michael Katz has documented, has a long American pedigree.[84] Since the colonial era, American elites have engaged in three obfuscations with regard to domestic poverty. The first is the denial that the "normal" functioning of protocapitalist and capitalist economies literally produces impoverished classes, independently of individuals' or groups' cleverness or willingness to work. Second, elites tend to create artificial distinctions between the "deserving" and "undeserving" poor: those for whom we should have compassion versus those—"sturdy beggars"—who must be punished, forced to work. Finally, Americans have repeatedly denied the history of state involvement in social welfare, from state subsidy of private philanthropy since its inception to governmental control of all aspects of economic life that both produce and ameliorate poverty.

Thus, the blame-the-victim trope is hardly new in American history (although the phrase itself was enshrined in American popular consciousness through William Ryan's wonderfully furious early 1970s polemic).[85] The particular symbolic strands that coalesced as full-blown underclass ideology in the 1980s were, however, historically specific to our era and uniquely symbiotic with notions of white ethnic community and women's culture.

As Frances Piven and Richard Cloward demonstrate in *Regulating the Poor,* American social welfare policy from the Depression into the 1970s evolved into an instrument for dealing with the urban reserve army—those poor people who, depending on the business cycle and other economic factors, were periodically employed, then unemployed, but always at the bottom rungs of the economic ladder. Federal spigots opened and closed in response to employers' desire for cheap labor, business cycle downturns, urban unrest, and, in the 1960s, the need "to reach, placate and integrate a turbulent black constituency" into the Democratic Party.[86] From the mid-1970s on, however, the Democratic Party increasingly abandoned minority, poor, labor constituencies, and the federal government pulled out of the business of regulating the poor. First Jimmy Carter, then Reagan drastically cut back social program spending, abandoned federal commitments to low-cost housing while allowing rapid-fire real estate speculation, and continued policies that encouraged, rather than slowed, big-city deindustrialization as firms relocated both regionally and internationally in search of the lowest possible labor costs.

The new ideology of the "minority urban underclass" arose during this period and functioned specifically, as had older culture-of-poverty formulations, to focus attention away from this political-economic production of poverty to the "pathological" behavior of the poor, whose characteristics were presumed (in the hard version) to cause or (in the soft version) merely to reproduce poverty. First articulated in sensationalized journalistic accounts, such as *Time* magazine's 1977 cover story "Minority Within a Minority: The Underclass," Ken Auletta's early 1980s *New Yorker* series, and the *Chicago Tribune*'s appalling 1985 series *The American Millstone,* underclass ideology was in 1987 given a scholarly (and a black) imprimatur with the publication of University of Chicago sociologist William Julius Wilson's *The Truly Disadvantaged.*[87] The journalists made near-biological arguments for the inferiority, criminality, and disorganization of the minority poor—*Time* asserted that "the brightest and most ambitious have risen," "leaving the underclass farther and farther behind."[88] Wilson, in contrast, argued for a series of sociological causes of what he termed a significant rise in minority "ghetto-specific behavior"—joblessness, teenage motherhood, welfare "dependency," street crime, drug use. Economic downturn and deindustrialization, Wilson argued, compounded by theflight of middle-class minorities who had offered credible role models, had led to "social isolation" and thus the proliferation of undesirable behaviors in inner cities. The solution was "macroeconomic policy designed to promote both economic growth and a tight labor market" and "measures such as on-the-job training and apprenticeships to elevate the skill levels of the truly disadvantaged."[89]

Pundits ignored Wilson's policy prescriptions while latching on to his accession to underclass ideology, and Wilson himself has now abandoned calls for tight labor markets, arguing instead that the inner-city poor need the discipline of any sort of employment, even at a subminimum wage. But it is not only this capitulation to continuing state-sponsored upward income redistribution that flaws Wilson's work: Just as there was no white ethnic community, no women's culture, so the underclass is itself a politically constructed category, undermined by any careful assessment of historical and contemporary data. Moreover, Wilson's passive-verb political economy, wherein jobs just leave cities and minorities "get concentrated," prevents any adequate assessment of the past and present creation and reproduction of urban minority poverty, indeed, entirely elides the narrative given previously.

And the invented traditions of white ethnic community and, to a lesser extent, women's culture are symbiotically linked to underclass ideology. The often-implicit argument that white ethnics were the good, innocent, oppressed poor, whereas today's impoverished minorities are somehow a different species, truly deserving the hatred and scorn of them now woven into American structures of feeling, finds its apotheosis in sociologist Philip Kasinitz's glowing review of *The Truly Disadvantaged:* "The long unfashionable notion of social disorganization may have been inappropriately applied to immigrant communities by the early Chicago sociologists. Yet Wilson argues convincingly that it has a place in the discussion of the underclass today."[90]

In other words, that was then, this is now. My grandparents are above criticism, but yours are beneath. (Somehow I am haunted here by the vision of farmer Fred Guelzow's leg cut off and stuck in his mouth—now why is that?) Similarly, journalists wax eloquent on the difference between their charming ethnic ancestors and how they all deserved a leg up (and a wink of the eye at occasional illegalities) and all those subhuman Others today who cannot possibly be apprehended similarly, even when they occupy the same space and are engaged in the same activities. Mike Royko, for example, the late *Chicago Tribune* columnist who played big-shoulders, salt-of-the-earth Joe Six-Pack, wrote in response to the threat to the historic inner-city (largely black and Mexican) open-air Maxwell Street market, "Don't Shed a Tear for Maxwell Street": "It's easy to get nostalgic about Maxwell Street. . . . I share some of this nostalgia . . . the first suit I ever bought. . . . There was some [stolen goods] . . . but not as much as people thought. . . . The old Jewish ghetto produced business tycoons, powerhouse politicians, federal judges . . . [but today] this area is a major catalyst for stolen goods, drugs, prostitution, etc. . . . It's also a myth that Maxwell Street is an incubator for small businessmen. . . . Maybe in the old days, but not anymore."[91]

Or take *The New York Times*'s Francis Clines waxing lyrical over a Sinatra-worshiping pizza restaurant owner who observed the Great Man himself peeling off $100 bills for down-and-out *paesans* and whose disabled son "got a spot in this great place" after he "put in one call to Sinatra."[92] Nowhere in the text is a hint of Sinatra's unsavory reputation—or the basic inequity of a system where one has to "put in a call" to Frank Sinatra to get a place in a publicly financed residential program. And would Sinatra have helped a black or Latino father get his son into one?

In contrast, Sam Roberts, one the *New York Times*'s more liberal reporters, actually openly refers to "the propensity toward violence among black Americans"—not impoverished, young, inner-city, *male*, black (and Latin, Asian, white) Americans in recent years since high-power weapons (neither manufactured nor sold by or for the profit of the poor) have become so widely available, and since increased government-created poverty has greatly enhanced the desirability of engaging in illegal, and therefore violent, economic activities.[93] No—"black Americans." The biologically inflected racist language of the Victorian and Progressive Eras, so often beaten back by political and intellectual will over the course of the post–World War II decades, returned as the public transcript of the 1990s.

The sign of the grandparent appears again, as an emblem of the past in the present, in model minority rhetoric. Model minorities—construed as various Asian groups and, more recently, some Latins—are those who "work hard," have "traditional family values," "respect their elders," and thus succeed in the United States without "extra help." Model minority discourse is thus simply an extension into the present, and onto different populations, of the ahistorical and antiempirical ethnic report card model. Steinberg, in fact, has pointed out how the "theory of Asian success is a new spin on earlier theories about Jews, with whom Asians are explicitly compared."[94] Political scientist Claire Kim charts two waves of model minority mythology in American popular political discourse.[95] The first, in the 1960s, is associated with anti–civil rights politics. By "the rules of ideological triage," Kim argues convincingly, citing the long history of American anti-Asian racism, Asians were for the first time defined as good citizens as *nonblack* and *noncommunist.* This new mythology was furthered by the 1965 Hart-Cellar Immigration Act's encouragement of well-off professional migrants, a significant "class drain" from the Third World. The 1980s Reagan revolution heralded the second wave, in which Asian Americans' "success" was used to legitimate "moving back the clock" on civil rights. Kim points out that model minority rhetoric is racist not only against blacks and Latins, but also against Asians themselves: It obscures their heterogeneous national origins, their actually limited professional success, the widespread economic difficulties of nonelite Asian migrants (heavier users of welfare than whites in California, for example, where more than two-thirds of Southeast Asians are on the state rolls), and continuing American violations of Asian Americans' civil rights. Suzanne Model, in her historical analysis of ethnicity and economy in New York City, effectively destroys the "Why can't blacks be entrepreneurs like Jews/Asians?" line of argument.[96] Steinberg starkly lays out the issue of privilege obscured by model minority claims:

> In demystifying and explaining Asian success, we come again to a simple truth: that what is inherited is not genes, and not culture, but class advantage and disadvantage. If not for the extraordinary selectivity of the Asian immigrant population, there would be no commentaries in the popular press and the social science literature extolling Confucian values and the "pantheon of ancestors" who supposedly inspire the current generation of Asian youth. After all, no such claims are made about the Asian youth who inhabit the slums of Manila, Hong Kong, and Bombay, or, for that matter, San Francisco and New York.[97]

Gender is woven—with thread extracted from the white ethnic community trope—into model minority and underclass narratives in insidious ways. The obsessive references to black and brown "female-headed families" versus Asian "small family businesses" evoke widespread racist images of feckless, lazy, hypersexualized black and Puerto Rican women in contrast to industrious, obedient, "family-oriented" Chinese, Japanese, and Koreans. The actual daily lives of the millions of black and Puerto Rican women clerical and service workers, for example, go virtually unrepresented in mass media. "There's nothing filthier than a black woman drinkin and cursin," exclaimed working-class Tony Ripetto in my late 1970s study.[98] And New York journalist Jim Sleeper, in his 1990 racist diatribe *The Closest of Strangers,* prescribes an alternative to affirmative action for black New Yorkers: "the recruitment and training of a few hundred young blacks prepared to work fifteen hours a day at low wages and in close family units, as the Koreans do, in order to pay their debts to immigrant lending societies."[99] Popular images locate Asian women inside women's culture—innately nurturant, locked into "close family units"—and black and many brown women aberrantly outside it, acting out "male," morally inferior behavior and thus endangering social order.

Underclass ideology and the symbiotically layered constructions of women's culture, white ethnic community, and model minorities are powerful popular modes of apprehending shifts in modern American life, of denying inequitable economic structures and public policies, of legitimating the status quo. They exist, however, in a complex ideological landscape also featuring constructs that, rather than stressing race/ethnic or gender differences among Americans, assert homogeneity and the need to reactivate American community. Thus, we return to the Bellah group and its political allies, the communitarians.

Both *Habits of the Heart* and *The Good Society* assume a white, middle-class United States that is in need of spiritual regeneration, a reanimation of a sense of community. Spiritual sickness has arisen through overemphasis on individual rights and pleasures, competition for status, the accumulation of consumer goods. The Bellah group, however, is rather more circumspect about the entailments of overcoming "rights talk" than many other prominent communitarians. Mary Ann Glendon, for example, would roll back abortion rights, and both she and the late Christopher Lasch would make divorce more difficult—Lasch actually proposed outlawing it for couples with children.[100] Amitai Etzioni, editor of the communitarian journal *The Responsive Community*, would use public policy not only to discourage single-parent families, but also to minimize nonparental child care.[101]

It is not difficult to perceive the distinctly antifeminist thrust of communitarian pronouncements. Given the enduringly sex-segregated occupational structure and the tortoiselike improvement in women's pay relative to men's (about which communitarians have little policy interest or recommendation), restrictions on reproductive rights and the availability of child care would simply imprison more women in homes with young children. Making divorce more difficult might discourage some men from absconding from their families but would certainly prevent many women from leaving abusive situations. What is more difficult to see clearly, however, is that communitarians and underclass ideologues have worked out a fascinating division of scholarly/political labor: Each is the other's obverse. Both groups want to reform and reorganize populations, to get everyone lined up and properly cumbered. Each group expresses nostalgia for a world it never really lost, an imagined social body prior to the onset of present-day disease. But for underclass pundits, the minority poor are the patients to be cured, whereas white middle-class America is the ghostly exemplar of social health. For communitarians, well-off whites are the patients, whereas the minority poor are invisible, the accident victims without insurance who must simply go elsewhere to obtain treatment.

Thus, the two discourse frames work symbiotically, playing on moral motherhood, for example, both to stigmatize poor minority mothers and to discipline those who are better off against making demands for improvements in pay or for a government-subsidized national child care system. Each discourse focuses attention away from capital and the tiny percentage of the American population in control of it, displacing concerns about the state of the nation from power and policy to the ghetto or shopping mall behaviors that are their epiphenomena. Each discourse is part of a long tradition of narrating the American temperament rather than American politics, of psychologizing what needs to be described in dollars and cents. The "politics of meaning" so hyped in the Clinton era, then, is only a more covert, 1990s version of earlier, explicitly white, male supremacist ideologies that stigmatized my immigrant grandparents. In our "musical chairs" national morality play, the music never stops for long unless the powerful are sitting in Baby Bear's chair.

3

The Great Family Fraud of Postwar America

Brett Williams

Like so many Americans, for me, family comes first. When family values are undermined, our country suffers. All too often, parents struggle to instill character in their sons and daughters, only to see their values belittled and their beliefs mocked by those who look down on America. Americans try to raise their children to understand right and wrong, only to be told that a so-called lifestyle alternative is morally equivalent. That is wrong.

Dan Quayle, Republican National Convention, August 1992

FAMILY VALUES RHETORIC seems to be everywhere, flailing about in search of the heterosexual nuclear family household. The 1992 Republican Convention sported vicious attacks on lesbians and "welfare queens," Marilyn Quayle's garbling of class privilege as domestic virtue, and Mary Fisher's bleak contrast between the comfort she found nestled in a supportive upper-class family and the grim ordeal endured by a gay man dying alone in his garret. Rhetoric has grown toxic across the mainstream political spectrum. Thus, Pat Robertson

I thank Micaela di Leonardo, Geoffrey Burkhart, Samuel Collins, Adolph Reed, Jill Wittmer, Kevin Gray, James Pitt, Stoney Cooks, Lucy Nerio, Roberta Spalter-Roth, Susie McFadden, Jenell Williams Paris, Sherri Lawson Clark, and Gina Pearson for helpful comments as I wrote this chapter.

charges that feminists typically "leave their husbands, kill their children, practice witchcraft, destroy capitalism and become lesbians."[1] Bill Clinton, in a monumental insult to a man who never spoke this way, says that if Dr. Martin Luther King Jr.

> were to reappear by my side today . . . he would say, "I did not live and die to see the American family destroyed. I did not live and die to see 13-year-old boys get automatic weapons and gun down 9-year-olds just for the kick of it. I did not live and die to see young people destroy their own lives and then build fortunes destroying the lives of others. . . . I fought for freedom, . . . but not for the freedom of children to have children and the fathers of the children to walk away from them as if they didn't amount to anything."[2]

And FBI director Louis Freeh, calling for more humanitarian solutions to crime, nonetheless shifts easily between family values and its new companion, the "culture of violence," as he lumps "hopeless poverty" with "unloved children."[3]

Journalists offer cultural commentary as well. *Time*, in a primitivist trance, speculates that Americans have grown too much like the Ik, a starving people who allegedly regressed to pure, primal, murderous greed.[4] The *New York Times* spotlights "Children of the Shadows," cast off, one imagines, by their invisible Ik-like kin.[5] The *Atlantic Monthly* trumpets, "Dan Quayle Was Right" to herald a cover story that accuses single parents of valuing their own ambitions and escapades more than their children's. This piece features such rigorous correlations as this: "North Dakota, for example, scores highest on the math proficiency test and second-highest on the two-parent family scale. The District of Columbia is second lowest on the math test and lowest in the nation on the two-parent-family scale."[6] The author, Barbara Whitehead, goes on to charge that children with only one parent are more likely to experience emotional and behavioral problems, drop out, abuse drugs, get pregnant, and have trouble with the law. She concludes with the rank notion that children are better off if their father dies, taking with him to the grave an uncompromised reputation as an authority figure.

These are only a few recent examples of today's family saga as told by politicians and the mainstream press. Despite the rainbow of family values rhetoric, clear themes run through it. Most conflate form and content, reading selfishness, cancer, and cannibalism into single-parent households, or self-sacrifice into marriage. Most are racist, sexist, and homophobic, running riot among poor black families and lumping reproductive decisions with murder in vilifying inner-city neighborhoods. Many guardians of family values portray themselves as victims of political correctness, tout the courage it takes to criticize the poor, and find in popular culture diabolical evidence that they are besieged. For example, Whitehead argues that American culture pathologizes the two-parent family, citing as evidence a bumper sticker she saw in Amherst, the television shows of David Lynch, and a Boston-area museum.[7]

As is often the case, these storytellers advance a single-minded story of family breakdown, ignore debates in promoting narrow social science, and in turn bolster research and writing that reaffirm what many Americans may believe they already know. This process shapes genres as diverse as the personal essay and the quantitative mystification. For example, Cornel West's heavily publicized *Race Matters* rests on no standards of evidence, selection, representation, or interpretation, but rather flaunts the "just look around you" approach to social research. Yet he feels entitled to claim and many reviewers feel moved to praise such prose as this: "And a pervasive spiritual impoverishment grows. The collapse of meaning in life—the eclipse of hope and absence of love of self and others, the breakdown of family and neighborhood bonds—leads to the social deracination and cultural denudement of urban dwellers, especially children. We have created rootless, dangling people with little link to the supportive networks—family, friends, school—that sustain some sense of purpose in life."[8] West writes, of course, about poor black Americans, and his quote has the sole virtue of helping to unmask the fact that family values rhetoric most often takes aim at them. Those personal essays that selectively but not self-consciously purport to do social research will most likely be championed if they tell West's kind of story.

Those quantitative mystifications that carry political weight also tell stories of family breakdown while obscuring the fact that they, too, are personal essays. Quantitative researchers may begin with the assumption, for example, that families are the same as households and that there is only one appropriate way to fill a home. They render other kinds of domestic groups invisible, pathological, or badly flawed. They must spin stories to make sense of their statistics, thus joining figures that seem weighty to stories that they simply concoct. For example, in a study that comes close to being compassionate and insightful, David Ellwood questions whether "we" should expect single mothers to act more like husbands or more like wives. If the former, then "there is no one to help when the child is sick, no one to take the child to the dentist, and no one to help with the day-to-day crises."[9] Ellwood thus sabotages his noble intentions with his self-satisfied sense that in the absence of a two-parent nuclear family, single mothers have no domestic relations at all.

All of these devices to pathologize the families of the poor converge on teen pregnancy: the misuse of statistics; the slippery path from social science to popular culture, political speeches, and back again; the smug fabrication of biographies; and the blackout of those who try to spin a different story. In addition, teen pregnancy rhetoric exposes the main argument of this chapter: that family values hoopla rests ultimately on a monstrous hoax that paints the postwar era as a golden age for American families. The message seems abundantly clear: The United States suffers from an epidemic of teen motherhood, harbinger of lost families. Most Americans, I believe, have heard that message.

Many will reply, when asked to name the peak year for teen motherhood, that it is now. Yet news reports consistently obscure how teen motherhood is measured. When researchers calculate the percentage of teenaged girls who actually give birth, they find that these percentages were much higher in the 1950s than today. In 1957, for example, 97 out of 1,000 women aged fifteen through nineteen had babies. Today only half as many do. The startling logic of the fact that with improved contraception and legal abortion teenagers might be less likely to have babies is surpassed only by the spectacular masquerade by which this logic is lost.

Social scientists, politicians, and journalists then proceed to concoct stories about the epidemic, often searching for a single cause that will in one fell swoop account for all pregnancies: the burdensome legacy of sharecropping or a quest for self-esteem. But they are asking silly and useless questions. Research that raises the initial alarm is based not on counting the teenaged girls who give birth, but on calculating the prospects of future children, who are more likely to be born to teenagers today than in the past, as many women wait longer to give birth and then have fewer babies (meaning that these older women thus make up a smaller portion of new mothers).

Their decisions to defer or forgo marriage and childbirth are key, but rarely scrutinized, and teenaged girls (mostly black ones) become the scapegoats for an imaginary collapse of family values.[10]

This smoke screen typifies the family values show: The reforms of the 1960s, which actually opened up more possibilities for many Americans, including greater reproductive choice, become savage spears skewering the American family, so that today its role relations are so blurred that children have children. The story rests on inventing a golden age for families: the postwar era culminating in the 1950s. Nostalgists evoke two separate and generic visions, one for blacks and one for whites, construct them differently, and use them to mask both historical and contemporary social processes. These two postwar Americas have become raced, mirror-image mystifications shoring up an appeal to family values. By addressing each in turn, I hope to reveal what they mask and how.

The Golden Age for White Americans

By all accounts, postwar white America was a nuclear family fest. Women and men married younger, had more babies, spaced their babies more closely, and lived together longer, in single-family homes, even after their children had moved on. Divorce rates, along with women's job prospects and educational parity to men, fell, and many Americans reported in polls that they hoped to find their life's satisfaction within the nuclear family. This ideal 1950s family serves as centerpiece to family values rhetoric today.

In wondering why this pro–nuclear family boost occurred (reversing in many ways the trends of the twentieth century), scholars have pointed to several possibilities. Death rates dropped after the turn of the century, eliminating early widowhood for many Americans. The Great Depression and World War II had reinforced extended family ties, encouraging people to move, pool, and share; separating married couples; intensifying intergenerational dependencies. Yet many people experienced these connections as suffocating and conflicted. Most importantly, government policies and postwar conversions financed these white householders' ambitions: This perfect family was heavily subsidized.

The GI Bill provided housing and educational assistance to white men. To bail out banks suffering foreclosures, Home Owners Loan

Corporation, Federal Housing Administration, and Veterans Administration loans reduced down payments on houses from 50 percent before World War II to 5–10 percent afterward, and the thirty-year mortgage (fixed at 2–3 percent) replaced the five-to-ten-year mortgage of the period between the wars. The federal government subsidized highway construction and encouraged industrial conversions to produce prefabricated suburban housing. Thus, government policy and low-cost loans underwrote much of the cost of all new suburban housing, making these families perhaps the luckiest welfare recipients in history (if one discounts the settlers of the west). In unspeakable irony, they stand today as emblematic of self-reliance and proof by counterexample that welfare creates dependency and sloth.[11]

Yet at the time, members of these families experienced them as troubled. Women faced conflicting messages about work and domesticity: Enthroned in their new kitchens, they were demonized no matter which path they took. The transformation of shell-shocked veterans into emasculated bureaucrats haunted cultural arenas from television sitcoms to psychiatric research. Observers such as Father Robert F. Drinan fretted about divorce—"Time is running out. The forces of barbarism are at the gates. The very future of the nation depends upon what happens to the family life of our country during the next generation"[12]—citing its disastrous consequences for the "half-orphans" who were its victims and who faced mental illness, personality changes, crime, and early death as a consequence. Concern surged over juvenile delinquency; social scientists and their populists sought its cause: Was it the working mother, parental abandonment, infection from across the tracks, or contamination from television shows such as *The Lone Ranger*? Were young delinquent girls actually lesbians? One judge sentenced defendants to read good books, so despairing was he of finding role models or family values in postwar society.[13]

The underbelly of the 1950s nuclear family peers out most disagreeably in the ways that medical and social service professionals conceptualized and managed teen motherhood, schizophrenia, and homosexuality. Doctors and social workers entwined and confused the three paths and blamed them on skewed or hypernuclear families (perhaps foreshadowing contemporary notions that welfare breeds degeneracy).

During the 1950s, psychologists discarded two prewar tenets: The biological mother is a baby's best bet, and a girl should pay the price for pregnancy by rearing an illegitimate child. Earlier the young woman might have been labeled retarded; today she allegedly lacks self-esteem. In the 1950s, she was supposed to be striking back at parents who did not provide appropriate gender role models. Bred of a man who could not curb his wife, boyish in appearance, aggressive in grabbing male prerogatives, she might well be a lesbian. However, she could be rehabilitated through the birth and adoption process. By renouncing motherhood, denying selfish pleasure, and making a gift of her baby to a needy childless couple, she closed one act of her small psychodrama and began the redemptive process, finalized by marriage to a man and rebirth as a true woman. In 1955, ninety thousand white babies were put out for adoption, up 80 percent since 1944. The value of white babies was assured with the diagnosis of the mother as only temporarily mentally ill. She was curable, not genetically inferior. Foundling homes and orphanages may have closed their doors,[14] but maternity homes and baby sellers blossomed, for waiting to accept her gift were couples under great pressure not to be childless.[15]

The 1950s were also a time of deep concern over schizophrenia, a diagnosis that strained to contain homosexuality, juvenile delinquency, the isolation of housewives, epilepsy, encephalitis, mental deficiency, endocrine disorders, developmental disturbances, aphasia, impairment of auditory perception, dyslexia, severe hallucinations, and paranoia. The management of schizophrenia reveals some of the same twisted logic that beset teen pregnancies, conflating mental illness, gender relations, sexuality, and the tensions plaguing reified patriarchal nuclear families.

Psychiatrists of this era believed that schizophrenics felt threatened by powerful emotional experiences and their own hostile impulses. They were responding—perhaps appropriately—to the early misery of their interpersonal contacts through anger and regression. Some were probably homosexual, or merely bisexual, having stalled just past the autoerotic stage on the proper path to heterosexual maturity. The problem lay in their early years, in their parents' skewed and noxious relations: a "weak, immature, quiet, retiring," "inadequate, indifferent, subdued" or "passive and masochistic" father unable to complement or control (the real culprit)—his "eccentric and paralogic," "domineering, aggressive, rejecting, critical and overdemanding" schizophrenogenic wife.[16] In 1956 researchers proposed an institutional heir for babies born in the Florence Crittenden homes for unmarried pregnant women:

> Perhaps the next phase will include a study of schizophrenia as a family-borne disease involving a complicated host-vector recipient cycle that includes much more than can be connoted by the term, schizophrenogenic mother. One could even speculate whether schizophrenia as it is known today would not exist if parthogenesis was the usual mode of propagation of the human species or if women were impersonally impregnated and gave birth to infants who were reared by state nurses in a communal setting.[17]

The schizophrenogenic mother was a strange concoction, the maternal counterpart to the frigid bitch of teenaged sexual competition. She was cold, domineering, overprotective, and rejecting. She conveyed hatred to her child but framed her hostility with a metamessage of love, thus rendering him speechless, for he could not react to either message or comment on the double bind. The more subtle her domination was, the more malignant it became. She was a martyr to motherhood, feigning self-sacrifice and demanding in exchange unquestioning conformity with her wishes and convictions. The child's father could be toxic, too, but he was never as pathogenic as the schizophrenogenic mother.

Fueled by research and policy machines led by Gregory Bateson at Berkeley and Theodore Lidz at Yale, this portrait of the virulent nuclear family and malignant hypermother seemed completely obvious to at least a generation of mental health professionals, despite its cruel parody of the suburban housewife's ideal road. Why was this caricature unquestioned by a profession that now rallies firmly around the diagnosis of schizophrenia as an organic disease of the brain? Why did the mental health industry see women as so demonic? Why were schizophrenic, institutionalized housewives, who claimed they had flipped because they could not stand the work, isolation, and stress, yielded so little industry time?

Since the pathology festered in the family, treatment (as for the teen mother) demanded that the patient be institutionalized (perhaps to sample radioactive foods). Commitment could be involuntary, and release laws ignored mental patients' civil rights. Moreover, mere psychotherapy was considered inadequate, making electroconvulsive or insulin shock, lobotomy, or lobectomy necessary to purge the toxic psychic waste. The cruelty of both diagnosis and treatment, to patients and their families, unmasks the 1950s milieu: Suburban households harbored thick contradictions and generated deep disease but nonetheless sheltered medical paradigms that upheld the idea of these households while tracking how they went awry. Established as frail, lonely outposts in suburbia, many could not do their work, and institutions had to do it for them.[18]

Finally, the 1950s were a trying time to come out as a lesbian woman or a gay man. Although lesbian women and gay men had much in common, including brutal sweeps and purges, persecution as communists, police harassment, and the pressure to marry, their experiences were different in some ways, including their representation in the medical and social service literature. Lesbians were nearly invisible in medical research, and criminal/sodomy laws did not take them very seriously. Rather, they popped up, unexamined, in a number of worrisome contexts as stand-ins for juvenile delinquents, teen mothers, and the mentally ill. Lesbianism appears to have been too taboo for medical researchers to examine seriously: Lesbian women posed a true suburban nightmare.

By contrast, much research focused on gay men, caught in a turf war between psychiatrists and police. Psychiatrists argued that homosexuality was not a biological problem after all, but probably a mental illness. Some linked it to the single-parent household, for a woman alone was likely to engender a homosexual son. Or perhaps homosexuality stemmed from restrictive maternal attitudes toward the child's emerging sexuality or an early environment that was "barren and affectless." Whatever the cause, the grown homosexual man, according to this view, had a deep fear of intimate sexual contact with females.

Some psychiatrists struggled for a more humane, medicalized approach to homosexuality than the punitive screening, surveillance, dismissal, and incarceration practiced by the government, military, and courts. They criticized government regulations calling homosexuality a symptom complex seen in schizophrenic obsessional reactions, a "psychopathic personality with pathological sexuality."

"Many homosexuals are markedly unstable individuals whose mental health is a precarious matter at best. The stresses of prolonged investigation and the anticipation of inevitable punitive discharge are sometimes too much for them. It is not infrequent for such persons to develop acute disorganization or severe neurotic reactions requiring hospitalization."[19]

These psychiatrists tried to sort male homosexuals into different types, differentiating the "psychopathic personality with pathologic sexuality that is well-developed and long-standing" from those whose "homosexual acts did not indicate a well-developed sexual perversion, but rather were minor by-products of emotional immaturity in one way or another."[20] Some psychiatrists fought the military's discharge procedures, its emphasis on identifying and disposing of homosexuals with no real evidence. Some pleaded for a general, rather than dishonorable, discharge for these men, arguing they would be branded, banned, and unable to earn a living ever after, an excessive punishment for those who were "not truly perverted."

Psychiatrists also entered the criminal debate, arguing that sodomy laws were applied too loosely to round people up and that perhaps sentencing was too stiff, citing such criminals as "a man who lived with another man as his wife" and a "48 year old Negro who allowed himself to be masturbated in a public park."[21] The black man went to jail for six months, but his partner was committed to a state mental hospital, suggesting the importance of race and class in the shielding or medicalizing of gay men. As another example, a psychiatrist studying homosexual pedophiles in Sing Sing concluded that most were using a schizophrenic adaptation resistant to therapy but that electroconvulsive shock was effective in redirecting their orientation.[22]

We may never fully understand the homophobia and misogyny of the 1950s, but we can recognize that this spurious golden age was marred by unspeakable cruelty toward the mentally ill, lesbian women, gay men, and teen mothers, all of whom foiled its idealized white household. While many people in suburban families may have prospered, many others felt miserable and trapped. They escaped from their historically anomalous, fragile, and restrictive households in a short generation, built more varied homes in the 1960s, and sometimes railed against the homes they had grown up in. Today's family values rhetoric transposes these decades to demonize the years when Americans won more options and civil rights, but at the price of an inclusive social history that would bolster support for real families today.

The Golden Age for Black Americans

The golden age for Black Americans surfaces very differently, resting on an urban myth that celebrates those downtown areas white suburbanites fled. Because they were racially segregated, many of these areas were integrated by social class. Political speeches and much academic writing today hallow them as repositories of 1950s family values: Women and men married, worked, went to church, and taught their children to obey the proper authorities. Poor people could look to wealthier people for models of how to live one's life and as living proof that racism was no obstacle to personal pride and professional success. Even if people seemed poor, they luxuriated in the blessings of family and community.

Sociologist William J. Wilson was perhaps the first and most forceful champion of these fanciful communities:

> In the earlier years, the black middle and working classes were confined by restrictive covenants to communities also inhabited by the lower class; their very presence provided stability to inner-city neighborhoods and reinforced and perpetuated mainstream patterns of norms and behavior. . . . Lower-class, working-class, and middle-class black families all lived more or less in the same communities (albeit in different neighborhoods), sent their children to the same schools, availed themselves of the same recreational facilities, and shopped at the same stores.[23]

Wilson has bolstered family values rhetoric through his analysis of how these communities have changed. With only the most perfunctory nod at mountains of scholarly material that documents the buffeting of central cities by an array of political and economic forces, he suggests that the real problem there today is the loss of role models. When those who could leave, did, they left the poor with no one to model obedience, marriage, and self-esteem. Thus isolated, the poor sank into family and community pathology. Many scholars (beginning with some who did move out) and popularizers have embraced and echoed this vision of a lost golden age, and many white Americans feel they know it to be true. Unlike the critics who have flocked to attack the white golden age, almost everyone seems to embrace this mythical black urban community. On its path to conventional wisdom, it has mislaid even the skimpy infrastructure Wilson built, leaving the loss of role models to stand on its own in explaining the poverty of our central cities.

To examine that explanation fully, we must begin with the mythical community. First, the idea excludes the possibility of diversity in these places, offering up a generic vision to capture social life in segregated cities all over America.[24] Second, it rests on no historical or ethnographic foundation. For example, Wilson cites as his only evidence for what segregated communities were like the monumental *Black Metropolis,* an ethnography of 1940s Chicago.[25] However, he furnishes no page number (out of 809) for his claim, and I cannot find it there. Attending to just a small portion of what people wrote and remember about actual places exposes this generic representation as shady, shoddy, and convenient.

First to fall is the overarching portrait of friendly, harmonious class emulation. Real communities experienced variety in class relations, mediated by job opportunities, property ownership, schools, and civic and religious organizations. Class relations were probably no worse among black Americans than among any other group, but the historical record and ethnographic record attest that at least some postwar black neighborhoods were bitterly divided. St. Clair Drake and Horace Cayton (the authors of Wilson's sole source) in fact report "invidious distinctions based on skin color" and much interclass animosity, including intense resentment of the "dicties, stuck-ups, muckti-mucks, tony people, strainers, strivers," and, reciprocally, the "shiftless," "low-class," "trash," and "riff-raff."[26] They recount one incident when a poor man called a black doctor at night, asking for help and finding the doctor's wife reluctant to call him:

> "That's the way you dicty niggers are. You so high 'n' mighty nobody kin reach ya. We kin lay here 'n' die. White doctors come right away. Yore own people treat ya like dogs." . . . Responding to the call, the doctor "felt sick at his stomach." "Are these my people?" he thought. "What in the hell do I have in common with them?" . . . and later complained to his wife, "Same old thing. Niggers cutting each other up over nothing. Rotgut whiskey and women, I guess. They ought to start cutting on the white folks for a change."[27]

Other black professionals and business people shared the doctor's hostility toward the poor, visualized sometimes "as a 'problem,' and always as an embarrassment" because they were "backward," "ha[d] never learned to patronize their own," "expect[ed] too much," demanded credit, and refused to pay their bills. Some complained of the "ignorance," "boisterousness, "uncouthness," and "low behavior" of the poor. Although some hoped to help speed up the processes by which the lower class might be transformed into a counterpart of middle-class America, they resented both the pressures they felt to be race leaders and the tendency of outsiders to "judge us by what all ignorant Negroes do."[28]

Other scholars examining this period in Baltimore and New York report myriad sentiments, including feelings of racial unity and the drive to organize, resentment toward black property owners, or, conversely, embarrassment at the ill-bred behavior of migrants from the South.[29] Steven Gregory quotes a New York doctor who linked the decline of his area to the influx of southern migrants before World War II: "The transition of Corona was devastating to watch. When they opened (LaGuardia Airport), they brought a lot of blacks from Newark, New Jersey, over here to work at the airport. That's when this town started going down the hill. That influx of blacks. Nothing to say about southerners, but most of them were southerners from Newark who came up here to take the jobs. And the complexion . . . the whole atmosphere of the community started to change."[30]

Historians and ethnographers also allude to separate class/cultural worlds, including very different clubs and churches. Regarding domestic life, Drake and Cayton write:

> Here, beneath Bronzeville's surface, were a variety of living patterns. The twenty households, sharing four bathrooms, two common sinks in the hallway, and some dozen stoves and hot-plates between them, were forced into relationships of neighborliness and reciprocity. A girl might "do the hair" of a neighbor in return for permission to use her pots and pans. Another woman might trade some bread for a glass of milk. There was seldom any money to lend or borrow, but the bartering of services and utensils was general. Brawls were frequent, often resulting in intense violence.[31]

Shirley Taylor Hazlip, describing her mother's childhood in Washington, D.C., writes:

> She grew up in a black Washington rigidly stratified by color and class. Her color allowed her to straddle the top of the light and the well-to-do, who strove to protect and replicate themselves. . . . They eschewed Southern-style food. They attended the 19th Street Baptist Church, considered a "high tone" temple of worship "that bore little resemblance to lower-class Baptist congregations scattered throughout the rural South or poor districts of cities." . . . They formed exclusive clubs like the Kingdom. . . . If the Kingdom was full, they might choose to join the Mu-So-Lit men's club. . . . With each succeeding generation, the group became more insulated and more secure.[32]

Joseph Jordan's interviews among poor people in two Washington, D.C., public housing developments asked people to recall the postwar years. They did not speak so bitterly of their middle-class neighbors, but their memories were more nuanced than the imagined community allows. People recalled the convenience of living near a doctor not because he was a role model, but because he was a doctor. Phyllis Martin spoke of the comfort of "having a family doctor" and other things she needed, such as stores and "a movie house." She also described playing in the streets (because she could not use the playground) until the police came by and then hiding until they left, and indeed she emphasized the inconvenience of being forbidden to go many places she would have liked. Medell Ford described how it felt to be "less than a first class citizen" while praising the institutions blacks built for themselves: "A lot of things you couldn't do. You couldn't go in restaurants, you couldn't go in theaters. But fortunately, in Washington, the blacks had a society within a society. We had our own theaters. We could go to our own clubs. And a lot of them were flourishing, they were doing really well."[33] It is worthy of note, however, that Black Washingtonians referred to their hospitals as "slaughterhouses."

Moreover, outsiders at the time (honoring a long tradition harking back to W.E.B. Du Bois's research in turn-of-the-century Philadelphia) were just as virulent as those today in railing about the pathology and bad behavior of the poor. For example, Constance Green complained that in 1960 nearly 84 percent of *all* blacks in greater Washington lived in the inner city in fetid conditions, where, because of the man-in-the-house rule for welfare recipients, the father deserted or hid out, and the children grew up in a broken home, went off to Junior Village, or learned to lie to bureaucrats.[34] Justice Edgerton, of the District of Columbia Circuit Court of Appeals, likewise noted "that enforced housing segregation . . . increases crowding, squalor, and prices in the areas where Negroes are compelled to live is obvious. It results in doubling up, scandalous housing conditions for Negroes, destroyed home life, mounting juvenile delinquency, and other indications of social pathology which are bound to have their contagious influence upon adjoining white areas."[35] And in 1954 the *Washington Post* weighed in with "The Wickedest Precinct": "Rats and wretches, prostitutes and panderers, slayers, and slashers, hopheads and 'winos,' mingle and fight and die in the Second Precinct—Washington's wickedest. . . . Its streets have been swelled for years by Negroes drawn from outside the precinct by the jazzy taverns, blood and thunder movie houses, pawn shops, second hand stores, take out lunchrooms and billiard parlors."[36] Even Drake and Cayton, describing the world of the lower class (sex and family), discuss wild children, babies without fathers, and hustling women, among other measures they saw of social disorganization.[37]

Are we to conclude that role modeling did not work? In any case, these neighborhoods never really existed as the static, sunny communities of family values mythology. The Black Belt was often a congested and vicious place, crammed with tuberculosis, nasty industrial facilities, and deteriorating buildings, slashed by freeways, viaducts, and overpasses that swept away suburbanites but scorned its residents' transportation needs.

Often, powerful real estate interests purposely constructed Black Belt neighborhoods (in a fair imitation of the Jewish ghettos some of these residents had fought to eliminate) with the assistance of government policies that restricted the suburbs to white homeowners. In Washington, for example, the 1930s expansion of government made D.C. real estate the most lucrative in the country, and the absence of an industrial base made the realty/banking/insurance/title/savings and loan interests unchallenged in political and economic leadership in the city. Profits relied, however, on a market of exclusiveness. As white residents spread out into Maryland and Virginia, blacks were barred and boosted out of places where they had lived for generations. Some people found their property condemned or cut up by new roads and subdivisions, and tenants were evicted so that landlords would remodel and rent or sell to white residents.

Black residents were thus herded from the alleys bordering white neighborhoods, civil war fort sites where they had once sought refuge, and up and coming neighborhoods such as Georgetown and Foggy Bottom and were confined tightly in a crescent a little more than two miles in diameter around a hollow white downtown (like a servants' quarters servicing the government, hotel, embassy, and business district). The congestion of this area helped realtors mobilize the myth of a black invasion and contain the Black Belt inside a ring of panicked white neighborhoods.

But even once there, the Black Belt did not stagnate because realty interests were roving and restless: developing luxury housing next to George Washington University, condemning black neighborhoods for government buildings, schools, highways, wartime housing, the expansion of the navy yard, and a superhighway network to transport white suburbanites in and out of the city and service the Pentagon and National Airport. Black residents were displaced repeatedly while concentrated downtown and crammed tighter and tighter into the already bursting ghettos, as new migrants from the South arrived, to fill wartime and segregated government jobs and to work as domestics.

There for the second time segregation was capitalized: Blacks paid higher prices for their own exclusion because the demand for housing was keener. The same real estate interests that made money by excluding Blacks from the new subdivisions collected inflated rents from the slums into which they were driven. Those who owned homes assumed exorbitant financing costs and staggering under the burden of those payments, with the low income provided by segregated jobs, had to take in roomers and subdivide their homes, no doubt contributing to harmonious class relations.[38]

Residents of Washington during these years remember a severe housing crunch. Forced to double up and overcrowd, they also moved frequently, sometimes because they went to live with other kin or seek new jobs or because they were burned or forced out. Residents of Washington during these years speak of moving "round and round" or "just moving around." They lived on different streets and in several quadrants. They left relatives, lived with others, rented rooms, tried with optimism the new housing projects, and at times saw their homes, blocks, and neighborhoods razed for urban renewal.

As Medell Ford told Theresa Trainor: "When I went into the army I was living at 236 L Street; prior to that we lived at 239 C Street, that was only about a block from the Willow Tree playground; 921 2nd Street; 133 D street; 125 F Street; 232 E Street. The reason I had so many addresses wasn't necessarily because we moved that often, but I lived with other members of my family. I lived with my grandmother a lot, and my great aunt, who was also my godmother."[39] And Joe Brown recalled: "We started out in Southwest and had to move because of the redevelopment. We moved to Northeast. And from there we moved to Southeast."[40] Thus, the bright neighborhoods constructed by scholars today seem to exist only in their imaginations.

Indeed, residents fought to break "the iron ring which now restricts most Negro families to intolerable, unsanitary conditions." Despite the glorious communities they allegedly lived in, black families seemed anxious to move out. They felt resentful, disliking "the ideology that they should have a community of their own" and "bitterly attack[ing] the forces that ha[d] created an overcrowded black belt."[41] These supposedly golden years between 1945 and 1960 saw fierce battles to register voters and to bust the segregation of stores, recreational facilities, jobs, schools, and housing.

Three-quarters of the black workers in the city worked in low-paying domestic, service, and unskilled laboring jobs. Blacks' median income was only 52 percent of that of whites in 1950. Both the District and the federal government enforced rigid job ceilings. In the Police Department, blacks were most likely to work as crossing guards. In 1957 black citizens still could not work in airlines, in banks, in the Big 5 Department Stores, as streetcar or bus drivers, in the Fire Department, or on the Washington Redskins. Advertisements in the *Uptown Citizen* newspaper boasted of repair and paint companies employing only white mechanics. Federal legislation exempted businesses, as well as religious organizations, private clubs, restaurants, and the federal government, from fair employment practices if they employed fewer than twenty-five persons. These exemptions covered most of the Washington workforce. In 1959 blacks were still excluded from jobs as laundry truck drivers, ticket sellers, desk clerks, retail sales personnel, distributors of dairy products and baked goods, and all jobs in finance, insurance, savings and loans, real estate, title companies, and hotels (except for an occasional bellman or "assistant housekeeper").

Civil rights activists thoroughly documented the operations of this job ceiling from the 1940s to the 1960s as they sought to puncture it. The Congress of Racial Equality organized eighty-five picket lines in protest during the 1950s. As late as 1964, civil rights activists termed this situation a "powder keg." That it posed a problem in urban management is evidenced by the long campaign—and lengthy, vivid testimonies about beatings and harassment—that the National Association for the Advancement of Colored People (NAACP) conducted to expose discrimination and brutality in the Police Department and to oust Chief Robert Murray. Citizens recall simply staying off the streets whenever they could during those years, and one officer appointed to serve east of the river recalled his instructions: "You'll have to plan on beating people up over here."[42]

If one wants to romanticize a golden age, for some black residents of Washington it might be the early 1960s. People speak of feeling bottled up, or piled up, during the earlier years. The 1960s, by contrast, were a time of opening up. In many interviews, people expressed a sense of greater space and freedom as restrictive covenants fell. Several people mentioned moving out of the central city, sponsoring kin, buying a house, getting a yard, riding the bus to a better school, shopping with greater comfort because they could use restaurants and restrooms, and going into business or becoming a manager.

Others were not so lucky. By the late 1950s, as part of a postwar dream to make Washington the most beautiful capital in the world, the District Commissioners, in collaboration with the Redevelopment Land Agency and the D.C. Housing Authority, had moved seriously to bulldoze the Black Belt and relocate its residents east of the Anacostia River in order to reclaim downtown properties for tourism, commerce, and the state. These interests escalated a tortured, long-term, everyday looting of homes and communities in Washington's Black Belt, through code enforcement and condemnation for unsanitary conditions, to make room for federal buildings, more expensive housing, parking garages and parking lots. Thus, many people moved not into the streetcar suburbs but into public housing. In the words of the NAACP, it was "a 40 or 50 million dollar building program on the shoulders of race prejudice."[43] As examples, twenty thousand families were displaced in 1955 and seventeen thousand in

1961. In 1962 more "large families" had to move to make room for the Northeast Freeway, the East Leg, and the "C extension."

In 1958 the *Washington Post* published an article about a police precinct east of the Anacostia River. In 1947 the Eleventh Police Precinct, which covered the entire eastern side of the Anacostia River, had been divided in two. In "Juveniles Harass 'Baby' Precinct," reporters Alfred Lewis and Harry Gabbett described the growth and transformation of Washington's newest police precinct, the Fourteenth, opened in 1948, when its first case involved the theft of two cows from nearby Benning Road. In 1950, the precinct's population had been sixty-six thousand; in 1958, ninety thousand, with "Negroes in a better than 3-to-1 majority. . . . The biggest landlord in the Fourteenth is Uncle Sam, operator of no less than seven public housing apartment projects in the area. It is estimated that nearly 14,000 persons live in these projects today and 474 new units are under construction to provide shelter for some 3000 others."[44] The precinct also sported an "intriguing cloud" from the "colorful city dump," and auto thefts had replaced the theft of cattle as a social problem. This open-burning dump posed dangers to people in its vicinity; one child died after being badly burned there. It serves as an appropriate metaphor for the transformations taking place.

The last wave of public housing seems particularly telling. Housing officials had fretted for years about their inability to find space for displaced citizens. As the 1950s passed, planning authorities grew more desperate for space to house the people they were displacing. In the 1960s, during the last throes of home rule, their public records indicate that they simply gave up. However, these records also reveal a last-gasp effort to wring profits from housing dislocation. These developments grew more and more monumental, farther both from the center city and from the garden apartment ideal, designed for "large families," necessarily on public assistance, in the far outlying areas of northeast and southeast Washington and in a new reservation south of the Capitol on the river's west bank. By 1964 the National Capital Housing Authority was the city's largest landlord, with eight thousand units housing forty thousand people and twenty-three hundred more units in the works. Between 1950 and 1967, the neighborhoods east of the Anacostia River experienced a population growth of nearly 50 percent, while the city as a whole grew by only 6 percent.

Within a decade, the area east of the river (like many other parts of the city) was racially transformed through almost total white flight in interaction with "black removal." The Committee to End Segregation in the Nation's Capital had seen this coming as early as 1945. Ironically, the committee assumed that these new settlements would be servants' quarters, or bantustans, when actually there was nowhere to work at all.

Marion Barry and the Anti–Family Values Melodrama

Many historians of the city have blamed its problems on the flamboyant rule of Marion Barry, and histories of the city between 1976 and 1996 inevitably focus on his personal follies, with little attention to others in power before or since. But until the 1970s, the District was ruled by Congressional District Committees, three appointed commissioners, and many layers of planners and public authorities. All public works and political reforms required a special act of Congress. Citizens could not vote, and place-based associations and civil rights organizations served as their primary means for petitioning the commissioners about social problems or social change.

The failure of the city government has allowed the return of the commissioners in the form of the Financial Control Board and numerous receiverships. However, a researching of the history of the 1940s through the 1960s reveals that the city was constructed to fail under commissioner rule through renewal, relocation, and an infrastructure devoted to commuting automobile traffic. Many people profited from the infrastructure that was put in place then: from the Wall Street investors who loaned city agencies money, through those who demolished sections of the central city, to the developers and land speculators east of the Anacostia River.

The hasty, unplanned, haphazard overdevelopment of the area east of the river is palpable in the grim overbuilding; disorderly street plan; overlapping, contested neighborhood names; and absence of facilities. Arterial highways slice through communities and bear no resemblance to Pierre L'Enfant's original plan for city streets. Huge public housing developments that seem almost like small towns devour parts of the landscape. People and buildings are crammed into spaces that are too small to hold them. In many places, the hasty, grafted overdevelopment has left a grim ugliness, which is difficult to navigate and to know. People are too crowded, the buildings too big. There is too dim a mix of commercial and residential uses. There are no sit-down restaurants, and abandoned theaters dot a landscape of pawnshops, discount shops, and boarded-up buildings. Family values are not the problem.

The golden age masks all these processes and leaves us with a simple-minded portrait of black American communities in the 1950s. The Black Belt is glorified, and the second ghetto is naturalized. The roles of capital and the state in constructing and destroying both are erased. Thus, President Clinton invokes family values in the name of Dr. King at Anacostia High School, which at the time of his activism was all white and violently resisted integration. The ahistorical imagery of the golden age allows us to construct, in turn, something we call "the ghetto" and its "underclass."

How did the silly and pernicious fiction of the postwar black community become, like its white counterpart, a moral touchstone by which to measure city life today? How could a suffocating, segregated time reemerge in cultural debates as an era when family values prospered? Although I cannot fully answer these questions, the last section of this chapter explores some possibilities: the processes of cultural inscription that mask social processes and the political convenience of elevating families so that class and race become epiphenomenal.

Mystification and the Policy Lag

The postwar era is inscribed in particularly powerful ways in American society, beginning with the suburban house that enshrines both family room and master bedroom for the emerging eroticized companionate family. Between 1948 and 1955, many of these American households acquired televisions. Early television faced several problems: how to move spectatorship from outside to inside the home and make it compatible with idealized white family life, how to counter charges that television would contaminate Americans with Jewish ideas from New York, and, most importantly, how to gather families together in their new homes around the *television*.

Much of early television was concerned with the self-conscious invention of families escaping to the suburbs. Situation comedies helped families reconstruct domesticity and family life under new conditions and to imagine proper gender and generational roles.

Television also helped these families build communities, even as they left friends, relatives, and denser city life. These communities excluded people of color, lesbian women and gay men, the unmarried, the mentally ill, the elderly, and the homeless. Television offered new suburbanites happy families, electrical towns, and sanitized space.

Thus, segregated social space was enshrined in a new medium of unprecedented powers. In fact, some argued at the time that television helped black Americans, for it gave them the chance to participate, too. David Reisman wrote, using odd analogies, "The social worker may feel it is extravagant for a slum family to buy a TV set on time, and fail to appreciate that the set is exactly the companion for substandard housing the family can best appreciate—and in the case of Negroes or poorly dressed people, or the sick, an escape from being embarrassed in public amusement places."[45]

Television has never been a monolithic force, and even in the 1950s the more macabre anthology and vaudeville shows competed for family time. Indeed, television's family mainstay, the bachelor father household, premiered during this time (raising continuing questions about television's relationship to reality). But the important point is that early television followed, tried to mirror, and also helped to invent, in segregated space, the white suburban family where Mother Stays Home and Father Knows Best. Programs such as *Ozzie and Harriet* or *Leave It to Beaver,* which neatly resolved problems of gender, generation, and togetherness, stand as iconic for these families, far outlasting the families themselves and even commanding their own cable television station today.

Black families did not appear on television until the 1970s, although individuals appeared as clowns and housekeepers. Even the genteel Nat King Cole was boosted from the air after only one season, for his integrated variety show could not withstand the anxiety surrounding civil rights struggles in 1955. The postwar golden age is, however, ironically inscribed in several cities through high cultural landmarks and gentrifying inner-city neighborhoods. These include Washington's Sumner School and Howard and Lincoln Theaters, even Old Anacostia (ironically a site of vicious white working-class resistance to integration) and Baltimore's Sharp Street Church, Douglass High School, and the Royal Theater. Often key to preservation and "revitalization" efforts, these landmarks are surrounded by lore of the area's heyday and often evoked to celebrate family values. Often these landmarks and their lore herald the displacement of those alleged to behave badly today. They stand as grand reference points, islands of authenticity inspiring nostalgia for better days. In effect, they sell Jim Crow.[46]

These mystifications may be powerful because they hide critical social processes that would be better symbolized by a house than a family. In postwar America, deliberate, unjust government programs subsidized upward mobility for many white people and inferior segregated jobs and houses for most blacks. To praise yesterday's white families for building self-reliance and the black families for nurturing community allows critics to blame today's poor families for a deteriorating social fabric. All three claims are scandalous. But when the family is holy, race and class become epiphenomenal. Phyllis Schlafly contends that we live in a two-class society, divided not between rich and poor but between those who hold decent family values and those who do not.[47] Or as Whitehead offers in what is meant to be her penultimate proof that Dan Quayle was right: "In intact families children share in the income of two adults."[48] However, it seems likely that many Americans do not buy into these mystifications. Most polls show variety, confusion, and conflict in how people feel about families and family values. Despite the rhetoric, there is no consensus regarding sexual orientation, legal marriage, or the timing of childbirth. And we have voted with our feet. Most of us will live in varied households, spending less time rearing children and more time building other kinds of connections than June Cleaver did. We fill our homes with friends and relatives, give refuge to our boomerang children who cannot cope or find work, sustain intergenerational households and interhousehold domestic networks, defer childbirth and marriage, cement sibling ties, build lifelong same-sex relations, create families blending blood relatives, partners, lovers, and friends. We negotiate with the parents of our children about how to share responsibilities when we do not live together, we share custody, we foster and adopt children from around the world, and we search for alternatives to biological reproduction within heterosexual marriage. Older women in public housing find daily security and support through telephone buddies. These arrangements are often riddled with the inequities of class, race, and gender, and many people still face immense problems in making their families work. But we would do better to help real families in what they try to do than try to wish them away.[49]

But for officials starved for public resources and unable to do their work, the focus on family values provides an excuse they can live with when there is nothing they can do. We see this again and again in the speeches and writings of urban politicians. As just one example, the Washington, D.C., public schools offer frequent workshops for administrators and teachers on the family crisis. Rather than concentrate on what they can do to build constituencies, fight for funding, and transform the schools, these workshops discuss such topics as profanity in the home and fetal alcohol syndrome. The massive sloughing off of federal and state responsibility for people in cities thrives on and drives city custodians to their romance with the days of segregation. They have no money, and little political power, to address the inability of the poor to find decent jobs, affordable housing, and stimulating schools. Family values and, increasingly, "culture-of-violence" rhetoric deliver them from this quagmire. Yes, indeed, "the District of Columbia is second lowest on the math test and lowest in the nation on the two-parent family scale."

In addition to inequality in schooling, all sorts of other social problems are masked by the reifying of families and the ignoring of class. Many middle-class people are sinking from the consumer debt that has allowed them to fake a self-reliant suburban lifestyle, yet credit card advertising relies on themes of mastery and freedom. Popular writers link teen suicide to divorce, ignoring the fact that it disproportionately afflicts young gay men. Teenagers need support when they struggle with sexual orientation or contraceptive strategies, try to combine parenting and education, look for jobs that are not there, or run afoul of the law. Some homeless people may suffer from addictions, but they need housing, and so do their struggling kin who may have been forced to triage them.

Many of those immiserated in the 1950s profited from changes in the 1960s and early 1970s. Black Americans and mental patients won civil rights. The American Psychiatric Association decided that lesbian women and gay men were not mentally ill after all, and some cities enacted domestic partnership legislation. Teen mothers are no longer routinely evicted from public housing. But the reforms that allowed some families greater flexibility stopped too soon, and other families were relegated to abysmal housing and schools in neighborhoods where there were no jobs. People's experiences are sharply polarized by race and class, and schizophrenics live both in nurturant group homes and on the street. Government programs increasingly blame and punish those who do not live out the suburban or Black Belt ideal, and family values rhetoric ultimately demonizes the black poor, the last sinkhole for these tired notions. We need to fight for programs that support the actual families and households Americans choose and build. We need to let the good old days go.

PART TWO

Race, Ideology, and Social Policy: Beneath a Mystified Rhetoric

4

Race in the American Welfare State: The Ambiguities of "Universalistic" Social Policy Since the New Deal

Michael K. Brown

You must start with three facts: Most poor people are not on welfare. Most people on welfare are white, female and young. Two-thirds of the poor are women and children. A black mask has been put on the face of poverty. We must "whiten" the face of poverty to change the dynamics of the debate.

Jesse Jackson, *The Nation,* January 22, 1996

ONE OF THE CURIOSITIES of the recent debate over welfare and the legacy of the Great Society is the way in which critics in both the conservative and liberal camps have implicated African Americans. Conservative politicians commonly lament the "grim harvest of the Great Society" and pronounce its policies the cause of inner-city devastation by producing the "breakdown of the family structure."[1] Rather than remedying black poverty, the policies of the Great Society induced dependence on welfare, eroded work incentives, and facilitated moral laxness. Some versions of this catechism attribute the policy failures to the warped incentives of cash transfer policies, but most eventually identify the behavioral predilections of the poor as the root causes.[2]

What conservatives have done is to give the early-nineteenth-century belief that relief and social welfare had debilitating effects on the poor a new twist by linking it to race. The culture of poverty has coalesced with long-standing racial stereotypes that are the residue of slavery and its aftermath—the portrayal of African Americans as lazy and African American women as sexually promiscuous and wanton that is endemic to contemporary images of black welfare mothers. Rhetorical manipulation of the image of "dependent but avaricious" black welfare mothers by conservative politicians and policymakers depends on such racial stereotypes for its saliency and power, a power readily demonstrated in Republican electoral victories throughout the 1980s and most recently in 1994.[3]

Liberal opponents responded by apologizing for the excesses of the Great Society, admitting to the "behavioral problems of the poor" and accusing African Americans, and, of course, the liberals of the 1960s, of undermining the possibilities for a broader, more inclusive welfare state with their emphasis on "race-specific" policies. By adopting group-specific, rather than universalistic, all-inclusive, social policies, which singled out race as the decisive barrier to economic advancement, Great Society liberals and blacks alienated the white working-class core of the Democratic Party coalition and wrecked whatever chance there had been for a broader biracial, class coalition in the 1960s. Many contemporary liberals believe that the Democratic Party cannot hope to reestablish itself as a vehicle for progressive social policies so long as it embraces the racial agenda of the 1960s; it will become a majority party once again only to the extent that it cultivates middle-class loyalties and sheds race-specific policies. In fact, Bill Clinton's 1992 presidential election victory has been attributed to his campaign proposal to give welfare mothers a choice of working or being removed from the rolls, which brought Reagan Democrats back into the party fold. Some writers believe that Clinton's failure to address welfare during his first two years was a proximate cause of the electoral debacle of 1994.[4]

The irony here is that both contemporary neoliberals and conservatives have erected a racial mythology of the American welfare state. This mythology of the Great Society turns on a conception of welfare, Aid to Families with Dependent Children (AFDC) to be specific, and other 1960s policies that obscures the true effects of American social policy. The conservative claim that welfare has led to the degradation of the black family is manifestly untrue, while the fact that AFDC—a means-tested but otherwise color-blind policy—has become identified as a program for black women counters claims that the unraveling of the New Deal coalition can be traced to race-specific policies. Liberal critics cannot explain why AFDC, the majority of whose beneficiaries have been white (blacks have never made up more than two-fifths of the beneficiaries), is central to debates over race and the American welfare state.

The Perils of Nonexclusive Social Policies

This story of the political failure of the post-1960s Democratic Party recapitulates the standard account of race and class in American history. Such narratives are sordid tales of how incipient working-class alliances are scuttled by the machinations of ruling elites that deliberately foment racial prejudice or of how blacks or Native Americans are mere pawns, and ultimately the real losers, in a mostly all-white class struggle. Where the most recent version differs is that African Americans have now assumed the role of spoilers, just as white workers once did. Demands to remove racial barriers to economic opportunity and redress long-standing grievances only embitter otherwise natural allies.[5] Any mitigation of economic inequalities necessitates social policies that will transcend racial divisions and preclude their political manipulation. The only sure way to do this, according to some writers, is either through universalistic social policies or through a "color-blind" politics. Although the former appeals to the class interests of whites, while the latter presumes that only policies morally justified on nonracial appeals will succeed, either approach presumably would overcome the limitations of race-specific policies, yet permit the redistribution of resources to inner-city communities.[6] Both arguments are based on dubious assumptions and evade the racial legacy of federal social policy.

The notion of universalistic social policy is ambiguous. It typically refers to non-means-tested policies, which are presumed to be politically insulated from attack because they are inclusive. European social democrats bitterly fought to eliminate means-tested policies in order to forge solidarity; the political success of the American Social Security program is attributed, both by its allies and detractors, to its universalism. Yet the political prowess of universalistic social policies may be exaggerated; nor is it always a reliable guide to the legitimacy and survivability of social policies. To juxtapose universalism to its supposed opposite, means-tested policies, is misleading. Means-tested policies lack legitimacy because they are exclusionary and separate taxpayers from beneficiaries. They inspire opposition from those excluded.[7] Yet no universalistic policy is truly universalistic, since most are implicitly exclusionary. Nonveterans obviously do not qualify for veterans benefits; neither single persons nor childless couples qualify for a family allowance. The popularity of either depends less on universalism than on a belief that veterans benefits and family allowances are socially worthwhile programs. Social Security is often taken as the paradigmatic instance of the political power of universalism, but its popularity depends less on its universalism than on the widely shared belief that benefits are "earned" and thus are different from other social benefits.

Means-tested policies have universalistic features in that they are supposed to apply to all eligible recipients; they are not race specific.[8] Nor is it the case that means-tested policies are always the most vulnerable to political attack. During the 1980s, universalistic employment policies for the nonaged were shredded in Europe, while most means-tested policies in the United States were protected after the 1981 budget cuts. The Gramm-Rudman-Hollins law, which imposed mandatory budget cuts when the deficit exceeds specified ceilings, exempted all federal means-tested programs but not all universalistic entitlements. Medicaid, food stamps, and child nutrition were all expanded after 1982, and Supplemental Security Income, the federal means-tested program for the elderly and disabled, emerged from the 1980 budget wars more or less unscathed.[9] Universalistic programs may have more staying power; politicians certainly operate on this assumption. Yet one should be wary of automatically concluding that so-called universalistic programs will always serve the poor and the rich well. There is perhaps no better example of a politically secure universal policy than America's surrogate housing policy, the mortgage interest deduction, but this policy contains an implicit reverse means test, rewarding only home owners and excluding renters and thus excluding most low-income households. Universalism sometimes punishes the poor.

William Julius Wilson argues, correctly I believe, that political conflict over social policy in America is not just a matter of the divisive effects of means testing, as many proponents of universalism assume. It is less important whether social policies are targeted or universalistic, he believes, than it is that any policy be "clearly race neutral."[10] The problem, Paul M. Sniderman and Edward G. Carmines suggest, is to gain the support of whites who do not oppose the welfare state as a matter of principle but do oppose race-specific policies or any form of racial targeting. Public opinion data indicate that any policy that smacks of racial targeting erodes public support. In one survey, for example, 70 percent of white Americans indicated they would favor special tax breaks for businesses in poor neighborhoods, but only 43 percent would favor tax breaks in the ghetto.[11] Like Wilson, Sniderman and Carmines think that race-neutral or color-blind policies would persuade many whites to support new or expanded social policies.[12]

But what constitutes a race-neutral social policy in a racially stratified society is unclear. Wilson assumes that universalistic policies will be race neutral, yet a tangled connection between racism and social policy has been at the center of the American welfare state since the New Deal, belying the very notion of race-neutral policies. Nonexclusive, race-neutral policies in America have a way of being particularized along racial lines. Historically, the most legitimate universalistic social policy has been public education, but it has also been, and continues to be, one of the most racially stratified. "Separate but equal" obviously did not mean racially neutral despite the tortured logic of *Plessy* v. *Ferguson* (1896); but neither is the contemporary acceptance of de facto school segregation, however the Supreme Court rationalizes it.[13] It is hard to see what would constitute a race-neutral policy for public schools in a society with deep and enduring residential segregation. White suburbanites, whatever their feelings about education, have been reluctant to raise their taxes to rectify the deterioration of inner-city schools.[14]

Means-testing matters less than racial stigmatization. Crucial evidence of this is the historical discrepancy in the legitimacy of the two main public assistance programs since the 1930s: Old Age Assistance (OAA) and Aid to Families with Dependent Children. The former remained popular with legislators into the 1950s and continued to inspire fear among federal officials worried that the states would turn the program into a universal old age pension, whereas the latter became the object of a never-ending controversy immediately upon the end of World War II. OAA's divergence from AFDC in the 1940s and 1950s is not entirely attributable to either the legitimacy of old age assistance or the electoral clout of the elderly; it also depended on the stigma attached to AFDC as the proportion of blacks on the rolls increased in both the North and South.

The difference between the two programs was most apparent in the South, where state legislators cracked down on AFDC mothers at the same time they loosened eligibility criteria for OAA and raised benefits substantially. A Budget Bureau report dryly noted that in Louisiana "relatively rigid standards as compared with OAA cases are applied to the determination of income and resources for ADC [Aid to Dependent Children] cases."[15] During the 1970s, any stigma associated with the Supplemental Security Program, which replaced OAA in 1974, virtually disappeared; AFDC remained racially stigmatized. There is abundant survey evidence that AFDC is believed to be of sole benefit to black families and that black women receiving welfare are viewed more negatively than white women. The welfare backlash of the 1970s turned on the racial stigmatization of social policies, not the divisive effects of means tests.[16]

The idea of the "undeserving poor," as the divergent treatment of OAA and AFDC suggests, is intimately connected to the history of race and racism in America. What differentiates the "deserving" from the "undeserving" poor is work, and work has been historically connected to race, both in terms of the effects of labor market discrimination—blacks' inability to work at decent jobs—and as the source of the ideology of the American work ethic. One mark of citizenship in America, Judith Shklar argues, is earning a living, a status historically defined in light of a fear of falling into the degraded state of a slave. To be a citizen was to be free, which meant to be an independent worker. The strength of the ideology of work in America derives from "the memory of slavery, rendered ever potent by racism, [and] still arouses predictable fears among white workers and haunts blacks."[17] One contemporary expression of that fear is the loathing of "welfare dependency."

The argument for race-neutral or nonexclusive social policies elides this history and the relationship between race and social policy at the core of the American welfare state, with consequent implications for any notion of a biracial class coalition. Racism and, more broadly, the relationship of blacks to the welfare state cannot be exorcised by a mere shifting to more universalistic, race-neutral policies, even if that were financially possible today. What Wilson and others avoid is the way in which racial distinctions have become embedded in social policies, whether means-tested or not, since the New Deal. Such distinctions are quite startling: As of 1986, white households received 90.5 percent of all non-means-tested transfers and 63.4 percent of means-tested payments, whereas black households received only 8.2 percent of non-means-tested payments and 32.3 percent of means-tested payments.[18] These distributional inequities, as important as they may be, are not of interest here. What matters are the divergent relationships to the welfare state, the basis of a group's connection to the system of public social provision, and the political perception of that relationship.

The reality of American social policy since the 1930s is that it is both inclusionary and exclusionary, disadvantaging blacks relative to whites at the same time that putatively inclusionary, racially neutral policies such as AFDC are racially stigmatized. America's welfare state is based on a pattern of racial stratification that is defined by a long-term overlap between racial and programmatic boundaries, particularly among the nonaged. This overlap depends on the relative exclusion of minority and female-headed families from the main non-means-tested and private forms of social provision and the disproportionately low benefits they do receive when included; it also depends on their disproportionate inclusion in means-tested programs. The racial stratification of federal social policy obscures the structural advantages and disadvantages that derive from differential access to the welfare state between blacks and most whites. And by linking dependency with race, it perpetuates the most invidious of racial stereotypes. What is most distinctive about the modern American welfare state, in my view, is the extent to which social policy has become racialized, or rather the way in which some social policies have become racially stigmatized.

It is commonly assumed that the racial stratification of federal social policy dates from the Great Society. Wilson observes that the Great Society was "modeled on the English poor laws" and established a racially bifurcated system of social provision in big cities.[19] This is usually understood to be a legacy of the New Deal. Exclusion of African Americans from the Social Security Act and other New Deal legislation left a tangled, bitter legacy that reinforced racial inequalities. Meanwhile, social and political changes ignited by the New Deal set the stage for the unraveling of Jim Crow in the South and the second great wave of migration from sharecroppers' shacks in the South to the tenements of northern ghettos. Lyndon Johnson and the Democrats responded to this migration and the civil rights movement by creating new social policies calculated to assimilate African American migrants into the economy: the War on Poverty, Model Cities, and employment training, among others. Yet despite these heroic efforts to overcome the limits of the New Deal and remedy the exclusion of African Americans from the welfare state by "tacking onto the social security system a whole new layer of programs especially targeted for the poor, both whites and blacks," the architects of the Great Society failed and made race the decisive cleavage in the ensuing struggles over social policy.[20]

The origins of the racial stratification of federal social policy cannot be found in the so-called race-specific policies of the 1960s. Very few of the social policies of the 1960s were race specific as that term is commonly understood. When used by Wilson and others, race specific refers to affirmative action policies. Food stamps, Medicaid, and educational and employment training programs were all putatively race neutral, though in some cases the various employment training programs were targeted to big-city ghettos. The expansion of AFDC, often taken as the significant development of the 1960s, was neither planned nor desired by Johnson administration policymakers. And even though it is true that federal funds were directed at big cities with identifiable black constituencies, white middle-class jurisdictions also benefited substantially from the Johnson administration largesse. The diversion of funding under the Elementary and Secondary Education Act of 1965, a hallmark of the Johnson policies, to middle-class constituencies is a case in point.[21] It is well known that the major beneficiaries of the Great Society were the elderly, most of whom are white.

The identification of the Great Society as of sole benefit to African Americans derives from the public perception of the intended beneficiaries of the War on Poverty and the rise in the welfare rolls, whatever the reality. Contrary to public perception, the connection between race and social policy embedded in the American welfare state stems from national policy decisions during the 1930s and persistent discrimination within the labor market or within unions that has made some groups less eligible for social insurance or the receipt of employee benefits.

Despite the statutory exclusion of African Americans from social insurance, the New Deal is taken as a model of what ought to prevail under color-blind, universalistic policies. Wilson, for example, draws an invidious contrast between the Great Society and the New Deal, arguing that the latter was based on a repudiation of the dole in favor of full employment, popular public works programs, and aversion to means-tested relief.[22]

Yet the significance of the New Deal, in my view, is that it illuminates the perils of "universalism" in a racially stratified society. The New Deal's social policies, when combined with persistent racial exploitation and discrimination, reconstituted the color line in America. This new color line derived from the reliance of African Americans on relief, which was grounded in their widespread occupational displacement and downgrading as white workers turned their racial fury on blacks in the depths of the Depression and in the failures of New Deal social policy. Franklin Roosevelt's fiscal and employment policies reinforced the occupational displacement and downgrading of black workers, relegating them to both federal and local relief rolls. The 1939 amendments to the Social Security Act, which distinguished between widows and other mothers, made access to social insurance or public assistance pivot on family structure and thus inadvertently made the black family an object of social policy. The effect of New Deal social policy was to incorporate blacks into the welfare state while preserving the color line.[23]

This account of the New Deal lays bare the problematic relationship between universalistic social policy and the promise of a biracial, class coalition. The New Deal does not fit the typical historical pattern of race-class dynamics, since it ideologically, and in some ways politically, sublimated race to class. What the New Deal revealed, however, was the tension between race and class and the sheer impossibility of a class strategy in the absence of a confrontation with racism in America. Rather than incorporating African Americans into the New Deal as working-class citizens, it reconstituted the color line and embedded racial distinctions in the welfare state.

The Antinomies of Race and Class in the New Deal

The foundations of the American welfare state were forged on the basis of limited but universal claims to provide security for all citizens and to establish a framework for the rehabilitation of economic opportunity. New Deal social policy sought to eradicate dependence by replacing it with the right to security. The Social Security Act of 1935 established work-related entitlements for the aged and nonaged, which were supplemented by "temporary" work relief and public assistance policies. Contributory social insurance was reinforced by the right to collective bargaining and, by the end of the 1930s, labor laws that provided a minimum wage and other legal protections in the workplace.

The New Deal appealed to the common fears of the destitute and near-destitute and to the collective aspirations and hopes of the "ill-housed, ill-clad, and ill-nourished." New Dealers equated a common plight with the common good. Roosevelt's jeremiads at economic royalists, Harry Hopkins's ruminations about "idle men, money, and machines," and Aubrey Williams's assertion of the right to work as "simply economic realism . . . the quickest and cheapest way to attain full economic recovery" articulated claims to work-related social rights.[24] These universalistic claims to economic security were based on social class and were so understood. Workers believed that by "voting Democratic and supporting the New Deal . . . they were affirming rather than denying their class status."[25] Class identity overwhelmed ethnic and racial status.

Neither race nor gender figured in the founding of the American welfare state, as white liberals during the 1930s suppressed or ignored questions of racial and gender inequality. They assumed that as class differences between blacks and whites diminished or as class unity prevailed, racism would evaporate and gender would be irrelevant. There was an ineluctable faith on the part of racial liberals within the administration that New Deal reforms would incorporate blacks into the new political order and alter their economic status, thereby removing the single most important source of racial prejudice. White hostility would diminish as black income and education rose.[26] White liberals and radicals outside the administration saw race as a diversion from more urgent issues and an impediment to the formation of a broad working-class coalition. Attention to racial identity was thought to be dangerous precisely because it would allow conservatives to divide the nascent working-class alliance, particularly in the South.[27] In either case, race was suppressed in favor of a nonracialized notion of social class. At the same time, New Deal liberals made family integrity central to social policy by defining female householders as unemployable and reshaping social insurance, by 1939, into a policy for "family protection." Race and gender were thus sublimated to social class and family.

The logic of class and family appealed strongly to many African Americans and women. Roosevelt's assiduous avoidance of racial issues, notably his refusal to back congressional efforts to pass an antilynching law, was overshadowed by the limited but important economic assistance provided to African Americans by the New Deal. Black voters responded both to the logic of class and to Roosevelt personally, and rather than hold him responsible for the failure to pass an antilynching law, they swelled the Democrat Party rolls in northern cities.[28]

Nowhere, however, was the growing salience of class consciousness more apparent than among black elites in the main African American political organizations—the National Urban League (NUL), the National Association for the Advancement of Colored People (NAACP), and the National Negro Congress (NNC)—which came to believe that only through a class-based alliance of black and white workers could economic deprivation be overcome. Youthful black radicals sought to modify long-standing policies of the NAACP in favor of an alliance with white workers; and leaders within the NUL, notably T. Arnold Hill, tirelessly pursued a biracial class coalition. Many black organizations broadened the base of their white alliances by including union leaders on their governing boards and minimizing racial consciousness. The fight against racism was not entirely abandoned. The call for an alliance of black and white workers was accompanied by demands from prominent African American intellecturals such as Ralph Bunche to exclude whites from black organizations and by strenuous efforts to counter racism in the administration of New Deal programs and in unions. Yet for a time, black leaders could be said to have put their faith in a class strategy for political change. Blacks were thus incorporated into the new political order as part of a class coalition rather than as an exploited racial group.[29]

For women, a similar result prevailed because New Deal social policy was ultimately grounded in the idea of family protection. The New Deal preoccupation with family security was reinforced by the widespread belief that families, first and foremost, should be protected from the storms of the Depression. Ironically, the many attempts to force women out of the labor market and the palpable gender inequities of New Deal social policy provoked not only opposition by women but also, and quite often, support by women. The salience of gender, Alice Kessler-Harris has argued, paled before a belief that justice entailed distributing jobs to family providers before all else.[30] Some of the strongest opposition to married women continuing to work came from other women searching for ways to preserve their families.

But the appeal to social class and family was contradicted by the realities of a racial and gender bias at the core of the emerging welfare state. Neither the appeals of racial liberalism nor the vision of a unified working class could conceal the realities of race. And the perception of the moral justice of family providers could not completely obscure gender. What mattered in the end was how New Deal social policy defined the relationship of black workers and black families to the new welfare state, the patterns of exclusion and inclusion.

The exclusion of black agricultural and domestic workers from unemployment and old age insurance, the Wagner Act, and the Fair Labor and Standards Act put almost three-fifths of the black labor force outside the main welfare state policies. When combined with the exclusion of black sharecroppers, who were considered to be self-employed, it is likely that three-quarters or more of African Americans could not gain entry into the permanent New Deal welfare state. Not even those African Americans working in industries covered by the 1935 Social Security Act were unaffected. Because of wage-related eligibility criteria, 42 percent of black workers who worked in covered industries and paid payroll taxes for old age insurance were uninsured, compared to 20 percent of white workers, at the end of 1939.[31]

Yet black workers and their families were disproportionately included in New Deal relief programs. In fact, what blacks largely got from the New Deal was relief: By the spring of 1935 when the federally subsidized relief rolls peaked, 22 percent of all black families were receiving relief, compared to 13 percent of white families. Table 4.1 shows that the gap was substantially higher in urban areas, where over one-third of blacks were on relief, compared to one-eighth of white families, and in northern cities than in the South. Fifty-four percent of black families in northeastern cities were on relief, compared to 14 percent of white families. The relief rates in midwestern cities

TABLE 4.1 Urban Relief Rates, by Race and Region, 1933–1940, Selected Years

	Cash Relief 1933		*Cash Relief 1935*		*Work Relief 1940*	
	White Families	*Black Families*	*White Families*	*Black Families*	*White Families*	*Nonwhite Families*
Urban U.S.	10.0%	30.9%	13.5%	36.4%	3.5%	8.2%
Urban Northeast	9.5	35.8	14.2	53.7	3.1	9.1
Urban North-central	10.9	42.1	13.5	51.3	4.0	14.3
Urban South	10.0	25.6	11.4	25.5	3.3	6.0
Rural South	12.3	10.8	12.3	7.3	5.2	2.6

General Relief 1937

Blacks	*New York*	*Chicago*	*Detroit*	*Philadelphia*	*Baltimore*	*St. Louis*
% of caseload	21.7	25.0	31.8	44.2	47.1	40.0
% of population	6.4	8.3	9.3	13.0	19.4	13.4

SOURCES: Federal Emergency Relief Administration, *Unemployment Relief Census, October 1933* (Washington, D.C.: GPO, 1934), Table 5; Philip M. Hauser, *Workers on Relief in the United States in March 1935* (Washington, D.C.: GPO, 1938) vol. 1, Tables 19, 20, 21 (data on the number of families are drawn from the 1930 Census); U.S. Bureau of the Census, 1940 *Population: Families, Employment Status, Regions, Cities, 1,000,000 or More* (Washington, D.C.: GPO, 1942), Tables 5, 13, 15; National Resources Planning Board, *Security, Work, and Relief Policies* (Washington, D.C.: GPO, 1943), 117.

were comparable to those on the Eastern Seaboard; in southern cities the relief rates were lower, although the rate for black families exceeded that for whites: 26 percent of black families were on relief, compared to 11 percent of whites. Only in the rural South did white relief rates exceed those of blacks and then only slightly.

The disproportionate concentration of blacks on relief continued into the early years of the war. By the late 1930s, black workers and their families were more likely to be on work relief than whites; indeed after 1938 the proportion of blacks on Works Progress Administration (WPA) rolls actually increased. The total number of workers on the WPA rolls declined substantially by 1940, but the work relief rates for black families remained three to three and one-half times those of white families in northern industrial states (Table 4.1). Among urban workers throughout the country, black workers made up 17.2 percent of work relief rolls in 1940, down slightly

FIGURE 4.1 Black Workers on Federal Relief in Northern Cities, 1935–1940

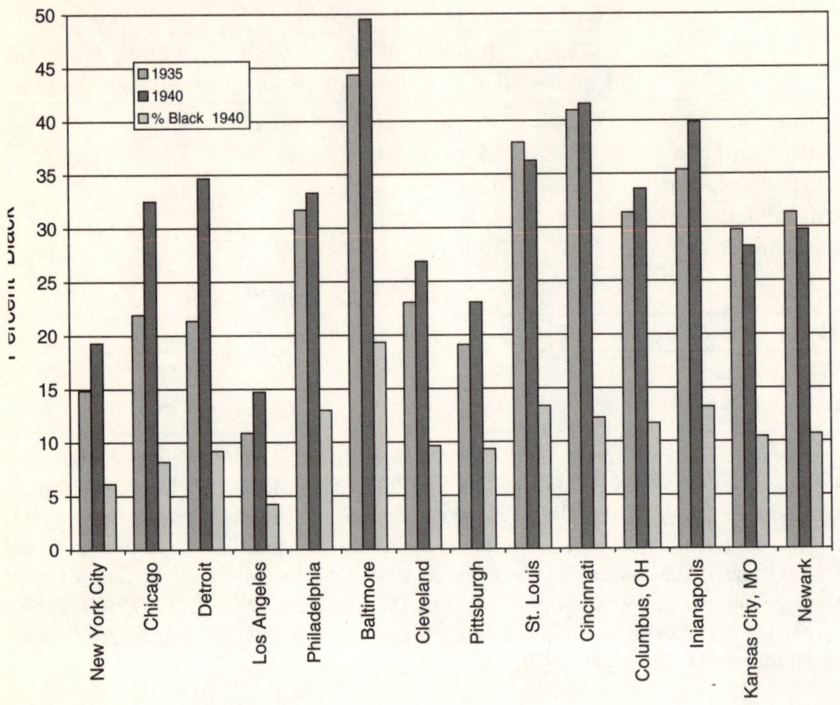

SOURCES: Philip Hauser, *Workers on Relief in the United States in March 1935* (Washington, D.C.: GPO, 1938), vol. 2, Tables 1–2; U.S. Bureau of the Census, *The Labor Force* (Washington, D.C.: GPO, 1940), Tables 41–47.

from 18.7 percent in 1935. But the proportion of black workers on the relief rolls increased in the north-central region and declined sharply in the South. As Figures 4.1 and 4.2 demonstrate, the proportion of black workers on work relief in large northern cities increased by an average of 3.3 percent between 1935 and 1940, with large increases in Detroit (13.4 percent), Chicago (10.6 percent), New York (4.4 percent), Indianapolis (4.5 percent), and Baltimore (5.2 percent). By contrast, in southern cities the proportion of blacks on relief declined by almost 10 percent on average, apparently because whites in the South were less likely to be forced off the WPA rolls than blacks. The proportion of blacks on relief in southern

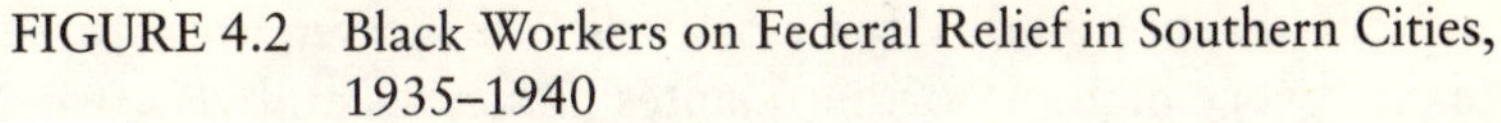

FIGURE 4.2 Black Workers on Federal Relief in Southern Cities, 1935–1940

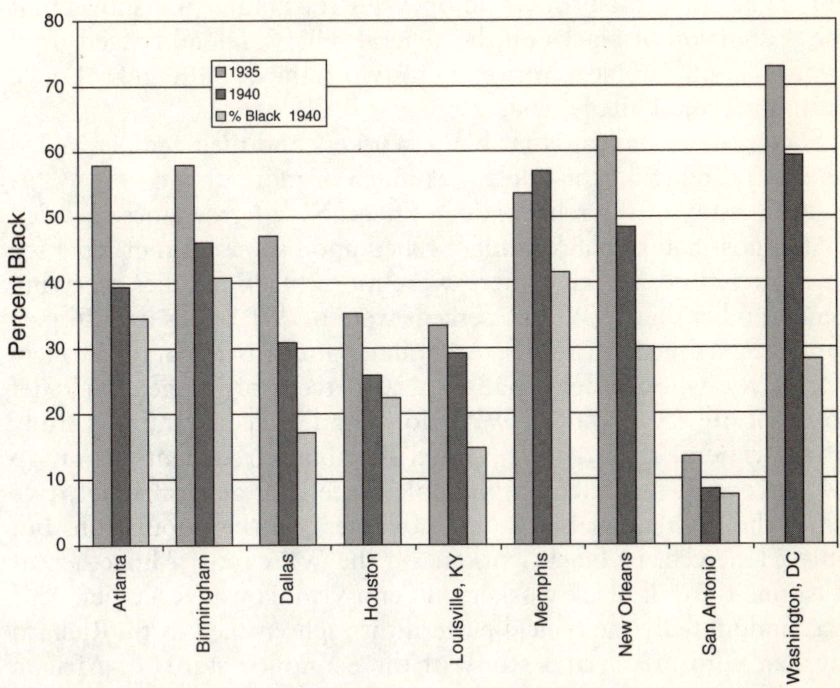

SOURCES: Philip Hauser, *Workers on Relief in the United States in March 1935* (Washington, D.C.: GPO, 1938), vol. 2, Tables 1–2; U.S. Bureau of the Census, *The Labor Force* (Washington, D.C.: GPO, 1942), Tables 41–47.

cities remained very high (38 percent) compared to northern cities (31 percent). Overall, black workers made up about one-third of the workers on relief in the nation's largest cities in 1940; this was greatly in excess of the proportion of blacks in these cities, especially those in the North.[32]

By the end of the decade, black workers made up a larger share of a much smaller federal work relief caseload, but this hardly tells the whole story. These data understate the number of black workers and families on relief in the late 1930s, since they do not include data on general, or local non–federally subsidized, relief. The proportion of blacks on general relief, which was the only source of assistance if one did not qualify for work relief or a categorical program, remained very high in northern states and cities and was usually higher than the proportion on WPA rolls. Table 4.1 shows that the proportion of blacks on the general relief caseload ranged from about one-fifth in New York City to two-fifths or more in St. Louis, Baltimore, and Philadelphia.

Some studies indicate that black workers and their families relied on general relief, or the "dole," as much or more than on the WPA. A 1938 study of the relief rolls in fifteen New Jersey cities revealed that almost half of black families relied upon some form of relief for their livelihood and that there were more black families receiving general relief than WPA (22 percent were on WPA rolls and 26 percent received general relief). A similar pattern is apparent in New York City, where blacks made up 20 percent of the general relief rolls but only 8 percent of WPA slots. And in Pennsylvania a study of the general relief rolls revealed that black recipients made up 24 percent of so-called employables receiving general relief, five times the number of black "employables" in the population, but only 11 percent of black workers on the WPA rolls. Altogether, at least one-third of black workers in Pennsylvania were on relief. This was undoubtedly the typical pattern throughout the North. Richard Sterner, who prepared a study of the economic status of African Americans for Gunnar Myrdal, captured their predicament when he observed that during the Depression "more Negroes obtain their main livelihood from relief . . . than from any single productive occupation except agriculture and domestic and personal service."[33]

The concentration of blacks on relief rolls, as important as it was to the survival of black families in the 1930s, stemmed from the widespread occupational displacement of black workers and the failure of New Deal employment and social policies. Blacks and women were cast as the villains of the Depression as it was presumed they took jobs from deserving (white) men; they were either forced out of the labor market or subject to occupational downgrading. White workers organized to force black workers from scarce jobs at the outset of the Depression, actions that local public officials often explicitly condoned. Skilled white workers displaced black workers by appropriating "Negro jobs" they had previously scorned. As the National Urban League told Roosevelt in a 1937 memorandum, "The area of so-called 'Negro jobs' had been steadily invaded by disemployed whites during the past decade, and this invasion, increased tremendously during the past five years, has practically eliminated any type of work 'reserved' for Negro workers."[34] Employment gains in manufacturing and personal service prior to the Depression were sharply reversed: Between 1930 and 1940, the proportion of blacks employed in manufacturing declined from 18.6 to 13.1 percent and in personal service from 19.3 to 11.7 percent. Accompanying the decline in the proportion of black skilled workers were increases in nonfarm labor and domestic service. The black unemployment rate was substantially higher than that for whites, and by the end of the 1930s the ratio of black to white unemployment had actually increased.[35]

New Deal social policies reinforced the effects of private labor market discrimination in forcing blacks on to the relief rolls. The wage policies of the National Recovery Administration led employers to impose color bans, relegating many black workers to the relief rolls. New Deal agricultural policies forced many black farmers and sharecroppers off the land, and many migrated to southern cities, swelling the relief rolls. But the most important New Deal policies forcing many blacks back onto relief rolls were the work and labor policies. Black workers faced the same job competition with white workers for work relief they encountered in the private labor market. Alfred Edgar Smith, an African American aide to Harry Hopkins who submitted monthly reports on the experience of African Americans under the New Deal, wrote that "Negro workers apparently have not been and are not being assigned to work relief in their direct relief proportion, and view with alarm the prospect of being left on state supported direct relief rolls."[36]

Black workers were excluded or displaced from public works projects either because doing so was a matter of policy or because local labor unions were allied with the officials running public works programs. The Civilian Conservation Corps, for example, imposed a quota on black participation, since many blacks were on relief and would have qualified. In other cases, skilled black workers were excluded from Public Works Administration (PWA) projects because of the pressure of local craft unions and the refusal of employment agencies to refer blacks. African American workers fared less well with the Civil Works Administration and the PWA when the aggregate unemployment rate was higher—and white efforts at displacement were more fierce—than with the Works Progress Administration. But even the WPA was not immune to such pressures. WPA subcontractors in New York City, for example, refused to hire blacks, and a NAACP survey discovered only forty-one black men employed on twelve construction projects.[37]

The subterfuges deployed to exclude black workers were numerous: African Americans were often denied work relief on grounds that since their standard of living was lower than that for whites, they did not need work and could presumably survive on cash relief; their applications were deliberately processed more slowly than those of white workers, which meant that the limited slots were given out to whites first. Such exclusionary practices were abetted by WPA policies. Harry Hopkins issued a policy directive in early 1936 requiring contractors to hire workers through union representatives and gave union members priority for work relief. The National Urban League protested, telling Hopkins and other WPA officials, "The average business agent would recommend first all the white men in the union who are on relief rolls, and would then seek by any possible means to avoid referring Negro union members, if there were any."[38] Hopkins subsequently issued a nondiscrimination policy, but local unions remained in control of job allocation to the detriment of black workers. There is also evidence of occupational downgrading. Black white-collar workers were often given unskilled WPA jobs so as to reserve available white-collar jobs for whites, a practice that evidently was common on PWA projects as well.[39]

Not only were blacks forced on to the relief rolls in greater numbers; they also were less likely to get off. More precisely, they shifted from relief to private jobs at a much slower rate than white workers. In the mid-1930s, the turnover rates for blacks were much lower than for whites, and when blacks were removed from the WPA rolls, they were less likely than whites to be reemployed.[40] By the late 1930s, many black workers and their families were caught in a relief cycle, which explains the increasing proportion of blacks on the relief rolls.

The general pattern is quite clear: As blacks were laid off or displaced from private-sector jobs, they were cycled onto cash relief and then off cash relief and onto work relief only as white workers departed for private-sector jobs. There is evidence that blacks were less likely to move from cash to work relief than whites were. After the creation of the WPA, two-thirds of white workers on the relief rolls in New York City moved on to the WPA rolls, compared to just one-third of black workers. Evidence from the New Jersey study of urban blacks demonstrates the prevalence of this pattern. In six cities, including Newark and Jersey City, black families made up 31.5 percent of the general relief rolls but only 19 percent of the cases transferred to the WPA rolls during 1938. If blacks were cycled from cash relief to work relief, white workers cycled from relief to work. There is some evidence that when whites were cycled off local relief rolls, they were more likely to move into the private-sector jobs than blacks. In Wayne County, Michigan (Detroit), 48 percent of blacks suspended from local relief rolls took WPA jobs, compared to 35 percent of suspended white workers, who were more likely to find work in the private sector.[41]

The relief cycle left black workers with few alternatives: They were forced onto relief, and their only alternative to cash relief was work relief. Life was especially difficult for black women, many of whom were worse off on general relief and public assistance after 1935 than they had been under the Federal Emergency Relief Administration (FERA).[42] The people abandoned when Roosevelt and Hopkins dismantled federal relief and reinstitutionalized local poor relief, it is worth remembering, were predominantly black and female.

If many New Dealers, among them prominent black officials and activists, thought the concentration of blacks on relief an "economic bright spot," others were far less sanguine. Acknowledging the importance of relief to the survival of black families, one black FERA official, Forrester B. Washington, believed long-term "dependence" on relief was as horrid a fate as the exploitation and discrimination that were the everyday lot of African Americans, since such dependence would only reinforce racial prejudices. Executives of the National Urban League had similar fears and adopted a policy of seeking jobs, rather than relief, for blacks. These fears fueled a strident effort by NUL leaders to create a permanent public employment program in the late 1930s. The warnings went unheeded as most New Dealers assumed that the social reforms of the 1930s would change the socioeconomic status of black Americans and usher in an era of racial harmony.[43] The reality, however, was that relief became an integral part of the color line in northern cities.

Even though the number of blacks on relief declined between 1935 and 1940 and the total number of blacks on relief was small—most

African Americans still lived in the rural South, where relief was mostly nonexistent—the rising proportion was regarded with concern and contributed to the perception that there was a link between blacks and dependence on relief. One indication of this concern was the appearance of fretful reports on African American migration toward the end of the decade. The report of the New Jersey commission investigating the plight of African American workers and their families reported that much of the public believed that blacks were migrating to the North for the "sole purpose of getting on public relief," something the commission was at pains to disprove. It commented, "The Negro population has consistently been treated as a dependent group to which relief of a sort must be given."[44] A report by Alfred Edgar Smith to Hopkins in the spring of 1938 mentioned apprehension in Chicago over a steady increase in the city's black population; efforts under way in Washington, D.C., to discourage southern migrants from settling in the District; and comments in a congressional debate on a relief appropriations bill that referred to black migration as "a disturbing factor in the relief situation to be reckoned with in the future."[45] By reinforcing the underlying dynamics of labor market discrimination, New Deal social policies contributed to the fateful connection between relief and race forged in the 1930s.

Politically, the onset of racially stratified social policies by the late 1930s eroded support for local relief and public assistance. There should be no illusions about the so-called ennobling qualities of work relief in the late 1930s. Work relief, although preferred to cash relief, was stigmatizing like the dole and resented; WPA workers were set apart as incompetent or worse. One informed observer said at the time that the WPA "has meant so much in hardship, humiliation, bad working conditions and jobs not in their own trade, that they want to get off the rolls as quickly as possible."[46] Given the pervasiveness of racist stereotypes about black workers, the increasing proportion of blacks on the WPA rolls could only have reinforced such impressions. There was consequently very little public support in the late 1930s for expanding WPA and relief expenditures, despite continuing high levels of unemployment. Large majorities opposed increased spending for either relief or the reduction of unemployment.[47]

Besides the absence of pressure to increase spending on work relief and public assistance, there was overt opposition to relief spending.

Local tax protests, widespread in the early years of the Depression, continued throughout the late 1930s. In Baltimore, for example, the Taxpayers League organized against the incumbent mayor when he proposed a tax increase to deal with unemployment and rising relief costs. Even though the mayor escaped defeat on a platform pledged to efficiency and reduced spending, the opposition to both relief and tax increases spread throughout the state. A familiar drama was played out in Maryland, one that pitted a conservative, rural-dominated legislature against urban jurisdictions, with rural opponents making a fateful connection when, in the context of the relief politics of the late 1930s, they objected not just to city profligacy but also to "the presence of 'large numbers of Negroes' who, after having sampled the pleasures of 'relief allotments, refused to work any more.'"[48] How widespread these sentiments were is difficult to tell, but the increasing presence of blacks on the welfare rolls did not go unnoticed and may well have contributed to the erosion of political support for employment policies.

Blacks certainly believed that enactment of tighter eligibility standards for relief and reduction of relief funds in the late 1930s were motivated by hostility toward them. A columnist for the *Chicago Defender* thought that "the belief that most of the migrants into Illinois were Race persons had something to do with the legislature's decision to lengthen the residence requirement for relief as a bar to migration. Probably the fact that large numbers of Race persons are on WPA had something to do with the decision of Congress to reduce the appropriation. In any event the appropriations have been reduced and the Race must suffer."[49] And prominent Republicans searching for ways to peel off voters from Roosevelt's coalition or repeal New Deal policies made the connection between relief and race a matter of public discussion. Robert Taft, a conservative Republican senator from Ohio, publicly commented that it is "virtually essential" that the Negro race escape from the "demoralizing help" of the WPA.[50] Other Republicans peddled this line during the late 1930s for the electoral benefits. Already by the end of the 1930s, conservative and anti–New Deal politicians were engaged in linking race, taxes, and welfare in the voters' minds.

That the racial stratification of New Deal relief policy persisted is partly due to the 1939 amendments to the Social Security Act, which made the black family, and hence the behavior of black women, an object of public scrutiny. These amendments expanded coverage of old age insurance to include the survivors (widows and dependents) of eligible workers and erected, as one of the architects of the law, J. Douglas Brown, put it, "a closely interlocking system of protection for both the aged and for dependent survivors of all ages," or for the social protection of families.[51] The addition of survivors and dependents benefits were justified as a necessary replacement for Aid to Dependent Children, or "Mother's Pensions," as the program was known at the time. The Social Security Advisory Council observed in its report that just as Old Age Insurance would replace Old Age Assistance, "the arguments for substituting [survivor's] benefits as a matter of right in the case of children are even more convincing than in the case of aged persons."[52] The Social Security Board had reported that in 43 percent of families receiving ADC, the father was deceased and thus would be eligible for survivor's benefits; adding the dependents of dead but eligible workers to social insurance was expected to reduce the future costs of public assistance.

The 1939 amendments put adequate social protection for nuclear, two-parent families at the core of social insurance and thus drew an arbitrary distinction between the married and unmarried, the legitimate and illegitimate. By reinforcing the notion that women's place was in the home, not the workforce, survivor's benefits fully institutionalized the dependency of women that until 1939 had been restricted to single mothers, thereby making gender a constitutive element of the welfare state. Without alterations in the coverage provisions, working women were at a singular disadvantage: They were precluded from attaining eligibility by exclusions in coverage and paid what amounted to a marriage tax, since single wage earners would subsidize families. Wives' benefits were superior to the realistic benefits that could be obtained by working women, whose survivors and dependents remained uncovered by the 1939 amendments. The wise woman would presumably favor patriarchy to work.[53]

Equally fateful, the 1939 amendments also drew a fine distinction between legitimate and illegitimate "widows" and the offspring of such relationships. Thus, the amendments incorporated a distinction based on marital status into the heart of the act. Neither divorced nor deserted women with dependent children were entitled to survivor's benefits; dependent children below the age of eighteen were eligible regardless, provided they had not been adopted and were dependent upon the beneficiary. "Illegitimate" children, that is, the children of "unmarried" women, were specifically excluded by the 1939 amendments. The law required that dependent beneficiaries demonstrate a legal relationship to the deceased but covered worker, which meant, Congress explicitly stipulated, that the relationship be recognized as legal under state intestacy or inheritance laws. Children born out of wedlock or in common law marriages were typically excluded from inheritances, though state provisions varied widely. Most states at the time required fathers to support "illegitimate" children, but, ironically, under the provisions of the 1939 amendments "benefits must be denied in many instances to surviving children who have been in fact supported by a father even though he has contributed to a system designed to protect fatherless children."[54] Family organization thus became a determinant of a person's relationship to the welfare state.[55]

Aside from ritualistic pronouncements that survivor's benefits would reduce ADC caseloads, little thought was given to the relationship between the two. What is clear, however, is that insofar as Mother's Pensions, which had been incorporated intact into the Social Security Act, was a social policy for "gilt-edged" widows, it was now replaced by survivor's benefits, leaving ADC for all other single mothers and thus altering the character and goals of that policy. Congress refused in 1935 to accept an administration proposal to provide public assistance payments for all families in need with children under the age of sixteen. This decision statutorily labeled single mothers as unemployable and excluded poor two-parent families from federally subsidized public assistance altogether.

Moreover, state governments, under the fiscal pressures of the Depression, acted to alter the goals of ADC. Massachusetts, for example, broadened the definition of "suitable mothers" in order to shift women and children to federally subsidized ADC and relieve pressure on unsubsidized general relief. As a consequence, the proportion of widows receiving a Mother's Pension declined from 71 percent in 1935 to 47 percent in 1942.[56] Mother's Pensions had historically aided white women and children, a pattern that began to shift during the Depression. The process of occupational displacement and the exclusion from social insurance operated here as elsewhere to increase the proportion of black families receiving public assistance except in the South. The proportion of black families receiving ADC rose from about 3 percent in 1931 to 14–17 percent by 1937–1940, slightly higher than their proportion in the population, although in southern states black children made up 12 percent of the ADC caseload but 38 percent of the children.[57]

The growing concentration of African Americans on work relief, general relief, and public assistance was accompanied by rising concern over the implications of prolonged unemployment for the structure of black families. Long before the Moynihan Report made illegitimacy and the structure of the black family central to the debate over welfare, New Dealers, social workers, and black elites were already using similar language. E. Franklin Frazier reported that anywhere from 10 to 30 percent of black families in the North were headed by women and that unattached black women made up a larger proportion of relief recipients than white women. The FERA apparently believed that black poverty, unlike white poverty, was a problem of "female dependency often involving children."[58] The Urban League documented a decline of employment for black men and the rise of black women to the status of bread winners. The St. Louis Urban League said the "increasing number of Negro women who are finding their way into domestic service as a way of taking up the slack resulting from the scarcity of jobs for men [was cause for concern]; that this development portends a bad future for Negro family life and the welfare of its children, no one can deny."[59] The Urban League's strong stand in favor of a permanent public employment program was undertaken in light of such fears. A Detroit social worker, in a chilling portrait of the effects of the Depression on black families that is all too redolent of contemporary commentary, said, "Negro women are frequently left as the economic heads of families when their husbands can neither contribute prestige nor security and drift away from the family scene."[60]

New Deal Legacies

The disproportionate presence of blacks among the beneficiaries of means-tested policies during the Depression, when coupled with the distinction between widows and other mothers after 1939, bequeathed an explosive legacy to the future. The war-induced prosperity provided many African Americans opportunities for employment and occupational advance and blurred somewhat the racial stratification at the heart of the New Deal welfare state. But this prosperity did not eliminate racial stratification. The joint effect of New Deal reforms and the continuing process of occupational discrimination relegated blacks and single women to a newfound status within the American welfare state that could not be easily undone. The racial and gender distinctions etched into the fabric of social policy in the 1930s not only persisted but also were elaborated, and by 1960 the image of indolent blacks lounging on relief forged during the Depression had been linked to illegitimacy.

Postwar employment changes worked to the disadvantage of black workers, as did the economic stagnation of the 1950s. In the postwar period, blacks, who remained concentrated in low-skill, low-wage jobs, faced increasing competition from white workers displaced from agriculture and a shrinking demand for unskilled labor in an economy dominated by an expansion of defense-related manufacturing, with its requirements for skilled technicians. Occupational discrimination and competition from white workers likely operated to limit the access of black workers to full-time, high-wage employment. These labor market dynamics had similar effects to those in the 1930s and limited access of African Americans to social insurance, thus relegating them to means-tested public assistance, primarily ADC and general assistance.

Black women were doubly disadvantaged. Not only was their access to middle-class policies undermined by labor market discrimination, but they also remained statutorily excluded from unemployment compensation. Nationally, 49 percent of working African American women in 1960 were employed as agricultural laborers or domestic workers, both of which remained uncovered by unemployment insurance. In the South, 60 percent of black women were affected by these occupational exclusions. Only 10 percent of white women, by comparison, were employed in these jobs, and they were two and a half times as likely as black women to be in manufacturing jobs.[61] Moreover, the unemployment rate for black females was almost twice that of white females. As a consequence, it is not surprising that so many African American women found themselves, from time to time, in need of ADC benefits.

The ADC caseload grew much faster than Old Age Assistance in the late 1940s as the racial composition of the ADC caseload shifted. Blacks, especially outside the South, were admitted to ADC at higher rates than whites in the early war years, and between 1942 and 1948 the number of black families receiving ADC increased by 46 percent.[62] Throughout the postwar period, the proportion of black families on the rolls rose rapidly even as the overall growth of the ADC rolls stagnated because of policies adopted in many states to exclude families from welfare. Most of the movement of African American families onto the ADC rolls took place prior to the Great Society, not during and after. By 1961, 40 percent of the ADC caseload (3 million persons) was composed of black families, up from 29.5 percent in 1948 and about what it is today. In some areas of the country the proportion was much higher: In northern industrial states black families made up 59 percent of the caseload; 45 percent in the Midatlantic states of New York, Pennsylvania, and New Jersey; and 57 percent in the South. Yet many poor black families that needed assistance did not receive ADC. Here the racial pattern was reversed: 80 percent of "illegitimate" nonwhite children did not receive ADC in 1960, compared to 20 percent of similar white children.[63]

Perversely, blacks were both underrepresented and overrepresented on the welfare rolls, and the sharp differences in the distribution of aid to blacks between urban and rural areas during the New Deal reappeared. Two-thirds of black families receiving ADC lived in cities of fifty thousand or more inhabitants, compared to 29 percent of white families. Once again, it was blacks in the rural South who bore the brunt of discrimination and exclusionary policies, while the presence of large numbers of African Americans in northern and southern cities attracted both hostility and concern.[64]

The rapid change in the composition of the ADC rolls was accompanied by prolonged, hostile attacks on welfare in many areas of the country as the New Deal's putative consensus on the need for family protection unraveled with a debate over illegitimacy that became entwined with race. The rise of illegitimacy as a political issue was fueled by perverse laws in some states and by well-known changes in the marital status of ADC recipients as the number of widows on the rolls declined and women whose husbands had left them or women who had given birth to children out of wedlock increased. In Illinois, for example, the law sharply distinguished between divorced/separated/deserted women and family, on the one hand, and those families with "illegitimate" children, on the other. Families of the former kind had to wait six months to receive benefits because of legal requirements to track down husbands and obtain support, whereas children of unmarried mothers were immediately eligible for a grant.[65] Some states began to impose restrictions, notably "suitable home requirements," and reformers and social welfare officials responded by asking whether categorical assistance to single mothers could be sustained given the increasing provision of ADC to families whose fathers were absent for socially unacceptable reasons. One national welfare official worried that "it high lights a condition frequently arousing such a strong suspicion and prejudice as to sidetrack the concern for the child's need."[66]

Local welfare and relief programs were under persistent political attack beginning at the end of the war, an attack that reached a national furor by 1952. Welfare policies were publicly attacked in sixteen states during 1947–1948, and in many cities prolonged investigations were undertaken. The charges have a familiar, contemporary ring. A New York Budget Bureau report said, "The welfare department appears to have no standards of morality for relief recipients but condones immorality and even abets it." A Detroit judge proclaimed that welfare was a "free love racket" that paid unwed mothers to have babies. And in Baltimore the Commission on Governmental Efficiency and Economy reported that "it certainly appears that the welfare policies have had the practical result of condoning and in effect encouraging dependence upon the government, idleness, pauperism, desertion, illegitimacy, dishonesty and irresponsibility."[67] Illegitimacy and welfare chiseling became a national cause, with otherwise staid national publications reporting on the squalor of unwed mothers, very often reputed to be working as prostitutes on the side while collecting the taxpayers' money, and deadbeat husbands.

Race was the ever-present subtext to these reports. Coded language conveyed unmistakable meanings. One *Saturday Evening Post* exposé of "welfare fraud" managed to avoid mentioning race, but practically every picture accompanying the story was of black women and children.[68] A fixation on black migrants coming North to take advantage of generous welfare payments dates from the 1930s. A New York City welfare report of the late 1940s revived the charge and gave it currency in the postwar period, suggesting that "the relief allowances . . . granted in New York City has and will continue to encourage migration to this city of people without any visible means of support, including those whose sole purpose is to receive public assistance."[69] The perils of migration also surfaced in other cities and were allusively linked to illegitimacy and the African American family.

Conservative politicians in the North and white supremacists in the South fused race, sex, and welfare in the 1950s by exploiting racial fears and concern over rising welfare expenditures. They depicted black unmarried mothers as "women whose business is having illegitimate children" and who used ADC as the means to their ill-chosen ends.[70] It was less a matter of welfare dependence than welfare corruption, a problem of "black women, sex, and money" that was portrayed, as Rickie Solinger puts it, as "a direct financial loss for whites."[71] Federal social policy was directly implicated as the progenitor of "illegitimate" black children. The National Urban League reported that "The Truth Seeker, a Negrophobic smear-sheet" appeared on the streets of New York City, headlining, "UNCLE SAM: BLACK BASTARD BREEDER SUPREME—Unwed Negro Mothers Battle New Orleans, Mississippi, and Newburgh, New York."[72]

By linking race, sex, and money, politicians and others hostile to welfare revived stereotypes of African American women that can be traced to slavery. Black women in slavery were portrayed as sexually promiscuous and wanton, stereotypes that justified sexual assaults during slavery and thereafter. Efforts to undo these images have historically failed, and after the Depression they were joined to an image of morally corrupt welfare chiselers—the hypersexual, greedy, black welfare mother who produced children for profit at the expense of white taxpayers. The irony, here, is that compared to black unwed mothers, twice as many white unwed mothers who refused to give their children up for adoption were receiving ADC. The lurid but erroneous images of black welfare mothers reestablished the connection among race, taxes, and welfare that was apparent at the end of the 1930s, and many states made concerted efforts to purge black families from the welfare rolls through suitable home laws and laws withdrawing support from "illegitimate" children.[73]

The racial bifurcation in social policy that forms the core of so much commentary was firmly established prior to the launching of the Great Society. It is no small irony that the decade blamed for the failures of American social policy actually sought to replace welfare with job training, education, health care—all of the remedies that are part of practically any contemporary political agenda. More ironic perhaps is that the welfare explosion of the 1960s was of principal benefit to white families. By the time the AFDC rolls began exploding in the late 1960s (the largest increases took place between 1967 and 1973), the proportion of eligible black families enrolled in the program was far higher than that of white families, and the average monthly caseload for white families increased by 80 percent, compared to just 2 percent for black families.[74] The proportion of white female-headed families that received AFDC tripled between 1961 and 1977, rising from 11 to 34 percent.[75] In many northern states, the proportion of black AFDC recipients declined. In the heartland states of Illinois, Michigan, Ohio, Indiana, and Wisconsin, for instance, the proportion of blacks dropped from 59 to 47 percent, and in New England states the drop was 7 percent. The explosion of the black ghettos in the mid-1960s was of extraordinary benefit to poor white women, who, though eligible, had been deterred from applying for assistance. It is not the first time in American history that the struggle for racial justice has meant a more just society for everyone.

My tale of the New Deal and its legacy for post–World War II social policy serves as a warning to those who think that race-neutral policies offer a way to break the historical link between race and social policy. Large-scale universalistic social policies such as Social Security make sense, but not for the reasons often advanced. The political success of a social policy depends on more than its inclusiveness. The reason to support more inclusive social policies is that they are more equitable and less likely to be discriminatory. By the same token, universalism is not likely to remove race from social policy. Social insurance policies that put employment at the core, as Old Age and Survivor's Insurance do, will perpetuate racial inequities so long as labor market discrimination persists.[76] More importantly, universalistic transfer programs would have to be very large and very expensive to have any appreciable effect on ghetto poverty. Even if the Democrats were to regain congressional majorities (itself problematic), investors' fears of rising federal deficits and inflation, along with widespread opposition to taxation, would make the adoption of comprehensive programs impossible. For any new social policy some form of targeting will be necessary.

New social policies might be nonexclusive and color-blind, but they are unlikely to remove race from social policy. Would these policies continue to be viewed as part of a legitimate safety net, even as it became clear that the need for them would continue long into the future and that a disproportionate number of the beneficiaries would be racial minorities? Proposals for neo-WPA programs illustrate the problem. Mickey Kaus believes that work relief would be both more acceptable to the American public and more effective in remedying urban poverty simply because it responds to the ideology of the work ethic.[77] But if the experience of the New Deal, or even of the public employment programs of the 1970s, is any guide, Kaus's new WPA will inevitably be seen as relief for poor blacks. It is worth recalling that the one social program eliminated outright in 1981 was public service employment, a program in which blacks were disproportionate beneficiaries.[78] Any new programs to remedy inner-city poverty, moreover, will compete with other needs—for example, retraining of workers displaced by global economic competition—and very likely reproduce the New Deal pattern of racially biased allocation of public resources combined with the stigmatization of whatever assistance is provided for the poor.

Any severing of the link between race and dependence, a connection grounded in the legacy of slavery and the experience of the Depression, will require more than policy engineering. It will come about only as part of a transformation of the racial practices of this society. Racism cannot be removed by ignoring it, despite the ideology of a color-blind society; nor will black and white workers comprehend a common fate by sublimating race to class. To do so is to succumb to the myopia of the racial liberals and radicals of the New Deal. Justice Thurgood Marshall's eloquent defense of affirmative action policies in the *Bakke* case made clear the necessity of confronting racism in a principled way: "It is unnecessary in 20th century America to have individual Negroes demonstrate that they have been victims of racial discrimination; the racism of our society has been so pervasive that none, regardless of wealth or position, has managed to escape its impact. . . . It is because of a legacy of unequal treatment that we now must permit the institutions of this society to give consideration to race in making decisions about who will hold the positions of influence, affluence and prestige in America."[79] So, too, must the legacy of racism in our social policies be confronted.

5

Symbolic Politics and Urban Policies: Why African Americans Got So Little from the Democrats

Dennis R. Judd

An assessment of the benefits that African Americans derived from participating for more than a half century in the New Deal coalition must include an analysis of the federal government's urban policies. I am willing to assert that outside the South the constellation of federal urban policies enacted from the 1930s to the 1960s has exerted a more enduring and far-reaching impact on race relations and the well-being of African Americans than even the civil rights legislation of the 1960s. Viewed from the perspective of black Americans, the federal role in the cities was consistently perverse and detrimental, for almost all of the federal policies had the effect of reinforcing and sometimes even mandating racial discrimination and segregation. For northern blacks, any dividends paid for their

---

Some material in this chapter is based on research also reported in *City Politics: Private Power and Public Policy,* 2d ed., which I coauthored with Todd Swanstrom. I thank Todd Swanstrom for granting me permission to use some material from that book. I also thank Mike Goldfield for thoroughly reading and critiquing an earlier version of this chapter.

participation in the New Deal coalition were offset by the negative consequences of urban policies sponsored by the Democratic Party. The effects of these policies are never figured in the balance sheets kept by liberals who might claim that blacks have not been sufficiently appreciative of the benefits of interracial coalitional politics.

Political Spectacle, the Democrats, and Urban Policy

The importance of African Americans to the New Deal coalition was immediately connected to their voting strength in northern industrial cities. Few cities of the North had many black residents in 1910, but by the 1930s the situation had changed dramatically. Between 1910 and 1930, more than 1 million blacks left the southern states for such places as Chicago, Detroit, Cleveland, New York City, Pittsburgh, Philadelphia, and the smaller industrial cities sprinkled throughout the Midwest and the Northeast. Black populations in the big cities rapidly increased during the Great Migration (as historians called it), rising from 1.9 percent of New York's population in 1910 to 4.7 percent by 1930, from 1.5 percent to 8 percent in Cleveland, and from 5.5 and 6.4 percent to more than 11 percent in Philadelphia and St. Louis.[1] By 1930, blacks made up 18 percent of the population of Gary, Indiana, and 16 percent of East St. Louis's population. These numbers make it plain why Democratic politicians in the North began to court African American voters in the 1930s.

The New Deal made efforts to respond to the concerns of black voters. In addition to the material benefits that flowed through relief and public works programs, the administration made some important symbolic gestures. Franklin Roosevelt placed blacks in several visible positions, and he generally followed the recommendations of the National Association for the Advancement of Colored People when he appointed race relations advisers to a few federal departments. Partially as a result of such gestures, for the first time since Reconstruction blacks turned their backs on the Republican ticket in the 1936 election and gave more than two-thirds of their votes to the Democrats. In the presidential elections to follow, the proportion of blacks voting Democratic rose steadily.

After the Roosevelt years, northern Democrats generally embraced the cause of civil rights. In 1946 Harry Truman's Justice Department recommended the enactment of a federal antilynching law. A month after the Democrats suffered heavy losses in the 1946 congressional races, Truman signed Executive Order 9008, which established a presidential commission on civil rights. In February 1948, the president proposed a civil rights bill that would have established a permanent civil rights commission, made lynching a federal crime, authorized the Justice Department to sue for infringement of voting rights, reestablished the Fair Employment Practices Commission, and prohibited discrimination on buses and trains that crossed state lines.[2] A few months later, after an impassioned speech by Hubert Humphrey, the delegates to the Democratic National Convention narrowly endorsed the civil rights bill. Subsequently, Truman issued executive orders prohibiting discrimination in the federal civil services and segregation in the armed forces.

I offer this brief account as the outline of the standard narrative describing how the Democrats became allies of African Americans in their struggle for political equality and representation in the American political system. By labeling this recounting a "standard narrative," I do not intend to denigrate the efforts of liberal Democrats who fought to break down the legal edifice enforcing a second-class citizenship for blacks. Several prominent liberals were willing to, and did, take significant political risks in defense of civil rights remedies. When the Dixiecrats walked out of the Democratic Convention in 1948, it was generally assumed that Truman's reelection bid was doomed, as indeed it was if southern politicians had refused to return to the fold just before election day. However, it should also be noted that Truman would have lost the election if the big cities had not tipped the scales in his favor in the industrial states.

A persuasive case can be made that African Americans reaped huge benefits when they abandoned the Republicans and began voting Democratic. In exchange for their votes, northern liberals "came through." This version of the story, however, obscures as much as it reveals because it is based on a recounting of the dramatic events played out on the political stage—party conventions, political posturing, speeches, elections—what Murray Edelman has called the "political spectacle."[3] But the day-to-day implementation of policy was completely uncoupled from the spectacle. At the level of "deep politics"[4] beneath the Sturm und Drang, policy implementation proceeded according to its own logic. In the case of urban policy, racism was a fundamental premise of that logic. While northern liberals publicly proclaimed their commitment to civil rights, immensely important housing and urban development policies were being carried out that systematically discriminated against and segregated blacks within metropolitan areas.

Federal Urban Policies: The Suburbs

When large numbers of blacks began streaming into northern cities in the years before World War I, white home owners and developers reacted by blanketing residential areas with restrictive covenants. By the 1920s, the owners of a large proportion of homes in major metropolitan areas were barred from selling to blacks. Deed restrictions were almost universal in exclusive subdivisions. The precedent for enforcing them was established by the enormously influential Kansas City developer Jesse Clyde Nichols, who developed the Country Club district of Kansas City from the early years of the century to the mid-1920s. To help developers escape the vagaries of the marketplace and achieve control over their subdivisions, Nichols devised the self-perpetuating deed restriction. Such restrictions were enforced by home owner associations (or by individual home owners going to court), which could wield the significant threat of suing any individual home owner for violating a restriction. In the Country Club district, the deed restrictions specified minimum lot sizes and setback distances, the building materials and style of houses, and even paint colors and landscaping.[5] By signing these deeds, buyers also automatically promised to resell only to whites.[6] Blacks were, in effect, treated as a threat to property values in precisely the same way as an unapproved room addition or wild paint scheme was. Nichols's innovation quickly spread to other cities and to neighborhoods that lacked home owner associations, with the restrictions enforced in these areas by neighbors or by realtors.

By the 1920s, the real estate industry had accepted as a fundamental law of economics the principle that the value of property was connected to the homogeneity of neighborhoods. From 1924 until 1950, article 34 of the realtors' National Code (circulated to realtors everywhere by the National Association of Real Estate Boards) read: "A Realtor should never be instrumental in introducing into a neighborhood a character of property or occupancy, members of any race or nationality, or any individual whose presence will clearly be detrimental to property values in the neighborhood."[7] In addition, most local real estate boards were guided by written codes of ethics prohibiting members from introducing "detrimental" groups into white neighborhoods. The textbooks and training materials used in real estate training courses were careful to point out that realtors were ethically bound to promote homogeneous neighborhoods. The leading textbook used in such courses in the 1940s, for example, compared some ethnic groups to termites eating away at sound structures:

> The tendency of certain racial and cultural groups to stick together, making it almost impossible to assimilate them in the normal social organism, is too well known to need much comment. But in some cases the result is less detrimental than in others. The Germans, for example, are a clean and thrifty people. . . . Unfortunately this cannot be said of all the other nations which have sent their immigrants to our country. Some of them have brought standards and customs far below our own levels. . . . Like termites, they undermine the structure of any neighborhood into which they creep.[8]

Any realtor found breaking the code by selling to suspect groups in the wrong areas was subject to expulsion from local real estate boards. Even nonaffiliated brokers felt compelled to accept the realtors' guidelines because most of their business depended on referrals.

The housing industry's policy of preserving residential segregation became a foundational principle for two of the most influential and expensive federal housing programs ever enacted. The National Housing Act of 1934 funded the well-known loan program administered by the Federal Housing Administration (FHA). In 1944, Congress supplemented this legislation by the more generous Veterans Administration (VA) loans made available to returning GIs by the Serviceman's Readjustment Act. Whereas FHA loans typically required a 5 to 10 percent down payment, VA loans required no down payment at all.

A reading of the 1934 Housing Act does not make it obvious that federal policy would tilt toward the suburbs at the expense of the inner cities. Title I of the 1934 act provided FHA insurance for loans used for "permanent repairs that add to the basic livability and usefulness of the property."[9] Section 203 set up the FHA's home loan program for new construction. City officials hoped Title I would be a catalyst to entice affluent people to stay within the city limits and remodel their homes rather than move to new homes in the suburbs. Downtown business interests wanted Title I to bolster the value of the central business districts. But most banks, savings and loans, realtors, and contractors saw Section 203 as a way to finance new construction beyond the built-up city. In lobbying for the housing legislation, they had agreed to Title I only as a compromise necessary to ensure congressional approval.

As actually implemented, the new federal programs came to mean new housing construction outside the cities. Very little money was ever appropriated to implement the inner-city Title I provisions. In contrast, over the years the FHA loan guarantee program for new construction exerted a huge impact on the housing industry. Fully 79 percent, about 9.5 million units, of all FHA-insured units from 1934 to 1975 were insured under the 203 program, representing a face value of more than $109 billion.[10] About one-third of all homes purchased in the 1950s were financed through FHA or VA loans. By 1972, FHA had helped almost 11 million families become home owners.[11] In 1984, the FHA-VA share of home loans fell below 10 percent for the first time since World War II.

Federal administrators reflected the values and assumptions of the housing industry for the simple reason that they were recruited from the industry. As was the case for all the regulatory agencies created during the New Deal years, the regulated industry supplied most of the federal personnel with whom they would have to deal, and federal administrators shuttled freely back and forth between private industry and government jobs. As a consequence, the main effect of federal policy was to give official imprimatur to the way the housing industry already operated.

Almost all of the new homes underwritten by FHA-VA loan insurance were built in the suburbs. Throughout the 1940s and 1950s, the FHA exhibited an overwhelming bias in favor of the suburbs, as indicated by the fact, for example, that in its first twelve years it did not insure a single dwelling on Manhattan Island. In part, the FHA's suburban bias reflected a preference for single-family, middle-class neighborhoods, as opposed to densely settled city neighborhoods. But the FHA suburban preference went far beyond a simple matter of geography. FHA administrators assiduously promoted the idea that housing, and therefore neighborhoods, must remain racially segregated. When the FHA issued its *Underwriting Manual* to banks in 1938, one of its guidelines reminded loan officers of the FHA's belief that property values and racial segregation were closely connected:

> Areas surrounding a location are [to be] investigated to determine whether incompatible racial and social groups are present, for the purpose of making a prediction regarding the probability of the location being invaded by such groups. If a neighborhood is to retain stability, it is necessary that properties shall continue to be occupied by the same social and racial classes. A change in social or racial occupancy generally contributes to instability and a decline in values.[12]

Any bank that ignored this instruction might have its authorization to participate in the FHA insurance program withdrawn.

The FHA's administrators derived their views about the connection between racial segregation and property values from reports by real estate analysts. A revealing glimpse into how sensitive FHA administrators were to the issue of race can be gained by the reading of some startling language from a 1933 report submitted to the agency by one of its consultants, Homer Hoyt, a famous sociologist and demographer. Hoyt's professional opinion was that

> if the entrance of a colored family into a white neighborhood causes a general exodus of the white people it is reflected in property values. Except in the case of Negroes and Mexicans, however, these racial and national barriers disappear when the individuals of the foreign nationality groups rise in the economic scale or conform to the American standards of living. . . . While the ranking may be scientifically wrong from the standpoint of inherent racial characteristics, it registers an opinion or prejudice that is reflected in land values; it is the ranking of races and nationalities with respect to their beneficial effect upon land values. Those having the most favorable effect come first in the list and those exerting the most detrimental effect appear last:
>
> 1. English, Germans, Scotch, Irish, Scandinavians, North Italians
> 2. Bohemians or Czechoslovakians
> 3. Poles
> 4. Lithuanians
> 5. Greeks
> 6. Russian Jews of lower class
> 7. South Italians
> 8. Negroes
> 9. Mexicans[13]

FHA administrators routinely advised developers of residential projects to draw up restrictive covenants against nonwhites in order to obtain FHA-insured financing.[14] As a consequence, between 1946 and 1959 less than 2 percent of all the housing financed with the assistance of federal mortgage insurance was purchased by blacks.[15] In the Miami area, only one black family received FHA backing for a home loan between 1934 and 1949, and there is "evidence that he [the man who secured the loan] was not recognized as a black" at the time the transaction took place.[16]

In 1948, in the case of *Shelly* v. *Kraemer,* the U.S. Supreme Court ruled that racial restrictive covenants could not be enforced in the courts.[17] Following that decision, the FHA began to change its policies, at least as conveyed to banks through its manuals and booklets. In 1950, the FHA reissued its *Underwriting Manual* so that it no longer overtly and in writing recommended or required racial segregation or restrictive covenants. The agency did nothing, however, to reverse the effects of its previous policies. Federal administrators took no actions to discourage realtors or lending institutions from discriminating against blacks. Builders and banks were free to operate as they always had, without fear that they might run afoul of federal policy. When the largest developer in the East, Levitt and Sons, decided to build the huge Levittown project outside Philadelphia in the 1950s, restrictive covenants were attached to deeds even though, unlike Nichols's Country Club development, Levittown was designed for ordinary middle-class families. Deed restrictions could no longer be legally enforced, but this proved to be inconsequential; the Levitt firm simply refused to show houses or to accept applications from blacks. William Levitt argued that economic realities required him to recognize that "most whites prefer not to live in mixed communities."[18] In 1960, not a single black family lived among Levittown's eighty-two thousand residents.[19]

Even without racial covenants, the housing industry found it easy to keep blacks from moving into white neighborhoods. Realtors either refused to work with African American home buyers or steered them to particular neighborhoods. Lending institutions continued to discriminate against African American loan applicants. Banks and insurance companies redlined large areas of inner cities and suburbs where blacks lived.

In the 1960s, civil rights activists finally succeeded in calling attention to these practices, and in 1968 Congress passed legislation barring racial discrimination in housing. Provisions of the Civil Rights

Act of 1968 proscribed discrimination by lenders through "either denying the loan or fixing the amount, interest rate, duration, or other terms of the loan."[20] The statute also mandated that each of the federal regulatory agencies involved with the real estate industry take affirmative steps to enforce both the spirit and the letter of the law.[21] In the same year, Congress passed the Housing and Urban Development Act. Section 235 of this legislation was intended to encourage home ownership for lower-income people previously excluded from the housing market. The Equal Opportunity Act of 1974 and the Home Mortgage Disclosure Act of 1975 were meant to stop redlining.[22] However, all this legislation came too late, and it did too little to reverse the patterns of racial segregation in urban areas that had been initially sponsored and sanctioned, and later ignored, by federal policies.

Federal Urban Policies: The Cities

The federal policies that helped to segregate urban areas formed a complex matrix. One part of the matrix was the FHA/VA loan policies, which virtually sealed the suburbs off to blacks for decades, followed by halfhearted, ineffectual liberal remedies of the 1960s and thereafter (these policies are discussed later in this chapter). A second part of the matrix comprised powerful policies that financed inner-city revitalization, slum clearance, and public housing. Blacks were closed off from the suburbs and thereby artificially contained within slums or diverted into neighborhoods "in transition" by realtors sowing panic among white residents through the use of blockbusting tactics. A third dimension of the matrix was the subjection of blacks to federally funded policies intended to remove them from the limited turf they already occupied.

The failures of the urban renewal and public housing programs of the 1950s are well understood, partly because of the furious reaction that finally burst forth in the 1960s. Notably, the first and most influential exposé of the urban renewal fiasco was published in 1964 by a conservative Republican, Martin Anderson. In *The Federal Bulldozer,* Anderson described how urban renewal had become a means of subsidizing corporate designs on downtown real estate at the expense of small businesses and working-class and poor people.[23] The only people who could possibly have been surprised by

Anderson's book were those who continued to believe overblown rhetoric about the virtues of slum clearance.

The political coalition that secured the landmark postwar redevelopment legislation, the Housing Act of 1949, was composed of Republicans and Democrats, liberals and conservatives.[24] Democratic mayors of the big cities, downtown business interests, and those who owned real estate in the urban core were concerned about the economic consequences of blight. They lobbied hard for federally assisted slum clearance. Liberals and the organizations they represented fought for both urban renewal and public housing on the premises that housing shortages and dilapidated housing constituted social evils and that the clearance of slum housing provided an opportunity to build decent and adequate housing in its place. The compromise that made congressional approval possible was a bill that contained something for both liberals and conservatives.

The loud debate over the legislation made it appear that economic and social goals were both going to be accomplished. Once the law was placed in the hands of federal administrators and local urban renewal authorities, however—that is, when the spectacle gave way to ordinary, more mundane politics—economic priorities quickly trumped social objectives. Implementation relied upon local governments and upon the private marketplace, strategies embraced by both liberals and conservatives. The national objectives of the legislation, which specified a clear priority that public housing be built on land cleared of slums, was immediately undermined when local urban renewal agencies implemented the clearance part of the program.

Mayors and downtown business interests, as a result of their successful efforts to secure federal backing for urban renewal, "engineered a massive allocation of private and social resources" in the cities.[25] The federal effort leveraged an astonishing volume of private investment. By 1968, $35.8 billion had been committed by private institutions in 524 renewal projects.[26] All across the country, hundreds of square blocks in inner cities were reduced to rubble. The redevelopment of run-down business districts and the clearance of nearby slums made downtown areas more attractive to prospective investors. Simultaneously, across the country hundreds of thousands of lower-income residents were removed from neighborhoods close to the central business district.

The social costs of renewal fell disproportionately on poor people and on African American slum residents. In the first eight years of the urban renewal program, blacks made up more than three-fourths of those who were displaced by clearance projects.[27] Blacks who were forced to move typically moved into dilapidated housing in slightly more distant slums that might next be targeted for clearance. The cruel new game in town became known as "musical slums." A (lucky?) few were able to move to public housing constructed on cleared land still surrounded by the slums. Barriers to moving elsewhere—for example, to the suburbs—were kept in place, as we have seen, by the housing industry and by federal administrators. "Given the realities of the low-income housing market . . . it is likely that, for many families, relocation [meant] no more than keeping one step ahead of the bulldozer."[28]

An entire generation of mayors launched their political careers by adroitly using federal urban renewal funds to remake the inner-city landscape. Richard Lee of New Haven, David Lawrence of Pittsburgh, Raymond Tucker in St. Louis, and Joseph Alioto in San Francisco—these and many other Democratic mayors presided over "directive regimes" composed of business leaders, local politicians, and, sometimes, labor unions.[29] Energized by the idea that they were implementing a national project of civic renewal—and even more by the prospect of mutual material gain—the urban renewal coalition typically became a juggernaut capable of overwhelming any opposition that dared to oppose its version of progress. Most mayors and urban renewal administrators would have agreed with M. Justin Herman, who headed San Francisco's redevelopment agency, when he was quoted as saying (in reference to one of his projects), "This land is too valuable to permit poor people to park on it."[30] Herman was cited in a major publication in 1970 as "one of the men responsible for getting urban renewal renamed 'the federal bulldozer' and negro removal" because he was so effective at moving blacks out of the neighborhoods near San Francisco's downtown.[31] Even in cities where effective opposition was mounted by black leaders and black neighborhoods, a politics of divide and conquer generally won the day. In Atlanta, for example, "in the case of blacks, city actions not only failed to encourage solidarity, they explicitly discouraged it. . . . Policy measures and administrative practices . . . were used to afford *particular benefits* to the black community in order to fragment opposition to the city's renewal program."[32] Through all of this period, federal administrators rarely raised objections to the tactics used by local renewal authorities to move projects forward.

In announcing urban renewal programs, mayors typically mentioned clearance and public housing in the same breath, but slum clearance was always the real meat in the sandwich. White Democratic aldermen who ruled in the big cities rarely allowed public housing projects in their own wards. The mismatch between clearance and the rate of construction and the siting of public housing meant that relocatees typically had to pay higher rents when they moved. Finding a place to live was often extremely difficult, since the number of low-income units torn down drastically reduced the supply of housing that poor families could afford. By the end of 1961, 126,000 housing units had been torn down through urban renewal, but only 28,000 public housing units had been built to replace them.[33] Blacks who were able to move into public housing found themselves living in a more densely packed segregation than before. In virtually all cities, public housing was segregated as a matter of policy. The federal government did not question these practices until 1963. By then, city after city had constructed clusters of high-rise fortresses that became enduring symbols for whites of a failed effort by the national government to help blacks. Public housing joined welfare as an evocative symbol of wasted money.

The FHA/VA and urban renewal/public housing programs interacted in complex ways to shape patterns of residential segregation. On the one hand, the federal government helped millions of middle-class Americans flee the cities for the suburbs. On the other hand, the fact that middle-class blacks could not buy suburban homes insured by federal loan guarantee programs meant that they could find good housing only in neighborhoods adjacent to black areas or in areas targeted by realtors for blockbusting. Because they were so frequently used as the opening wedge by realtors looking for a way to accelerate home sales, the movement of a black family onto a white block became a symbol of neighborhood decline. Realtors made money by exploiting whites' fears, buying low from whites desperate to move and selling high to blacks desperate for a nice home and neighborhood. Inevitably, the white middle class learned to associate the presence of blacks with residential change and lower property values.

By reducing the supply of inner-city housing, clearance projects exponentially increased the pressure on existing housing at the margins of slum areas. African Americans in poverty were forced to cluster together in densely packed, run-down areas where rents were cheap, or they were afforded the option of moving to high-rise public housing projects that were even more thoroughly segregated from the rest of society than the slums they had left behind. White families moving to the suburbs were pursuing the American dream of home ownership. Black families were effectively barred from making the same move, and if they were poor and lived in the slums, they lived in constant fear of the bulldozer. The complicated web that ensnared blacks in this way was woven at least as much by federal policies as by the actions of private entrepreneurs in the real estate and housing industries.

The Weak Policies of the Post–Civil Rights Era

In 1968, Congress passed the Federal Fair Housing Act, which contained the first antidiscrimination measures of any consequence in the area of housing.[34] According to some evidence, the degree of racial segregation in urban areas declined marginally in the 1970s and 1980s for African Americans, though the pattern was extremely uneven, with the most significant decreases occurring in new metropolitan areas of the South and West, which had high rates of housing construction.[35] For older urban regions, the level of segregation mostly did not fall in the 1970s, and in quite a few cases (and even overall) it increased in the 1980s.[36] In the St. Louis area, for instance, where the level of segregation declined between 1980 and 1990, nonracial factors such as housing cost and economic factors seemed to have become less important in explaining racial segregation than in any previous decade. These findings led a researcher investigating St. Louis to conclude that "race may matter even more than in the past" in explaining segregation.[37]

The persistence of high levels of residential segregation should not seem surprising. For decades the federal government had sanctioned or enforced racial discrimination in the housing market, and these policies were reinforced by the practices of developers, realtors, and lending institutions. New policies designed to end racial discrimination could hardly be expected to reverse segregation overnight, no matter how aggressively such policies might be enforced. We will never know what strong policies might have accomplished, however, because when the federal government finally enacted antidiscrimination legislation, the new policies were weak and enforcement was anemic. For decades public and private institutions had expended enormous resources in the cause of racial segregation. When the time came to reverse the effects of earlier policies, no equivalent expenditure of resources was forthcoming.

The Housing and the Civil Rights Acts of 1968 and other measures initiated in the 1960s were supposed to reverse decades of discriminatory behavior in the housing industry. There can be little doubt that Democratic liberals fought hard for antidiscrimination legislation. Beginning in 1964, Lyndon Johnson urged Congress to outlaw discrimination in housing. All eyes were focused on the more basic civil rights legislation, however, and in any case the idea of applying civil rights remedies to housing touched a raw nerve—the belief that individual property rights should not be curbed. In both 1966 and 1967, a fair housing bill died in the Senate. Finally, in 1968 a civil rights bill was passed that covered housing. Under Title VIII, housing discrimination was outlawed. Its provisions were quite sweeping, covering sales and rentals, provision of information about cost and availability, advertising, purchasing, constructing or repairing, and real estate services and practices.

We might ask why this legislation has had so little effect on the overall incidence of racial segregation. There are two keys that yield an answer. First, the enforcement provisions contained in the act were weak. The Department of Housing and Urban Development (HUD) was given the responsibility of receiving complaints initiated by citizens. By thus being limited to a passive, rather than an advocacy, role, HUD could easily stay out of controversy by treating each case as basically isolated and nonpolitical. Presidents Richard Nixon and Gerald Ford carefully steered clear of enforcement efforts; Nixon even took the step of overruling his HUD secretary, George Romney, when it looked as if HUD might challenge local zoning laws in 1971.[38] Nixon's statement that "to force integration in the suburbs, I think, is unrealistic" might have seemed like a distinctly Republican view,[39] but during the 1976 campaign Jimmy Carter made his famous "ethnic purity" statement when he said: "I see nothing wrong with the ethnic purity [of neighborhoods] being maintained. I would not force racial integration of a neighborhood by government action. But I would not permit discrimination against a family moving into a neighborhood."[40] Perhaps because of the uproar caused by his remark, during his presidency Carter invested some rhetoric reminding local governments that they were obliged to promote housing desegregation. He successfully pushed through amendments to the Housing Act of 1968 that strengthened antiredlining legislation. HUD's basic role did not change, however, and no federal grants were ever cut off because of noncompliance by local governments.[41]

Interestingly, it was Ronald Reagan's HUD secretary, Samuel Pierce, who took some steps to raise public awareness of the remedies available under the 1968 Housing Act. Possibly as a result, the number of complaints received by HUD rose sharply in the 1980s. In line with a philosophy of decentralizing authority, the Reagan administration moved much of the responsibility of adjudicating the complaints to state and local civil rights agencies. The number of conciliations and the volume of monetary awards increased sharply;[42] nevertheless, most administrators at the state level felt they could actually do little for their clients. It made more sense for citizens to bypass these governmental agencies entirely and go directly to the courts.[43] By continuing to focus on individual remedies rather than on the large-scale politics of housing discrimination, the Reagan administration was keeping the governmental role in fair housing enforcement small, inconsequential, and uncontroversial. That the Reagan administration nominally did more than any administration before it to enforce fair housing laws may seem ironic unless it is understood that the laws were never intended to significantly change the structure of the housing market itself.

Without intruding into the housing industry, the government's stated goals of breaking down housing segregation were not likely to be accomplished. No other program illustrates this point better than the Section 235 program of the 1968 Housing Act, which was meant to promote home ownership by lower-income, primarily inner-city, residents. Democratic liberals proclaimed that the Section 235 program was supposed to do for the poor what the FHA programs previously had done for the middle class. That inner-city blacks were the principal target of the program was clear from the congressional debates, which made frequent reference to the urban riots sweeping the country in the wake of Martin Luther King Jr.'s assassination in April 1968.[44] Democratic liberals and some Republicans were attracted to the idea of home ownership by the poor on the assumption that home ownership was the main expression of the American Dream, but with a twist: These same members of Congress also thought home ownership could be used as an instrument of social control. Representative Henry Reuss, a liberal Democrat from Wisconsin, argued that "we think a man who owns his home is not likely to burn it down."[45] Though the debate revolved around the desirability of helping the poor buy homes, Congress followed its usual pattern of providing the biggest housing subsidies to upper- and middle-income home buyers, with little going to the poor.

There were two steps involved in making housing allegedly affordable to lower-income buyers. First, Congress established a new high-risk mortgage fund to be administered by the FHA. This fund would virtually eliminate risks for banks in extending loans to applicants as long as the applicants showed a basically worthy credit history and record of employment. Second, the FHA would contract with lenders to pay the difference between what buyers could pay (limited at 20 percent of the buyers' income) and a mortgage rate payment amortized at 1 percent interest (with the rest of the interest to be paid to the lending institution by FHA).

Several things went wrong with the Section 235 program, most of them entirely predictable. Congress limited the amount of the subsidy for each mortgage, so that many buyers found that they had to pay much more than 20 percent of their income if they wanted a loan. Lending institutions both encouraged this practice and made loans carelessly, realizing that the federal government would be responsible for covering most losses anyway. Appraisers and developers seized their opportunity for making money; they quickly discerned that FHA inspectors looked the other way at shoddy repairs and substandard new homes with inflated prices. Corruption greased the process from beginning to end, with lenders, appraisers, federal inspectors, builders, and lenders all conspiring to get money out of the program.[46] Of course, low-income home buyers were the victims of this scam, being induced, as they were, to buy homes that required immediate, expensive repairs. Finally, and significantly, builders found that suburban governments used zoning and other regulations to keep subsidized property out, so that most of the homes sold to blacks ended up located within segregated, generally run-down neighborhoods.[47]

FHA ended up holding a huge number of foreclosed properties sold to buyers who could not afford the payments or who abandoned their homes because of defects in construction. The reason federal administrators allowed the Section 235 program to deteriorate into a scandal is that they "followed the familiar bureaucratic career pattern of shuttling between the private and public sectors."[48] FHA inspectors were willing to approve substandard houses in segregated neighborhoods both because this avoided controversy with local officials and because it conformed to their continued bias in favor of segregated housing patterns.[49]

Despite the Section 235 fiasco, subsidies to promote home ownership for lower-income people continued, but they constituted a tiny proportion of the overall housing market (always less than 0.5 percent). Efforts to promote home ownership for minorities and lower-income people moved on two fronts—small subsidy programs and a challenge to so-called redlining practices by financial institutions, which routinely refused to loan in areas with lower property values and areas characterized by "social problems." Section 108 of the Community Development Block Grant program made funds available for loan guarantees and for small-interest subsidies. HUD's requests for these programs for the 1999 budget year show how extremely small they are: If Congress approves, $100 billion will be available for loan guarantees (the money goes to banks if loans have to be foreclosed) and $11 million for credit subsidies. As part of President Bill Clinton's National Homeownership Strategy, funds are also available for education and counseling—$25 million are requested for 1999, up from $20 million in 1998. Under this initiative, as of 1996 six Homeownership Zones had been designated, with five to seven more planned. The federal commitment requested in 1999 was $25 million. In June 1998, HUD secretary Andrew Cuomo claimed that this program was resulting in the construction of two thousand units of low- and middle-income housing in Louisville, Cleveland, Sacramento, Buffalo, Baltimore, and Philadelphia.[50] This averaged out to a total national commitment of 333 houses for six cities.

When federal policies shifted toward the goal of nondiscrimination in the late 1960s, the spotlight began to focus on the private institutions of the housing industry. The Equal Credit Opportunity Act of 1974, the Home Mortgage Disclosure Act of 1975, and the Community Reinvestment Act of 1977 were all designed to change some of the most basic ways that real estate and banking institutions did business. The 1977 legislation said that mortgage lenders had "a continuing and affirmative obligation to help meet the credit needs of the local communities in which they are chartered . . . consistent with safe and sound operation of such institutions."[51] Community-based organizations were empowered to challenge applications for branch banks, mergers, acquisitions, and other business undertakings if banks seemed to be neglecting local needs. After the 1977 legislation, banks were subjected to repeated protests and a substantial amount of litigation from community groups protesting apparent redlining practices. According to one estimate, by 1991 approximately $18 billion in reinvestment commitments had been negotiated with banks in seventy cities.[52] These concessions no doubt made some difference, but a clear pattern of discrimination seemed to continue. A 1992 study by the Federal Reserve Bank of Boston found that minorities were roughly 60 percent more likely to be turned down for a mortgage, even after thirty-eight factors affecting creditworthiness, such as credit history and total debt, had been controlled for.[53] This pattern reflected not only the fact that some measure of racial discrimination continued to persist, but also the fact that minority applicants were often seeking loans on property in areas considered a bad investment by the banks.[54]

By the late 1990s, there was evidence that the situation might be turning around. Between 1993 and 1996, loans to blacks rose by more than 50 percent (compared to a 14 percent increase for whites), and the home ownership rates among blacks rose from 42 to 45 percent from 1993 to 1997. Just as significantly, over the same period home loans in low- and moderate-income areas increased at a one-third faster rate than loans in middle- and upper-income neighborhoods and in neighborhoods with more than 10 percent minority residents.[55] No doubt the surging economy accounted for the rise of home ownership among blacks and other minorities, but community-based organizations that pooled federal money with other sources contributed to some degree. Did this mean that the sins of the past were finally being redressed?

It is pointless and misleading to recount such statistics without articulating an understanding of how they fit into the totality of national housing policy. Considered as a whole, the federal housing policies of the last three decades have surely contributed more to housing segregation than to its reduction. Subsidized home ownership programs have provided success stories for individual families, but they have made up an insignificant proportion of federal housing subsidies. And few of those subsidies have gone to the poor. Budget authority for assisted low-income housing (what Congress authorizes in expenditures) fell from $71 billion in 1978 to $16.3 billion in 1997 (in constant 1996 dollars).[56] Beginning with the budget cuts of the Carter years, HUD experienced the largest cuts of any cabinet-level department in the federal government; its share of the total federal budget fell from 7.5 percent in 1978 to 1.3 percent in 1990, a level it has been stuck close to ever since. At the same time that HUD budgets shriveled, tax breaks for home owners soared. The cost of home owner tax deductions to the federal treasury increased from $34 billion in 1978 to $87 billion by 1997, with 44 percent of the deductions in 1997 being claimed by home owners in the top 5 percent income bracket. In 1996, the wealthiest 20 percent of American households received 82 percent of home owner tax breaks; by contrast, the bottom 60 percent received less than 4 percent of the subsidy.[57] As in the past, housing subsidies continue to work as a powerful tool for transferring federal aid to affluent suburban home owners at the expense of lower-income rental households.

Ironically and perniciously, the housing programs earmarked for the poor have had the effect of reinforcing racial segregation. In an analysis of HUD's first national study of segregation in public housing, in 1977 two researchers reached the rather dismal conclusion that public housing projects "represent a federally funded, physically permanent institution for the isolation of poor minority families by race and class."[58] By segregating blacks in larger numbers on less real estate than in private-market neighborhoods, public housing raised the overall level of racial segregation of entire metropolitan areas.[59] Unfortunately, many years later it became obvious that this process had continued. In December 1994, HUD released a second report and found again that public housing tended to intesify the segregation of African Americans receiving housing subsidies. According to the HUD researchers, "The most striking feature of the results is the virtually inverse relationship between the percentage of a census tract's population that is African American and the occupancy of projects within that tract by whites."[60]

The replacement of government-built and -administered housing with certificates that could be used by landlords or vouchers distributed to individual renters provided a possible way to overcome the resegregative effects of public housing. Partially in reaction to accumulated media exposure of such high-rise disasters as Pruitt-Igoe in St. Louis and Cabrini-Green in Chicago, in the 1970s Congress began to experiment with certificates and vouchers. In 1974, Congress created the Rental Certificate Program (Section 8 of the Housing and Community Development Act). In 1987, Section 8 was amended to allow the issuance of vouchers directly to tenants. By 1994, approximately 1 million certificates and 294,000 vouchers had been issued by HUD, and in 1988 and 1990 Congress passed legislation that allowed certificates and vouchers to be transported out of the jurisdictions that issued them.

To assess the effects of these programs, in 1992 Congress passed the Housing and Community Development Act, which instructed HUD to gather information about programs that encouraged mobility among assisted-housing recipients. HUD's report to Congress, filed in April 1995, showed that the attempts to promote mobility for the recipients of assisted housing had proved to be largely ineffective. The HUD study of four metropolitan areas showed that rental assistance recipients experienced somewhat less concentration in impacted areas than tenants living in public housing, but "sharp disparities remain." According to HUD, "Black recipients are much more likely than whites or other minorities to live in areas of high black poverty."[61] The study showed that 18 percent of blacks with rental assistance ended up living in areas with poverty rates of 20 percent or more, compared to 1 percent for whites and 5 percent for other minorities. Nevertheless, blacks living in assisted housing were significantly more likely than the general population of blacks to live outside areas with concentrated poverty and in racially mixed neighborhoods.[62] In contrast to these findings, a study of the St. Louis area found that Section 8 recipients were more likely to live in segregated neighborhoods than were those living in public housing units.[63] Thus, it is difficult to generalize from the HUD study.

HUD's study relied upon a comparison of Section 8 and public housing projects in only four metropolitan areas—Washington, D.C., Wilmington, Seattle, and Oklahoma City. A separate HUD study of residential mobility programs in eight urban areas found that these programs succeeded in helping black tenants to find housing outside poverty-impacted and segregated neighborhoods. The first and largest such effort at desegregation started in Chicago, Illinois, in 1981, after more than a decade of litigation against the Chicago Housing Authority and HUD. By the spring of 1994, the program resulting from the landmark *Gautreaux* decision had placed more than fifty-six hundred families in nonsegregated neighborhoods.[64] As a result of court orders, seven other cities have implemented much smaller programs, and HUD has evaluated them positively.[65] These programs seem to show what can happen with enough effort—but the overall effort has been small indeed. As of 1994, about eleven thousand people had been assisted through mobility programs in all the cities subject to court orders and other judicial remedies or agreements. The numbers will not have grown significantly since then. The *Gautreaux* consent decree in Chicago will be satisfied when seventy-one hundred people of the "plaintiff class" have been moved, at the rate of 150 certificates per year. The number of certificates involved in the other cities is extremely small; only Cincinnati, Memphis, and Dallas have agreed to assist more than two hundred people.[66] Obviously, such programs hardly amount to a significant national (or even local) commitment.

It would be naive to suppose that residential mobility programs tied to low-income housing assistance can ever promote desegregation on a consequential scale. Falling budgets guarantee that only a very small percentage of people needing housing assistance will ever get it. The number of Section 8 vouchers was frozen from 1995 to 1998, when Congress began to consider approving an increase of eight thousand, which were likely to be targeted to the elderly. In most metropolitan areas, waiting lists are two to four years long—and growing. In 1998, 5.4 million renters spent over half of their income on housing,[67] and two families were competing for every privately built low-income unit that came onto the market.[68] The worsening housing shortage for the poor could be juxtaposed with the fact that virtually all the new minority home owners have bought in the suburbs.[69] The combination of falling budgets for low-income housing and the boom in home ownership for more affluent minorities is contributing to the concentration of the very poor in the inner cities.

If we do a mind experiment and imagine increased federal spending for low-income housing (truly a fantasy), we must ask whether it is likely that the federal government would show the political will to push for desegregated assisted housing on a significant scale. As the Yonkers controversy of the 1980s illustrated so well, such efforts have always been explosive.[70] The federal government long ago backed away from challenging local zoning laws. In a rather typical case, in the 1990s the St. Louis County, Missouri, housing authority ignited intense opposition when it proposed to provide one unit of assisted housing near an unincorporated white area. In response to this and one other similar incident, residents organized two new municipalities, and the county backed away from any further efforts to disperse assisted housing.[71] When this kind of controversy occurs when only a few units or tenants are involved, it is not hard to imagine the response to more significant efforts. In any case, it is not only the poor who remain segregated. The black middle class, including those who have moved to the suburbs, continues to live primarily in segregated neighborhoods.

The Persistence of Residential Segregation

The federal government's programs for moving the white middle class out of the central cities in the 1930s and beyond interacted in complex ways with its urban renewal and public housing programs to more intensely segregate blacks than before. Federally insured loans made it possible for the white middle class to achieve the Everyman version of the American Dream that treats home ownership as a symbol of social status and success. But vastly more was at stake than symbolic status. For most middle-class Americans, home ownership became the main source of capital worth and savings, the means by which a family could send children to college and leave something for the next generation. Home ownership and the appreciation of property values, in other words, became intimately tied, for the middle class, with life chances. Blacks were locked out of this mechanism long enough that patterns of residential segregation became written in stone. Only strong, probably politically infeasible policies could have made much of a dent, and as we have seen, such policies have not been forthcoming.

It was not possible for African Americans to begin moving to the suburbs in any numbers until the mid-1960s. Between 1970 and 1980, the number of blacks who lived in suburbs grew by almost 50 percent, an increase of 1.8 million persons.[72] One in ten blacks living in central cities in 1970 moved to the suburbs during this period, and the percentage of urban blacks living in suburbs increased from 16 percent to 21 percent.[73] In the 1980s, the trend continued. By the 1990 census, about one-fourth of urban blacks were living in the suburbs. Though blacks are still far behind whites in their rates of suburbanization, they are catching up and in many metropolitan areas are suburbanizing at faster rates than whites.

As with whites, blacks who suburbanize tend to have higher incomes than blacks who stay behind in the central cities. They move to the suburbs to escape the problems of the inner city and to find a better environment in which to raise children. To a limited extent, African Americans are able to improve their condition in the suburbs. The rapidly expanding suburban economy, for example, provides more job opportunities. When occupation is controlled for, blacks who live in suburbs earn more money than blacks who live in central cities.[74]

The suburbanization of African Americans, however, cannot be used as a measure of blacks' progress. It is a myth that black suburbanization has been a significant vehicle for upward mobility and that it signals the removal of barriers to residential segregation. Suburbanization of blacks, while not making things worse, "replicates the racial and class disparities found within cities."[75] For the most part, black suburbanization does not represent integration; rather, it is an extension of racially segregated living patterns in the central cities into close-in suburbs. The older the suburb is, the greater is the black population growth. Blacks are moving into older inner-ring suburbs, such as Oak Park, Maywood, and Bellwood outside Chicago; Oak Park and Southfield outside Detroit; Shaker Heights bordering on Cleveland; and Yonkers north of New York City.[76] Suburbs tend to fall into "black" suburbs and "white" suburbs. Most suburban whites have little contact with blacks: 86 percent of suburban whites live in suburbs with a black population of less than 1 percent.[77]

Even those suburbs that are racially mixed tend to be highly segregated internally. Overall, though residential segregation in the suburbs is less extreme than in central cities, it is still very high. One index of segregation varies from scores of 0 to 100, with the numbers indicating the percentage of either whites or blacks who would have to move in order to achieve an integrated living pattern. Uniform distributions of each race across all spatial units would yield a score of 0, indicating no segregation, and complete segregation would be indicated by a score of 100. A study of segregation in the St. Louis metropolitan area found that the city had a segregation index of 90.3 in 1980. The three suburban counties with substantial numbers of blacks (St. Louis, Madison, and St. Clair Counties) had segregation indexes of 79.9, 86.5, and 91.4, respectively.[78] Thus, although segregation, overall, is lower in suburbs than in central cities, the suburbs are still highly segregated.[79] Only one suburban area, El Paso, Texas, was classified as having "low" segregation (less than 0.5) in 1980.[80] In metropolitan areas with large black populations, suburbs are highly segregated. Moreover, it appears that racial segregation intensified in the 1980s.[81]

It is clear that economic differentials between white and African Americans do not account for racial segregation. Suburban blacks would be much more evenly distributed among suburbs if class determined residential location, instead of being concentrated in a small number of suburbs, as they actually are.[82] In the St. Louis metropolitan area, for instance, socioeconomic differentials between blacks and whites accounted for less than 15 percent of the segregation among suburbs in 1980, and a follow-up study of 1990 census data showed that nonracial factors accounted for an even smaller proportion of segregated patterns than in previous decades.[83]

Racial and economic segregation between central cities and suburbs became well established in the 1950s. For the six largest metropolitan areas, the median income of central city residents (according to the 1950 census) was 95 percent of the income of the suburbanites in those areas. Ten years later, city residents earned only 88 percent as much as the people living in the suburbs, and the gap has steadily widened. By 1980, the average family in the six central cities made only 75 percent as much as families living outside the boundaries in those cities. A study of central city–suburban disparities in fifty-five metropolitan areas, measured by income, unemployment levels, the number of dependent persons, and educational attainment, found that central cities lost ground relative to their suburbs in the 1970s. According to more recent evidence, the gap continued to widen in the 1980s. The study also found a dynamic effect: The greater the disparity was between a city and its suburbs, the more rapidly the city declined because jobs and population were attracted out to the suburbs.[84]

Not only are African Americans segregated in suburbs; they also live in political jurisdictions that have many of the same fiscal problems as the central cities. A study of Philadelphia's suburbs for the period 1977–1982 found that predominantly black suburbs had a per capita tax base that averaged 30 percent less than the tax base of white or mixed suburbs; in addition, municipal debt per capita in black suburbs averaged almost twice that of mixed and white suburbs. In general, black suburbs tend to have lower tax bases, higher debts, poorer municipal services, lower socioeconomic status, and higher population densities than do white suburbs.[85] The current movement by blacks and other minorities to the suburbs does not necessarily—indeed, it probably does not—foreshadow a new era of neighborhood integration. It surely does, however, mean that the blacks living in poverty will be even more isolated from both whites and the black middle class.

The Legacy of Federal Urban Policy

In symbolic terms, African Americans derived considerable benefit by joining the New Deal coalition. In party platforms and on every oratorical opportunity, Democratic liberals expressed their opposition to racism and offered their unstinting support for equality. And there was more than mere posturing; substantial, controversial, historic policy was forthcoming. By any reasonable standard, the civil rights laws of 1964 and 1965 were historic, watershed events in American national history.

In the case of urban policy, the record is far more ambiguous. Whatever the stated policy objectives might have been, taken as a whole and over the long run urban policies harmed, more than helped, African Americans. If these policies might be considered "rewards" for blacks' participation in the Democrats' coalition, it is hard to imagine a worse payment on a debt. The federal government's programs, when considered in their entirety, constituted a powerful strategy of metropolitan development. The present pattern of residential segregation is a legacy of this strategy. A second legacy is even more insidious and perhaps more difficult to remedy than segregation itself: Federal policies helped to shape contemporary racist attitudes, fears, and stereotypes.

If poor, African Americans could find safe and adequate housing only by moving into public housing. Demand always exceeded supply, so that for many poor families the big challenge was to keep one step ahead of the bulldozer. For those who outlasted the waiting lists, the reward must have seemed puny, indeed: Forced into dense clusters of high-rise buildings constructed on land cleared of slum housing, blacks living in the "projects" often found themselves living in the worst of the slums. The "concentration effects" much debated today were set in motion by a program intended to help the poor find suitable housing. The confirmation of racist stereotypes was a perverse, damaging consequence of the way public housing was implemented: For whites, public housing became a handy cultural symbol for blacks on welfare.

Ironically, racist stereotypes were also encouraged when the black middle class tried to break out of the inner-city ghetto. Shut off from the new housing in the suburbs, middle-class black families inherited the housing left by whites fleeing the cities. Typically, they displaced whites who lived in areas close by all-black neighborhoods, and just as typically, they bought into neighborhoods targeted by realtors for blockbusting. Because this process was so often repeated, the white middle class developed the habit of associating declining property values with an "invasion" by blacks (an impression that became a self-fulfilling prophecy). By reducing the supply of inner-city housing, clearance projects exponentially increased the pressure on the existing housing stock at the margins of all-black areas.

One way to understand the effect of this dynamic is to imagine what might have happened if middle-class blacks had been as free as middle-class whites to leapfrog to suburban housing tracts. No doubt a high degree of racial segregation would have continued to exist. Even if it had, however, African American home owners would have been able to (1) find affordable and desirable housing by buying new homes rather than buying from white home owners and

(2) benefit from the dynamics of the housing market as white home owners did. With this scenario in operation, the presence of African Americans in a neighborhood would not have been automatically equated, in whites' imaginations, with dilapidated housing or with declining property values.

Federal law shifted dramatically in the late 1960s, and the private housing industry was forced to follow suit. It appears that new governmental policies and private practices have, to a degree, helped the black middle class become home owners and move to the suburbs, albeit mostly to segregated black neighborhoods. Of course, the programs that helped blacks buy homes were insignificantly small compared to the subsidies going to the richest (mostly white) home owners. At the same time, blacks in poverty have been increasingly concentrated in inner-city ghettos. Between 1970 and 1990, the proportion of census tracts in the central cities classified as "extreme poverty," where more than 40 percent of residents were officially poor, more than doubled.[86]

What kinds of policies are needed to effectively challenge patterns of residential segregation? For federal policy to significantly reduce residential segregation and the concentration of poor blacks in poverty in the central cities, the federal government would have to be willing to challenge local zoning and land-use practices. Perhaps even more importantly, the federal government would have to be willing to intervene directly in the housing market to change some of its principal dynamics. Rather than merely regulating lending institutions, for instance, the government could become a primary lender. It could also, in principle, impose reparations and damages on landlords and home owners found violating antidiscrimination laws. But all such speculation ignores political realities. It is difficult to imagine a circumstance in which a Democratic president would propose policies to desegregate housing that would be equivalent, in strength and in effect, to those once used to promote segregation.

The case for a policy of affirmative action in housing can easily be made, not primarily because African Americans historically suffered discrimination at the hands of realtors, developers, and banks, but because the federal government itself helped to create the present patterns of residential segregation and is therefore obliged to enact policies of equal force to reverse the effects of its earlier actions. This argument is exactly parallel to that used by the federal courts from the 1950s right up to the present in a large number of school desegregation cases. A voluntary interdistrict desegregation plan in the St. Louis metropolitan area continues in effect because the state of Missouri operated dual school systems for decades and because the courts found that governments throughout the region had played an active role in preserving residential segregation.[87] Obviously, in the political climate prevailing at the turn of the century it would be unrealistic to suppose that a similar logic might be applied in an attempt to reduce the incidence of housing segregation in metropolitan areas. This fact speaks volumes about the terms that African Americans are still expected to accept as "partners" in the post–New Deal Democratic coalition.

6

Playing by the Rules: Welfare Reform and the New Authoritarian State

Mimi Abramovitz and Ann Withorn

In August 1996, Contract-with-America Republicans joined with Clinton Democrats to pass the Personal Responsibility and Work Opportunity Reconciliation Act (PRWORA). In one fell swoop this devil's bargain fulfilled Bill Clinton's promise to "end welfare as we know it." It replaced Aid to Families with Dependent Children (AFDC) with Transitional Aid to Needy Families (TANF). The historic change effectively abolished the sixty-year-old meager but real federal entitlement to family assistance. It achieved a states' rights agenda with 1990s panache by proudly "devolving" responsibility for society's poorest, darkest, and newest arrivals to the states, capping federal welfare spending, and imposing a myriad of behavioral controls on poor women.

Many observers now agree that welfare reform represented part of the Democratic electoral strategy designed to win votes by bashing the poor. Traditional conservatives believed that the best way to defend capitalism and restore patriarchal controls was to weaken the welfare state and promote "family values." Clintonian neoliberals planned to win and stay in office by becoming a "new kind of Democrat." The New Democrats defended capitalism and patriarchy by investing in health, employment, and family life for the middle class. To avoid the label "old-fashioned" or "tax-and-spend liberal," they hoped to "bring the state back in" without appearing to do so.[1] To this end, the New Democrats offered the middle class small changes, predicated their support for "working people" on doing less for the poor, and systematically attacked welfare, the program for single mothers and their children.

This chapter places welfare "reform" in historical context and provides a brief overview of the latest "reforms." It examines the ways in which social scientists wittingly or not justified the regressive social policy initiatives. We argue that social scientists encouraged punitive welfare policy by proposing ideas that legitimized the old view of poor people (especially people of color) as lazy, immoral, irresponsible, and in need of social control. Social scientists also theorized that policies targeted to the middle class would trickle down to the poor. The combined impact of maligning the poor and proposing that the government limit positive social programs to those who "work hard and play by the rules" made it that much easier to repeal welfare.

The systematic attack on welfare might have been another round of historically conservative reforms had it not been passed with so much liberal support. "Liberal" lawmakers, the "liberal" media, and "liberal" social scientists embraced welfare reform uncritically, justified its thrust, or consented to it by their silence. Once Congress passed the bill, both mainstream advocates and progressive critics of welfare reform engaged in reactive damage control. They tinkered with marginal features of the bill in hopes of salvaging a threadbare cushion for poor women and children. With hindsight they might have done better by presenting a politicized alternative to the full-scale reversal of social and economic rights sold to the public as welfare reform.[2]

A Brief Overview of Welfare Reform

The AFDC program, or "welfare as we knew it," was part of the original 1935 Social Security Act. This landmark legislation launched the modern welfare state by, among other things, shifting major social welfare responsibilities from the states to the federal government. It created two different types of benefits: the popular Social Security and Unemployment Compensation program and the unpopular public assistance programs then called Aid to the Aged, Aid to the Blind, and Aid to Dependent Children.[3] In the mid-1950s, Congress added Aid to the Permanently and Totally Disabled to both the social insurance and public assistance plans.

From the start, the welfare state punished some groups for not playing by the rules of a game from which they were barred by reason of gender, race, class, personal history, and/or market economics. The legislation defined middle- and lower-income people who worked and formed two-parent families as "deserving" of aid and rewarded them with access to the more generous, less stigmatized, and nearly universal social insurance programs. At the same time, the emerging welfare state regarded single mothers, those unable to work, and most persons of color as "undeserving" of aid. Congress relegated them to the less adequate, unpopular, and means-tested AFDC program. By treating people differently based on their compliance with prevailing work and family norms, Social Security and most other welfare state programs perpetuated the fault lines of class, race, and gender that, according to liberal political theory, the welfare state was supposed to bridge.

These welfare state distinctions fell heavily on women, who have always been overrepresented on the rolls. This is especially so for poor, husbandless woman who turn to the AFDC program as inadequate but essential respite from the failures of workplace and family. They have had the hardest time because the system rewards married women, previously married women, and those viewed as lacking a breadwinner through no fault of their own, such as widows or wives of sick, disabled, or temporarily unemployed men. At the same time, the system punishes single mothers, abandoned wives, and women connected to poor men.

The history of AFDC provides too many examples of how social policy has penalized poor women because of their class, race, and marital status and how it has used its programs to try making them change their ways.[4] From the start, Congress provided lower benefits for AFDC than for the other public assistance programs created by the Social Security Act. It did not even include funds for the mother until 1950. Many states implemented AFDC only reluctantly. In the 1930s and 1940s, some states refused aid to black women to keep them working as field hands and domestic help. In the 1950s and 1960s, the states denied aid to many single mothers and women of color using "suitable home," "man in the house," and "midnight raid" policies that equated unwed motherhood with unfit motherhood.

In the early 1960s, pressure from the civil and welfare rights movements limited the use of these moralistic behavioral standards. Backed into a corner, Congress used the increased labor force participation of women as justification for adding mandatory work programs to AFDC. The Community Work Experience Program and the Work Incentive Program became the punishment of choice for poor single mothers. Not coincidentally, the new work rules helped to press wages down by supplying the labor market with more low-paid workers.

Despite an intensification in the 1970s, these work programs—the forerunner of today's workfare—never met their own goals. Child care shortages, labor market barriers, and lack of funds to implement needed training and social services stood in the way.[5] In addition, the coerciveness of these programs deterred applicants. It also sent a clear message about what happens to poor women who do not comply with gendered behavioral norms.

During the 1980s, the Reagan administration intensified the assault on poor people and welfare programs for political and ideological gain. It mounted this attack even though in the mid-1970s the AFDC caseload had stabilized at about 10 million individuals (two-thirds of whom were children) and never exceeded 2 percent of federal spending. Indeed, the program's already low benefits, bureaucratic practices, and punitive polices ensured that only the most desperate women would choose welfare over work or marriage. Instead of easing the burdens of poor women, the 1982 Omnibus Budget Reconciliation Act tightened AFDC rules and threw thousands of the "working poor" off the rolls. In no state did the combined value of AFDC and food stamps raise a family of three (the average size of a welfare family) above the poverty line.[6] The cuts further isolated women on welfare and discouraged more low-wage workers from thinking of welfare as a benefit that might cushion their precarious standard of living. Despite AFDC's relatively low expenditures and small caseloads, liberal supporters, including those in new left economic justice coalitions, began to accept some of the punitive welfare reforms. Politicians took the silence of the wider middle class as consent.

During the rest of the 1980s, the Reagan administration continued to malign the poor, cut welfare programs, and grant waivers to states to experiment with new models that would make welfare even less accessible to the poor. These state "experiments" paved the way for the 1988 Family Support Act (FSA). Its new work mandates and moralistic behavioral rules led critics to refer to the FSA as the "new paternalism." In 1996, Congress went even further. It passed the Personal Responsibility and Work Opportunity Reconciliation Act, which followed the Republicans' Contract with America and ended welfare altogether.

From Paternalism to Abdication

The Personal Responsibility and Work Opportunity Reconciliation Act of 1996 appeared revolutionary. But, in fact, the 1996 law basically intensified the logic initiated by the FSA, which was the first of the new bipartisan initiatives to use government dollars to dictate the work, maternal, childbearing, and parental behavior of poor women. The new paternalism policies made little pretense of cushioning the effects of poverty or even of cutting federal spending.[7] The FSA also took an early potshot at AFDC's status as an entitlement program based on need. For the first time, the government required recipients to participate in a "social contract" in which they exchanged welfare benefits for activities intended to lead to employment and "self-sufficiency."

The FSA transformed AFDC from an income maintenance entitlement that allowed women to stay home with their children (but with increasing pressures to become employed) into a mandatory work program offered in exchange for income support. Its centerpiece, the Job Opportunity and Basic Security (JOBS) program, was fueled by negative stereotypes of women on welfare as lazy, living high on the hog, and cheating the government. Reflecting these stereotypes, JOBS required women on welfare to go to work, to enroll in school, or to enter training programs. The FSA also mandated states to provide some backup services, along with stricter collection of child support payments. Nonexempt welfare mothers who refused to participate in JOBS faced the reduction or loss of benefits. The law did not, however, sanction states for failing to provide adequate services.

The FSA won praise from both sides of the aisle despite twenty years of research showing that welfare-to-work programs had little success. JOBS, however, proved to be less than a resounding success.

Even with wide variation in state-designed welfare-to-work programs, evaluators consistently reported only "modest" income and employment gains and a slight, if any, drop in the welfare rolls.[8] Congress promised but never provided the states with the extra money needed for job supports, including education, training, and child care programs for public assistance recipients. Only the less costly but most coercive measures, such as job clubs, job search, and sanctions, remained in place. Without supportive services, punishment and control became the most dominant features of programs for the poor.[9] When skewed economic "growth" failed to provide enough low-skilled jobs at breadwinner wages, not surprisingly, the welfare rolls grew.

The FSA's work mandates, which controlled the employment behavior of women on AFDC, represented the top side of the new paternalism. The flip side included a series of state initiatives by which the government sought to control the marital, childbearing, and parenting behavior of women on welfare. New Jersey, followed by many other states in the early 1990s, passed a family cap. Also known as the child exclusion, it denied benefits to children born after their mothers went on welfare—although the typical welfare family has two children, as do most families. Other states provided cash rewards for welfare recipients who married (i.e., "wedfare"). Still others considered a similar bonus for women who accepted Norplant, the long-lasting contraceptive implanted in a woman's arm. At the same time, most states did not counter the Hyde Amendment, which denied Medicaid-funded abortions to those same women. The FSA also imposed exceptional controls on unwed teen mothers. They could not receive support unless the young mother lived with the child's grandparents or in a group home.

Like the work rules, the measures targeted to poor women's marital and childbearing behavior reflected a host of unproved and pernicious assumptions about women and welfare. They implied that welfare caused family breakup, that poor women had babies to increase their welfare check, that husbandless women were promiscuous and sexually irresponsible, and that marriage was an effective antipoverty strategy for poor women.

The FSA also initiated Learnfare and Healthfare, which called the parenting skills of women on welfare into question. Learnfare programs linked welfare benefits to school attendance and punished families whose minor children missed school without an acceptable excuse. Healthfare docked the welfare check if children did not follow a prescribed schedule of doctor visits. Most insidiously, both made documentation of compliance the mother's responsibility. This imposed yet another round of bureaucratic checkpoints for women to address if they stooped so low as to seek welfare. Since 1988, the states have been allowed to withhold additional government dollars from AFDC families that move from states with lower benefits.

Many states adopted these programs despite twenty years of research that failed to find conclusive links between welfare and an individual woman's marital or childbearing behavior.[10] However, these behavior modification proposals played well in the political arena and showed signs of spreading to other social service arenas, such as public housing.

Many observers believed that the FSA had ended the decade-long effort to reform welfare once and for all. Nonetheless, bipartisan support for another round of even more restrictive welfare reforms emerged during the 1992 presidential campaign. The Clintonian New Democrats proclaimed that AFDC should be a "second chance, not a way of life." Their new idea—a two-year cap on AFDC, after which recipients must work—differed little from earlier Republican proposals to increase "personal responsibility." The Democrats promised even more punitive measures than those authorized by the FSA. They insisted that the new welfare reform would put "government back on the side of citizens who play by the rules." The Republicans promised more cuts and greater behavioral controls to ensure that poor people met their "obligations."

Once in office, Clinton initially focused more on health care than welfare reform. To prove, however, that he remained committed to changing welfare, Clinton adopted the Reagan policy of encouraging the states to experiment with punitive AFDC changes. But even before the 1994 election of the Contract-with-America Congress, the idea that AFDC should be only a brief respite from unemployment and a path to employment had won the day. Aided and abetted by social science research and dreams of political gain, pundits from both parties campaigned against welfare. They convinced the public that AFDC should not be the means by which underemployed, unemployed, or never-employed single mothers could provide for their families when jobs that provided adequate wages, benefits, and time for family care could not be found. Nor should the program be allowed to "reward" single mothers, now defined as the cause of all the nation's social problems, from school dropouts to drive-by shootings to the deficit.

By 1996, the Contract with America and a looming election brought Republicans and most Democrats together behind the PRWORA. Clinton signed the bill after two earlier vetoes and some brave but small opposition from certain Democrats. To make sure that everyone knew where he stood, Clinton scolded Democrats for being "too partisan" in opposition to the PRWORA. After all, he noted, "we all agree that welfare has failed and that we need reform."[11]

The coldhearted new welfare law turned welfare into a temporary program and proscribed certain work and family choices of poor women. The provisions fell into three main categories: work enforcement, family regulation, and an end to entitlements. The first two tightened the work and family mandates already put in place by the FSA. The third added something new: It ended welfare altogether!

The PRWORA intensified the already strict work requirements created by the FSA with two unprecedented changes. It limited AFDC eligibility to a maximum of five years (shorter at state option) and required most welfare recipients to be at work within two months of receiving aid—either in some type of (low-)waged employment or in a workfare program in which they "earned" their welfare grant. Clinton's early welfare reformers had promised that the more coercive features of the federal law would be muted by a host of services to help women on welfare follow the rules. These services would include health care reform, expanded child care services, and the earned income tax credit, among other nonwelfare reforms that were to surround the more punitive welfare program.

Instead, Congress cut the child care, education, and training services that had been included in the FSA to enable single mothers on welfare to go to work. The historical record confirms what Clinton's advisers should have known: When it comes to poor women and welfare, only the least costly and most punitive programs ever survive the inevitable political, funding, and bureaucratic constraints. Knowing this, the welfare reformers should not have allowed welfare to be reformed until Congress had assured them that the needed supports were in place. The PRWORA's lack of backup services downgraded welfare reform to its most coercive provisions.

The PRWORA also intensified the FSA attempts to impose a singular set of family values on welfare mothers. Congress made no secret of its intentions. The preamble to the new welfare law declared that it sought to reduce out-of-wedlock pregnancies and to encourage the formation and maintenance of two-parent households. To this end, the law (1) included the child exclusion, which permitted the states to deny aid to children born to a woman receiving welfare; (2) created a $20 million "illegitimacy" fund to be shared by up to five states that decreased their out-of-wedlock births without increasing abortions; (3) allocated funds for abstinence programs but not sex education; and (4) eliminated almost all direct aid to unmarried teen mothers and to immigrants.

However, the PRWORA's most horrific and historic change involved stripping AFDC of its entitlement status. The new welfare law converted AFDC into a state-run block grant and capped federal funding to the states. This reform effectively destroyed the sixty-year-old presumption that families in need had a "right" to welfare. For the first time, states could deny aid to poor women even though they qualified under the program's eligibility rules. The new name for AFDC—Temporary Aid to Needy Families—signaled the intent of the harsh revisions. Since then, wherever poor women turn, they find increasingly punitive programs that avoid, rather than address, their basic needs. In the words of one Boston woman: "I've got lots of problems. I've got no money and my housing is bad, my older boy is acting up, the schools are failing, and its not safe in my neighborhood. The rest of my family has big troubles too. Sure I want to work, but I need time to cope and more education before I can get a decent paying job. So don't just immediately start talking about child care and employment. Right now they are way down on the list of the things I need to take care of my family."[12]

New Liberal Rationales

The 1996 reform embodied a successful merger of recent "liberal," Clintonian ideas with the most conservative proscriptions for poor women. A Democratic administration, spurred by a Republican majority in Congress, passed some of the more punitive welfare reforms in recent history. This time around mainstream social science came to the ideological rescue. In 1962, social scientists had helped to write a report for the Department of Health, Education, and Welfare that justified government social spending with the theme "Having the Power, We Have the Duty."[13] By the 1980s, the work of many liberal social scientists provided rationales for demonizing the poor while creating social protections for the middle class. The studies provided veneer for policies that rewarded work and responsibility while depriving people of the jobs and income needed to play by the rules. In the end, the research justified the ongoing assault on welfare and other social programs.

Support for punitive welfare reforms became especially evident in several poverty discourses. This support included discussions that (1) defined the poor as an underclass, (2) insisted that welfare provision contradicted "core" American values, (3) argued that AFDC was not feasible because it could not win political support, and (4) promoted the idea that a two-tiered welfare set would help the poor. The justificatory arguments contained in this research resonated well with the traditionally conservative American culture. But they also signaled the end of a commitment to the ideals of a liberal welfare state, however limited and unequal it had been.

The Urban Underclass

The popular but ultimately racist "theory of the underclass" supports punitive welfare reforms by defining the underclass as people living in neighborhoods characterized by high rates of poverty, crime, drug dealing, hustling, school dropouts, joblessness, as well as high rates of female-headed households, teenage pregnancy, out-of-wedlock births, and welfare use.[14] These theories depict the underclass, unlike the ordinary poor, as a rootless population functioning outside mainstream values and institutions. By way of conclusion, these theories maintain that the poor transmit so-called dependency and antisocial behavior from one generation to the next (in homes headed by women) and that this "culture of poverty" remains stubbornly resistant to change.

Conservatives blamed the existence of an underclass on unproductive values and behavioral traits, an absence of "normal" male-headed families, and an expanded welfare state.[15] Liberals explained the behaviors as pragmatic, if irresponsible and destructive, adaptations to isolation, discrimination, and blocked opportunities, as well as to problems inherent in single-parent families.[16] But many of the 1990s liberals and conservatives agreed that the underclass was not merely poor, disorganized, and marginal, but also deficient and deviant. Liberals joined with conservatives to conclude that use of AFDC by itself constituted dependence and that dependence became socially harmful exactly because it provided financial support for the underclass. Even though liberals claimed more sympathy for the poor than conservatives did, they, too, regarded the poor as irresponsible, as unwilling to play by the rules, and as otherwise unable to abide by the social contract. These arguments drowned out more radical analyses that linked the problems of deepening poverty to the contradictions of capitalism, in particular to the international, profit-driven need for low wages and high unemployment rates. Feminist arguments that recognized the strength of women who raise families in the face of poverty, gender and racial discrimination, and male violence were never acknowledged. And with most of the research and media coverage focused on inner-city ghettos, most people heard underclass and thought black or Latino.

It does not take much listening to conservative and liberal pundits to recognize that the underclass has been feminized. The message became all too clear that crime, drug use, school dropouts, and teenage pregnancies were among the "tangle of pathologies" recklessly passed on from one generation to the next by women (of color) heading families without a male at the helm—or that mother-only families kept their households mired in poverty and dependent on the state. Christopher Jencks actually posited a "reproductive underclass" of women whose inability to make responsible reproductive decisions was underwritten by the presence of an AFDC subculture that separated poor women from normal society.[17] Scholars and "experts," from liberals such as David Ellwood and Senator Daniel P. Moynihan, to conservatives such as Charles Murray and Lawrence Mead, asserted that AFDC helped to create this increasingly feminized underclass.[18] They called for limiting, if not eliminating, the program to advance women out of poverty. Punitive approaches to the poor—from capping benefits to fingerprinting recipients—were invited as well by those who discussed welfare mothers in the same breath as drug users, criminals, and other antisocial groups, as if no differences existed. Such thinking, in turn, incited the view that the existing meager and class-biased welfare programs were not punitive enough. It also denied any credence to arguments that benefits could and should be *increased*.[19]

This "new consensus" among liberals and conservatives conveniently dismissed the traditional liberal view that economic insecurity stemmed directly from the dynamics of a profit-driven market economy. It also undercut the long-standing recognition that loss of income resulting from old age, illness, disability, and/or unemployment represents one of the normal risks of living and working in a capitalist economy over which people have little or no control and therefore merits government protection.[20] Feminist arguments that women need viable options besides dependence on men also receded before the liberal call to "value families," if not to promote family values.[21]

The welfare reformers twisted feminist demands and the massive entry of women into the workforce into an attack on single mothers. Poor women typically chose welfare over low-paid work when they needed to directly supervise their children, receive medical care, pursue educational goals, and/or preserve some degree of control over their lives. The welfare critics declared that they could no longer defend welfare because so many other women had become employed, albeit at dead-end, low-paid, often dangerous jobs with few benefits. There was no hearing for the arguments of welfare activists that, given such options, it made more sense for many women to stay home with their children, to help them navigate the drug- and crime-plagued streets that deindustrialization and its attendant poverty had helped to create.[22]

Finally, William Julius Wilson argued that the dynamic of class, more than race, created the underclass.[23] This analysis paved the way for many other social scientists to downplay how racism helped to deepen poverty. By dismissing the significance of race, social science made the theory of the underclass and the politics of welfare reform more creditable. Ironically, the "deracializing" of the underclass enabled social policy debates and outcomes to become even more racist.[24] For example, the repeal of welfare ostensibly targeted all poor single mothers who dared to seek assistance for themselves and their children. However, serious racial undercurrents drove the debate. Supporters declared that the new program represented "a second chance, not a way of life,"[25] and that it would instill "responsibility" in culturally adrift welfare mothers, especially unwed teen mothers. These ideas became a thoroughly permissible racial code. They moved race from the right to the center of public policy discourse.

Core American Values

In addition to positing an undeserving, largely criminal, and black underclass sustained by female-headed households, some liberal intellectuals created support for coercive reforms by arguing that welfare violates core American values.[26] Ellwood, the former assistant secretary of planning and evaluation for the Department of Health and Human Services and architect of the Clinton administration's welfare reforms, advocated this perspective in his writing and policymaking. While claiming sympathy for AFDC recipients, Ellwood, along with communitarians such as the sociologist Amitai Etzioni, argued that income support programs, especially AFDC and general assistance, conflicted with America's universal core values. Ellwood identified these values as individual autonomy, the virtue of work, the primacy of the family, and the desire for community. Past "experts" had called for expanding income support programs by creating some kind of guaranteed income. In contrast, Ellwood insisted that social policy must "come far closer to the American ideal . . . of a guarantee that people who strive and who meet reasonable social responsibilities will be able to achieve at least a modest level of dignity and security."[27] Ellwood equated meeting reasonable responsibilities with abiding by his version of core American values.

By universalizing values, Ellwood's work also obscured the ideological roots and hegemony of the dominant set. He denied that the interpretation of core values may vary with race, class, gender, and ethnicity, and he ignored how sexism, racism, and classism interfere with the realization of these values. (If social policy must pass a "core values" test, why not ensure that all new initiatives do not support racism, the family ethic, and other widespread, harmful "values"?) Finally, Ellwood's view of policymakers as the final arbiters of core "American" values implies that they should become responsible for setting levels of dignity and security. This stance belies the historical record, which shows that progressive social policies and values are far more likely to emerge from political struggle than from academic policy analysis.

Political Feasibility

The belief that welfare contradicts core American values also underpinned arguments about political feasibility. The political feasibility discussion held that the majority of voters would not support programs that contravened these universal core values. Therefore, it would be futile to improve AFDC or seek some of the progressive changes long demanded by welfare rights advocates, which included replacing the welfare system with a guaranteed family wage.[28] Instead, in this view, to secure white middle-class support, it was necessary to build a coalition based on policies that all can agree upon, a strategy also known as the lowest common denominator. The lowest-common-denominator approach risks ignoring or subsuming the needs of poor women and all other marginalized groups.

Christopher Jencks made the consummate political feasibility argument. He concluded that it would cost some $35 billion to make all single mothers eligible for welfare regardless of employment status. The actual cost at the time was $24 billion. "Despite the advantages" of liberalizing welfare eligibility, Jencks concluded, "it would be politically impossible because single mothers are a relatively small, unorganized and unpopular group." Therefore "a program aimed at them will never be generous." In contrast, Jencks argued that a social policy focused on making low-wage work economically attractive could "win broad political support."[29]

The implication that any job is better than welfare, that it is better to be working poor than welfare poor, denied the realities of poor women's lives. The stress and invisible poverty that accompanied low-waged employment could actually worsen the plight of single mothers and their children.

Mickey Kaus and others expanded the political feasibility argument. They urged liberals to abandon the search for full economic justice and social equality while they had a "window of opportunity" with the Clinton administration.[30] Kaus and company encouraged liberals to jump into the policy stream as it flowed by. This meant developing programs to benefit the majority of waged workers (i.e., voters) without challenging the latter's negative and hostile images of welfare mothers or the urban underclass. But, we can only ask, how high did they jump? Which way was the stream going?

And how far did they swim while denying the messy questions about racism and the lack of real options for single mothers?

A Two-Tiered Welfare State Helps the Poor

Harvard sociologist Theda Skocpol offered the essential justification of the strategy for serving the middle class at the expense of the poor. After describing a reasonable set of proposals for the middle class—indeed, reforms far stronger than the Clinton agenda—Skocpol asked:

> But can the American poor really be helped by the program I have outlined? Wouldn't this set of policies help principally the middle and working classes, along with the most privileged and least troubled of the poor, leaving behind many of the extremely disadvantaged, disproportionately people of color, who require intensive services to break out of cycles of social pathology and despair? Initially, this might happen. Yet, an ever-deepening course of hope and improvement might soon unfold among the poor. Once genuinely new and non-stigmatizing incentives, social supports and ways of providing job opportunities were in place, the example of a few go-getters who took advantage of new policies and forged better lives for themselves might well propagate among relatives, friends and neighbors. After the word really got out that work really does lead to rewards, a certain amount of social despair that now pervades the very poor might well begin to dissipate. In a way this could be the greatest gift the new universalistic family security policies could give to the most disadvantaged among American poor, for it would facilitate their moral reintegration into the mainstream of national life.[31]

The New Democrats followed the trickle-down theory and then some. They offered the middle class new government programs, such as managed health care, college loans, family leave, and other investments in human capital. At the same time, the New Democrats reformed welfare and slashed many other programs for the poor. Indeed, officialdom used the existence of huge budget deficits to justify less social spending. The new middle-class programs therefore competed for government dollars with existing programs for the poor. Time and again, those programs serving the poor lost out. In a very short time, it became very clear that these work-based initiatives had little likelihood of ever reaching the poor people for whom few, if any, well-paid jobs existed at all.

The argument that it is all right to serve the middle class while the poor wait for hope to trickle down was fatally flawed conceptually as well as practically. First, no one can live on hope; nor does it usually trickle down. Second, Clinton, Skocpol, and others reinvented the original Social Security Act compromise, which conditioned *all* income maintenance benefits on employment rather than providing them as a right based on need. However, the presumption that paid employment is the only legitimate means for individuals to meet personal and societal obligations has become even less true now than it was in 1935. Deindustrialization and the rise of the "service economy" have meant that higher-paid manufacturing jobs have given way to lower-paid, part-time, nonunion jobs. The new jobs fail to lift people above the poverty line, much less provide a decent standard of living. Corporations have used downsizing, foreign competition, and export of production abroad to exert an additional downward pressure on wages at home.

By making employment the only legitimate source of economic security, social theorists and politicians ignored women's unique circumstances. It led scholars and policymakers to malign women on welfare without jobs as irresponsible adults and to devalue women's caretaking in the home and all other forms of unpaid labor. They also ignored sex discrimination in the workplace, sex-segregated occupations, and the gendered division of labor, which assigns women near-exclusive responsibility for the home even when they work outside it.

Welfare-bashing drew from the new liberal agenda to bring the state back in on behalf of the working and middle classes. It also reflected the traditional conservative hostility to a state that seeks social justice for the poor. This combination hit poor women with a one-two punch from friend and foe alike. Poor women found themselves left friendless at a time of greater and greater need, as Trudy Condio observed at a Boston speak-out: "I don't know who to trust anymore. My family and the people on the talk shows hate me for being on welfare and for not being married. But even my social worker and my teachers seem to think there is something wrong with me for not trying to find a job tomorrow. But I've got a lot to do, taking care of my daughter, trying to go to school, thinking about the future. Why doesn't anybody recognize that too?"[32]

It seems both cruel and absurd for liberals to have abandoned women's meager protection from a job market increasingly unable to provide jobs at a living wage. Liberal experts might have left this role to its historic players—conservative Republicans and racist Democrats. Instead, *they* themselves defined employment as the basis for benefits and held it up as the only "secure" option for welfare mothers. In sum, liberals delivered the ultimate rationale for ending welfare altogether. According to Jencks: "If a mother does not have a God given right to stay home with her children, if paying her to do so does not make economic sense, and if it does her children more harm than good, the case for welfare collapses. . . . The moral case for helping welfare mothers rather than working mothers rests on a factual mistake."[33]

The Politics of Welfare Reform

Welfare-bashing was neither accidental nor harmless. Rather, it served economic and political ends. On the economic front, the campaign for welfare reform helped to deflect attention from the failure of the market to provide both enough jobs and a livable wage. The leaders of both parties encouraged the increasingly anxious middle class to blame social programs, the deficit, and the poor, instead of the profit-driven policies of business and the state, for a falling standard of living.

Welfare reform can best be understood as part of a broader strategy launched by President Ronald Reagan and continued by Presidents George Bush and Clinton to promote economic recovery by cheapening the cost of labor for employers. Time limits, stiff new work rules, and workfare programs have thrown thousands of welfare recipients into the low-wage labor market, where they must compete for work with many other desperate job seekers. The increased competition for jobs makes it easier for employers to press wages down and harder for unions to negotiate good contracts. If "any job is a good job," then unions cannot organize. Cheapening the cost of labor and weakening trade unions have lowered the standard of living in the face of a new world economy.

The overall economic recovery strategy also included weakening the power of social movements to fight back. Welfare reform plays a role here, as does the erosion of the value of Unemployment Insurance and other cash benefits. Like a strike fund, access to social welfare benefits provides an economic backup that emboldens workers to resist exploitation on the job. Cash assistance weakens the power of unemployment to depress wages and limits the ability of employers to use fear of joblessness to keep workers in line.[34] As an alternative wage, government benefits create the potential for employed workers to fight for better pay and working conditions and for jobless workers to hold out for better-paying jobs. Access to cash assistance increases the bargaining power of women at home, as well as on the job. Welfare, in particular, has made it easier for women to avoid violent and abusive relationships. By increasing women's economic autonomy, welfare enables them to raise children on their own.[35]

Finally, welfare-bashing has served political ends. A demonstrated hostility to the poor and a willingness to cut "failed" social programs became a "bottom-line" ticket of entry into "responsible" politics in both parties. Welfare-bashing also became a useful race card in electoral campaigns. Politicians have regularly wooed voters by pandering to racial fears. Nixon had his southern strategy. Reagan had his welfare queen. Bush had Willie Horton. Clinton's political advisers bashed welfare to show white people that Democrats can be tough on blacks without saying so.[36]

Between a Rock and a Hard Place

Bashing of welfare recipients, the old welfare system, and the idea of a dependable welfare state continues. But it has grown more complicated as Clintonian compromises lurch forward. If bashing the poor was part of a broader strategy to use government dollars on behalf of the working and middle class, this bargain with the devil seems to have failed on its own terms. Most notably, health care reform lost out to private insurance companies. The public's mounting hatred of drive-by delivery of new babies and all the other service constraints favored by health maintenance organizations (HMOs) has forced the free-market government to consider a patient's bill of rights and other regulation of the profit-driven health care industry. This inevitable turn of events happened much faster than most critics of HMOs ever expected.

To make the case for welfare reform in the early 1990s, the reformers blamed recipients for every social ill. Today, the success of welfare reform depends on the placement of thousands of recipients in paying jobs. Indeed, Clinton must convince employers to hire the poor single mothers that his administration and its followers previously maligned as lazy, immoral, and fraudulent. To reverse the false stereotypes that his own people perpetuated, the president has been trying to "sell" recipients to employees. He bills them as "new workers" who, having been freed from expecting a handout, will serve their companies well.

Of course, room still exists to bash recipients who do not "succeed" in the new system. After all, if they cannot find a job or take advantage of these new "work opportunities," then their poverty must *really* be their fault. They then deserve any punishment they get. Taking away a poor women's children if she cannot find a job may emerge as an easy next step in a society that has historically distrusted the parenting capacity of poor single women and that has blamed poverty, juvenile delinquency, schizophrenia, and most other social problems on mothers.[37] A continuing attack on those who will inevitably fail to live up to an idealized version of womanhood will take the blame off unreasonable policies. It will further frighten others into continuing to pursue the myth.

Alternatively, if the new programs fail, which they are likely to do, social workers and administrators can always be blamed. Shortly after Clinton signed the welfare bill, a proreform columnist predicted that the new strategy would fall short because social workers would be insufficiently punitive.[38] Blaming public program staff also fuels the drive toward privatization. In fact, the government seeks to privatize the very social programs that it once concluded did not work. Under the ennobling pressure of the profit motive, government officials expect the same programs to make highly sensitive decisions about job matches and other service options.[39] Conversely, the government periodically "reinvents" public programs, so that they escape the old "soft" social work mentality. Meanwhile, new rules free the programs from having to monitor the effects of their new policies.[40]

Meanwhile, the programs designed for the poor continue to be belittled and cast off. Both the New Democrats and the Republicans stepped up their attack on the old system to justify their joint efforts to dismantle it. They could not allow the public to think that the problems in the existing social programs might have been fixed with simple remedies, such as adequate funding, trained staff, and the provision of other needed resources. The public had to be prevented from suspecting that the old programs did not have to be destroyed. In the end, the books had to be cleaned of all evidence that officialdom had once praised public programs as a social achievement that protected everyone from market forces over which individuals have little or no control.

The New Democrats wanted to bring the state in not as a beast to be tamed but as a tool to build the economy and to serve the middle class, if not the poor. They hoped to mediate the negative impact on the middle class of fifteen years of public and private retrenchment. However, the Clinton administration's own effort to match the antistatism of the conservatives got in the way. After the defeat of health care reform, it became virtually impossible to enact comprehensive social programs. The populace, whose conservative views reflected years of national rhetoric hostile to the welfare state, needed reeducation on the merits of government programs. Instead, the Clinton administration's welfare-bashing sent an antigovernment message. And in a State of the Union address, Clinton advanced public hostility to the very programs he sought to establish by declaring that "the era of big government is over."

Not surprisingly, the gains in social investment have been small. The main new program the New Democrats have managed to get through Congress turned out to be tax relief for the upper (not lower) middle classes. In addition, the success of welfare-bashing has paved the way for an assault on the popular entitlements that serve the middle class. Shortly after Congress passed the PRWORA, the President's Commission on Social Security released a report that included three different ways to privatize Social Security—all linked to Wall Street. The question was not, Should Social Security be privatized? Rather, the question was, How and when? (Medicare is on the privatization chopping block in the form of medical savings accounts.)

Finally, welfare reform undercut Clinton's chosen role as a "healer." Unlike the Republican rhetoric that thrived on divisiveness, the Democratic Leadership Council had once called for "unity." Instead, the attack on welfare fueled the politics of hate that is tearing this nation apart. The Clintonian Democrats' strategy to win votes by attacking poor women on welfare implicitly sanctioned the bashing of other "outsiders," be they gays, leftists ("domestic socialists," in conservative parlance), or immigrants. It also opened the floodgate to the justification of ever-more-punitive programs for whomever comes next in an ever-widening search for those who break the rules.[41]

Toward a More Authoritarian State?

Left unchallenged, the divisive trends outlined here risk paving the way for the more authoritarian state promoted by the triumphant Republican right in 1994. Unfortunately, arguments made by social scientists to validate punitive welfare reform have contributed to this possibility in several ways.

Many mainstream social scientists perpetuated traditional conservative explanations of social problems. By focusing on individual values and behavior, rather than institutional classism, racism, and sexism, they effectively blamed "the victim" rather than the "system." These culture-of-poverty theories also heightened public tolerance for government intervention in the work, marital, childbearing, and parenting behavior of women on welfare. By implication, they endorsed new state controls on any of us. Once legitimized for one group (in this case, the most vulnerable), these controls can more readily be extended to others whom the powers that be choose to define as "undeserving," "deviant," or "too demanding." The current short list seems to include immigrants, gays and lesbians, the disabled, the drug addicted, the mentally ill, and "recipients of Affirmative Action." The long list includes anyone and everyone who fails to play by the rules.

Social science findings that maligned the poor and devalued government also helped politicians to undercut the liberal tenets of entitlement, self-determination, and federal responsibility. Yet these had been the very principles that for the past sixty years had fueled hope for social, economic, and political progress within our imperfect market economy and our deeply compromised democracy. Their replacements—the standard conservative notions of contract, control, compulsion, and states' rights—shift the balance of political power from the people to the state.

Welfare-bashing brought the state back in—but in ever-more-dangerous ways. Taken to a logical extreme, welfare reform may become the jumping board for the abandonment of hard-won democratic rights—rights that represent a real, if compromised, achievement of our society. The strategy to save the white middle class at the expense of the poor inherently endorses punitive proposals. We fear it contains the potential to make room for a more authoritarian state.

Postscript: In Struggle

Despite all the dangers, we do not lack optimism. In this post–cold war world, it may be more possible to look to other countries for models—witness the health policy debates. Existing international studies challenge the alleged "value consensus" that social programs do not work to lessen poverty and increase the standard of living. Indeed, comparative research has found that during the 1980s income maintenance programs in Canada, Australia, and five northern European countries reduced poverty by 16.5 percent, compared to only 6.6 percent in the United States. Despite similar pretransfer poverty rates, poverty dropped less than 4 percent for children in single-parent families in the United States but plummeted nearly 30 percent in other nations. Similar effects appear in cross-national comparisons of tax policies.[42] U.S. voters may be value-bound. If so, such information will make no difference. We believe, however, that informed voters can evaluate new, yet reasonable choices. If so, they can also support candidates and policies that promise to address basic human needs.

Even more importantly, women on welfare are rising up angry and finding new allies as the PRWORA cuts its wide swath through social democracy. Like the welfare rights movement of the 1970s, activists have begun to lead the fight for a more expansive and just state. Unwilling to take the blame, the punishment, or the coercion lying down, welfare mothers in many states are protesting the whole set of programs associated with reform: lowered benefits, time limits, abusive fraud investigations, workfare, and family caps. The National Organization for Women and its Legal Defense Fund worked with the National Welfare Rights Union in the effort to defeat welfare reform. They argued that welfare was an issue for all women. Some of the new women politicians, especially women of color in state and national offices, appear interested in an alternative vision of welfare reform. They, too, have concluded that the treatment of poor women foreshadows the treatment of all women.[43] Labor/welfare coalitions are forming in many states. They have opposed welfare reform, exposed the prowealth agenda of the right, and insisted that social security and economic security are necessities for democracy. Some religious and human rights groups have begun to define welfare reform as an abuse of human rights.

The efforts to thwart the welfare reform blitzkrieg—and the chilling future it forebodes—are definitely long shots. In the short run, we are losing. The right has won. It is consolidating its strength and making the denigration of poor people a central principle of unity. Better professional policy proposals can make a difference. But they will not save the day. We stand a better chance by reviving a broad-based movement. To succeed, such a movement must be built upon a women's movement linked to progressive labor, civil rights, and welfare rights organizations, to name only a few. Poor women must play leadership roles in this new coalition, whose politics is fueled by deeply felt demands for justice, power, and equality. Such a movement is needed because social policy rarely changes for the better unless pressured to do so from below. If not now, when?

7

The New Face of Urban Renewal: The Near North Redevelopment Initiative and the Cabrini-Green Neighborhood

Larry Bennett and Adolph Reed Jr.

THE CABRINI-GREEN PUBLIC HOUSING DEVELOPMENT, located just a mile north of Chicago's downtown "Loop," is a complex of over seventy buildings erected in three principal phases between World War II and the early 1960s. The Frances Cabrini Homes were completed in 1942, providing just under six hundred apartments in a network of two- and three-story "walk-up" buildings. The Cabrini Homes stretch north of Chicago Avenue to Oak Street, lying to the west of Hudson Street. Adjoining the Cabrini Homes on the north is the Cabrini Extension, completed in 1958 and until recently including fifteen structures between seven and nineteen floors in height (and holding just under nineteen hundred residential units). After World War II, the Chicago Housing Authority (CHA) committed itself to high-rise building construction, as reflected in the Cabrini Extension, as well as the final segment of Cabrini-Green, the William Green Homes. The Green Homes are north of Division Street and west of Larrabee Street. The eight Green high-rises, completed in 1962, hold nearly eleven hundred apartments.[1]

The Cabrini-Green development is at the western end of Chicago's Near North Side community area (which extends from the Chicago River north to North Avenue and from Lake Michigan west to the North Branch of the river), which historically has been among the city's most ethnically and economically diverse locales. Sociologist Harvey W. Zorbaugh studied this part of Chicago in the 1920s, entitling the resulting book *The Gold Coast and the Slum.*[2] During this period, the area west of Wells Street and below North Avenue was occupied mainly by Italian Americans and known variously as Little Sicily or Little Hell. Adjoining Little Hell on the south were several blocks where African Americans resided.

Historian Thomas Lee Philpott, in *The Slum and the Ghetto,* notes that it was the presence of this small North Side African American neighborhood that, in part, gave impetus to one of Chicago's early philanthropic housing experiments. In 1928–1929 the Estate of Marshall Field built the Marshall Field Garden Apartments along Hudson Street to the south of North Avenue: "By the time the Field Gardens opened, upwards of four thousand black people were living in the Lower North Side. Whites in the area hoped to contain the Little Black Belt below Division Street. The Field project, on the white side of that emerging line, cleared away 'substantial housing which it was an advantage to be rid of.' It was just the sort of property that landlords were willing to turn over to black tenants."[3] In spite of the Marshall Field Garden Apartments' architecturally advanced courtyard design and the management's sponsorship of a variety of community activities, the project experienced great difficulty in attracting and holding tenants. According to Philpott, this was because the Field Gardens' management insisted on charging rents that were beyond the means of local residents.

In any event, when the CHA constructed the Francis Cabrini Homes in the early 1940s, the Near North Side's polyglot character remained. Nonetheless, throughout much of the 1950s and 1960s—as the complex was greatly enlarged and indeed transformed through the construction of the Cabrini Extension and Green Homes high-rises—Cabrini-Green did not have the reputation of public housing wasteland that it later achieved. The turning point in the project's reputation probably occurred in July 1970 when two Chicago Police Department officers were shot and killed on the Cabrini-Green grounds.[4] During the next few years, security systems in Cabrini-Green were upgraded, but many longtime residents recall that in the aftermath of the 1970 police shootings the Police Department adopted a stay-clear-of-Cabrini approach to local patrolling.

Cabrini-Green once again won headline attention in March and April 1981. For a few weeks, Chicago mayor Jane Byrne moved into an apartment at 1150–60 North Sedgwick, ostensibly to bring attention to increasing criminal violence in the complex.[5] Mayor Byrne was more than likely seeking to reverse a growing sentiment among the city's African American electorate that she had reneged on campaign promises offered during her uphill election victory of 1979. In early April 1981—as Mayor Byrne held press conferences to discuss the problems of public housing, or as she attended social gatherings in Cabrini-Green—the complex became a familiar locale for many Chicagoans. However, when Byrne returned to her Gold Coast condominium in mid-April, Cabrini-Green dropped off the local media screen.

Yet even as Cabrini-Green's notoriety was amplified by events such as the Byrne sojourn, the Near North Side's reputation as gold coast and slum, port of entry, and ethnic phantasmagoria was shifting. Through urban renewal, in particular the development of the huge Sandburg Village complex between LaSalle and Clark Streets, the affluent lakefront Near North Side was preserved as a high-income enclave.[6] Above North Avenue, the real estate development and gentrification of the Lincoln Park neighborhood were in high gear by the 1960s. And beginning in the 1970s, the old warehouse and light manufacturing district on Cabrini-Green's southern flank was recast as a gallery district—well on the way to winning its new identity as River North. In short, Cabrini-Green centered a huge north side area undergoing aggressive real estate investment and physical upgrading.

By 1986, a former aide to Mayor Richard J. Daley, Ed Marciniak, had published a short book that formalized a rumor already in wide circulation among the city's political and economic elites:

> The future of Cabrini-Green and the fate of the Lower North Side are entwined. As the Lower North Side fades away, the Cabrini-Green project, more visible and vulnerable, becomes the chief concern of reformers who live inside or outside the project. In the near future, therefore, the Cabrini-Green high-rises will be at the center of a classic confrontation between political constituencies with clashing interests;

> between onrushing affluence and defensive poverty; between spunky owners of small properties and spineless bureaucracies; and between urban revival and inner city stagnation. . . . At one time Cabrini-Green was viewed as the Near North Side's Rock of Gibraltor, but no longer. Hence, the Cabrini-Green public housing project faces an unsure future. Inevitably, Cabrini-Green's high rises will be recycled or torn down, their residents relocated.[7]

Census data reveal that the 1980s were indeed a decade of significant change in the Near North Side community area. And the outset of that ten-year span of time, and reflective of the area's long-standing status as gold coast and slum, the median income of local residents was about 25 percent above the citywide figure. In effect, although the blocks east of Clark Street were home to some of the city's wealthiest residents, as one moved west of Wells Street, the large low-income population substantially reduced the community area's median income figure. But by the end of the decade, the Near North Side community area's median income had risen to twice the citywide median. Correspondingly, during the same ten-year period the median sale price of single-unit homes in the Near North Side increased from $138,000 to $700,000. As recently as 1977, the city of Chicago issued only 59 residential building permits within the Near North Side community area. By 1990, this figure had reached 173.[8]

This spurt in the Near North Side real estate market was strong enough to generate a parallel shift in neighborhood demographics. From the World War II era until the 1980 census, the African American proportion of the Near North Side population hovered around 30 percent. In the next decade the area's African American population declined from twenty-two thousand to fifteen thousand (that is, from 33 to 23 percent of the community area total) and the number of whites, in turn, increased by about four thousand.[9] The Near North Side—which had always retained its posh lakefront enclave—was beginning to experience significant gentrification in areas west of LaSalle Street.

Cabrini-Green is not simply a poor residential area within the gentrifying Near North Side. Its fortunes have also been affected by the shifting circumstances of the Chicago Housing Authority. In 1937, the state of Illinois, responding to the passage of federal public housing legislation, authorized a new local agency, the CHA, to build and manage public housing units within Chicago. Like other public housing authorities around the United States, during the CHA's first decade of existence it produced a relatively limited stream of housing developments. By the 1950s, and in response to increased congressional authorizations for public housing and the approval of the new urban renewal program, the CHA's building program had expanded dramatically.[10] However, as the CHA's development activities grew, the agency also began to encounter considerable public and political resistance. Especially under the leadership of Elizabeth Wood, the CHA pursued a policy of careful racial integration (both with regard to site location and tenant placement), which by the mid-1950s had earned it many enemies around Chicago. During that decade, the city's African American population growth—which had accelerated greatly during the war years—continued, and many neighborhoods on the city's south and west sides were undergoing racial transition. In the short run, the city's political leadership removed Elizabeth Wood from the CHA. Over the longer run—from the mid-1950s until the mid-1960s—the mayor, City Council, and the CHA pursued a public housing siting protocol that guaranteed the location of all new CHA developments in exclusively black or racially changing areas.[11]

This policy and related CHA internal procedures were challenged in the *Gautreaux* v. *Chicago Housing Authority* lawsuit of 1966, which resulted in a federal court order to "open" the entire city to public housing development.[12] The CHA, at the behest of Mayor Richard J. Daley, responded to the *Gautreaux* ruling by ceasing to build new "family" public housing units. Historian Arnold Hirsch reports that, having built more than 1,000 units of housing per year between 1950 and 1966, the CHA built 114 such apartments from 1969 until 1980.[13] Moreover, with the end of its mandate to build public housing, the CHA quickly became an administrative backwater. From the mid-1970s until the late 1980s, the CHA's executive leadership marched in and out of a revolving door, the agency's finances collapsed, and on the ground—in public housing developments across the city—the quality of life deteriorated.[14]

In 1988, following the release of a blistering report produced by a mayoral committee examining local public housing, Mayor Eugene Sawyer appointed developer Vincent Lane to head the CHA's board and administrative operations.[15] Lane assumed his dual role bearing a well-publicized mandate to clean up CHA's internal operations and, possibly more importantly, to define a new "vision" for public housing in Chicago. During Lane's tenure, the CHA developed its Mixed-Income New Communities Strategy, first implemented at Lake Parc Place on the South Side and the original model for Cabrini-Green redevelopment.[16]

In late May 1995, following months of press reports detailing internal mismanagement at the CHA, the U.S. Department of Housing and Urban Development (HUD) took over the operations of the local housing agency.[17] Vincent Lane resigned as CHA chair and was replaced by a HUD official, Joseph Shuldiner. In June 1996, Shuldiner and Chicago mayor Richard M. Daley announced the Near North Redevelopment Initiative (NNRI), a neighborhood improvement plan that would demolish more than thirteen hundred units of Cabrini-Green housing, build approximately half as many replacement public housing units, encourage market-rate private housing and commercial development in the Cabrini-Green area, and physically upgrade local schools and other public facilities.

The NNRI represents both an extension of and break with plans to redevelop Cabrini-Green dating from 1993. At that time, the Vincent Lane–led CHA won a $50 million Hope VI grant from HUD to initiate rehabilitation of Cabrini-Green. By 1995, when Lane was ousted as CHA head, the Cabrini-Green redevelopment process had stalled. However, in announcing the NNRI in 1996, CHA executive director Shuldiner and Mayor Daley proposed to use the remaining Hope VI grant funds. More generally, their vision of the new Cabrini-Green neighborhood carried over Vincent Lane's mixed-income community philosophy. However, the NNRI anticipates that private developers will rebuild the Cabrini-Green area, and the geographic scope of the present plan far exceeds the original Hope VI proposal to rebuild slightly less than ten acres of the Cabrini-Green site.[18]

In October 1996, the Cabrini-Green Local Advisory Council (LAC)—the development's official tenants' organization—filed a federal lawsuit against the CHA and city of Chicago. The LAC's suit charged that the CHA and the city had excluded Cabrini-Green residents from the NNRI planning process and that the effect of the NNRI would be to remove many Cabrini-Green residents from the neighborhood.[19] In the following pages, we first examine the sociological grounding of the NNRI by linking the details of its neighborhood analysis to predominant themes in contemporary sociological discourse. In subsequent sections, we offer a "counterportrait" of the Cabrini-Green neighborhood—based on interviews with local residents and the examination of various accounts of neighborhood life—that challenges the governing assumption of the NNRI, namely, that the Cabrini-Green public housing development is a hopelessly pathological "ghetto underclass" area. We conclude our analysis by noting the parallels between the NNRI and the long-discredited urban renewal program, and we offer a series of suggestions for transforming the NNRI into a truly inclusive neighborhood improvement process.

The Mixed-Income Ideology and Neighborhood Development

The NNRI proposes to reshape the Cabrini-Green area through the construction of over two thousand units of new housing, commercial development along Division Street, and a number of public projects, such as a recently opened branch library on Division Street. The CHA and city of Chicago have proposed a 30/70 percent ratio of subsidized to nonsubsidized housing, although the NNRI does not detail how the low-income housing will be developed or managed. The NNRI further outlines a physical vision of the Near North Side reflecting many of the principles associated with the "new urbanist" movement in city planning and architecture. In fact, the NNRI is grounded in a poorly thought-out understanding of the Cabrini-Green area that is itself derived from a questionable chain of sociological analysis. Indeed, the plan's 30/70 ratio of subsidized to nonsubsidized dwellings seems to revive the real estate industry's old and discredited notion of neighborhood racial "tipping points" (the level of black presence that would make an area unattractive to white), and although new urbanist planning has won many admirers across the United States, the NNRI does not demonstrate any degree of sophistication in linking physical design elements to the on-the-ground social conditions of the Cabrini-Green neighborhood.

Social Isolation, Concentrated Poverty, and Neighborhood Viability

From the moment that Vincent Lane began his campaign to redevelop Cabrini-Green, public officials, planning documents, and various real estate groups have framed an empirically inaccurate and analytically inconsistent portrait of Cabrini-Green and its residents. Time and again, officials such as Lane and Mayor Daley have asserted that the basic elements of urban neighborhood life—family and friendship networks, neighborhood-based organizations, and responsible leaders—are absent from Cabrini-Green and, moreover, that local residents suffer from extreme social isolation. There is a simple enough explanation for the excessive labor dedicated to drawing this misleading picture: to legitimate the NNRI by appropriating a set of presumably unassailable sociological arguments. In practice, the sociological grounding of the NNRI is far less solid than the CHA and city of Chicago realize.

At the core of the NNRI's interpretation of the Cabrini-Green area are the linked propositions that current residents suffer from social isolation—that is, lack of contact with outside people and institutions—as well as overly homogeneous internal social structure, and "concentration effects" produced by the unhealthy proportion of low-income people in the neighborhood. For example, the CHA's 1993 Hope VI application identifies "isolation and concentration" as Cabrini-Green's defining features.[20] This document subsequently details the consequences of social isolation and concentration of poverty:

> A plethora of socio-economic ills makes distress a predominant characteristic for the families housed in the Cabrini Extension . . . all of which propel and perpetuate the generational cycle of poverty and dependency. The dense concentration of very low income and racially homogeneous residents in a geographically isolated area establishes a basic condition of distress, hopelessness and lack of opportunity for the Cabrini population. The monolithic nature of the population deprives the community of valuable role models, strong community and family supports and creates insurmountable obstacles to the socio-economic mainstream.[21]

Having determined that what ails Cabrini-Green are its residents' social isolation and concentration of poverty, the CHA/city of Chicago planning agenda has single-mindedly sought to root out these conditions. In 1995, Vincent Lane reiterated that the agency's objective in reorganizing the delivery of low-income public housing was to create "stable, mixed income" neighborhoods.[22] The CHA's commitment to that objective remains central to the rationale of the subsequent NNRI. This plan states that the "Cabrini-Green development is a pocket of isolated and concentrated poverty surrounded by wealth, and the challenge is to end years of isolation for public housing residents through integration of public housing in a vibrant revitalized Near North Side neighborhood."[23]

The neighborhood analyses produced by prospective Cabrini-Green area private developers have been even more dramatic in emphasizing isolation, concentration, and resulting social pathology as the area's defining features. Even while complimenting the virtue of individual Cabrini-Green residents, the North Town Community Partnership proposal of 1995 matter-of-factly describes the housing project as "warehouses of terminal poverty" and as "crime-plagued, prowled by dope gangs, unsure of today, desperately uncertain of tomorrow."[24] This document repeatedly sounds the theme of Cabrini-Green residents' isolation, noting that "seen from 40 floors up in a luxury tower across town, Cabrini-Green's apartment slabs brood like tombstones on quarantined turf."[25] In recounting the project's history, the partnership plan even harkens back to the old notion of uncultivated migrants "dependent on welfare and often unaccustomed to city life."[26] A Draper and Kramer analysis of market-rate units likewise describes the area as "an isolated enclave" and notes, approvingly, the announcement of plans to demolish Cabrini-Green's high-rises, which "has reinforced the perception that public housing will not continue to dominate the area as it has."[27]

A Tracy Cross and Associates market analysis, in particular, reveals the slippery, ideological character of Cabrini-Green's "isolation." The Tracy Cross study asserts, paradoxically: "While isolated to ethnically-oriented convenience shopping within the immediate vicinity, areas contiguous to the Near North Planning Area include a vast variety of retail establishments extending from grocery stores anchored by Jewel and Whole Foods to 'big box' retailers like Home Depot, Sam's, Best Buy, the Electric Company, Homemakers, Super Crown, The Gap, Bed Bath and Beyond, Crate & Barrel, and Cost Plus, among others."[28] By thus compromising its own presumption of Cabrini-Green's disconnection from the surrounding city, the Tracy Cross description reveals that the area's putative isolation is more rhetorical than geographical.

Another revealing element of the Tracy Cross analysis is its equivocal attitude toward mixed-income development. In consecutive paragraphs this study cautions that the mixed-income strategy dampens market-rate development because "homebuyers tend to prefer developments that are more insular in nature and more restricted in their socio-economic composition," then describes the Cabrini-Green area negatively, and, with the standard implication of pathology, observes that Cabrini-Green is, "for all practical purposes, an isolated part of the city."[29]

This way of construing Cabrini-Green's isolation is more a matter of presupposition than locational reality. After all, the extensive array of commercial facilities—and by no means all upscale—in the vicinity of Cabrini-Green is not a matter of contention. Furthermore, our conversations with Cabrini-Green residents reveal that they view proximity to commercial, recreational, and other facilities as one of the area's principal attractions. For planners, developers, and evidently some city officials, what makes the area seem so strikingly separate from its surroundings is the prior presumption of the public housing population's isolation, as well as the allied (but only inadvertently articulated) expectation that white, more affluent Near North Siders want to maintain distance from public housing residents. The latter notion underlies the amazingly counterfactual assertion in the CHA's 1993 Hope VI application that Cabrini-Green residents' isolation "is more profound than other CHA communities"—that is, in comparison to residents of the Ida B. Wells and Robert Taylor Homes, which "sit within the poorest neighborhoods of the city."[30] Yet unlike these other CHA developments, "Cabrini-Green, due to its location, over time became surrounded by wealthy communities that are racially diverse."[31] In keeping with this strange line of argument—that the most extreme social isolation is found in an area of considerable demographic, commercial, and residential diversity—this document persists in the claim that "Cabrini-Green resembles an island—cut off from nearby resources by vast and insurmountable racial and social boundaries, as well as physical ones."[32]

The sociological source for much of the thinking that structures the NNRI can be found in the work of Harvard University (and former University of Chicago) sociologist William Julius Wilson, who, in particular, has identified social isolation and concentration of poverty as key elements explaining the contemporary plight of inner-city, African American neighborhoods.[33] It is Wilson's contention that when the proportion of very poor people in a neighborhood rises to a certain level, institutions atrophy and social organization breaks down. At this point neighborhoods lose a crucial "'social buffer' that could deflect the full impact of the kind of prolonged joblessness that plagued inner-city neighborhoods in the 1970s and early 1980s."[34] More recently, Wilson has indicated what he means by social organization:

> When I speak of social organization I am referring to the extent to which the residents of a neighborhood are able to maintain effective social control and realize their common goals. There are three major dimensions of neighborhood social organization: (1) the prevalence, strength, and interdependence of social networks; (2) the extent of collective supervision that the residents exercise and the degree of personal responsibility they assume in addressing neighborhood problems; and (3) the rate of resident participation in voluntary and formal organizations. Formal institutions (e.g., churches, and political party organizations), voluntary associations (e.g., block clubs and parent-teacher organizations), and informal networks (e.g., neighborhood friends and acquaintances, coworkers, marital and parental ties) all reflect social organization.[35]

Wilson further asserts that in neighborhoods of this sort, social networks wither. As a result, resident supervision of youths and of the neighborhood's affairs in general deteriorates. Adults in the neighborhood no longer "assume responsibility for maintaining standards of public behavior even on the part of children who are not their own."[36] Moreover,

> the significance of increasing social isolation is not that ghetto culture went unchecked following the removal of higher income families from many inner-city neighborhoods, but that the increasing exodus of these families made it more difficult to sustain the basic institutions in these neighborhoods (including churches, stores, recreational facilities, etc.) in the face of increased joblessness. . . . As the basic institutions declined, the social organization of inner-city neighborhoods (sense of community, positive neighborhood identification, and explicit norms and sanctions against aberrant behavior) declined. This process magnified the effects of living in highly concentrated urban poverty areas—effects that are manifested in ghetto-specific culture and behavior.[37]

By "ghetto-specific culture and behavior," Wilson means relatively high rates of teenage childbearing, out-of-wedlock births, female-headed households, drug abuse, welfare dependency, weak labor force attachment, and violent crime. These are the substantive phenomena that constitute what Wilson and others refer to as the widespread social pathology in many inner-city areas.

The CHA/city of Chicago presumption that the problems of Cabrini-Green result from the social pathology of the public housing population reflects the limitations of the social isolation/concentration of poverty theses in which it is embedded. Both are grounded on much older stereotypes about poor people. These stereotypical ways of characterizing the very poor have a long history, and by representing the very poor as radically different in their behavior, values, and motivations from other, supposedly normal people, these stereotypes have often been associated with the stigmatizing of specific racial and ethnic populations.[38] Over the last generation, they have become distinctly racialized in American popular and policy discourse. Today, when commentators speak of an intergenerationally self-reproducing urban "underclass," normatively and behaviorally different from the mainstream American population, they typically refer to black Americans, or in some cases to Latinos. Contemporary pronouncements that such an alien population exists among us ultimately restate with slightly different language and rationales earlier and similarly racialized formulations concerning the self-reproducing "culture of poverty."[39] In turn, both culture-of-poverty and underclass formulations derive from even older and more overtly prejudiced patterns of stigmatizing the very poor by attributing their poverty to putative defects of character or moral laxity.

William Julius Wilson's theory of social isolation and the harmful effects of demographically concentrated poverty is built on a set of concepts—social disorganization, social pathology, the notion of an intergenerationally self-reproducing cycle of poverty, and the study of neighborhoods as discrete ecological systems—derived from a school of sociological thinking and research that originated at the University of Chicago early in this century.[40] Scholars associated with this analytical approach helped to create the study of urban sociology, and one of its early and most substantial products was, in fact, *The Gold Coast and the Slum,* Harvey Zorbaugh's 1929 study of the Near North Side. Wilson himself recognizes his theory's links to the Chicago School.[41]

Subsequent scholarship has pointed out that, despite important contributions to the study of urban life, the Chicago School's approach is biased in four ways that tend to distort research findings. First, the focus on pathology and disorganization can presume a static and narrow model of healthy social organization, one that naively treats certain social practices and forms of social organization as the "norm" and all others, by definition, as "deviant." This is a problem of moral judgment and ethnocentrism that can cloud interpretation of social practices.[42] Second, by imposing a narrow model of appropriate forms of social organization, this approach can overlook other, functional patterns of organization or misinterpret them simply as evidence of "breakdown."[43] Third, the Chicago School's examination of neighborhoods as coherent ecological systems rests on a conceptually questionable foundation. The boundaries of "natural areas" defined geographically or physically may or may not overlap with the sociological boundaries of "neighborhoods." Research in the Chicago School tradition has been largely insensitive to this distinction, as it has to the reality that neither sort of boundary, even when determinable, necessarily conforms to the boundaries of the social and cultural worlds of the individuals who live within them.[44] This problem with the Chicago School approach is exacerbated by a fourth significant limitation. Because it focuses on the relation between individual or family behavior and the determinative force of a naturalized environment, this research orientation does not take into account the role of political actions, public policy, and larger structural forces in shaping the context of options available to people in communities.[45]

The conceptual link bridging the classical Chicago School approach and Wilson's formulation of an urban underclass defined by social isolation and concentrated poverty is the notion of a self-perpetuating culture of poverty. As propounded by Oscar Lewis in the early 1960s,[46] the culture-of-poverty idea built on Chicago School–like premises concerning the pathological patterns of social organization and behavior that characterize specific populations. Lewis, however, asserted that these patterns emerged as more or less rational adaptations to a shared position of disadvantage within larger systems of inequality and as such were not simply the product of social dynamics purely endemic to the neighborhood or natural area.

Yet despite this divergence from the prototypical Chicago School interpretations, Lewis's culture-of-poverty idea retained two of the Chicago School's deepest theoretical commitments. Lewis contended that, although those patterns of organization and behavior may be adaptations to external forces, they are dysfunctional with respect to the goal of improving the socioeconomic conditions of those who express them. This perception, which is a central claim justifying attention to a culture of poverty, carries on the Chicago School's focus on social pathology. Similarly, Lewis argued that those pathological adaptations reproduce themselves inertially—independently of changes in or interventions upon the external structures in relation to which they developed—and therefore become proximate and intergenerationally durable sources of impoverishment. This view preserved a fundamentally ecological interpretation, even as Lewis acknowledged an ultimate etiology in broader patterns of inequality and injustice. Although Lewis's ecological analysis centered on shared values instead of the classical Chicago School's emphasis on sociologically coherent geographical zones, their common commitment to an ecological model—which stresses endemic bases of impoverishment and dysfunction—has exercised a parallel influence on discussions of antipoverty policy.

Lewis's value-based notion of a self-perpetuating poverty culture converged with the Chicago School view of the crucial causal links producing urban poverty, which ultimately derive from the normative and behavioral defects of the poor.[47] The result of this interpretive predisposition is a self-fulfilling prophecy in which an overly narrow definition of the universe of investigation leads inevitably to a behavioral understanding of the proximate sources of inequality and poverty. This, in turn, skews the focus of social policy—as contemporary discussions of public housing alternatives, and the redevelopment of Cabrini-Green in particular, clearly demonstrate—in favor of strategies giving priority to a presumed need to counteract or correct deficiencies among poor people.

The biases that shape this analytical perspective are problematic not only because they stigmatize people unfairly, but also because their distorting lens misspecifies causes and effects of poverty and inequality and therefore leads to misdirection of policy interventions in ways that are both ineffective and unnecessarily punitive. One striking example of this problem is the conventional wisdom that teenage childbearing is a major cause of inner-city poverty and is an epidemic form of social pathology that creates a self-reproducing underclass. The empirical evidence, in contrast, is that black rates of teenage childbearing declined steadily from 1960 at least through the mid-1980s.[48] And there also is clear evidence that teenage childbearing is far more an effect than a cause of poverty.[49] Nevertheless, concern with reducing teenage childbearing remains a disproportionately prominent item in the agenda of antipoverty policy.

The conceptual flaws that underlie and misshape the behavioral approach to poverty research and social policy are obscured because they are consonant with deeply ingrained ways of thinking about poverty. The stereotypes thereby reaffirmed resonate with a longstanding ideological and moralistic tendency to make invidious distinctions between those who are supposedly worthy or deserving and those who are not.[50] This tendency dates at least to the English Poor Laws of the sixteenth century and has shaped American social welfare policy since its inception. Between the New Deal and the 1960s, this invidious distinction became increasingly racialized, with black Americans, in particular, becoming identified with the lazy, defective, or otherwise undeserving poor.[51]

To some extent this shift simply grafted common stereotypes of black shiftlessness and hypersexuality onto the domain of social welfare policy, where they meshed with a familiar stereotype of the lazy, feckless, or improvident beggar. Lewis's culture-of-poverty formulation gave those who were uncomfortable with frankly racial stereotypes a way to embrace a fundamentally racialized theory of the defective poor while avoiding the stigma of racism. Culture became a proxy for race. Although Oscar Lewis did not wish either to stigmatize black Americans or to argue that the supposed poverty cultures were entirely maladaptive or causal of impoverishment, his general characterizations of the poverty culture were negative; and his contention that the culture is self-regenerative fueled the view that it is more cause than effect of inequality.[52]

This notion was quickly taken up by those who did define the poverty culture as more or less flatly pathological and with evidently racial sources. Most prominently, this included then Labor Department official Daniel Patrick Moynihan, whose 1965 report on the

Negro family made the most direct and extensive argument that black poverty was primarily a function of black cultural pathology.[53] Significantly, Moynihan adapted an interpretation of the Negro family that had been originated in the 1930s by black sociologist E. Franklin Frazier, a product of the Chicago School.[54] Moynihan's influential argument explicitly racialized the discussion of urban poverty and paved the way for a steady shift in the focus of research and policy toward correcting presumably defective behavior and values among poor people and away from redistributive approaches that challenge what Lewis had identified as poverty's ultimate sources—systemically reproduced inequality and disadvantage.

William Julius Wilson's linking of extreme social isolation and concentration of poverty to the emergence of an urban underclass in various American inner-city neighborhoods reflects the behavioralist grounding of Lewis's culture of poverty and Moynihan's black cultural pathology, while reasserting the early Chicago School's emphasis on the relation of neighborhood ecology to disorganization and social pathology.[55] Like Lewis and Moynihan, Wilson defines his inner-city underclass in terms of individual values and behavior; also like Lewis and Moynihan (at least perfunctorily), Wilson indicates its ultimate origins in social structures of inequality external to the underclass milieu he describes. Yet by giving analytical primacy to the role of social isolation and the effects of concentrated poverty, Wilson combines behavioral and ecological views to present a picture in which very poor people suffer most immediately from bad individual behavior stemming from moribund social networks. From this perspective, improving people's condition requires altering their patterns of behavior and interaction by, among other ways, dispersing them throughout neighborhoods in which the very poor do not predominate—in which, that is, more affluent residents can act as social buffers against disorganization and as role models discouraging pathological behavior.

Neighborhood Diversity and Racial Tipping Points

The NNRI proposes demolishing 1,324 existing units of low-income housing in tandem with a neighborhood development plan to build over 2,000 units of new housing, of which 30 percent will be set aside for public housing families. The net effect of the NNRI will be to eliminate 624 low-income units in the area, that is, just under 50 percent of the demolished Cabrini-Green units. The CHA has stated, "The 30% ratio was arrived at by the City planners through consultation with market analysts and a developer/financiers' focus group."[56] More specifically, "Tracy Cross and the members of the focus group agreed that at least 50% of the units would need to be market rate in order to attract purchasers. They felt that 30% public housing and 20% affordable housing would be appropriate ratios and would not compromise sales of private market housing."[57]

In fact, no explanation has been offered by the CHA, city of Chicago, or anyone else for how the precise 30/70 formula was derived. However, this formula likely rests on the assumption that the low-income residents will be black and therefore reflects a concern to avoid the racial tipping point (that is, the level of black presence that would make the area unattractive to whites).[58] Estimates of this tipping point typically locate it between 25 and 33 percent black occupancy.[59] Tracy Cross, the CHA's sole identified source, explicitly links race and market potential, asserting that the Near North Planning Area's character as "poor, predominantly African American" means that it "cannot, at least during the near term, enjoy the full compliment of market-rate housing demand that the Near North Primary Market Area as a whole has to apportion."[60]

Recent work by sociologist John Yinger has challenged the idea of an absolute tipping point, citing evidence that the levels of black presence that whites will accept vary across time and place, even within a given city, and are "subject to some control and manipulation."[61] He also argues that it is a mistake to view expressed white preferences as natural or immutable; he identifies such mitigating forces as the "degree of white prejudice in the neighborhood" and the effects of past and current discrimination in housing and other markets.[62] "For the most prejudiced neighborhoods, tipping will occur as soon as the first black moves in, but in the least prejudiced neighborhoods integration might be sustained at a composition of 50 percent black or more."[63] And Yinger notes that race is usually only one of a complex of factors that shape a household's neighborhood preferences.

By insisting that public housing not exceed 30 percent of new construction, the NNRI in effect pursues a strategy of reducing the black population in the Near North Planning Area in order to make the neighborhood more attractive for white occupancy. That strategy, in turn, means that the NNRI is bound to ignore the needs of the low-income residents of the Cabrini-Green community. The NNRI glosses over these issues with a coating of new urbanist rhetoric, which promises to fix problems of inequality and poverty via physical design innovations.

The New Urbanism and Neighborhood Diversity

For the CHA and city of Chicago, the NNRI's principal selling point is its adherence to new urbanist city planning principles. Although the leading exponents of new urbanism, including architects Andres Duany and Elizabeth Plater-Zyberk, have produced their most notable work in nonurban settings such as Seaside, Florida, the new urbanist penchant for small-scale architecture, congenial public spaces, and pedestrian convenience has begun to influence planning practice in big-city environments.[64] Here is how *Chicago Tribune* architecture critic Blair Kamin describes the NNRI's physical scheme:

> The plan reinstates the street grid that existed before modernist planners turned Cabrini-Green into superblocks. . . . Cabrini-Green will not only look like the rest of the city if the grid is put back, it will have a chance at working like the rest of the city, with small blocks creating a more intimate scale. . . . There are other positive features, such as the use of small parks, even a traffic circle, to delineate districts, so the new Cabrini-Green no longer seems like one vast project and instead becomes a series of small neighborhoods.[65]

In effect, the CHA and city of Chicago are proposing that low-rise residential development, the reintroduction of the local street system, and the provision of more "intimate" public spaces will set the proper tone for the new Cabrini-Green/Near North Side area. As a model for neighborhood revitalization, this strategy shares with Wilson's social isolation/concentration theses, as well as with the early Chicago School, the presumption that the physical environment is determinative of social relations. In reality, the new urbanism represents the beautiful box into which the NNRI seeks to pack a contested neighborhood.

The core intention of new urbanist city planning is to stimulate communal relations by way of physical design. For example, new urbanist architecture typically uses traditional domestic design elements, such as front porches, to bring residents outside of their houses and into physical contact with one another. In Celebration, Florida, the new urbanist town that the Disney Corporation is developing near Orlando, the downtown is within walking distance of every residential neighborhood. Journalist Michael Pollan writes that principal architect Robert A.M. Stern's street plans have sought to create "an outdoor room—a public space in its own right, not just a connector."[66] By creating such spaces, the new urbanists intend, first, to instill the habit of public socializing and, second, out of this habit of public socializing, to elicit the development of rooted social ties.

However, as Pollan's recent analysis of Celebration indicates, the forging of community by physical means is not nearly so straightforward a process. Although residents of Celebration offer nearly universal praise for their physical surroundings, the town has already experienced a sharp conflict over the agenda and curriculum of its local public school. New urbanist architects wish to build community through congenial design, but in practice their design strategies can stimulate only certain types of informal socializing, which may not be the most important factor contributing to broad civic participation or the building of a community's organizational life.

In regard to the NNRI, the precepts of new urbanism have not been tested in a diverse urban environment. The new urbanist towns "of record" have been upscale resort and second-home communities with demographically homogeneous populations. Not only will the new Near North Side be far more racially and economically diverse than Seaside or Celebration, but also the very process of planning and rebuilding the Cabrini-Green area has engendered intense social conflict that will continue, for some time in the future, to influence local attitudes and public behavior. Furthermore, the NNRI as presently constituted simply assumes that the physical proximity of residents who are black, brown, and white, as well as rich and poor, will produce the mentoring and inculcation of correct behavior deemed essential for harmonious community life. Without devoting attention to the associational and institutional bases for building community, such an expectation is fanciful. As such, the NNRI presents a new physical model for the Near North Side and without further elaboration rests its case.

In this latter respect, the NNRI does indeed recall the defects of urban renewal. Once again, physical design precepts are proposed as the "magic bullet" of neighborhood salvation. Moreover, just as the opponents of urban renewal were often characterized as narrow-minded, "private-regarding" parochials, Cabrini-Green residents—who have a multitude of good reasons for distrusting the CHA—have been characterized by public officials and press alike as selfish obstructors of neighborhood improvement.[67] And ultimately, though the face of the NNRI's new urbanist physical plan is ever so benign, execution of the plan promises to yield the unwilling dislocation of hundreds of Cabrini-Green families.

The NNRI proposes that a set of untested physical design techniques, coupled with upscale residential investment, will produce a new and better Near North Side. To carry through what might otherwise look like a simple land grab, as well as to offer the assurance of a congenial environment for incoming, affluent homebuyers, the proponents of a new Near North Side have devoted great energy to scapegoating the incumbent Cabrini-Green residents. This latter task has been accomplished by their borrowing from a body of sociological work that in recent years has received much public exposure as well as been subject to serious challenge. Furthermore, as deployed by NNRI advocates, this line of sociological analysis legitimates the CHA/city plans to reduce very substantially the Near North Side's low-income and racial minority population. Interestingly, its "casting" as the "villain" in the CHA/city rendition of the decline and fall of Cabrini-Green has not been lost on local residents. Note this observation drawn from the "*Vision 2000*" report on the Cabrini-Green LAC–sponsored neighborhood planning workshops of 1993:

> The dominant theme emerging from this planning process was the need for change in terms of how the residents are perceived and treated by outside authorities, such as the CHA and other human service system providers. The HOPE 6 application as developed by CHA for Cabrini-Green focused primarily on the deficiencies and needs of the community. From this point of view, the kind of community development as envisioned by the Cabrini-Green residents would be impossible to achieve.[68]

This is a remarkable observation. Even as the CHA, city of Chicago, and various urban affairs commentators have systematically misconstrued the nature of the Cabrini-Green neighborhood and its residents, these same residents possess a nuanced understanding of the methods committed to the task of removing them from their homes.

The Complexities of a Public Housing Community

Cabrini-Green has achieved legendary status among public housing projects in the United States. For many years, Chicago-based newspaper reporters and television news crews have visited the neighborhood to examine its physical decay or to post updates on its periodic waves of gang violence. In 1981, during Mayor Byrne's brief stay in Cabrini-Green, the neighborhood won a flash of national attention. More recently, a number of widely publicized violent criminal incidents, notably the Dantrell Davis shooting in 1992 that set in motion Vincent Lane's redevelopment campaign, have occurred on Cabrini-Green's grounds. Since the Davis murder, the project has received ongoing national news coverage as a barometer of the efforts to regenerate public housing in major American cities.

Invariably, the journalists and public figures who have sought to characterize Cabrini-Green have emphasized its physically appalling, socially deviant features. For example, Vincent Lane once vowed that his Hope VI redevelopment proposal would substitute a "normal neighborhood" for the existing public housing complex.[69] In the more carefully bureaucratic prose of the CHA's 1993 Hope VI proposal to HUD, Lane's view is elaborated: "This isolation, over time, is also reflected in an absence of external public, private and social service resources available to the community. Like many of Chicago's public housing and low income communities, the Cabrini-Green area and families are chronically underserved."[70]

Another characteristic view of Cabrini-Green was expressed by journalist Steve Bogira, who in the mid-1980s visited a number of Cabrini-Green families touched by gang violence and titled his resulting article in the *Chicago Reader* "Prisoners of the War Zone." Kevin Coyle, author of *Hardball*, a book chronicling the fortunes of a Cabrini-based Little League baseball team, emphasized the project's physical harshness in his initial description of Cabrini Green: "From afar, each building appears to have been formed out of a single gargantuan brick and shoved endlong into the earth. The only signs of life come from the windows, many of which display shades, greenery, or in a few cases, lace curtains. Many others, however, are burned out, empty, hollow. It is the empty windows, particularly those on the upper floors, to which the eye is instinctively drawn."[71]

Abnormality, danger, emptiness: These are the terms that key most Chicagoans' understanding of Cabrini-Green. Aside from the consistently negative quality of these depictions, they share another feature: Each is the product of a visitor to Cabrini-Green—possibly a well-intentioned visitor—but nonetheless someone who spends a limited time in the neighborhood and then withdraws.

A survey of the poems, stories, and essays that appeared in the local newspaper *Voices of Cabrini (VOC)*, which was produced from early 1993 until mid-1994 (and briefly revived the following year), communicates another sense of Cabrini-Green. For example, in "A Mother's Prayer," Margaret Smith begins:

> I raised my children
> with a smile, hugs, love,
> and lots of good food.
> We sing and dance
> and swing our hair to
> the beat of our favorite raps.
> O' Lord I pray that they
> finish school that's the hope
> I have for them that it
> will become a reality one day...[72]

However, *Voices of Cabrini* is not simply a compendium of warm sentiments. In "Untitled," another Cabrini-Green mother, Gloria Corkrell, observes:

> I live in the ghetto, But I won't
> let the ghetto live in me.
> Through the bullets, the drugs, and the
> crime trying to raise a family of kids . . . three.
> Alone and on my own without a man
> raising my children as a single Parent I know I can.
> Though my job is tough, hard and a heavy load,
> All I can do is my best to keep my children
> On the right road...[73]

Cabrini-Green residents require no reminder of the hazards offered by their surroundings, as well by some of the other tenants in the public housing complex. Nevertheless, CHA and city of Chicago decisionmakers should not suppose that there are not thousands of family-oriented, law-abiding residents of Cabrini-Green or that these Cabrini-Green residents have not fashioned a working community.

Social Networks and Neighborhood Institutions

The residents of Cabrini-Green, and most assuredly their social networks, their institutions, and their neighborhood's physical environment, do indeed bear the marks of the project's turbulent circumstances. Nevertheless, Cabrini-Green is a community dense in social ties and the home of many committed residents. Without the material affluence of middle-class people, Cabrini-Green's low-income residents routinely depend on relatives and neighbors for short-term use of household items and articles of clothing, child care, shopping assistance, and advice and companionship. As one of our informants (who, though wishing to remain in Cabrini-Green, recently moved into an apartment a few blocks away) put it: "It was a family. . . . If somebody died, family would come and see about you; if you're hungry, they feed your kids; if the kids are outside and they're getting their kid a popsicle, they'll get all of them a popsicle; if you come upstairs with your hands full of groceries, everybody'll help to take your groceries in. That's in Cabrini . . . PERIOD."[74] Another informant estimated that he had about fifty local relatives in Cabrini-Green, "plus their kids." This same individual, who is the father of seven, emphasized how important it is for him to be able to depend on neighbors to watch after his children—a favor that he is more than willing to return when he has the time.

Beyond the family and friendship networks that give structure to the lives of many Cabrini-Green residents, the neighborhood—quite contrary to the depiction offered in the 1993 Hope VI proposal—is served by a variety of churches and social service agencies. Among the *Voices of Cabrini* features was a church directory, which included as many as twenty local congregations. Some of these churches represent very small congregations, but others, such as Saint Joseph's Roman Catholic Church on North Orleans Street, play a significant role in the larger community's life. There are ten to fifteen social service agencies operating in and near Cabrini-Green. Table 7.1 identifies some of the more important agencies and congregations in the neighborhood.

Locally based agencies offer a wide array of services: medical treatment, youth-oriented sports programming, individual and family counseling, and legal assistance. Bounding the Cabrini-Green area on the north, the New City YMCA's LEED Council offers a variety of educational and workforce preparation programs. The staffs of most (possibly all) of these organizations would agree that the local demand for their services stretches their resources to the limit, but this is quite a different situation from the one presented in

TABLE 7.1 Selected Cabrini-Green Area Social Service Agencies, Religious Congregations, and Community-based Organizations

Organization	*Main Program/Services*
Chicago Center for Law and Justice	Legal Services
Al Carter Youth Foundation	Youth Sports
Fellowship of Friends	Tutoring, college preparation
Fourth Presbyterian Church	Center for Whole Life (pre-school)
Holy Family Lutheran Church	Day care, legal services, Cabrini Alive!
Lasalle Street Church	Day care, tutoring, family counseling
Lower North Center	Youth recreation, leadership development, Project Lead
St. Joseph's Roman Catholic Church	Youth and after-school programs
St. Matthews United Methodist Church	Girl Scouts, community meeting space
Montgomery Ward Tutoring Program	Primary- and secondary-level tutoring
Winfield Moody Drop-in Center	Family counseling, drug/AIDS awareness, pregnancy prevention, youth field trips
Winfield Moody Health Center	Health and social services

SOURCES: CHA documents; Cabrini-Green LAC.

the 1993 Hope VI proposal: that the current Cabrini-Green is "isolated" and lacking in social service resources.

The Cabrini-Green area's institutional network is not simply the consequence of programs developed to serve the public housing population or of coincidence—agencies located in the area before the arrival of public housing. Cabrini-Green's Local Advisory Council dates from the 1970s, and over the past quarter century it has dealt with issues such as management of building laundry rooms, architectural modifications (including the closing in of the high-rise building open-air corridors, or "ramps"), home appliance orders, and, in recent years, the evolving plans to redevelop the project and its adjoining neighborhood.

Since the 1980s, several groups of tenants have been working to develop the Resident Management Corporations (RMCs) that will soon provide most building services throughout the Cabrini-Green complex. The president of the Cabrini Rowhouse RMC estimates that a group of approximately twenty residents has worked to build that organization, which has taken shape, in part, through work accomplished at weekly meetings dating back to 1993. Since the spring of 1996, the four Cabrini-Green RMCs have been producing and distributing a newsletter.

Despite the Cabrini-Green LAC's growing distrust of CHA/city redevelopment plans for the neighborhood, many local residents have developed proposals or participated in initiatives associated with the Hope VI process. The residents' Human Capital Development Committee has funded an array of programs involving Cabrini-Green tenants in community service–oriented efforts. Cabrini Alive! predates the Hope VI era, bringing together Near North Ministerial Alliance volunteers and Cabrini-Green residents to rehabilitate project apartments. For several years in the early 1990s, Cabrini Greens, whose participants were mainly local teenagers, raised produce for sale to neighborhood residents and at a local farmers' market. Since 1994, several dozen Cabrini-Green teenagers have participated in Project Lead, a program that emphasizes youth decisionmaking and action to address community problems. Project Peace, which is directed by a team of local residents, offers conflict resolution training in two local schools. Also funded by Hope VI have been the training/licensing of a number of Cabrini-Green residents as professional day care workers and the training of volunteer tenant patrols. Participation in the Human Capital Development Committee has itself represented a significant commitment for its half-dozen members, who have attended weekly (and more recently, monthly) meetings since 1994.

Table 7.2 identifies ongoing tenant initiatives at Cabrini-Green. In the future, this list of projects is likely to expand. For instance, the RMCs are in the process of opening five laundromats. In addition, the Cabrini Rowhouse RMC will train and hire a team of energy auditors who will visit individual apartments to assess how efficiently residents' heat and other utilities are working and, when appropriate, suggest needed repairs.

Cabrini-Green and the Near North Side

Physical descriptions of Cabrini-Green—particularly those, such as Kevin Coyle's, that emphasize the Green Homes and Cabrini-Extension buildings—typically highlight the incongruence of the complex and its neighborhood environment. This is not an implausible way of viewing Cabrini-Green. If one sets out to the east of the complex, soon enough after passing under the Chicago Transit Authority elevated track—just as in Harvey Zorbaugh's time—one has left the slum for the Gold Coast. Heading north, west, or south of Cabrini-Green, one would—until very recently—encounter open space (south

TABLE 7.2 Cabrini-Green Resident Initiatives

Program	*Start-up Date*	*No. of Participants*
Cabrini-Green Textile Works	Early 1996	11
CADRE (Combating Alcohol and Drugs Through Rehabilitation and Education)	Late 1995	7
CHA Works job training	August 1995	45
Child care training	1996	14
Project Lead	1994	206
Project Peace	1996	5
Resident safety monitors	Early 1997	80
Volunteer tenant patrolling	1989	150

SOURCES: CHA documents; Cabrini-Green LAC.

of North Avenue), deteriorating industrial sites (along Halsted Street and the Chicago River's North Branch), and an obsolete commercial street (Chicago Avenue). In short, Cabrini-Green seemed to be isolated. One consequence of this way of viewing Cabrini-Green is to suppose that there is nothing there within the project. In the previous section of this chapter, we have highlighted what is there, in so doing noting a set of varied and well-established neighborhood social patterns and institutions quite like what is present in many inner-city areas.

There is a second consequence of viewing Cabrini-Green as a physical anomaly within its neighborhood context, which is to suppose that its residents are cut off from the surrounding area. This is not a point of view expressed by Cabrini-Green residents, though what they have to say about their neighborhood in relation to the larger Near North Side tells us much about the evolving character of this portion of Chicago. In the first place, our informants frequently characterize their neighborhood as including areas well beyond Cabrini-Green's boundaries. For one informant it was "North Avenue to Chicago, from Sedgwick all the way to Halsted." Another individual expanded the neighborhood far beyond these bounds by mentioning that he had lived in different parts of the city and that he had friends in each of these areas.

When we asked residents about community amenities, there was a comparable apportioning of items. Among the very local sites or facilities of note are Stanton and Seward Parks (but not in the evening), the public library, and the New City YMCA (just northwest of Cabrini-Green). However, the larger area includes amenities that are frequently visited by local people: Water Tower Place's movie theaters, the lakefront, and Lincoln Park (with several individuals mentioning the zoo's special attraction for Cabrini-Green youths). One informant noted the convenience offered by the number 29 bus, which allows her to go to the Loop for shopping or to use the Harold Washington Library. Nor is this more expansive sense of neighborhood defined only in terms of what a person can take from the larger community. In discussing the area adjoining Cabrini-Green, one informant noted that she often volunteered at Saint Joseph's school. In short—and even while noting various Cabrini-Green physical and social shortcomings—Cabrini-Green residents often think of their part of Chicago as a good place to live.

Aside from the Cabrini-Green area's amenities, there is another environmental point about which local residents tend to agree. At present, the Cabrini-Green area is not awash in economic opportunity. Some long-standing local employers, such as Montgomery Ward, have reduced hiring. Others, notably the Oscar Mayer plant that stood just to the east of Cabrini-Green, have shut down altogether. In essence, the economic and geographic restructuring of the Chicago metropolitan region since the 1960s has yielded a series of destabilizing changes in the Cabrini-Green area: Relatively well-paying manufacturing and warehousing jobs in the Near North Side and along the North Branch of the Chicago River have been lost; during the 1970s and 1980s considerable physical deterioration and building abandonment resulted from the downturn of the "old" local economy; and in the 1990s upscale residential development (promising few, if any, jobs for incumbent low-income residents) has become the engine of economic change.[75] For many Cabrini-Green residents, the much-heralded revival of the Near North Side is a bitter-tasting remedy for the neighborhood's various ills. Having persevered through decades of CHA mismanagement, and having learned to make the best of their neighborhood, many long-time residents expect that they will be pushed to another part of the city now that real estate developers have taken an interest in the Cabrini-Green area.

Cabrini-Green and Crime

For a substantial part of the Chicago population, Cabrini-Green and other notorious CHA projects, such as the Robert Taylor Homes, embody urban crime and lawlessness. Books such as *Hardball* virtually rhapsodize the audacity and persistence of local gang activity. In the year or two following the shooting of seven-year-old Cabrini-Green resident Dantrell Davis in late 1992, Chicago's daily newspapers time and again ran such headlines as "Gangs Call Shots Despite CHA's Security Force," "CHA to Get Security Funding," and "CHA Sweeps Plan Set." Indeed, the amended 1997 CHA/city of Chicago Hope VI proposal takes for granted this looming sense of Cabrini-Green criminality: "Law-abiding residents feel trapped in their homes as the incidence of crime increases."[76] In fact, CHA figures indicate that Cabrini-Green is not an especially violence-prone public housing area, and in the last few years there is some evidence of a decrease in local criminal activity.

One of the ironies of early 1990s urban crime hysteria across the United States is that so far as official figures can determine, this period marked the onset of a downturn in criminal activity.[77] For example, a 1994 CHA report indicated that by 1993 crime in Chicago public housing developments had fallen below the level of five years earlier.[78] Between 1992 and 1993, Cabrini-Green's incidence of crime (that is, annual homicides, criminal sexual assaults, serious assaults, robberies, burglaries, thefts, and vehicle thefts per one hundred residents) fell from 10.3 to 8.2. In the latter year, this meant that Cabrini-Green's crime rate was only slightly above the CHA overall figure (7.7) and well below the figures for Rockwell Gardens (12.7), the ABLA complex of developments (12.4), and Robert Taylor Homes (11.4). More recent data, provided by the Police Department's Special Functions Unit, also indicate a downward trend in Cabrini-Green crime. Using month by month tabulations of Part I crimes (homicide, criminal sexual assault, robbery, battery, assault, burglary, theft, vehicle theft, and arson), we calculated the 1995 and 1996 volumes of reported criminal activity at Cabrini-Green as 557 and 481, respectively.

In the spring of 1993, the *Chicago Tribune* reported a particularly graphic indicator of declining local criminal activity during the early 1990s: the first quarter (January–March) decline in gang-related shootings in Cabrini-Green's Police District Eighteen (East Chicago). Between 1991 and 1993, this figure dropped from 76 to 27.[79] More generally, crime figures for the Eighteenth District are sharply at odds with the popular perception of Cabrini-Green. Criminal activity in this district is far less common than in the Second (Wentworth), Eleventh (Harrison), and Seventh (Englewood) Districts, and indeed, the Eighteenth District's incidence of major crimes tends to fall below the citywide average.[80] Of course, the Eighteenth District is a mixed area, including affluent neighborhoods to the east and north of Cabrini-Green, in which one might expect to find a low incidence of crime. Nevertheless, a further implication of this very point ought to be noted: Criminal activity within Cabrini-Green does not appear to spill over into adjoining areas; nor does it appear to pose a threat to the security of these adjoining areas.

Interestingly, community area crime data reveal that Cabrini-Green's local area, the Near North Side, is substantially safer than the six community areas presently housing the bulk of Chicago's Section 8 tenants. In terms of violent crimes (that is, homicide, robbery, simple battery, aggravated battery/assault, criminal sexual assault against females, and domestic violence against females), for 1994–1995 the Near North Side ranked forty-second among the city's seventy-seven community areas. The rankings for the "big six" Section 8 areas are Woodlawn (eight), West Englewood (nine), Austin (fifteen), South Shore (seventeen), Rogers Park (thirty-four), and Uptown (thirty-six).[81]

The point, however, in discussing the relationship between the Cabrini-Green neighborhood and local criminal activity is not to justify quarterly gang shooting figures of seventy-six, or even twenty-seven, as acceptable. Nor is it to claim that local perceptions of gang-promoted violence or other forms of criminal activity are exaggerated. Rather, the point is to discuss the problem of local criminality in a realistic context. Several features of crime in many inner-city neighborhoods, and Cabrini-Green in particular, are incontestable. First, as the older, manufacturing-based economy of many inner-city neighborhoods has declined since the 1960s, crime rates have soared. Second, during this same period gang membership and mobilization have climbed, and more than in the past gangs have centered a flourishing underground economy trading drugs, firearms, and other illicit commodities. Third, with particular reference to Cabrini-Green, as the CHA's tenant screening and building maintenance standards collapsed after the 1960s, public housing projects became a haven for gang-related action (offering many unoccupied apartment units and virtually boundless interior and outdoor spaces for doing business or evading the police).[82] Fourth, again with particular reference to Cabrini-Green, police patrolling of the project has been episodic, often induced only by after-the-fact reports of violent criminal activity. In essence, the Chicago Police Department has adopted a containment policy in dealing with public housing crime.

Since some time in the 1970s, residents of Cabrini-Green have simply had to come to grips with a transformed local environment. The overall level of criminal activity increased during the 1970s and much of the 1980s, with a considerable portion of the increase in violent crime related to the staking out/defending of economic turf by competing gangs. Public housing violence also has a distinctly seasonal quality, tending to peak during the warm summer months and ebb during the remainder of the year. Over the years, most Cabrini-Green residents have been either directly or indirectly touched by violence. Young men growing up in the project experience particular pressures: Just like everyone else, they run the risk of getting in the way of a stray bullet; they are also likely to be the objects of aggressive recruitment by local gang units.[83]

In spite of these conditions, law-abiding Cabrini-Green residents have attempted to sustain a livable community. Many parents engage in extremely vigilant supervision of their children in order both to protect them from gang violence and to block gang recruitment. It is a commonplace for public housing parents to prohibit unsupervised outdoor play by their smaller children. Over the years, many tenants have sought security jobs within Cabrini-Green, and security provision is one focus of the RMCs. In the fall of 1997, Cabrini-Green residents and representatives of the Near North Ministerial Alliance developed a "safe passage" program to provide security in the vicinity of Jenner Elementary School.[84] And possibly most interestingly—and despite the generally strained relationship between local residents and the police—there is much evidence of local support for improved policing. When asked to identify influential people within Cabrini-Green, several of our respondents noted particular police officers (individuals who tended to move beyond the role of law enforcement officer and offer more personalized assistance to local people or programs). In a notable example of this kind of mutual respect, 172 Cabrini-Green area residents signed a petition early in 1977 seeking to retain Sergeant Percy Coleman as head of the local community policing unit.[85] Many of the petition signers were residents of 624 West Division Street, a building whose gang activity had been substantially reduced through Coleman's efforts.

Cabrini-Green in Voices of Cabrini

Voices of Cabrini offers an extraordinary glimpse of life in Cabrini-Green.[86] The newspaper's staff numbered about ten local residents, headed by coeditors Mark Pratt and Henrietta Thompson. Five thousand copies of each *VOC* issue were distributed within the housing complex. One of the newspaper's particular aims was to tap the literary talent/aspirations of local residents; the anniversary *VOC* (April 24, 1994) identified eighty-nine contributors to the first year's issues.

A review of *VOC* issues reveals what is in many respects a typical community newspaper. Among the regular columns are a food/

recipe guide, local church notes, and a popular music survey (heavily weighted to hip-hop). There are occasional obituaries, and in several issues articles pay tribute to individuals who have made special contributions to the community (for example, school crossing guards and an assistant school principal). The issue preceding Christmas in 1993 included a page of "Dear Santa" letters (for example: "Dear Santa: My name is Paris Dani. I am 8 years old. I want a puzzle for Chrismas and a Easy Bake oven and a game. The end. I love you/Paris"). During the summer months, *VOC* included Near North Little League team standings, on whose two dozen teams approximately 450 local girls and boys performed.

However, the most characteristic feature of *VOC* issues were the half-dozen or more poems, short stories, and essays submitted by Cabrini-Green residents. It is by reading these entries that one encounters the particularity of Cabrini-Green. Younger people produced most of this work, which ranges from the hopeful imaginings of some very young writers to the rather stark accounts of local life by older residents. Cover essays in late 1993 and early 1994 (December 19, February 27, and March 27) were entitled "My Transformation: From Addiction to Involvement," "Forever Free: My Battle with Alcoholism," and "Drug Addiction," respectively. In each instance, older residents recounted their battles with substance abuse. In these and many other articles by older (and some younger) writers, the narrators used their accounts of personal experience to extrapolate moral lessons: Do not give up on school, resist gang recruitment, stay off drugs, and the like.

VOC's news stories confronted other neighborhood realities. The cover story of the May 16, 1993, *VOC* provided a short account of Cabrini-Green's history. The October 24, 1993, issue included articles on the gang truce of 1993, as well as several commentaries on the CHA's antigang "lockdown" strategy of the same period. On June 26, 1994, *VOC*'s cover articles discussed the neighborhood redevelopment plan. The newspaper looked at each of these issues from multiple perspectives. Most of the contributors expressed reservations regarding Vincent Lane's policies, but there were clear variations in the individual interpretations of whether to support neighborhood redevelopment or to comply quietly with the 1993–1994 security lockdown. In short, what *VOC* reveals is not just a community as portrayed by some of its more committed and talented residents, but also a community, like most others, in which there is a range of views about local virtues and problems, as well as about how the community's problems ought to be addressed.

The Real Costs of Relocation

The CHA/city of Chicago Near North Redevelopment Initiative proposes to reduce the Cabrini-Green housing stock from thirty-six hundred to twenty-three hundred units. Approximately seven hundred new units scattered through the NNRI area have been promised to displaced Cabrini-Green residents. Beyond these local relocations to "hard units" (that is, CHA-owned dwellings), the CHA proposes to offer Section 8 rent assistance to additional displaced Cabrini-Green residents for use in obtaining private-sector housing. The philosophy animating the Section 8 rental assistance program—offering market choice to low-income families, and permitting them to seek housing outside of racial ghettos—is certainly convergent with the rhetoric driving the NNRI. However, the empirical features of Chicago's real estate market and the local record of the Section 8 program suggest that for Cabrini-Green relocatees "market choice" will be more illusion than reality. Furthermore, their dispersal via Section 8 certificates or vouchers is viewed by many Cabrini-Green residents as an exercise in community seeking via community destruction.

For low-income families, the housing market in the Chicago area is very tight. In a 1994 report on rental housing in Chicago, the Metropolitan Tenants Organization noted that the number of rental apartments in the city had decreased by 10 percent between 1980 and 1990. Furthermore, demand pressures especially drive up rents for apartments suited to large families, just the kinds of family groups that the NNRI will move from Cabrini-Green. The result of these market conditions is that landlords, particularly when screening larger families, can be very choosy in selecting their tenants. The Metropolitan Tenants Organization report comments, "Discrimination based on familial status is often coupled with gender, marital status, and racial discrimination."[87] The acuity of this observation is borne out by two features of the Chicago-area experience with Section 8 vouchers and certificates. First, approximately three in ten Section 8 recipients are unable to use their certificates or vouchers.[88] That is, they simply cannot find housing to suit their needs, coupled with a landlord willing to rent to Section 8–assisted tenants. Second, the bulk of Section 8 recipients locate housing in city neighborhoods or suburban communities that are quite racially segregated.[89] For example, among Chicago's six community areas with the greatest concentrations of Section 8 tenants are South Shore, Austin, West Englewood, and Woodlawn—each with an African American population approaching or exceeding 90 percent.[90]

These problems with the Section 8 program are well known to Cabrini-Green residents. The Voorhees Center (University of Illinois–Chicago) report on the Section 8 program and Cabrini-Green redevelopment, released in May 1997, notes that residents already displaced by the vacating of Cabrini-Green buildings have experienced considerable difficulty in using Section 8 assistance. These residents have complained not just about the difficulties of using Section 8 vouchers or certificates in the Chicago rental market, but also about ineffective relocation advice and counseling by the firm hired by the CHA to assist relocation.[91]

The local record of the Section 8 program cautions against high expectations that displaced Cabrini-Green residents will be well served in finding new places to live. At the same time, the rationale driving the NNRI's tenant relocation provisions rests on the most dubious of foundations. Moving residents from Cabrini-Green presumes that they suffer from an absence of the institutions and other social supports essential for satisfactory community living. Yet the wholesale displacement of residents has the immediate effect of pulling apart the very networks of social and family ties that allow the low-income population of Cabrini-Green to survive. As we have documented in the preceding pages, there is a vital Cabrini-Green community; and as is typically the case in low-income inner city neighborhoods, the quality of local life is largely sustained by informal, friendship- and family-defined social networks.[92] The NNRI fails to recognize this feature of the real Cabrini-Green. Instead, it proposes a strategy of neighborhood upgrading via upscale real estate investment that promises to destroy the neighborhood's intricate network of community-sustaining ties, practices, and commitments.

Real Neighborhood Revitalization in Cabrini-Green

During the 1950s and 1960s, municipal officials across the United States used the urban renewal program to reshape their cities. In urban renewal's heyday, slum clearance was expected to rid cities of their worst neighborhoods; and subsequently, through the magic of progressive city planning and modernist architecture, new and untroubled communities would emerge from the ashes. In reality, city officials were not always careful to ensure that clearance areas were incapable of more incremental, possibly locally driven upgrading; and in many instances their specification of areas requiring demolition more directly reflected calculations of prospective development potential than objective measures of neighborhood decay.[93]

Among the consequences of urban renewal's overambitious agenda and frequently mishandled implementation were countless neighborhood–city hall conflicts and the devastation of many viable inner-city communities. Few, if any, contemporary Chicago officials would hail urban renewal as a great success, nor is the CHA or the city of Chicago eager to draw parallels between urban renewal and the NNRI. Yet in crucial ways the NNRI looks like urban renewal's lineal descendant, reappearing in the guise of public housing reclamation and new urbanist city planning. Since the 1980s, residential gentrification has proceeded to the north and east of the Cabrini-Green area, while the city's political, civic, and economic elites have discussed how removing this aging, physically decayed public housing development might further contribute to the real estate upgrading of the Near North Side. And in a fashion that recalls the worst of urban renewal, the city and CHA have repeatedly fumbled efforts to involve Cabrini-Green residents in a meaningful neighborhood planning process.

The high-handedness of the CHA/city approach to Cabrini-Green residents is attributable, in part, to the persistent effort by some officials, ably assisted by members of the media and a handful of other urban affairs experts, to demonize the area's public housing residents. The logic of this effort takes the following course: If we can manage to convince the public at large that Cabrini-Green is a chaotic jungle whose residents do not deserve to be involved in discussions about the future of their neighborhood, then we can proceed with wholesale demolition and new, upscale residential development. It has been the aim of the foregoing analysis to demonstrate the inaccuracy and wrongheadedness of this scenario. It is, indeed, time for the CHA and the city of Chicago to recast the NNRI process and commit themselves to the following four-point planning scheme.

First, the NNRI must be redefined via new, all-parties-included negotiations. With private developers already building new housing in the Cabrini-Green area, and with new residents arriving on Cabrini-Green's northern flank, the negotiations must become fully inclusive, embracing representatives of the city of Chicago, the CHA, Cabrini-Green residents, other incumbent neighborhood residents and locally based organizations, private developers, and new residents. The central issue to be addressed in such an inclusive planning process is the overall character that the new Near North Side will take.

To set the appropriate tone for these new negotiations, the CHA and the city must come to the table prepared to support the wishes of all those Cabrini-Green residents who want to remain in the new neighborhood. In this case, the implementers of the NNRI will be doing nothing more than complying with Mayor Daley's commitment as expressed in his letter of support for the 1997 Hope VI reapplication: "Also critical is the commitment that my administration, along with the CHA, has made to accommodate every lease-compliant family that will be displaced . . . that wants to remain in the Near North community."[94]

Second, the new NNRI must not limit the planning agenda to questions of physical design and indeed must give equal attention to the crucial issues of institution-building, social services, and economic development. The CHA/city program has reduced the NNRI process to physical design matters: new urbanist architecture as an antidote to the failings of Cabrini-Green's high-rise milieu; the related virtues of front yards, stoops, and a traditional street layout; and the siting of new public facilities. The working presumption seems to be that if "everything is in its place," then community will flourish. This is seldom true.

The most important matters to be addressed before a new, effectively multiracial and multiclass community can be formed are neighborhood institution-building and economic opportunity for Cabrini-Green residents. Participants in the planning process must investigate what social services, community organizations, and even local businesses are likely to fuel the development of community ties. An associated problem is the linking of new development to job opportunities for those in need of work and income. Nonetheless, as we have demonstrated in the preceding pages, the existing Near North Side community possesses considerable resources to bring to bear on these matters. Given a forthright approach to negotiation, practical solutions to institution-building and economic development matters can be identified.

Third, beyond the completion of new development work and rehabilitation of existing structures in the Near North Side, the "new neighborhood" will require the formation of a community forum for airing various points of view. The CHA/city NNRI rests on the largely unexamined and inherently contradictory assumptions that something new is in the works for the Near North Side, yet when currently envisioned physical developments have been completed, a fully "operational" and harmonious community will spring into existence. As the last several years of conflict-laden planning surely indicate, this is a very unlikely scenario.

For the new Near North Side to be a community that includes all who live and work there, it will need to maintain an institutionalized "space" that encourages the discussion of local conflicts, the success/nonsuccess of new and long-standing local social initiatives, and different parties' shifting views of the future of the neighborhood. In essence, the CHA and the city must take their own rhetoric seriously. If indeed the development of a truly mixed-income neighborhood on the Near North Side is a social experiment, then it will require an institutional mechanism for negotiating the ongoing trials that will confront residents of this new model of inner-city community.

Fourth, the City of Chicago and CHA have proceeded with the NNRI as if major rehabilitation work in Cabrini-Green were not imperative now. In fact, such a commitment is long overdue, and the city of Chicago should reserve for public housing rehabilitation a substantial portion of the tax increment finance revenues (estimated to be $300 million) that will result from private development in the area. This commitment of rehabilitation funds is required to return major portions of the project to physical habitability, and from the standpoint of the Cabrini-Green residents, such a commitment will represent a much-needed signal of good faith on the part of the CHA and the city.

PART THREE

Ideology and Attacks on Antiracist Public Policy

8

Occupational Apartheid in America: Race, Labor Market Segmentation, and Affirmative Action

Stephen Steinberg

No greater wrong has been committed against the Negro than the denial to him of the right to work.

A. Philip Randolph, *What the Negro Wants*

The core of the civil rights problem is the matter of achieving equal opportunity for Negroes in the labor market. For it stands to reason that all our other rights depend on that one for fulfillment. We cannot afford better education for our children, better housing, or medical care unless we have jobs.

Whitney M. Young Jr., *To Be Equal*

If there is any one key to the systematic privilege that undergirds a racial capitalist society, it is the special advantage of the white population in the labor market.

Robert Blauner, *Racial Oppression in America*

THE ESSENCE OF RACIAL OPPRESSION is *not* the distorted and malicious stereotypes that whites have of blacks. This is the *culture* of oppression, not to be confused with the thing itself. Nor is the essence of racism epitomized by a person having to sit in the back of a bus. In South Africa this was called "petty apartheid," as opposed to "grand apartheid," the latter referring to the political disfranchisement and banishment of millions of blacks to isolated and impoverished "homelands." In the United States, the essence of racial oppression—*our* grand apartheid—is a racial division of labor, a system of occupational segregation that relegates most blacks to work in the least desirable job sectors or that excludes them from job markets altogether.[1]

The racial division of labor has its origins in slavery, when some 650,000 Africans were imported to provide cheap labor for the South's evolving plantation economy. During the century after slavery, the nation had the perfect opportunity to integrate blacks into the North's burgeoning industries. It was not southern racism but its northern variant that prevented this outcome. This point is worth emphasizing because it has become customary—part of America's liberal mythology on race—to place the blame for the nation's racist past wholly on the South. But it was not southern segregationists and lynch mobs that excluded blacks from participating in the critical early phases of industrialization. Rather, it was an invisible color line across northern industry that barred blacks categorically from employment in the vast manufacturing sector, except for a few menial and low-paying jobs that white workers spurned. Nor can the blame be placed solely on the doorstep of greedy capitalists, those other villains of liberal iconography. Workers themselves and their unions were equally implicated in maintaining a system of occupational apartheid that reserved industrial jobs for whites and that relegated blacks to the preindustrial sector of the national economy.[2] The long-term consequences were incalculable, since this closed off the only major channel of escape from racial oppression in the South. Indeed,

---

The original version of this chapter appeared in a special issue of *The Nation* as "Occupational Apartheid," December 9, 1991, 744–746. The current version incorporates material from subsequent work: Chapters 8 and 9 of Stephen Steinberg, *Turning Back* (Boston: Beacon Press, 1995); and Stephen Steinberg, "The Role of Racism in the Inequality Studies of William Julius Wilson," *Journal of Blacks in Higher Education* 15 (Spring 1997):109–117.

had the industrial revolution not been "for whites only," this might have obviated the need for a civil rights revolution a century later.

The exclusion of blacks from the industrial sector was possible only because the North had access to an inexhaustible supply of immigrant labor. Some 24 million European immigrants arrived between 1880 and 1930. A 1910 survey of twenty principal mining and manufacturing industries conducted by the U.S. Immigration Commission found that 58 percent of workers were foreign-born. When the commission asked whether the new immigration resulted in "racial displacement," it had in mind not blacks but whites who were native-born or from old immigrant stock. Except for a brief examination of the competition between Italian and black agricultural workers in Louisiana, nothing in the forty-volume report so much as hints at the possibility that mass immigration might have deleterious consequences for blacks, even though black leaders had long complained that immigrants were taking jobs that, they insisted, rightfully belonged to blacks.[3]

If blacks were superfluous so far as northern industry was concerned, the opposite was true in the South, where black labor was indispensable to the entire regional economy. Furthermore, given the interdependence between the regional economies of the South and the North, occupational apartheid had indirect advantages for the North as well. The cotton fiber that Irish, Italian, and Jewish immigrants worked with in mills and sweatshops throughout the North was supplied by black workers in the South. In effect, a system of labor deployment had evolved whereby blacks provided the necessary labor for southern agriculture and European immigrants provided the necessary labor for northern industry.

This regional and racial division of labor cast the mold for generations more of racial inequality and conflict. Not until World War I were blacks given significant access to northern labor markets. In a single year—1914—the volume of immigration plummeted from 1.2 million immigrant arrivals to only 327,000. The cutoff of immigration in the midst of an economic expansion triggered the Great Migration, as it was called, of southern blacks to the urban North. Industries not only employed blacks in large numbers but in some cases also sent labor agents to the South to recruit black workers. Between 1910 and 1920, there was a net migration of 454,000 southern blacks to the North, a figure that exceeded the volume for the previous forty years combined. Here is historical proof that blacks were no less willing than Europe's peasants to uproot themselves and migrate to cities that offered the opportunity for industrial employment. To suggest that blacks "were not ready to compete with immigrants," as the author of a recent volume on immigration does, is altogether fallacious.[4] The simple truth is that northern industry was open to European immigrants and closed to African Americans. Whatever opprobrium was heaped upon these immigrants for their cultural and religious difference, they were still beneficiaries of racial preference.

It is generally assumed that World War II provided a similar demand for black labor, but this was not initially the case. Because the war came on the heels of the Depression, there was a surfeit of white labor and no compelling need to hire blacks.[5] Indeed, it was blacks' frustration with their exclusion from wartime industries that prompted A. Philip Randolph and his followers to threaten a march on Washington in 1941 unless Franklin Roosevelt took steps to lower racist barriers. Roosevelt pressured black leaders to call off the march (just as John Kennedy did in similar circumstances two decades later), but Randolph persevered until Roosevelt agreed to issue an executive order enunciating a new policy of nondiscrimination in federal employment and defense contracts. The opening up of northern labor markets triggered another mass migration of southern blacks—1.6 million migrated between 1940 and 1950—and by the end of the war 1.5 million black workers were part of the war-production workforce. This represented an unprecedented breach in the nation's system of occupational apartheid—one that set the stage for future change as well.

Nevertheless, as recently as 1950 two-thirds of the nation's blacks lived in the South, half of them in rural areas. It was not the Civil War but the mechanization of agriculture a whole century later that finally liberated blacks from their historic role as agricultural laborers in the South's feudal economy. By the mid-1950s, even the harvest of cotton had become mechanized with the mass production of International Harvester's automatic cotton-picking machine. The number of "manhours" required to produce a bale of cotton was reduced from 438 in 1940, to 26 in 1960, to only 6 in 1980.[6] Agricultural technology had effectively rendered black labor obsolete and with it the caste system whose underlying function had been to regulate and exploit black labor.[7] Thus, in one generation white planters went all the way to Africa to import black laborers, and in another century the descendants of those southern planters gave the descendants of those African slaves one-way bus tickets to Chicago and New York.

When blacks finally arrived in northern cities, they encountered a far less favorable structure of opportunity than had existed for immigrants decades earlier.[8] For one thing, these labor markets had been captured by immigrant groups that engaged in a combination of ethnic nepotism and unabashed racism. For another thing, the occupational structures were themselves changing. Not only were droves of manufacturing jobs being automated out of existence, but also a reorganization of the global economy resulted in the export of millions of manufacturing jobs to less developed parts of the world.

The fact that the technological revolution in agriculture lagged nearly a half century behind the technological revolution in industry had fateful consequences for blacks at both junctures. First, blacks were restricted to the agricultural sector during the most expansive periods of the industrial revolution. Second, they were evicted from rural America and arrived in northern cities at a time when manufacturing was in a steep and irreversible decline.

William Julius Wilson has argued that deindustrialization is the principal factor in the genesis of the black underclass in recent decades.[9] According to Wilson, blacks migrating to northern cities not only encountered a shrinking industrial sector, but also lacked the education and skills to compete for jobs in the expanding service sector. For Wilson, this explains why conditions have deteriorated for the black lower classes during the post–civil rights era, a period of relative tolerance that has witnessed the rise of a large and prosperous black middle class.

There can be no doubt that deindustrialization has exacerbated the job crisis for working-class blacks. In the case of New York City, for example, the manufacturing sector was cut in half between 1955 and 1975, involving the loss of some five hundred thousand jobs.[10] As recently as 1990, New York City lost thirty-four thousand jobs over the summer, including fifty-two hundred jobs in manufacturing, fifty-six hundred jobs in construction, and sixty-five hundred jobs in retailing.[11] If these jobs could be magically restored, many blacks would surely benefit.

Nevertheless, there is reason to think that Wilson places far too much explanatory weight on deindustrialization as the reason for the job crisis that afflicts black America. As Norman Fainstein has argued, blacks were never heavily represented in the industrial sector in the first place.[12] Fainstein's data indicate a pattern of "employment ghettoization" involving the exclusion of blacks from whole job sectors—not only job sectors that require the education and skills that Wilson assumes to be lacking among young blacks, but also service-sector jobs that require minimal education and skills. Fainstein concludes that "the economic situation of blacks is rooted more in the character of the employment opportunities in growing industries than in the disappearance of 'entry-level' jobs in declining industries."[13]

It is a leap of faith on Wilson's part that, if not for the collapse of the manufacturing sector, blacks would have found their way into these jobs. There is nothing in history to support this assumption, since, as we have seen, the entire thrust of northern racism has been to exclude blacks from blue-collar jobs in the primary sector. Even if 3 million manufacturing jobs had not disappeared, what basis is there for assuming that they would have gone to blacks, rather than to working-class whites or, as in the past, to the new immigrants who have been pouring into the nation's cities despite the collapse of the manufacturing sector? The lesson of history is that blacks have gained access to manufacturing only as a last resort—when all other sources of labor have dried up. Now we are asked to believe that blacks would have finally gotten their turn, except that the jobs themselves have disappeared.

Wholly absent from Wilson's analysis is any consideration of the role that racism plays in restricting employment opportunities for blacks. In his resolve not to "'trot out' the concept of racism" to explain the job crisis among blacks,[14] he has taken the illogical and dangerous step of eliding racism altogether. Although Wilson's foregrounding of "class" and the role that race-neutral economic forces played in exacerbating inherited racial inequalities had liberal intentions, his theme that racism was of "declining significance" not only constituted a gross distortion of reality but also was seized upon by elites inside and outside the academy that wanted to get "beyond civil rights" and take race off the national agenda.

The Elision of Racism in Social Science Scholarship

Given the vast literature on racism, one might suppose that there are countless studies of employment discrimination. This is not the case. As Joleen Kirschenman and Kathryn Neckerman, the authors of a recent study, comment, "Despite intense interest in the relation of race to employment, very few scholars have studied the matter at the level of the firm, much less queried employers directly about their views of black workers or how race might enter into their recruitment and hiring decisions."[15] Instead, the extent of discrimination is gauged through examination of racial differences in employment rates or wages within given job sectors. Because discrimination is not measured directly, the methodological door is left open for some to claim that blacks are underrepresented not because they are subject to discrimination, but because they lack the requisite "productive capacities." The counterclaim is that blacks have lower "payoffs" than whites even when they have the same productive characteristics. Ultimately, this issue can be resolved only with studies that measure employment discrimination directly.

One such study was sponsored by the Urban Institute in 1991. The authors, Margery Austin Turner, Michael Fix, and Raymond Struyk, conducted 476 "hiring audits" in Chicago and Washington, D.C. In the hiring audit, two testers, one black and one white, were carefully matched in terms of all attributes that could affect a hiring decision. The sampling frame consisted of help-wanted ads in major newspapers; only low-skilled, entry-level jobs requiring limited experience were selected. The basic finding was as follows: "Young black job-seekers were unable to advance as far in the hiring process as their white counterparts 20 percent of the time; black testers advanced farther than their white counterparts 7 percent of the time. Blacks were denied a job that was offered to an equally qualified white 15 percent of the time; white testers were denied a job when their black counterparts received an offer in 5 percent of the audits."[16]

As Turner et al. acknowledge, these are conservative estimates, since employers who discriminate against blacks are not likely to advertise in newspapers. Instead, they rely on employment agencies or employee networks, often for the express purpose of avoiding black job seekers. Furthermore, the auditors were all college students with "conventional appearance," defined as "average height, average weight, conventional dialect, and conventional dress and hair." But it is precisely blacks who may not be "average" in height or weight, or who do not conform to "conventional" styles of speech and self-presentation, who are most apt to be victims of discrimination. Although these estimates of the frequency of employment discrimination are unrealistically low, the audit study yields incontrovertible evidence that employment discrimination is widespread, even when candidates for a position are identical in everything but skin color.

Other direct evidence of employment discrimination comes from periodic revelations about the racist practices of employment agencies. In 1990, for example, two former employees of one of New York City's largest employment agencies divulged that discrimination was routinely practiced against black applicants, though concealed behind a number of code words. Clients who did not want to hire blacks would indicate their preference for applicants who were "All American." The agency, for its part, would signal that an applicant was black by reversing the initials of the placement counselor.[17]

Such revelations are shocking less because they uncover facts that were previously unknown than because they breach the conspiracy of silence that surrounds employment discrimination. Although there is little in public discourse to suggest that employment discrimination is rampant, a different picture emerges from surveys of employers and rank-and-file workers. In 1990, the *National Law Journal* asked a national sample of adults whether they believed that "employers practice some form of discrimination in their hiring and promotion practices regardless of their official policies." Half of whites (48 percent) and two-thirds of blacks (64 percent) said that all or most employers are discriminatory.[18] It thus appears that employment discrimination is openly acknowledged by the public at large. It seems to elude only certain armchair theorists who wish to believe that racism is virtually a thing of the past and that in today's racially enlightened society people are hired primarily on the basis of merit.

The elision of racism is, of course, a very old story. As Richard Wright observed in 1945, "American whites and blacks both possess deep-seated resistance against 'the Negro problem' being presented, even verbally, in all of its hideous fullness, in all of the totality of its meaning."[19] What was unique about the 1960s and 1970s was that the black protest movement ruptured the wall of denial and indifference and thrust "race" to the center of political consciousness and action to an extent unprecedented since Reconstruction. The ensuing backlash over the past two decades may thus be seen as a return to "normalcy"—"to evade and to elide and to skim over," as Charles Mills has compellingly written in *The Racial Contract*.[20] This is the context in which several recent books have promulgated the idea that racism is no longer the demon that it was in times past.

The tendency to downplay racism had its origins with the 1978 publication of Wilson's *The Declining Significance of Race*. This line of thought was ultimately carried to its logical and absurd extreme with the 1995 publication of Dinesh D'Souza's *The End of Racism*. Note that the only reason D'Souza is able to proclaim the end of racism is that (like Wilson) he has restricted the meaning of racism to intentional discrimination based on racial animus. There is no place in his scheme for "institutional racism," which he in fact dismisses as "a nonsense phrase" that "radicalized the definition of racism to locate it in the very structures of society."[21] By denying that the deep inequalities between blacks and whites are themselves racist, or rooted in white racism, D'Souza has set the stage for attributing these inequalities to black cultural pathology.

Essentially the same analysis, albeit in more muted tones, is advanced by Stephan and Abigail Thernstrom in *America in Black and White*.[22] According to the Thernstroms, blacks have been on a trajectory of racial progress since the 1940s and the passage of civil rights legislation in the 1960s removed the final parapets of structural racism. This construction of race history serves their ulterior purpose: to discredit affirmative action policy. The Thernstroms argue that affirmative action is (1) unwarranted because America is no longer the racist society that it once was, (2) unnecessary because blacks have made enormous strides without affirmative action, and (3) counterproductive because it exacerbates relations between blacks and whites.

The Thernstroms choose to ignore evidence showing that a decade after the passage of the 1964 Civil Rights Act, there were entire industries and whole job sectors where blacks were excluded by an impenetrable color line.[23] Indeed, this is what engendered the political pressures that led to the Philadelphia Plan and the other policy initiatives that came to be known as "affirmative action." The Thernstroms also ignore studies demonstrating that blacks have made the greatest progress in firms and job sectors where affirmative action has been implemented—in government, in major blue-collar industries, and in corporate management and the professions.[24] With inverted logic, they cite the very facts that are outcomes of affirmative action policy as proof that affirmative action is unnecessary.

In *When Work Disappears,* William Julius Wilson confronts a disjunction between theory and fact. With funds from a dozen foundations, Wilson and his students conducted a series of ethnographic studies and surveys in poor black neighborhoods on Chicago's South Side. Wilson found that, despite a massive loss of manufacturing jobs in Chicago, there were still scores of firms engaged in light manufacturing, some of which were located in Chicago's Black Belt. Wilson interviewed the owners of 179 firms in Chicago and Cook County that provided entry-level jobs. What he found was that 74 percent of the employers had negative views of black workers and preferred to hire immigrants.[25] Alas, immigrants from Central and South America had a better chance at being employed by manufacturing firms in Chicago than did the "native sons" in the surrounding neighborhoods.

This discovery presents Wilson with a quandary. His entire theoretical edifice has been founded on the premise that the flight of industry explained the high rate of black unemployment. From this empirical premise, Wilson goes on to argue that "racism" does not explain the plight of the black underclass, and he has emerged as a public champion for "universal," as opposed to "race-specific," public policy. How then is he to reconcile this paradigm with the finding that Chicago's employers were unwilling to hire blacks? Could racism—the R-word that rarely appears in Wilson's disquisitions on race and class—be the reason?

Wilson's first line of defense is to invoke the stock argument that immigrants are willing to work for lower wages than inner-city blacks are. Again, his empirical findings do not support his theoretical suppositions. Wilson found that the so-called reservation wage—the lowest wage at which workers are willing to sell their labor—was actually *lower* for blacks than for immigrants.[26]

When interrogated about the reasons for not hiring blacks, employers spewed forth with negative characterizations about black workers. Here is Wilson's summary: "Employers' comments about inner-city black males revealed a wide range of complaints, including assertions that they procrastinate, are lazy, belligerent, and dangerous, and have high rates of tardiness and absenteeism, carry employment histories with many job turnovers, and frequently fail to pass drug screening tests."[27] Wilson allows that "many readers will interpret the negative comments of the employers as indicative of the larger problem of racism and racial discrimination in American society."[28] But he admonishes us not to jump to any conclusions: "The degree to which this perception is based on racial bias or represents an objective assessment of worker qualifications is not easy to determine."[29] In effect, Wilson has backed himself into a logical corner, and there is only one way out: to give credence to the employers' claims that blacks are unproductive, untrustworthy, and undesirable workers.

Thus, Wilson makes much of the fact that twelve of the fifteen African American employers who turned up in his sample were reluctant to hire blacks. On the dubious assumption that their melanin renders them immune to racial stereotypes, Wilson concludes, in effect, that it is not the racism of employers but the problematic traits of black workers that render them unemployable. Wilson's position here is indistinguishable from D'Souza's claim that employers who refuse to hire blacks are engaged in acts of "rational discrimination."

Note that Wilson's many studies provide no basis for testing the "objectivity" of the employers' assessment of black workers. Nor has Wilson observed workers on the job in particular work sites or industries. Nor does he query his black subjects about *their* perceptions of employers or their experiences with racism. Nevertheless, Wilson reaches the startling conclusion that "the issues are complex and cannot be reduced to the simple notion of employer racism."[30]

This statement prompted me to retrieve Gordon Allport's *The Nature of Prejudice* from a dusty bookshelf. Here is his definition of prejudice: "An avertive or hostile attitude toward a person who belongs to a group, simply because he belongs to that group, and is therefore presumed to have the objectionable qualities ascribed to the group."[31] Allport allows that real differences exist among groups in the frequency of particular attributes. Indeed, this is the stuff of social science. But the nature of prejudice is such that preconceived judgments about groups are applied to particular individuals so as "to place the object of prejudice at some disadvantage not merited by his own misconduct."[32] In effect, Wilson has had to define prejudice out of existence in order to reach the conclusion that the patently discriminatory behavior of employers is not racist. Once again, he has engaged in a rhetorical shell game in order to defend his paradigm from the discrepant facts churned up by his own research. The alternative is simple: to reject what Mills calls "an epistemology of ignorance" and to acknowledge the simple truth that provides the logical underpinning for antiracist public policy—namely, that racism is still a significant factor in restricting the employment opportunities of blacks, all the more so for those at the end of the hiring queue.[33]

The Myth of the Black Middle Class

In propounding the "declining significance" thesis, Wilson does not summon evidence that racial prejudice and employment discrimination are on the decline. Rather, he *infers* this based on the success of the black middle class. Wilson is struck by the fact that in recent years "educated and talented" blacks have enjoyed unprecedented mobility in terms of occupations and income. According to Wilson's logic, racism cannot explain why the underclass has increased in size at a time when the black middle class is larger and more prosperous than ever.

But does this conclusion follow from the premise? After all, racism has never been indifferent to class distinctions, and it may well be the case that blacks who have acquired the "right" status characteristics are exempted from stereotypes and behavior that continue to be directed at less privileged blacks. There is nothing new in this phenomenon. Even in the worst days of Jim Crow, there were blacks who owned land, received favored treatment from whites, and were held forth as "success stories" proving that lower-class blacks had only themselves to blame for their destitution. The existence of this black elite did not signify that racism was abating (though illusions to this effect were common even among blacks). On the contrary, the black elite was itself a vital part of the system of oppression, serving as a buffer between the oppressor and the oppressed and fostering the illusion that blacks could surmount their difficulties if only they had the exemplary qualities of the black elite.[34]

To take an analogous example, in recent years women have made great inroads into the professions. However, this hardly means that the legions of women who still work in "female" occupations are not victims of institutionalized sexism, past and present. By the same token, the success of the black middle class is not evidence that racist barriers are not as impenetrable as ever insofar as lower-class blacks are concerned. As Derrick Bell has shrewdly observed, his son would not be hired as a waiter in the same restaurant that gives him red carpet treatment.[35]

Nor can it be assumed that this black middle class signifies a lowering of racist barriers in middle-class occupations. To be sure, the existence of this middle class signifies a historic breakthrough. Never before have so many blacks been represented at the higher echelons of the occupational world—in the professions and in corporate management. Never before have so many blacks found employment in core industries, in both the white- and blue-collar sectors. Nor can this new black middle class, given its size, be dismissed as "window dressing" or "tokenism." Yet there are other grounds for doubting that the existence of this large black middle class signifies the demise of occupational apartheid.

First, insofar as this black middle class is an artifact of affirmative action policy, it cannot be said to signify the deracialization of labor markets. In other words, the black middle class does not reflect a lowering of racist barriers in occupations so much as the opposite: that racism is so entrenched that without governmental intervention, there would be little "progress" to boast about.[36] Second, although a substantial segment of the new black middle class is found in corporate management, there is a pattern of racial segregation *within* these structures (similar to racial tracking in many "integrated" schools). Studies have found that many black managers work in personnel functions, often administering affirmative action programs. Others function as intermediaries between white corporations and the black community or the black consumer.[37] Cut off from the corporate mainstream, these black executives often find themselves in dead-end jobs with little job security. By outward appearances, they have "made it" in the white corporate world, but their positions and roles are still defined and circumscribed by race.

Much the same thing can be said about the black business sector. In an incisive analysis, Sharon Collins provides the following account: "Black entrepreneurs are concentrated in segregated rather than generalized services. In 1979, 68 percent of black-owned businesses were in retail and selected services that marketed their wares almost exclusively to black consumers. In 1979, 99 percent of all minority business was based on federal procurement or sales to the minority consumers."[38] In her analysis of data on Chicago-based minority professional service firms, Collins finds a similar pattern of racial segmentation, even with firms doing business with the government:

> Personnel service firms provided workers for units with racial concerns, such as the Office of Manpower. Black law firms were hired for contract compliance and labor-management issues in segregated services such as Housing and Urban Development. Certified public accountant firms performed pre-grant and general audits for segregated sites such as Cook County Hospital. Management consulting firms provided technical assistance primarily to agencies such as Chicago's Department of Human Services or the Federal Office of Minority Business Development. Engineers provided professional services to predominantly black sites such as Chicago's Northshore Sanitary District.[39]

In short, the much ballyhooed growth of black-owned business has generally occurred within the framework of a racially segmented economy.[40]

Finally, there is the double-edged sword associated with public-sector employment. On the one hand, the fact that government employment has opened up to blacks marks another change of historic dimensions. For two decades after World War II black representation in government was largely restricted to the Postal Service and to low-level clerical and service positions. Today some 1.6 million blacks, constituting over one-quarter of the entire black labor force, are employed by government. Indeed, this is the source of much of the "progress" that we celebrate.

On the other hand, this statistic shows once again that racial progress has depended on the intervention of government, in this instance as direct employer. Within the ranks of government, furthermore, there is a great deal of internal segregation. For the most part, blacks are employed as social welfare providers in such areas as education, welfare, health, employment security, and public housing. Essentially, they function as intermediaries and buffers between white America and the black underclass. As Michael Brown and Steven Erie have argued, "The principal economic legacy of the Great Society for the black community has been the creation of a large-scale social welfare economy of publicly funded middle-income service providers and low-income service and cash transfer recipients."[41]

To conclude, as Collins does, that "the growth of a black middle class is *not* evidence of a decline in racial inequality in the United

States" is perhaps an overstatement.[42] After all, the sheer existence of a large black middle class means that blacks are no longer a uniformly downtrodden people. But this fact may signify not a dissolution so much as an artful reconfiguration of caste boundaries in the occupational world. To control the disorder emanating from the ghettos of America, a new class of "Negro jobs" has been created. They are not the dirty, menial, and backbreaking jobs of the past. On the contrary, they are coveted jobs that offer decent wages and job security. Nevertheless, they are jobs that are pegged for blacks and that function within the context of racial hierarchy and division.

Precisely because the new black middle class is largely a product of government policy, its future is subject to the vagaries of politics. Already it is apparent, as economists John Bound and Richard Freeman have concluded, that "the epoch of rapid black relative economic advance ended sometime in the late 1970s and early 1980s and that some of the earlier gains eroded in the 1980s."[43] Evidence already exists that recent court decisions restricting minority set-asides are having a severe impact on black businesses.[44] The unrelenting attack on affirmative action will inevitably lead to a further erosion of black socioeconomic gains. Finally, just as blacks benefited disproportionately from the growth of government, they will certainly be severely affected by the current movement to cut the size of the government and the scope of governmental services. Black public-sector workers are especially vulnerable to layoffs because they are concentrated precisely in job sectors heavily dependent on federal subsidies.[45] Indeed, a recent front-page story in the *New York Times* appeared under the headline "Black Workers Bear Big Burden as Jobs in Government Dwindle."[46]

The Strange Career of Affirmative Action

The civil rights revolution was fundamentally a struggle for liberty, not equality. That is to say, it secured full rights of citizenship for African Americans, but it did little to address the deep-seated inequalities between blacks and whites that were the legacy of two centuries of slavery and another century of Jim Crow. Despite the emergence of a wealthy black elite, there remains an enormous gap in economic condition and living standards between the black and white citizens of this nation. For example, in 1988 the median income for whites was $25,384; for blacks, it was $15,630.[47] Thus, on the whole black income is roughly 60 percent of white income, a ratio that has not changed substantially since 1980.

Furthermore, as Melvin Oliver and Thomas Shapiro have shown in *Black Wealth/White Wealth,* the racial gap in income is far exceeded by the racial gap in wealth (which includes home equity and financial assets).[48] In 1988, the median net worth for white families was $43,800; for black families, it was only $3700. Whites with a college degree had a net worth of $74,922, whereas blacks with a college degree had a net worth of only $17,437. This latter figure points up the utter precariousness of the so-called black middle class. Insofar as the racial gap in wealth translates into differential access to good housing, schools, and other resources, it provides a rough indication of how unequal the playing field is between blacks and whites.

The disjunction between rights and equality entered public discourse even before the legislative goals of the civil rights movement were attained. A common refrain among civil rights leaders was that "there is little value in a Negro's obtaining the right to be admitted to hotels and restaurants if he has no cash in his pocket and no job."[49] This was the logic for forging a praxis that went beyond the attainment of political rights and attacked the institutional inequalities that were the product of racism, both past and present.

Long before affirmative action entered the political lexicon, black leaders were demanding "compensatory treatment" for blacks in jobs and education. No sooner was this idea broached, however, than it aroused intense opposition. That opposition emerged initially not from the political right, but from liberals, many of whom had been active supporters of the civil rights movement.[50] Indeed, liberal disaffection with the rhetoric of compensatory treatment precipitated a split within the liberal camp as some prominent liberals declared their opposition to the "radical" direction that the civil rights movement was taking.[51] Here was an early sign that the nation would not go much beyond the grudging passage of civil rights legislation. Thus, it is not surprising that affirmative action policy did not develop through the legislative process. Rather, it evolved through a series of executive orders, court decisions, and administrative policies. At every stage it was liberals, some of whom had defected to the nascent neoconservative movement, who provided the most vocal and adamant opposition.

A key example is the liberal opposition to the Philadelphia Plan. Originally developed in President Lyndon Johnson's Department of Labor, the Philadelphia Plan was shelved after Hubert Humphrey's defeat in 1968. It was Arthur Fletcher, the black assistant secretary of labor during the first Nixon administration, who maneuvered to resurrect the plan. The other unsung heroes of affirmative action are Charles Shultz, then secretary of labor, who gave Fletcher indispensable backing; Attorney General John Mitchell, who successfully defended the plan before the Supreme Court; and Richard Nixon himself, who expended considerable political capital heading off a Democratic challenge to the plan in the Senate. One of the great ironies of racial politics in the post–civil rights era is that the Philadelphia Plan was implemented by Republicans over the opposition of the famed "liberal coalition" and without notable support of the civil rights establishment.[52] Indeed, some black leaders—notably Bayard Rustin—sided with labor leaders in opposing the plan.

There has been considerable speculation over the reasons that Nixon, who got elected on the basis of a southern strategy that appealed to popular racism and who later nominated two southern racists to the Supreme Court, was willing to champion the Philadelphia Plan. Contemporaneous opponents of the plan, most notably Rustin, contended that its aim was to split the "progressive" coalition between the labor movement and the civil rights movement. This idea has also been given some credence by Hugh Davis Graham in his history of the civil rights era. According to Graham, as Nixon pondered Shultz's proposal to resurrect the Philadelphia Plan, he was swayed by "the delicious prospect of setting organized labor and the civil rights establishment at each other's Democratic throats."[53] More recently, Graham has been even more explicit in postulating that "Nixon wanted to drive a wedge between blacks and organized labor—between the Democrats' social activists of the 1960s and the party's traditional economic liberals—that would fragment the New Deal coalition."[54]

This "theory" has assumed mythical proportions, invoked by writers on the liberal/left to provide political cover for their retreat from affirmative action. However, there is reason to doubt Graham's account of why Nixon threw his support behind the Philadelphia Plan. One must begin by putting this decision in historical context. In 1969 the Vietnam War was reaching a critical stage, and Nixon had to worry about an escalation of racial protest "on the home front." This was a period when memories of the "riots" following Martin Luther King Jr.'s assassination were still fresh, when black militancy was at its height, and when there were strident job protests in Philadelphia, Chicago, and numerous other cities against racism in the construction trades.[55] This was the context in which Fletcher and Shultz seized the opportunity to resurrect the Philadelphia Plan, whose main objective was to enforce the hiring of blacks in building trades controlled by lily-white unions.[56] From the perspective of the White House, there was little political liability in "sticking it" to the mostly Democratic unions. And there was clear political advantage in neutralizing black protest and in preempting the liberal agenda on civil rights with a policy predicated on contract compliance.

Whatever tangle of motivations were at work, Nixon actively fought off a congressional attempt to pass an anti–affirmative action rider that had the support of many Democrats, and Mitchell successfully defended the Philadelphia Plan before the Supreme Court. Subsequently, the Department of Labor issued a new set of rules that extended the Philadelphia Plan to all federal contractors, including colleges and universities. Thus, the scope of affirmative action policy expanded beyond anything contemplated when the Philadelphia Plan had been disinterred in 1969. Furthermore, the Philadelphia Plan embodied none of the "liberal" elements that were ideologically anathema to Republicans. It envisioned no new government programs, no make-work schemes, no major public expenditures.[57] However, as the backlash against affirmative action mushroomed, Nixon did an about-face and, as Graham points out, railed against the very "quotas" that he had put into place.[58]

Politics aside, affirmative action was unquestionably the most important policy initiative of the post–civil rights era. It drove a wedge into the structure of occupational segregation that had existed since slavery. And affirmative action achieved its principal policy objective, which was the rapid integration of blacks into occupational sectors where they had been excluded historically.

A society with a deep and abiding commitment to racial justice would have celebrated this historic achievement and expanded affirmative action into job sectors and job sites where blacks still have meager representation. Instead, affirmative action has been the object of unrelenting attack. A steady outpouring of books, many of them funded by conservative foundations and think tanks, have found erudite reason for relinquishing the single policy that has been effective in reversing the pattern of occupational apartheid.[59] Political scapegoating assumed a new face as politicians made affirmative action a lightning rod for working-class insecurities over falling wages and corporate downsizing. Liberal equivocation and bad faith served notice that even those putative "friends of the Negro" would offer little resistance in defense of affirmative action. As opposition mounted, more liberals threw in the towel, declaring that affirmative action was "too costly" politically.[60] In February 1995, *Newsweek* ran a cover story proclaiming "The End of Affirmative Action." Though President Bill Clinton made a much-publicized stand to "mend it, don't end it," the cynical view was that this only provided a public facade for the quiet dismantling of affirmative action programs and the enforcement mechanisms on which they depend.[61]

Having eviscerated affirmative action policy in a series of rulings, the Supreme Court today seems poised to deliver the coup de grâce. Like *Plessy* v. *Ferguson* (1896), which marked the end of Reconstruction three decades after the abolition of slavery, the gutting of affirmative action marks the end of the Second Reconstruction. In the first instance, blacks did not go back to slavery, but they lost rights that had been supposedly secured by the Reconstruction Amendments. Today there is no danger of blacks again being relegated to the back of the bus. However, the gutting of affirmative action will certainly lead to a steady erosion of many of the social and economic gains of the post–civil rights era. The sobering lesson of history is that when the First Reconstruction was ended, it took seven decades to recover the ground that had been lost.

9

The Voting Rights Movement in Perspective

Alex Willingham

SINCE THE MID-1980S, our expectations have grown about the prospects of a voting rights movement that could have broad impact on democracy in the United States. This little understood movement—focusing on electoral officeholding—grew during the 1980s to become a bone fide successor to the great civil rights movement and the main avenue for political advancement by racial minorities. Mass protests were replaced with political organizing, and the struggle for empowerment became a priority in communities never before involved in public decisionmaking. This movement has been a key factor in the politicization, since midcentury, of American racial minorities and directly responsible for the expansion and realignment of all forces active in politics.

The voting rights movement is not well understood today. It is seldom seen as a distinctive political activity or credited for its impact on the election process. When we do examine the movement, however, we find a classic American reform effort that responds to inequities and to dreams of a better day. It engages, and expands, the nation's thinking about a defect in the body politic. It is driven by forceful agitation, acquires legitimacy, and enjoys formal concessions from the political powers. The voting rights movement has become a rich arena for intellectual work in jurisprudence, intergovernmental relations and federalism, policy analysis, democratic theory, and the potentials and constraints of popular mobilization. I argue that it is time—after three decades—to integrate voting rights advocacy into our teachings about American democracy on a par with such vintage efforts as abolitionism, women's suffrage, the great labor organizing movements of the 1930s, and, indeed, the civil rights movement itself.

The Form of the Movement

The voting rights movement is primarily legalistic. It combines two distinct but parallel election issues: race discrimination and the parity of individual ballots. The race work is concerned with implementing the prohibition on discrimination in voting established by the Fourteenth and Fifteenth Amendments to the Constitution. The main agent for the race work has been federal voting legislation in the period since 1957, especially the Voting Rights Act of 1965, which was enacted in response to the demonstrations in Selma, Alabama. That 1965 act was a comprehensive initiative originally promoted to address conditions in registration and voting in the biracial Old South states where discrimination had been common despite the amendments. The law has evolved since then and by the 1990s had come to include a number of fundamentals that set the framework for voting rights work: The act identifies national minorities to be protected under its provisions; establishes a process to challenge, and void, any "voting qualification or prerequisite to voting or standard, practice, or procedure" that discriminates against covered populations; and requires that, in sensitive jurisdictions, any election change be subjected to federal evaluation for adverse impact on these groups.

The weight of the individual vote is practically and analytically distinct from the race question. It has been driven by attention to malapportionment and other arrangements that result in "dilution" of some votes relative to others. Such an outcome resulted when the population of districts—changing through normal growth and migration—became widely disparate. The main activity here has been to identify, correct, and then prohibit the use of malapportioned election districts in the U.S. House of Representatives or the multimember elected bodies (such as state legislatures, city councils, county commissions, and school boards) in state and local jurisdictions. This reform was made possible by legal reasoning against involving the 1922 amendment, finding such a "political question" to be justiciable under the federal Constitution. The pivotal event here was the U.S. Supreme Court's 1962 decision in *Baker* v. *Carr.*[1]

The voting rights movement combines the race and reapportionment efforts so as to invoke the authority of federal courts to pass on the merits of complaints about local elections systems. The practical effect of this "reapportionment revolution" is to ensure regular redistricting in response to shifts in population. The reconfigurations are then subject to review (or challenge) under Section 2 or 5 of the Voting Rights Act. A natural corollary to the legalistic emphasis is a reliance on specialized skills. The movement has little of the spontaneity, mass mobilization, protest, or appeals to conscience that drove the civil rights movement. Judicial and administrative procedures, legislative process, and legal standards place a premium on expert counsel.

The legalistic character of voting rights work can also be seen in the way it responds to the federal structure. Thus, even though the federal courts remain the main arena for resolution of claims, the main outcomes occur at state and local levels. This preoccupation with local decisionmaking structures is one noticeable departure from the national, and federal, focus of the civil rights movement. During the 1960s, protest, finding itself consistently frustrated in the localities, turned increasingly to national opinion and federal policy to press its claims even while continuing to act locally. But the successes at the national level were often subverted by the decentralized nature of the federal system, where crucial powers allocated to state governments provide a basis for obstruction. Among the most important of these powers is voting policy itself—local apportionment, election district arrangements, voter eligibility criteria, design of the structure of offices, and administration of elections.

By the l990s, the legal protection of voting was remarkably stable compared either to the panoply of Great Society social justice legislation or to its own status when at last there was a national census and attention was given to these issues. Congressional statute and legal opinion identify discrimination in voting as unconstitutional and set standards for defining this condition. Administrative practice prescribes effective remedies. A number of states are covered in whole or in part by the special preclearance provisions of the act, and all states are subject to sanctions where their procedures result in minority race vote dilution. On the eve of the 1990s, a powerful federal statute and effective mode of advocacy supplemented traditional constitutional protections. The decennial census serves as a trigger guaranteeing reexamination of election issues according to questions of equity and race. The special provisions of the act were renewed to extend to the year 2007.

What Is a Discriminatory Election System?

Generally speaking, no election device is discriminatory per se. The problem comes from the way the device interacts with a particular set of circumstances to affect voting strength. For purposes of illustration, we may recall the years after enactment of the 1965 Voting Rights Act, during which, as voting restrictions were removed, black citizens began to register and turn out in much higher numbers. But this turnout had little impact on the racial composition of those winning office. A decade after the enactment of the law, nearly all of the governing bodies continued to be all white even in communities of substantial biracial population. Registration and voting became merely a condition whereby blacks chose among candidates put forth by the active sector of the white community. For a range of offices, that condition remains true today, with notable exceptions, and no strategy has been effective in changing that outcome.

These conditions marked a crucial threshold in thinking about race and suffrage: Officeholding became a discrete issue resurrecting, and legitimating, an inquiry about why white politicians continued to dominate, despite the removal of voting barriers. (This process had matured by the mid-1970s.) Investigation uncovered a dismal picture of the black community at a competitive disadvantage. It was difficult for black communities to field candidates or meet the rigors of campaigning. Their candidates were routinely shut out of the key circles where they could cultivate useful acquaintances or negotiate reciprocal exchanges; on election day the best of them did well among their own race but failed to receive white support. The black candidate's campaign would be confronted with sometimes overt, other times subtle racist appeals. These appeals came in several forms designed to mine the racial images in the memory of the voting public. One tactic was to define an opponent as a representative of the "bloc vote." Another was to charge that civil rights groups "controlled" an opponent-candidate. Sometimes a token black would win. But the pattern of near total white race dominance continued.

The strategic considerations a potential candidate had to face in deciding to offer for election became agonizing because serious attempts to win office could further isolate active voters from public decisionmaking by "wasting" their vote on one of their own. The right to vote, apparently secure, was disconnected from power, influence, or change. Meaningful participation in the political process could be denied even with relatively free access to the ballot. Registration and voting could overcome neither the vestiges of vicious discrimination (meager economic resources, employment dependency, anxiety about the significance of public agencies, acquiescence in underparticipation) nor the preemptive advantages that accrue to a monopolistic political class (hard campaign experience, incumbency, and the pivotal role of white racial attitudes and bloc voting). After the initial spate of activity (in the four or five years after the enactment of the Voting Rights Act), disparities settled in that reproduced the historical pattern of disadvantages now seeming to neutralize the energies unleashed at Selma.

Civil rights groups seized upon these conditions to establish a proactive stance emphasizing minority officeholding. Large sectors of the public—official and lay—came to value the creation of opportunities for the election of minority officials and to see that as a logical requirement of suffrage policy. Indeed, in the new voting discourse social justice is explicitly and directly linked to the prospect of empowerment. The goal is to open access to political office and the exercise of authority attendant thereto. Because this discourse deploys a language of power, it does not exhibit the innocence associated with the civil rights movement. The new empowerment discourse can be expected to invite criticism from three sources: those who disapprove of sharing power, political opponents, and others who understand racism in terms of the restricted moralist discourse of the 1960s.

The idea of a discriminatory election system—and one that contravened the voting law—took form in response to these circumstances. It became the burden of voting rights litigation to account for these election outcomes and to persuade community leaders and civil rights groups that more was needed than the formal right to vote. The courts increasingly acted on the pleas of black communities to acknowledge that their failure to win office was a problem rooted in everyday practices and structures that, while neutral on their face, had a discriminatory racial impact that incumbents either developed, intentionally maintained, or benefited from through passive neglect. And, these communities argued, practical remedies were available to address the issue in elections to the U.S House of Representatives and multimember bodies in state and local jurisdictions. The decade after the Voting Rights Act saw guarded but dramatic change in legal thinking, and in 1986 a watershed opinion from the U.S. Supreme Court ruled that the use of at-large and multimember systems to elect such bodies was discriminatory insofar as these systems were used in places where minorities have not been elected, where minorities are sufficiently concentrated and cohesive, and where white racial bloc voting is significant. Such systems would be replaced by one where each member elected came from a separate district. This would free planners to draw smaller districts and target protected populations.

Single-member districts were well suited to the cause. They had rapidly acquired a new legitimacy in the maneuvering around "one person, one vote," becoming a practical solution in the drive to ensure equal weight to all votes. To comply with the focus on population equity, effective use of such districts often meant a disregard of county or incorporated municipality boundaries.

Spatial Remedy: An Unintended Consequence

The single-member district is crucial to modern voting reform and may be used to remedy infirmities in two ways. In one, district voting replaces at-large voting; in the other, one district configuration is replaced by another. When at-large voting is replaced, two benefits can be realized: The formal weight of the vote can easily be equalized by election authorities evening out/up (or avoiding disparities in) the population among the districts; and a viable political minority, or community of interest, submerged in a winner-take-all arrangement can claim its voice. When one district pattern is replaced by another, the benefits are similar except that attention shifts to the placement of boundaries that guarantee sufficient voters to respect the interest involved. At the congressional level, the practice has always been to elect in single-member districts. Congressional redistricting therefore has been exclusively a matter of selecting among alternative boundaries—the second option.

However, at local levels the situation was more complicated, often involving the replacement of existing systems with entirely new single-member arrangements. At the start of the civil rights movement, for example, many state legislatures elected their members from complex multimember schemes. City councils and county commissions were often elected at-large. Congressional and legislative representation was often assigned according to county or other jurisdictions without concern for population disparities. Such practices frustrated efforts to equalize the individual vote across the whole and became increasingly suspect as efforts to comply with one person, one vote occurred in the same communities where there was a demand for single-member districts or partisan minority voting opportunities or other communities of interests. The drive to eliminate population disparities increasingly took the form of a drive to eliminate at-large (or multimember) districts in favor of single-member districts.

Multimember districts also became suspect because in biracial communities the submergence intrinsic to multimember systems where there is some sort of racial diversity functioned to reinforce a pattern of discrimination covering not merely the minority political voice, but the minority race voice as well. Though developed on separate tracks, the logic of the movement to equalize the ballot and the crisis in black political empowerment dovetailed to intensify the attack on at-large elections and to affirm the single-member district as the ideal option.

The marriage was not a simple one, however. The use of single-member districts intensified the shift in thinking that had already begun. Civil rights groups—already overwhelmed by persistent low voter participation—saw the utility of the single-member district in addressing racial representation. They abandoned their minimalist efforts to protect the right to cast a ballot.

This shift played to the very strength of the single-member district because residential segregation—another legacy of racism—provided a handy basis for configuring election systems. Indeed, it was the historic and recurring neighborhood segregation among the nation's peoples that made the new reform so compelling. It is simple to design boundaries around these clusters, and voters therein can elect persons of their choice. Not surprisingly, in most cases this results in the election of a member of the clustered racial group. Over the years, the Voting Rights Act was increasingly construed and reapplied to appropriate the remedy used to ensure one person, one vote. During the 1970s, the remedy was increasingly used to secure the election of blacks to office, and in the late 1980s it was the overwhelming remedy of choice in the voting rights community.

The adoption of the single-member district was a penultimate pragmatic choice reacting to the nation's tradition of electing its public officials from geographic regions. The appropriation of this remedy in the modern voting rights movement has been justified on several grounds. Minority race communities with large numbers of poor and undereducated voters are able to manage better with single-member districts. Cost benefits result from a candidate campaigning in smaller areas. The prospect of victory enhances the argument that the vote is relevant. In some areas single-member districts encourage candidates to affirm some sense of a bond of interest that can further argue for the significance of the ballot. In other areas the same result may be accomplished because already existing community bonds are given new political expression.

Single-member districts also simplify election choices. At-large elections require additional use of multiple choices. Such ballots are more likely to produce such "mistakes" as spoiled ballots or "roll off," where the voter either makes an error or fails to enter a selection for the full list of offices. In some cases at-large elections discourage the voter from making any but the minimum selection. For better-educated voters, this is merely an inconvenience of the democratic process; for the disadvantaged it amounts to an absolute barrier to effective participation.

The special conditions of mobilizing in poor communities raises another issue influencing the utility of single-member districts—the problem of where to set the percentage of the population minorities need to create a viable district. Although the percentage varies, a simple majority is seldom sufficient to provide choice to the minority. Age structure and rates of participation make it necessary for election planners to compensate by including extraordinary majorities in these districts. Although this situation may decline in importance as minority officials come to enjoy the benefits of incumbency or seek to deploy their political skills (and resources) more widely, it is now reasonably certain that a typical minority community will need some supermajority within the district in order to prevail.

The appropriation of single-member districts has been successful because of simplicity and effectiveness. These districts are particularly exciting as a way to address racial exclusion, giving immediate political force to the formal right to vote. Voting law does not require creation of these districts, but the presumption of their remedial impact is overwhelming. The impact has been dramatic. When Gloria Molina was elected to the five-person Los Angeles County Board of Supervisors in 1991, she was the first representative from the area's Spanish-speaking communities. In biracial Burke County, Georgia, where whites have made up as little as 20 percent of the population, no black was elected to the governing commission until one hundred years after ratification of the Fifteenth Amendment! In Dallas County, Alabama (where Selma is located), blacks were not elected to the governing commission until 1989. These elections were all secured by single-member districts and are only a minuscule number of such cases. Pointing to these results, minority empowerment activists continue to praise single-member districts, and some even argue that multimember elections should be abolished altogether.[2]

Wider Application?

The hegemony of the single-member district provokes two kinds of questions. First, given the continuing limits on minority access to the political process, are there other ways in which the remedy can be expanded for wider, more decisive impact? Second, are there characteristics of spatial districting that limit its use in voting rights reform, and do we have the critical perspective, and tools, to uncover such limits?

To the first question the answer is a qualified yes. The single-member district can be expanded beyond its current use to maximize minority representation within existing systems. This will require consciously crafted plans and the extension of current thinking to a point where districting is used to *maximize* minority representation.

Wider application can also be accomplished in conjunction with the reorganization of governing bodies. This may result from such internal rules as rotating chairs or committee assignments, which enhance the influence of minority elected officials, or may involve actually expanding the size of agencies so that districts could be constituted with smaller numbers. The case of *Yolanda Garza* v. *County of Los Angeles* (1989) illustrates the possibilities.[3] At the time of the lawsuit, that county's government had just five persons serving a population of nearly 9 million—a number that exceeded that of all but a handful of states. Yet even with a growing minority population, the board remained all-white males. The *Garza* lawsuit was filed on behalf of Latino Americans to challenge their submergence within an at-large system and resulted in a typical change under the Voting Rights Act, namely, the adoption of a single-member system. An alternative approach would have expanded the size of the board to increase the chance of officials reflective of the diversity of the citizenry being elected.

The size of such bodies varies widely. The L.A. County board contained five persons, for example, but Chicago's city council had fifty members elected from wards. In this context, the typical voting rights remedy was applied in a mechanical way that constrained its impact. Such an approach may become a tool to avoid the more radical restructuring that its own successes seem to make necessary if the voting rights movement is to evolve.

Limitations of the Single-Member District

The answer to the second question, about the possible limits of spatial districting, is more involved and even less certain. It will require a more systematic sorting among a number of concerns about the use of single-member districts and thus of the limits of the voting rights movement that emerged during the 1990s. In my own view, there are several specific issues that identify the limits of the strategy used so far.

1. *Failure to empower a range of legitimate constituencies.* These voting reforms hold little promise for communities historically populated by the white poor where the election apparatus remains a monopoly of dominant elites. Economic discrimination in voting continues to stand outside the law. Nor is there a basis for litigating underrepresentation of women, another group not elected in sufficient numbers. Nor can the effort directly address the status of large numbers in the popu-

lation who do not have formal citizenship. Better representation of the poor and working people does often occur as a result of these election reforms, although such improvement is a by-product.

2. *Limited impact on single-person offices.* Districts do not apply to single offices, and the persons elected to these are seldom drawn from minority communities. This limitation is inherent to the electoral arrangement, although governmental reorganization can have a remedial impact. Improving the number of minorities on these offices raises questions of voter turnout levels and effective coalitions, and these require revisiting a set of questions abandoned when the civil rights groups committed to the new movement.
3. *Restrictive policy impact.* Where minority representation has been secured, and even where this may result in effective control of the body, the impact of minority representatives on policy can be limited. This limited impact results from the difficulty any public agency encounters in conducting the public's business in a fragmented governmental system. In public education, for example, delivery of services through local school districts can frustrate the best efforts of officials elected to these bodies.
4. *Overall instability of the remedy.* Election based on geographical concentrations is inherently unstable because of the mobility in a society of such uneven wealth and social circumstance. Districts that ensure minority representation at one time may not do so at another time. "Silent gerrymanders" may occur, involving declining population or regentrification. There are differential voting levels and life expectancy, as well as immigration from foreign countries, special institutional populations, and real estate conniving. These conditions invite attempts to draw districts that will appear more viable than they are.
5. *Conflict with other civil rights goals.* The remedy may conflict with other civil rights goals. Thus, although diverse communities remain a priority in race relations, the single-member district is dependent on one-race neighborhoods. This has implications for such issues as how to site public housing or the status of practices, such as "steering" by real estate agents and redlining, long opposed by civil rights groups.

The scale can be significant. Some districting is centered at the neighborhood level, which may elect a local councilor, but other districts will involve the half million inhabitants needed for a congressional seat or for some statewide bodies. Several key goals are involved, including residential diversity, quality housing, and school attendance zones. Districting invites trade-offs that involve troubling choices.

6. *Failure to eliminate partisan gerrymander.* The elimination of multimember districts drawn along city or county boundary lines opened possibilities to gerrymander that were not possible before. In effect, the growing use of single-member districts aggravates this process. Some argue that the partisan advantage shifts away from the party most likely to address minority concerns in the larger polity. For critics, this represents that bogeyman of racial reformers: the unintended consequence of benign intentions.

The plot thickens under additional scrutiny. White male Democrats held most of the offices in the communities under challenge and became defendants in the lawsuits. This monopoly provides opportunities both for minorities, which generally register as Democrats, and the GOP: The former must consider how to negotiate their positions with the party, and the Republicans can imagine opportunities to gain new adherents. This is particularly relevant in the old one-party South—still a mainstay of the Democrats—where the same structure was used for partisan as for racial discrimination. Because of Republicans' success in presidential elections, they have had a unique opportunity to administer the federal voting law so as to get at partisan barriers under the color of benign racial concerns. (Though enacted by a bipartisan congress under the Democrat Lyndon Johnson, the Voting Rights Act has been under Republican administration for twenty of the first twenty-seven years of its existence. Crucial court opinions have been written by Republican-appointed judges.)

Racial Preference? Betrayal of Liberal Ideals?

The effort to reform election systems to the advantage of racial minorities and the actual increase in the power of these minorities have been greeted by some as a betrayal of broader civic goals. This attitude developed gradually over the late 1980s, replacing the less articulate defenses of local white officials. Abigail Thernstrom pulled the arguments together in a 1987 book where she ripped apart the 1982 amendments and argued that blacks and Mexicans were abusing the act by focusing on actual token representation rather than voting.[4] This argument found further elaboration in works by Carol Swain focusing specifically on the partisan implications of the minority voting demands.[5] These writings were not widely read outside the voting rights community. When the 1990 census adjustment arrived, the process caught a lot of attention in more popular opinion journals and editorial pages, where writers such as Stuart Taylor voiced objections and others, such as Mary and Thomas Byrne Edsall, expanded the Swain argument regarding politics.[6]

These writings were usually, perhaps smugly, dismissed by persons familiar with the details of the litigation, especially the detailed proof developed, case by case, in adversarial proceedings. This dismissal was perhaps borne of a certain confidence based on a record of dramatic decisions won in cases handled by the southern office of the American Civil Liberties Union, the Legal Defense Fund of the National Association for the Advancement of Colored People, Mexican American Legal Defense and Educational Fund, and the southern office of the Center for Constitutional Rights. These successes were the result of meticulous argument before southern judges who were seldom enthusiastic about the proceedings.

But the new argument opposing minority voting rights was getting attention in official circles. Thernstrom was mentioned by lawyers seeking to find a defense for systems marked by a clear record of racial exclusion, lucid appeals for fair representation, and continuing racial bloc voting. These lawyers were desperate to shift the argument away from political practice and onto more abstract ideological grounds. In time dissenting judges picked up these themes, especially in the southern courts. Then in a 1993 opinion, *Shaw* v. *Reno,* the U.S. Supreme Court adopted the arguments in a case involving North Carolina congressional redistricting.[7] The majority opinion, written by Justice Sandra Day O'Connor, adopted a line of opposition, weaving a tale of a deracialized America threatened by black congressional representation. The opinion culminated an evolution in thinking and opened a new line of contentious litigation involving challenges to minority representation now derided as "race based."

With the imprimatur of the highest court, strange bedfellows began to emerge. Lani Guinier, who had toiled on behalf of voting rights, now theorized a replacement strategy involving some form of alternative voting procedure unrelated to districts.[8] At the time of her misappointment to the Clinton team, she was represented as a loner on this issue, but her thinking reflected ideas then percolating in a renewed advocacy of proportional representation (PR). This movement had enjoyed a heyday in American reform thought because of its forthright criticism of first-past-the-post, winner-take-all systems. Enjoying a reservoir of goodwill among thoughtful people, proportional representation lacked an effective politics of conveyance. Nevertheless, many believed PR to be a logical heir to the voting rights movement. It still may be. But the *Shaw* era has corrupted PR's prospects considerably; its value now may be not as a real choice but as an alternative to a critical discourse designed to resolve racial discrimination. Ironically, Guinier and the new PR may represent another voice of mistrust, even though they act as friends of minority representation.

We may now look at the elements in the thinking of these critics and skeptics. They say the voting rights movement has been excessive in several ways. First, it strays from the original intent of the civil rights movement and the Voting Rights Act. Second, it creates disunity and threatens a larger sense of national purpose. Third, it violates cherished civic values by conceptualizing representation in terms of cultural groups rather than individuals. In this argument the current emphasis on racial empowerment is deemed illegitimate.

But this emphasis on original intent is idealist. It assumes we can recover some controlling first event and that such an event should function as a moral absolute to command our allegiance and govern present behavior. In fact, the reconstruction of the intent of the civil rights movement is no more than a contested notion, just as every initiative in that movement itself was contested in practice. These observers, for example, usually conduct clearly self-serving reconstruction depicting the political goals of the civil rights movement as a minimalist drive to eliminate discrimination.

The national unity aspect is equally idealistic. They invoke larger liberal-democratic values, as well as those of racial justice movements. On the one hand, opponents invoke the notion of core civic values as a precondition for a workable polity. They say such unity, exemplified, again, in the consensus around civil rights work, is absent from the present movement and its tendency to use the language of power. They express concern about the way minorities themselves have intensified their struggles for political power. Such behavior secures the election of members of their own race but raises a question as to whether they are sufficiently attuned to the general good. This attitude, menacing enough when purveyed in the opinion journals, found explicit statement in official circles in the majority opinion in *Shaw* v. *Reno*.

The other angle on the unity theme involves politics more directly. Opponents say the voting rights movement undercuts the political base, and voice, of liberal advocacy. The base is threatened because liberal-Democratic districts will lose their minority voters, and the voice loses clarity as the language of group self-interest vies with the universalist discourse of New Dealism. At issue is the New Deal coalition—an advantageous partisan arrangement whereby biracial voting constituencies have benefited the Democratic Party. The other party is given a weapon in the partisan battle. It can use minority empowerment as a "wedge" to divide the progressive coalition. The increase in minority elected officials is discounted because victories reward the wrong cravings among racial minorities, who, at any rate, remain mere tokens on the governing bodies. And when one considers that the districts created to elect minorities actually subtract minority voters from coalition districts, the election of minorities amounts to a net loss for the larger cause.

This commentary amounts to a challenge to the core strategies used to gain some measure of access to the political process. In the 1990s, this commentary took an ominous path: energetic public debate about crucial minority aspirations dominated by writers and editors in the white majority population. It is also taking a familiar path in American political science: hostility to people's struggles couched in terms of the discipline's misguided reform zeal and its addiction to the simplistic logical truism that structural reform will have unintended consequences. The situation is all the more troubling because any effort to empower groups with a history of disadvantages is an enormous undertaking; "failure" will result in any reform short of a total overhaul.

The argument also suffers on conceptual grounds. The form of the criticism, for example, is adopted from the opposition to affirmative action. But the contestation over qualification at point of entry at the heart of that discussion is out of place in considerations of political status in a democratic system. The effort to separate the right to vote from the right to hold office is just so much sophistry, and if anything, the fundamental recognition of equal rights we readily accept in the political arena ought to be the template for our relations in other spheres of social life. Indeed, one good reason to give more attention to the voting rights movement is precisely this possibility.

The national fabric is merely an idealist construction that reduces to a hegemonic politics based in a fictive "white nation" whose claim to general allegiance is what should be scrutinized. The idealization of the civil rights movement is static, drawing on the consensus of a historical moment where progressive reformers operated with an image of community that was essentially acultural and biracial. Both these simplicities have given way in the face of sustained critical reanalysis of the American people in theory and the unequivocal demands for protection under voting law by all historically disadvantaged populations in practice.

Missed Opportunity?

Spatial representation—even when mediated by single-member districts—has certain shortcomings. This is occasion for engaged critique, as well as simplistic opposition from those who do not accept the goals of the movement. This condition makes it improbable that a consistent critical perspective will arise even among the best-informed observers. A major casualty of this condition is the insight associated with proportional representation. The triumph of the single-member district distracted from the movement for proportional representation and the larger effort to counteract the traditional winner-take-all feature of American politics. PR was the unrealized moment in Progressive Era reforms, and its significance is often unappreciated because of the attention to the recent period.

PR devices aim to ensure an impact in elections proportionate to the diversity of voices in the voting population. The proportionality, of course, does not depend on spatial conditions or on predefined racial (or ideological) groupings, although the broad community of contemporary and historic PR advocates has assumed that racial or other minorities would get elected in higher numbers under PR. Rather, proportionality is a condition where the distribution of preferences—and the intensity of those preferences—among elected officials equates to the distribution among the voters. This is secured by a process where options are provided to individual voters without regard to residence.

A succinct description of the mechanics of PR is difficult—a not inconsiderable factor in its limited use today. To attempt a summary description would require attention to two closely related concerns: first, that the voter not be locked into accepting one set option and, two, that the voter is allowed to express some measure of the strength of preference for candidates and that this be taken into consideration in the tabulation. The system is fit for multimember (at-large) election districts. Recent discussions of PR often look at it as some form of "cumulative voting," where the voter is given as many votes as there are candidates and then allowed to allot then freely.

The appeal of PR was never strong in America, although it is more common in other nations and is widely used in private decisionmaking. Some form was used in a number of municipalities, including New York City, Cincinnati, and several other Ohio towns, in the years after World War II. Illinois used a form in its state legislative elections. Both New York and Cincinnati voted these systems out. Today, Cambridge, Massachusetts, is the only major city with a PR system. Elections to the New York community school boards use a form of PR. Advocacy remains, and, though unsuccessful, referenda were held on proposals to convert to PR in Cincinnati and San Francisco in recent years. Settlement negotiations in voting rights cases often raise the option, and there has been some use in small communities as a result.

Historically, proportional representation was burdened with suspicion that its call for a "better" representation reinforced hegemonic designs of a WASP elite. The hope for the election of more women and racial minorities did not fit the times when PR enjoyed its most articulate advocates. Moreover, PR was avoided by leaders of both major political parties, by machine hacks, and by reformers alike. Finally, PR rested on an easy assumption about the availability of the free ballot and thus was not a credible sell in areas of egregious voter discrimination. Black voters emerging in the American South did not enjoy such access and increasingly geared their empowerment strategy to the prevailing institutions, focusing on the right to register and to participate even in the hated one-party systems. After *Baker,* proportional representation lost appeal rapidly.

Evaluation of contemporary voting reforms could benefit from a reconsideration of PR. We have not been so lucky, however, and when proportionality is discussed, the focus is on group representation. Some writers emphasize this notion of "proportional representation" and are antagonistic to its use. The antagonists have been effective. Their rhetoric is infused throughout opposition texts and was even included in a special proviso of the pivotal 1982 amendments to the law. Here the notion is corrupted into an epithet for preferential treatment of racial groups in elections. The prospect is set that this will overshadow the legitimate claims by proportionalists. And because the neo-PR criticism is so thoroughly racialized, it stands to be yet another occasion when race serves to divert attention from the main issues.

The Next Stage: Political Analysis of Voting Rights

We have a pressing responsibility to draw on current practice to evaluate the goals and structure of the voting rights movement. Integral to that evaluation is another task that extends beyond paradigm-dependent puzzles concerning wider application or clarification of internecine disputes; this is the task of identifying and accounting for political consequences. What is the impact of the new constituencies on popular participation in minority communities? How well do they contend in the political process? What counterstrategies have developed? What is the larger ideological character of the new constituencies? How well do they incorporate the legacy of progressive reform? A political analysis of the voting rights movement is necessary, and it requires a kind of thinking that relates these outcomes to civic agency and to prospects for reconstitution of a popular majority coalition.

There is reason to be cautious when we turn to political analysis. The voting rights movement has unfolded almost entirely within a two-party system that, by the 1980s, was operating less on a popular mandate than on a restrictive electorate. The antipopular tendency is reflected in voting work itself, which, in becoming so litigious, is increasingly disconnected from grassroots mobilization and accountability. Tension raised by litigation may lose its creative function and become mere top-down maneuvering. The litigation focus requires extensive resources and skills that are in short supply in disadvantaged populations. Where such counsel does exist, it is always expensive to support. Some legal assistance is provided by the U.S. Department of Justice, which will review election changes in certain areas or bring lawsuits on behalf of minorities. Other help is provided by the mainline civil rights organizations, whose cadre of lawyers can handle cases for communities at minimum expense.

Securing these resources diverts attention from community-based organizing for voter registration and education where efforts have not kept pace. Indeed, the Voter Education Project, an early pioneer in community-based registration, declined over the 1980s and ceased to operate altogether in the early 1990s. Voting levels remain low generally—even in districts where minorities select representatives of their choice. Election politics contains numerous barriers to voter participation (including the voter registration requirement), thereby aggravating the difficulty of minorities mobilizing within their own communities. Powerful bipartisan alliances operate to protect these policies.

With the new offices, minorities are better positioned to express and protect themselves. The arrival of minority elected officials has opened new avenues for communication across racial lines. But they remain at a disadvantage because of long-established attitudes. Age structure, for example, enhances the influence of just those parts of the white population most attuned to traditional race and social prejudices. Retrograde racial attitudes are at the base of the successes of politicians from Massachusetts to North Carolina who see the effectiveness of the Willie Horton appeals and exhibit a troubling inability to pursue electoral majorities without playing the racial theme. These long-established attitudes leave the recent success to be read negatively as a distraction from positive politics.

The election reforms in voting rights have propelled us beyond the state of empty minority ratification of one or the other contending white candidate. But that success is, in effect, another threshold with its own limitations. Thus, even though the number of black elected officials has grown, it has occurred in certain kinds of constituencies: all- or majority-black inner cities or single-member election districts (which amounts to the same thing). The later increases in other minority communities are following a similar pattern.

The prospects for moving beyond the latest threshold require the recasting of reform strategies. It will be necessary to incorporate the single-member district into a dynamic agenda. In politics there is a need to move on to another level of competition, one geared to electoral success at higher offices. In communities there is a need to generate accountability mechanisms that express community interests to affect the agendas of the elected officials. The larger goal is to see that the remarkable achievement in guaranteeing minority representation is realized in the reconstitution of a strategy where the popular will can be reestablished at the center of the political process.[9]

PART FOUR

A New Black Accommodationism

10

"Self-Help," Black Conservatives, and the Reemergence of Black Privatism

Preston H. Smith

THE TERM "SELF-HELP" was used by political commentators, politicians, and ministers during the Reagan-Bush era to indicate a shift in black politics. Often invoked, self-help was associated with phrases such as "self-reliance" and "individual responsibility" to indicate that the source of black social problems came, and certainly their alleviation should come, from *within* the black community. The term was used to designate a shift toward activity that is voluntarist, private, and inward-looking. Currently, President Bill Clinton has advocated more personal responsibility among black citizens to convey the same message: Black people should stop looking to the state for aid and solutions to *their* problems. They must instead look within their own communities for the "solutions" and, increasingly, for the *source* of their problems as well.

Calls for self-help and internal solutions to black social problems emerged during the Reagan-Bush era as the federal government backed away from its commitment to assist the needy and vulnerable of our society.[1] A self-help ideology has become widespread in the 1990s, culminating in the recent Million Man March. A dominant self-help approach has facilitated the corresponding growth of a new black privatism, exemplified by an increased faith in the capacity of private institutions and voluntary action, for example, the church, market values, and entrepreneurialism, to improve black social conditions. Not unlike an earlier occurrence one hundred years ago, the recent reappearance of black privatism is not accidental; rather, it signals an ideological and social adjustment to new political-economic arrangements in the United States.

Black conservatives are in the forefront of establishing a self-help ideology that appeals to nationalism, individualism, and traditional private authority and that dominates black political discourse on strategies to arrest debilitating conditions among black populations. These ideologues, such as Robert Woodson and Glenn Loury,[2] have taken advantage of a black legitimacy crisis that stems in part from the divergent social conditions experienced by affluent and poor groups and from the failure of black urban administrations to deliver material improvement to their impoverished constituents. In this chapter I examine the foundation, substance, and implications of this recently prominent "self-help" ideology. Although many blacks do not reject the government as a crucial factor in reconstructing black communities, as do black conservatives, black liberal and ostensibly progressive leaders nevertheless increasingly call for individual, voluntarist, private, and community-based approaches to the usual litany of black social problems—poverty, unemployment, crime, drug abuse, teenage parenthood.

This new black privatism was best expressed in the 1980s by an ideology of "black conservative populism," which combines a suspicion of government-based approaches to black subordination with a concern for the plight of poor urban blacks. This ideology's disdain for government aid places this strain solidly within a conservative, free-market notion of individual responsibility for upward mobility. The expressed concern for poor blacks gives this populism racial legitimacy, while simultaneously disarming out-of-touch, elite-oriented civil rights organizations and black politicians. The concern for poor blacks' well-being and autonomy allows this ideology to support "market-based solutions" to ending poverty. Concern for the poor's autonomy—not being treated as victims—is used to criticize "enforced dependency" by government, as evidenced in the notion that initiative and responsibility for individual action and change are sapped by government programs.

Once the poor's ability to act for themselves is established in principle, then their behavior becomes fair game and can be identified as an important cause of their own plight. And the concern with what poor blacks do *for* themselves as subjects is easily shifted to what they do *to* themselves. Black conservative populist ideology restricts the poor's legitimate actions to either private, bootstrap activities or self-destructive behavior.

Those who reject a conservative label nevertheless find ideological kinship with this focus on the black urban poor's behavior. Moreover, this preoccupation facilitates the attempt to reestablish traditional black authority as the source of social renewal by relegating public action to the evil designs of colonizing white men. As black liberals and black "progressives" shift more of their focus to the black poor's self-destructive behavior, they inevitably assert the moral authority of black voluntarist, private groups such as the church and fraternal orders to combat black pathology.

I first explicate the differences and similarities between traditional civil rights organizations and black conservatives regarding the importance of self-help for racial advancement. Second, I examine the black conservatives' attack on the welfare state and suggest that the language of their attack gives us insight into their real agenda for reestablishing traditional institutions of social authority, for example, the nuclear family, the church, and businesses in the black community. Last, I argue that black conservatives use self-help to shape new normative orientations that help to underwrite and adjust to the massive Reaganite disinvestment, private and public, in black communities. Such disinvestment has led to the impoverishment of that very group, the black poor, whose interests black conservatives claim to advocate. Black conservatives have used self-help's populist and democratic allure to shroud its socially regressive agenda for poor African American citizens.

Black Conservatives, Civil Rights Organizations, and Black Privatism

African Americans have had a long history of self-help efforts. A large part of this history has incorporated self-help in the racial uplift ideology of civil rights organizations such as the National Urban League (NUL) and the National Association of Colored Women (NACW).

Black conservatives attack these civil rights organizations for eschewing this self-help tradition in favor of depending on governmental assistance for racial progress. In response, civil rights organizations have joined black conservatives in promoting "role-modeling" as updated racial uplift and have focused on poor blacks' behavior as an obstacle to their upward mobility.

Tradition of Black Self-Help

Historically, self-help emerged in the form of mutual aid among free blacks during the antebellum period. Living in a hostile and violent racist environment necessitated blacks' depending on themselves for important goods and services. Booker T. Washington remains the black figure most associated with self-help.[3] For Washington, self-help meant that blacks should advance themselves through the work ethic and through accumulation of capital in landed property and small businesses. He contended that these efforts were more important than agitating for civil and political rights. Washington's self-help, however, relied enormously on private philanthropic contributions by robber barons.

Early-twentieth-century organizations such as the National Urban League and the National Association of Colored Women adopted Washington's advocacy of self-improvement for poor blacks. The NUL engaged in negotiations with business elites to create economic opportunities and to subsidize segregated institutions and services. Although the NUL did not shrink from exposing racial discrimination (it was, however, more circumspect than W.E.B. Du Bois and the National Association for the Advancement of Colored People [NAACP]), it sought to improve race relations safely within the bounds of the dominant political economy.

The racial uplift ideology of organizations such as the NUL and NACW shared in "the black self-help tradition." In this context, self-help meant moral instruction in the personal habits that would supposedly ensure social success, both for the individual and, by extension, for the race, once broader opportunities existed. Since these organizations believed that not all blacks were as yet qualified, either in job skills or in moral character, this approach also entailed reform efforts aimed at the moral tutelage and social control of black popular classes.[4] Thus, adopting self-help as a form of moral rehabilitation signaled blacks' readiness for entrance into American society.

Blacks would now be prepared to take their rightful place in society once the artificial barriers of race were removed. Proponents of this earlier self-help appealed first to white private elites and later to a reluctantly interventionist government to ensure nondiscriminatory access to public goods and opportunity for private gains. This self-help tradition assigned a special role for "talented" blacks. As the middle-class NACW's motto "Lifting as We Climb" suggests, the "better classes" had a responsibility to help their lowly brethren improve themselves as individuals and members of the Negro race.

These earlier efforts at black self-help were the products of necessity in the absence of a developed welfare state.[5] In the post-Reconstruction era, Washington's self-help was underwritten by white private philanthropy. Northern elite aid attempted to make up for the woeful services provided by segregated local governments to taxpaying black residents. While southern, rural African Americans were being encouraged to adopt self-help by black and white elites, the federal government was distributing a "half-billion acres of public land to speculators and monopolists" through land grants.[6] Economic and social elites seized upon "successful" black self-help efforts to survive as reason to "deny the necessity of broader public responsibility for major social needs."[7] Thus, even though the black self-help tradition espoused self-reliance and self-determination, circumstances forced dependence on white corporate paternalism. Prior to the Great Society, poverty, mitigated only by mutual aid and private charity, was a way of life for many black Americans. The poverty rate for blacks, as late as 1959, was 55.1 percent.[8] Black self-help not only failed to alleviate black poverty. It also imposed an added burden: The myth of the self-made man further burdened blacks, who had to demonstrate their moral worth in order merely to qualify for a portion of public resources and formal access to economic opportunity.

Black Conservatives' Attack on Civil Rights Organizations

Black conservatives have been stridently critical of civil rights organizations. They claim that these organizations represent the exclusive interests of the black middle class, which benefited from the civil rights movement, while its "foot soldiers"—poor blacks—sacrificed and got little in return.[9] The middle class benefited from the expansion of the public sector through the War on Poverty. This expansion resulted in what black conservatives identify as the chief problem of black poverty, namely, overdependence on the welfare state. Robert Woodson, president of the National Center for Neighborhood Enterprise (NCNE), states, "New efforts must focus on ending dependence on government and encouraging the growing movement among blacks to rely on themselves for an improved life."[10] Black conservative intellectuals indict the traditional civil rights organizations with facilitating welfare state expansion by making incessant appeals for aid to the black population. Instead of finding creative and self-reliant means to meet the needs of the poor, these organizations, so the argument goes, have become complacent through a steady diet of public-sector subsidies. Worse, black conservatives accuse civil rights organizations of using poor blacks' misery as capital to be exchanged for social programs that mainly benefit black middle-class professionals. Civil rights organizations are reproached for being either self-interested and not caring about the urban poor or completely devoid of fresh ideas about how to rectify poor blacks' predicament.

The popular press has taken black conservative opposition to civil rights organizations at face value. Black conservative opinion is treated as novel, a sign of new ideological diversity among African Americans. The popular characterization of black conservatives and civil rights groups as polar opposites exaggerates their differences and obscures what the two groups share in their approach to the poverty of urban blacks—black privatism.[11]

What is at issue for black conservatives and civil rights leaders is the role of racial discrimination in causing black poverty and the role blacks themselves should play in solving their social problems. Civil rights organizations feel that black social problems are largely created by institutionalized racial discrimination. But they also contend that people, especially the poor, sometimes respond to this racism inappropriately or "dysfunctionally." Black conservatives acknowledge that racial discrimination exists but downplay its relevance for current problems. Woodson points out that "if racism ended tomorrow, the plight of poor blacks would remain largely unchanged."[12] At other times, black conservatives consider racism as part of the "natural" environment: permanent, unchanging, something to adjust to but not waste time trying to change or attempt to eliminate.[13] The problems faced by the urban poor today, conservatives conclude, are due less to racism than to a paternalistic government bureaucracy in alliance with a complacent black leadership.

There appears to be more agreement between civil rights organizations and black conservatives on who is responsible for alleviating the problems of poverty. Civil rights organizations argue that society is responsible for helping but that leadership and initiative must come from within the black community. Blacks as citizens should get their fair share of aid, like any other group. As victims of institutional racial inequality, they are due special assistance. The government provides for other citizens in special circumstances, civil rights activists argue, so why should blacks be treated differently? Yet while civil rights organizations seek governmental and "private-sector" responsibility for assistance, John Jacob, former president and chief executive officer of the National Urban League, reminds us "that Black America is not standing still waiting for others to come to its rescue. It recognizes that its salvation lies within itself."[14] Jacob's position resonates with that of black conservatives who argue that blacks themselves should take responsibility for solving their own problems and not look to government for cues or direction. His moralistic discourse clearly indicates that the control and direction of reform should be dictated by the "black community."

Loury insists we must distinguish between the responsibility of white racism for black social problems and "the responsibility for relieving that condition" that should be borne by blacks themselves.[15] But Loury does not himself include white racism or any "external" factors when discussing current black problems and what threatens black America. He chides the black middle class for its reluctance to talk openly about "values, social norms, and personal attitudes," to confront "the difficult, internal problems which lower class blacks now face."[16] He argues that this black elite's moral leadership is crucial for "improving the life conditions of poor blacks by reducing the incidence of problematic behaviors among them."[17] His notion that low-income blacks' behavior represents an "enemy within" that is abetted by the middle class's abdication of its tutorial role unmistakably places the blame for black poverty on blacks themselves.[18]

Role-Modeling and the Problem of Behavior

Civil rights organizations today attempt to reappropriate the self-help tradition through a refashioning and updating of racial uplift ideology. The reincarnation of this form of middle-class-led self-help has assumed the various guises of "role-model" support for indigent blacks.[19] Civil rights leaders contend that black conservatives ignore the continuing contribution of civil rights organizations to self-help: everything from the NACW's "Black Family Day" to the currently fashionable mentoring programs that pair black professionals with black poor youths.[20] Jacob boasts of the NUL's having been first to come up with programs for teenage pregnancy prevention and male parental responsibility.[21] Law professor Roy L. Brooks, not satisfied with an ad hoc approach, goes so far as to call for a massive self-help program that has black middle-class families "adopting" black "underclass" families to teach them "survival strategies" in negotiating a racist environment.[22] This approach was anticipated by the Chicago Urban League in the 1920s when it advocated an adoption of "abnormal" black families by "normal" middle-class black families.[23] Black conservative Woodson reportedly has investigated "other self-help ideas that appear to be working," such as the adoption of poor black families by a group of black professionals in California.[24] Loury's lament supports this notion of elite responsibility for impoverished blacks. He writes regretfully: "Having achieved professional success, they [middle class blacks] appear not to recognize that their own accomplishments are rooted in the kind of personal qualities that enable one best to take advantage of the opportunities existing in American society. As a result, the opportunity for their lives to stand as examples for the lower class of the community goes relatively unexploited."[25]

Role-model ideology values the kind of voluntarist activity that emphasizes elite-led moral uplift in self-help. In addition, this ideology reinforces the notion that blacks are responsible for blacks, Jews for Jews, women for women, and so on. Although mentoring is meant to encourage low-income blacks to emulate the success of black professionals, it shifts the focus away from the questionable availability of adequate employment opportunities for the "dependent poor."[26] Moreover, role-model ideology confers moral superiority on those who have economic resources. It assumes that if a person has a respectable income, he or she has wholesome moral habits or "survival strategies," not privileges from middle-income parents or, sometimes, the luck of circumstances that have made success possible. Such a person is now entitled to "mentor" a person with lower status, who is assumed *not* to have those values.[27] This ideology flatters the black middle-class individual who has succeeded.[28] It inflates the social importance of affluent blacks, whose absence in inner cities is purportedly the reason that low-income blacks who were "simply" poor during the segregated era have been transformed into the "concentrated" and "isolated" poor of today.[29] The black middle class is touted by role-model ideology as the major force for relieving the wretchedness of impoverished blacks.[30]

Despite the superficial differences between civil rights organizations and black conservatives, their shared embrace of role-modeling forges a new consensus on the source of black social ills and the responsibility for their alleviation. Loury suggests that black middle-class people assert "moral leadership" by dealing with "the behavior of [poor] individuals . . . [and] the role such normative influences might play in the perpetuation of poverty within the group."[31] William Raspberry, a black syndicated columnist, commented recently that "the most important barrier to our progress now has to do with our own behavior."[32] Clearly, the problem for both civil rights organizations and black conservatives has become the behavior of poor blacks.

In our post–civil rights era, civil rights organizations such as the NUL attempt to have it both ways. They reassert their commitment to an activist government, while valorizing private, voluntarist activity through self-help, role-modeling, and mentoring. In a context of federal retrenchment and corporate irresponsibility, their commitment to self-help, despite their protestations of "not letting government off the hook," overshadows other programmatic thrusts and undermines the groundwork necessary for collective mobilization of black people to pressure the government to support an agenda for black community reconstruction.[33] Civil rights leaders' endorsement of self-help gives ideological quarter to black conservatives' concern with enhancing poor people's moral development. The embrace of role-modeling by both groups projects the black poor's behavior as the pivotal source of deterioration within black communities.

Black Conservatives' Attack on the Welfare State

Even though black liberals and conservatives agree to focus on the behavior of the black poor as an important obstacle to resolving poverty, each group assigns a different responsibility to government. Civil rights organizations still see an important need for government action. Sometimes governmental efforts should even approach the scale of the Marshall Plan that helped to reconstruct postwar Europe.[34] Black conservatives, in contrast, reject any proposals for a massive infusion of governmental aid because they feel that such an effort will duplicate the failed policies of the past. They envision minimal government efforts only in support of black-directed self-help programs in local black communities. Black conservatives criticize the welfare state for being ineffective in two ways: (1) social programs are too centralized and overly bureaucratic, and too little of the money designed for the poor ends up in their pockets; (2) social programs will increase dependency and encourage behavior that is not conducive for mainstream work and family responsibilities.

The Poverty Industry

Woodson criticizes civil rights organizations for "reflexively call[ing] for an expansion of the welfare state to accomplish what civil rights legislation has failed to do."[35] He is particularly critical of the "poverty industry" spawned by a paternalistic welfare state. Woodson claims that currently seventy cents of each poverty dollar go not to the poor but to those who serve them.[36] This asserted disparity, in his view, is further evidence that only the middle class gained ground in the War on Poverty. Worse, there has not been any "fundamental welfare reform" because middle-class social service providers have an interest in maintaining the current system in order to keep their jobs. Although the welfare state and its middle-class bureaucrats may not cause poverty, Woodson claims that they retain an interest in not alleviating poverty.[37]

Woodson's critique is not new. The critique of the "poverty establishment" has been made by left social scientists who see social programs as dehumanizing, stigmatizing, and conferring penurious benefits. Furthermore, they argue that these programs were used to coopt disruptive minority and poor activists into the federal patronage system. At the same time, these critics defend the idea of adequate social provision as a standard by which to judge the shortcomings of a stingy welfare state.

Woodson's account of the failed War on Poverty is selective at best. He neglects to point out that overbureaucratization was largely a result of conservative politicians' imposing rigid eligibility criteria and a punitive monitoring apparatus to police the so-called profligate poor. Also, top-heavy administration and diminutive benefits enforce labor market discipline through stigma and insufficient income.[38] Perhaps an even more glaring neglect in Woodson's account is his failure to ask how poverty is produced. Who or what is responsible for creating poverty? Is it pathological behavior? Is it racism? Is it economic exploitation and exclusion? Woodson and other black conservatives discount racism and see behavior as at least perpetuating poverty. What causes poverty is apparently beside the point. What causes dependency is of more interest to black conservatives.

Welfare State and Dependency

Black conservatives attack the welfare state as responsible for the moral breakdown of black "inner-city families." Loury says that "the easy availability of financial support for women with children without fathers present has helped to create a climate in which the breakdown in the family could be accelerated."[39] Justice Clarence Thomas concurs that the welfare state "doesn't offer any incentives for families to stay together. And it certainly accommodates the disintegration of the family."[40] Woodson thinks "[the welfare state] is a very big contributor" to family dissolution.[41] He points out that problems such as "teenage unemployment," "teenage pregnancy rate," and "welfare dependency" increased dramatically during the 1960s, whereas the rates only "reflected the national average" in the 1950s.[42] He avers, "I think the change is associated with the expansion of the welfare state and the poverty industry."[43] He frets that "public welfare and other social programs promote dependence and destroy individual initiative."[44]

It is not surprising that dependency on government is denounced in a liberal capitalist society that must support the myth of free-floating, autonomous individuals. But conservatives are particularly hyperbolic when equating dependency with human bondage. Loury gushes, "We may be witnessing the beginning of a great emancipation, the second emancipation: the freeing of the inner-city poor from the stifling confines of the politics of dependency, envy, and guilt-based claiming."[45] The imagery of a crisis of dependency is, moreover, gendered; the problems associated with the behaviorally focused "underclass" are predominantly identified with females.[46] But the concern for "intergenerational poverty"—the key element of the dependency claim—is overstated. Most women utilized Aid to Families with Dependent Children (AFDC) intermittently, shifting between earning poverty wages and getting public assistance. Studies have shown that daughters of AFDC mothers did not disproportionately receive welfare.[47] Moreover, two out of three black women were poor *before* becoming single mothers.[48] Despite the small percentages of welfare recipients that actually fit the description of "permanent welfare dependent," we are told that welfare dependency represents a crisis tantamount to slavery. What is behind this overwrought claim?

The criticism of dependency by black conservatives is selective and ideological. First, it underestimates the fact that "independent" male earners generally are not able to expend themselves at a workplace without a "dependent" wife to take care of household and child care work. In other words, independent wage earning relies on the unpaid work of dependents in order to reproduce itself.[49] Second, dependence on public assistance, for a woman, is assumed to be worse than dependence on a male breadwinner or a low-wage job. Yet dependence on an abusive male breadwinner is not a dependence we would encourage, nor is holding a job that is low paying, provides minimal benefits, and occurs in a demeaning and dictatorial work environment.[50] In a racially and sexually segmented labor market, employment possibilities for poor black women are located largely in this low-wage, unstable secondary sector.[51] Moreover, the ideological targeting of households headed by poor black females had consequences during the Reagan years. The number of black families with children living in poverty increased by 26 percent from 1979 to 1987. This increase is largely attributable to the fact that reduced government transfer programs lifted fewer black families above the poverty level in 1987 (one out of twelve) than in 1979 (one out of six).[52] The whole point of providing public assistance is to lessen dependence on unstable work or on an irresponsible husband/father to provide for a woman and her children.[53] For black conservatives, it appears that any job or any man would be better for black women than living on the "dole."

Black conservatives are oblivious to market coercion. Having a job, any job, is tantamount to independence, self-reliance, and "freedom," no matter how oppressive the work conditions or how low the pay. So important is merely having any job that Woodson charges Representative Bruce Morrison with being "antipoor" because he wants "to require all public housing residents to conform to prevailing wage laws and union rules" in competing for construction jobs. Woodson argues that this standard is antipoor because it prices unskilled tenant labor out of the market.[54] The consequence of Woodson's plan is to depress the wages of all workers by introducing low-wage competitors for stable jobs during a time of declining real wages (in 1987 black unemployment rates returned to the lower 1978 levels, but black earnings levels actually declined to pre-1972 levels).[55] This emphasis on employment and neglect of income ignore important sources of black poverty.

Indeed, black conservatives have a critical blind spot about the real workings of the American political economy: Their reconstructed accounts of welfare state failure never mention the changes in urban economies—caused by corporate and state restructuring—that have polarized labor markets between high-wage positions and low-wage service jobs and industrial jobs declining in number, pay, and rates of unionization. Reindustrialization in the cities has usually meant sweatshops with new immigrant women workers in the informal economy.[56] Perhaps the main consequence of mandatory workfare—a typical antidote proposed for dependence—is to force poor black and other women to compete for jobs in this expanding low-wage sector, thereby further depressing wages.[57]

Self-Help, Nationalism, and Gender

Black conservatives' self-help ideology, despite its populist rhetoric aimed at "empowering" poor black females and others in the inner city, uses terms of criticism that suggest an attempted reassertion of masculinist authority within the black population. In addition, the use of nationalistic appeals toward this end is instructive.[58] Loury asserts that "no people can be genuinely free so long as they look to others for their deliverance."[59] At another point he calls for a "move beyond the politics of out-stretched-hand dependency to a position where black Americans can stand on their own two feet and hold their head up."[60] Talk show host Tony Brown explains how the Democratic Party has duped blacks into embracing a mythical role for government, that of helping its citizens, "and a misguided notion that white people will solve black people's problems."[61]

The whole notion of black leaders' "begging" for government "handouts" suggests an Uncle Tom imagery that is anathema to self-respecting black citizens. In this formulation, the welfare state becomes synonymous with "whites" or, worse, the "white man." Given this equation, one could see the admiration that Clarence Thomas would have for Malcolm X as a representative of defiant black manhood.[62] What Thomas admires is the "doing for self," that nationalist self-help that Malcolm and the Nation of Islam popularized in the 1960s.[63] But this formulation mistakenly suggests that seeking state aid and benefits that are due to African Americans as citizens is not legitimate public activity and is a sign of racial weakness. Rather than seeing the welfare state as a collective institutional agent *and* a site for competing and contesting claims, black conservatives prefer to see only the white father. Their racialization of the welfare state reads blacks out of the body politic.[64]

The very language used to denigrate efforts by civil rights leaders to make claims on the state is revealing of the underlying black conservative agenda. Black conservatives feel that the welfare state has infantilized blacks as helpless victims. Woodson tires of hearing civil rights organizations' "litany of despair" and their depictions of blacks "as lost children waiting for a government Moses to save them from racism and economic deprivation."[65]

Moreover, there is a gender subtext to these characterizations. For conservative proponents of self-help, decrying racism becomes "bitchin," "whining," and "moaning."[66] One can almost hear them say, "Real men don't beg or whine; they take what they want." In these versions, the welfare state emasculates "real men," making them dependent on "handouts." Men can become men only through the independence that comes from the challenge of entrepreneurship and competition in the "free enterprise system." The competitive market becomes a mechanism for a necessary remasculinization, with nationalism and self-help serving as important tropes for black conservative ideology and for the reassertion of black male, middle-class authority in black communities.[67] By contrast, the welfare state, where black women have gained jobs and some assistance, represents a barrier to reasserting that authority; thus it must be attacked, at least indirectly.

There is a deep-seated sexism underlying black conservatives' critique of the welfare state. We have seen that an indirect endorsement of patriarchy and the "invisible hand" accompanies their selective and ideological attack on welfare dependency. Yet their attack on the welfare state involves real targets, too. Some black women are both welfare mothers and service providers. Witness Thomas's attempt to display his ideological mettle through his scurrilous attack on his sister's welfare status, a status incurred by her having become a caretaker for an ill family member.[68] For black women, human service employment represented 58 percent of their job gains between 1960 and 1980.[69] The black conservative attack on the idea of social service carries an attack on the dignity and autonomy of black women.

Black Privatism, Self-Help, and the Black Conservative Agenda

Black conservatives believe that poor blacks can find moral rehabilitation by adopting entrepreneurial values and practices. They also argue that entrepreneurs have been displaced as natural community leaders by those who favor protest and politics. Black conservatives' agenda is to inculcate in grassroots community leaders a self-help orientation that favors better management of community resources rather than a political approach that attempts to extract more resources from the government. A key part of this agenda is the promotion of public housing residents owning and managing their housing developments as a solution to their self-destructive behavior and economic underdevelopment.

Entrepreneurialism and Moral Rehabilitation

Black conservatives' belief in the "inviolability of the market" underlies their assertion that improvement of the black poor's condition requires a revival of the entrepreneurial spirit of pre–welfare state, segregated black America. Their notion of "romantic entrepreneurialism" recalls Reaganite populism, which involved freeing swashbuckling, "antielitist" entrepreneurs from the shackles of big government.[70] Black conservatives feel entrepreneurship can be liberating for all black social strata, especially the poor. In a transparent appropriation of activist rhetoric from the 1960s, Woodson asserts that we need to "address the problems of poverty by empowering those at the bottom."[71] Empowerment for him, however, means helping indigent blacks "participate in the free enterprise system."[72] Woodson sees "deregulation" as a key to black business development among the poor. He says, "If you lower the barriers to starting up a business, more low-income people could start businesses like day care centers."[73] Woodson's group, the National Center for Neighborhood Enterprise, is involved in giving low-income blacks "the capital and the information they need to empower themselves."[74] In contrast to middle-class volunteers always serving as role models for poor blacks, Woodson feels the experience of entrepreneurship can bring about an "internal transformation" for the poor.[75]

Woodson's program for cultivating poor blacks' "capacities" is premised on the morally transforming experience of adopting entrepreneurial values. He draws heavily on the work of John Sibley Butler, an economist and adjunct fellow at the NCNE. In *Entrepreneurship and Self-Help Among Black Americans,*[76] Butler constructs what he calls the "truncated Afro-American middleman theory." He argues throughout his book that the black entrepreneurial tradition has been ignored and ridiculed, indicting E. Franklin Frazier's *Black Bourgeoisie* as the exemplary work in this black antibusiness attitude.[77] Butler sees himself resurrecting a "hidden" history of a black business renaissance during the 1700s and at the turn of the twentieth century. He asserts that "Afro-American middlemen" thrived within segregated southern black communities by building black institutions and by confining themselves to their own well-kept black neighborhoods. Such groups were similar to other middlemen groups, for example, the Jews in Europe and the Japanese in California, that adjusted to society's hostility by creating their own institutions and businesses. Such "enclave economies" served as a safety net for those who were severely discriminated against in the outside economy.

Butler thinks that the measuring of black business success in terms of capitalization or employment is misguided. More appropriate, he thinks, is to measure how entrepreneurs have prepared later generations. He claims that the values of hard work and sacrifice learned from the entrepreneurial experience of middlemen have helped their children succeed at higher education. Thus, the lesson to be drawn by all groups, but especially the black urban poor, is to adopt entrepreneurial values. The parents' experience will provide the necessary launching pad for the next generation's upward mobility.[78] Curiously, Butler makes little mention that these middlemen's resources pay for their children's nutrition, security, shelter, and higher education; the key to their success, presumably, lies only in transmitted values.

Self-Help and Black Community Leadership

Black conservatives believe that the tradition of entrepreneurship was lost through the civil rights movement and the subsequent expansion of the welfare state, that the movement for desegregation ensued in the loss of "entrepreneurial spirit" and "self-help institutions." Woodson surmises that "many black businesses became casualties of racial progress."[79] In this regard, Butler repeats the link between self-help and entrepreneurship, contending that the primary task today is to recognize "the importance of community organizations which, at one time, were so much a part of the self-help tradition in Afro-American communities."[80] He refers to organizations such as the National Business League and its affiliates, Greek letter organizations, and fraternal orders.[81] Butler does not expect that black entrepreneurs will be able to hire everyone in the inner city. But "community enterprises will help people to stay afloat economically and provide alternative sectors for employment" for those who cannot secure a job in the external economy.[82] "A deliberate return to self-help" therefore will "augment the overall attempt to create opportunities in American society."[83]

This return to self-help assumes that "business people are reemerging as leaders of [the] community, a position which they occupied when the tradition of self-help was strongest in the Afro-American tradition."[84] Butler criticizes those black social scientists who, following Frazier, denigrate bourgeois values in the black community. In this scheme, however, poor blacks are reduced to "buying black" with their meager incomes and taking their policy cues from a reascendant black business class.

A hidden assumption in Butler's and others' celebrations of black self-help is that the interests and needs of black businesses and of the black poor are the same. Questions about internal distribution of community resources or conflicting land uses, for example, a parking lot versus a playground, are left unexamined in these black conservative ruminations. Presumably, since the black poor *can* become entrepreneurs, there exists no conflict of interests. Accordingly, the poor would cherish the prerogatives of property owners because they have hope of becoming themselves property owners. Or Butler and his colleagues think that a hidden organic black hand will magically guide the various private interests of black business people and property owners to realize the common interests of the black community. Given Butler's romantic assumption, one would think there was never any social conflict within segregated southern black communities—or that these "middlemen" never defused opposition to Jim Crow in order to protect their social status and business interests.

It seems that for black self-help advocates, class conflict occurs only through the mediation of the welfare state, for example, through black middle-class service providers who perpetuate the dependency of black poor clients; but internal conflicts magically disappear when the "free" marketplace mediates these relationships. Each individual becomes a free private agent in the marketplace, autonomous and not subordinate to any other agent. It is no wonder that Butler sees salience only in racial oppression; class, for all intents and purposes, does not exist as a factor in the unequal distribution of resources, either in society as a whole or within the black community.[85] Yet why should we assume that black business people are best suited for community leadership? What would they provide that has been lacking? Does black conservative populism, under the guise of restoring the entrepreneurial spirit, mean simply establishing black business people as "natural" community leaders?

Black Conservative Agenda

Black conservatives, of course, are in the vanguard of the new black privatism. Examining their policy agenda therefore provides the clearest view of the practical implications of self-help ideology. Woodson and the NCNE present a useful template for considering this agenda. Founded in 1981, the NCNE is designed to provide technical assistance to grassroots leaders whose neighborhoods are attempting to become self-reliant, if not self-sufficient, and an organizational framework for incorporating these leaders into the public policy process. Woodson got the idea that he could link grassroots leaders with corporate and foundation resources while working as head of the Administration of Justice Unit of the National Urban League. Woodson felt that "public policy should come directly from the people, in some cases instigated by those closest to the problem."[86] At the same time, Woodson became involved in the American Enterprise Institute's (AEI) "mediating structures project," which was headed by sociologists Peter Berger and Richard Neuihaus. The project's main idea is that the "mediating structures" of the "family, church, and neighborhood associations" would provide individuals with values and a sense of control where "megastructures"—the state and corporate sector—had failed. This perspective shaped Woodson's conceptual approach to problems in low-income black neighborhoods.[87]

Woodson felt early on that the input of those most affected by the problems of crime had been missing in government-sponsored programs. He argued that "expertise" in community problems should be based on experience rather than on abstract credentials. He was hostile to what he called "parachuting" solutions in from the outside. (Woodson's skeptical attitude toward professionals is consistent with more therapeutic self-help programs, for example, Alcoholics Anonymous.)[88] As an AEI resident fellow, Woodson put together a "urban youth forum" where "nonprofessional, self-taught experts on youth problems" could share strategies and problems. This gathering became the vehicle for establishing Woodson's credentials as a poverty broker. At this forum Woodson, speaking to the participants about the significance of their contributions, remarked:

> If we're saying that what you do is different, then there has to be a public record of that . . . so that some of us who interpret what you do in the policy community will have evidence for what we believe in our hearts to be true. It's not enough for Bob Woodson to say this. . . . We have to be able to say that we have called together young people and their sponsors around the country and they have told us this. We're interpreting and trying to analyze what they have said and what they believe. Therefore, this information is not about an isolated case; their comments point this out.[89]

Woodson had found an alternative source for *his* expertise. Rather than studies or abstract policy analysis, he would collect the "authentic" experiences of street service deliverers and then represent them in policy circles. He could argue that his data had irreproachable legitimacy because his sources were the very people affected by the problems on the ground. Who in the policy community from northern Virginia would contest him? There are various forms of "capital" that can be exchanged for professional prestige and material comfort. Instead of using the poor's misery as capital, a charge he has persistently leveled against the civil rights establishment, Woodson uses their "indomitable spirit" and unlettered know-how as capital, all in a "bootstrap," "tough love" political environment to entice corporate and government dollars for his operation.[90] The NCNE has become the clearinghouse for this collection and dissemination of native experiences.

The four areas for which the organization claims expertise are economic development, family preservation, education, and crime prevention. The NCNE conducts its business through various subunits: The Neighborhood Leadership Development Institute (NLDI), along with its counterpart the Leadership/Management Institute in South Africa, trains grassroots leaders; the Neighborhood Policy Institute (NPI) coordinates the organization's policy activities and serves as its public relations arm; and the Neighborhood Capital Corporation is a for-profit subsidiary that attempts to provide seed capital and technical assistance to small businesses.[91] The NCNE's organizational apparatus and patterns of external linkage highlight inconsistencies and contradictions within contemporary self-help privatism.

One of Woodson's major complaints as a "youth crime specialist," for instance, was that grassroots leaders were not recognized and consequently did not receive funding from government agencies and foundations. He specifically singled out the Department of Justice's Office of Juvenile Justice and Delinquency Prevention (OJJDP), which, he claimed, had ignored the unique problems of crime and anticrime efforts of neighborhood groups in the black community.[92] This stance seems at odds with Woodson's later criticism of his civil rights counterparts for seeking governmental assistance. Nor is the contradiction reducible to a change over time. The OJJDP has been a consistent governmental source of funds for the NCNE since 1984. The organization's funding has supported a "minigrant program" that provided "technical assistance vouchers" to neighborhood-based programs.

Funding from OJJDP has also supported a conference on "minority youth crime" in 1985 and from 1988 to 1990 implemented an antidrug campaign. Recently, the NCNE received another three-year grant from OJJDP that provides technical assistance vouchers for neighborhood-based antidrug activities targeting "at-risk" youth.[93]

The NCNE boasts about the amount of private funding it has received from individuals, corporations, and foundations. In the organization's eleven-year history (1981–1992), its budget has gone from $366,183 to $2.3 million. The sources of this largesse have been corporate foundations such as Allstate, Amoco, Proctor and Gamble; the right-wing John M. Olin Foundation; and more mainstream contributors such as the Kellogg and Charles Stewart Mott Foundations and the Pew Charitable Trust.[94]

As continued support from the OJJDP indicates, Woodson's operation found an ally in the White House during the 1980s. Woodson was one of the few blacks who made repeated trips to the Reagan White House.[95] His advocacy of "market-based" policies for "empowering the poor" carried over to work with the Bush administration, especially with his friend Jack Kemp.[96] The NCNE's early programs on tenant management served as demonstration projects for the legislation that the former representative recommended as secretary of housing and urban development. The program enacted by Kemp with tepid support from George Bush was called HOPE (Homeownership and Opportunity for People Everywhere), and it offered "subsidies for public housing tenants to rehabilitate and convert their homes to resident-owned cooperatives."[97] The Amoco Foundation funded a three-year public housing resident management demonstration with a $1.9 million grant.[98] Woodson's financial and ideological support would seem to undercut charges by black conservatives that their views have been marginalized by an all-powerful "civil rights establishment." Indeed, much of the conflict between black conservatives such as Woodson and his former colleagues in the Urban League involves their competing for corporate and government support.

Woodson and Kemp's relationship predated the Bush administration. In 1986, they sponsored a conference whose proceedings were published under the title *Revitalizing Our Cities: New Approaches to Solving Urban Problems*. Loury, who wrote the conclusion, entitled "Freeing the Inner-City Poor," characterized the conference as "a merging of the important work that Bob Woodson has been doing in community organization and self-help with what I think is the cutting edge of some new ideas in social policy that revolve around the opportunity society theme that Jack Kemp has made so prominent."[99] Loury has made it clear what this conference, and the alliance it cements, means for a new agenda within the veil: "Something may be happening here of quite historic proportion: a decoupling of the interest of the poor from the agenda of the anticapitalist, envy-mongering left. I know that's an ideological statement and it has no place here, but let me just offer it as a possibility of what's really going on. I mean, if we get down to what the real politics of this event are, I think something like that is quite salient."[100]

Woodson's "black economic agenda" found a ready kinship with some of Kemp's privatization initiatives at the Department of Housing and Urban Development (HUD), although Woodson apparently declined to join Kemp as HUD undersecretary because he felt Bush was "cozying up" to traditional black leadership.[101] Woodson has sought out "private-sector alternatives" to black social issues; these alternatives include educational vouchers to support black independent schools, private-based adoption and child care, opposition to busing, church-based economic development, tenant management, enterprise zones, housing vouchers, and tax policies to support black business formation.[102] Woodson especially seeks "a more market-oriented delivery system for human services."[103] The policy area that most coincided with Kemp's urban policy initiatives and has been most actively promoted by Woodson's NCNE is the privatization of public housing through tenant-led residential management and ownership.

Tenant Management and Moral Reform

Tenant management and ownership during the Reagan and Bush years became favored policies of self-help empowerment for the black poor.[104] In nearly every publication by or about Woodson, the Kenilworth-Parkside Resident Management Corporation, which has managed the public housing project in southeast Washington, D.C., of the same name since 1983, is extolled as a black self-help success story of the 1980s. In 1990, it became the first resident management corporation (RMC) to purchase a public housing development.[105] Under the direction of activist Kimi Gray, rent collection was purportedly more efficient and repairs purportedly more timely.[106] Many residents were hired to work in management, clerical, and maintenance positions, and auxiliary service businesses were developed. The selling of public assets and contracting out of services to private businesses started by tenants particularly appealed to Woodson and other black conservatives. They argue that resident management corporations help public housing residents "create their own businesses, to keep money and jobs within the community."[107] But at another residentially managed development with employment created by spin-off services, the unemployment rate for the housing project was still over 80 percent.[108] Despite the inflated rhetoric, these entrepreneurial gains seem paltry in a context of systemic public disinvestment.

The efforts of the residents of Kenilworth-Parkside to control their own environment drew on a rich history of activities in the black community regarding planning participation, community control, and neighborhood development. Tenant management in particular has long been advocated by low-income housing activists. Gray was once an active member of the National Tenants Organization.[109] Also, resident management in St. Louis came out of the rent strikes in the 1960s.[110] But excessive focus on tenant management and ownership obscures the limitations of privatization of public housing as a means of providing affordable, low-income housing. The advocacy of tenant management under the New Federalism suggests that resident control will provide either better housing and housing services for the same price or savings to the public treasury.[111] To make the transition to ownership, however, would take an equal or larger public subsidy than the level provided for supplemental rent and public housing. One study estimates costs to be between $70,000 and $90,000 for each new home owner.[112] Because the economic resources of the tenants have not significantly increased, financing for this "privatization" is still subsidized by the public sector.[113]

Although economic development is supposedly part of the payoff, Woodson is even more excited by the reported moral benefits. He maintains that the "bureaucratic, command-control approaches transfer the will for self-achievement away from local people to bureaucracies."[114] In contrast, and a result of privatization's rekindling of that will, teenage pregnancies were allegedly down and some "wayward men" took jobs and became responsible for their families.[115] Woodson argues that these moral benefits occurred because it suddenly was "okay" for teenagers to say "no." Dr. Alice Murray, who runs the Substance Abuse Program at Kenilworth-Parkside, states that "what we're working for is a change of behavior and attitude. . . . One of the things that this community has brought back is a kind of old-fashioned shunning . . . a way of saying, 'This behavior we will not tolerate. Should it happen, then we put you through all the services, but we don't expect it to happen ever again.' It's done in a very kind and gentle and loving way, but there's a shame when it occurs—which is not the case in the outside community."[116]

Woodson argues that these dramatic changes occur because when poor people own property, they then have a stake in society. Property ownership facilitates a moral transformation among the poor. People become "responsible" and no longer engage in dysfunctional behavior. The evidence for these changes lies mainly in asserted anecdotes or self-referenced claims.[117]

A report done for the Twentieth Century Fund is less sanguine.[118] This study points out a number of negative consequences of tenant ownership besides continued and costly public subsidization for home owners. First, public housing units, often the most modernized, are withdrawn from an already scarce supply of affordable housing. Second, a creaming effect occurs because ownership schemes favor higher-income nonwelfare recipients and thereby essentially undermine mixed-income public housing developments, which are favored by the housing policy community; welfare recipients found ineligible for ownership, despite meeting income requirements, are displaced when units are sold. Third, there is no evidence that privatization leads to neighborhood revitalization. Fourth, tenuous home ownership makes the home owner more economically insecure and vulnerable—for example, the home owner has to keep up with rising property taxes.[119] One investigator concludes that "no evidence [has been found] that resident management organizations are any more democratic, efficient, or accountable than well-performing public housing authorities."[120]

Although the case for public housing privatization was always weak at best and is now moot since privatization has been jettisoned by the Clinton administration,[121] the rationales are nevertheless revealing. Woodson stresses the moral side benefits of privatization. Although these supposed benefits could be seen as icing on the economic development cake, they often appear to be the cake itself.

Woodson and his colleagues have made light of the limited economic gain that comes from entrepreneurship and have stressed the importance of *values*. Woodson advocates the formation of "Junior Achievement"–type clubs to teach "entrepreneurial values like thrift, hard work, and showing up on time."[122] Moreover, he says, "entrepreneurial values have application beyond just business; and I think that steps should be taken to spread them among low-income people."[123] At one point he stresses the importance of Mom-and-Pop stores because "certain values are communicated to the children so that they tend to go on to college."[124] Privatization of public housing is attractive because property ownership "changes behavior." Raspberry quotes Kemp as remarking approvingly: "Owning something changes behavior in ways that no amount of preaching middle-class values ever could. Democracy can't work without the component that goes to the heart of what freedom is all about—the chance to own a piece of property."[125] Clearly, the target of this agenda is moral rehabilitation, not economic development.

New Black Privatism and Self-Help

The emphasis on moral reform through self-help excites Woodson not only because it prompts poor people to engage in self-corrective behavior, but also because it makes self-help attractive for those who would eschew the conservative label. More liberal commentators advocate government's enforcement of equal opportunity while reserving self-help for the moral rehabilitation of indigent blacks.[126] Even progressive scholars such as Cornel West assign a central place to self-help. West calls for more moral responsibility, warning that black inner-city behavior is a threat to black civic life. He sees self-help arresting what he diagnoses as life-threatening "nihilism." Self-help supplies the basis for combating nihilism—"a politics of conversion . . . [to a] love ethic."[127] West mentions the contribution of corporate and state disinvestment to black deprivation but warns those who would draw too strict a causal connection to avoid "extreme environmentalism." Yet West generalizes from specific behaviors to the overall orientation of an entire community—nihilism. His characterization in this respect is not unlike Loury's "enemy within." West endorses the notion that "jobs are not enough" when it comes to confronting "the cultural decay and moral disintegration of poor black communities."[128] Even though West often attempts to balance behavioral and structural causes, his dramatic and sweeping recourse to an internal threat taps into a cultural reservoir of free will individualism that regularly locates the cause of black social problems in black pathology.[129] Thus, behavior, not conditions, inevitably becomes the target for reform or, simply, for policing. West, perhaps unwittingly, embraces a black conservative populism with the prominent causal status he assigns to the destructive behavior of poor blacks. For West, this behavior represents the "major enemy of black survival."[130] His attempt to highlight the black poor's own responsibility, a position that links him with Woodson and Loury's populism, provides ideological space to introduce the notion that the black poor's behavior causes or perpetuates their own oppression.

The populism of black conservatives and scholars such as West divests the public of its authority in order to transfer authority to traditional private sources within the black community. Thus, West seeks salvation in the same groups or institutions as Woodson—"private voluntary associations" and "grassroots leaders." West hopes to rebuild damaged black psyches and, by extension, black civic life, with "intermediate institutions such as Christian churches, Muslim mosques, and character-building schools."[131] He concedes this agreement with black conservatives concerning the redemptive potential of the voluntary sector. But he also asserts that he differs from them because he sees these institutions' "role as both oppositional to and transformative of [the] prevailing class subordination of American capitalist social relations."[132]

Although some individuals and neighborhood groups have made heroic, if sometimes necessarily defensive, contributions, it is not axiomatic that these intermediate institutions perform in an emancipatory manner. Nor does West provide any hints about how these groups will function as oppositional and transformative forces or what conditions must exist in order to favor such contributions. We need to gauge carefully the dangers of incorporation and the preconditions for community mobilization. For these institutions can also function as social control entities that reinforce the social quiescence of marginal populations, a possibility that West does not acknowledge. West's apparent blind spot allows black conservative populism to assert a new normative orientation of black communitarian self-reliance, especially in the context of the fiscal retrenchment of the

1980s and 1990s and especially when the maldistribution of social goods and services remains weakly contested.

Even though West attempts to distance his position from that of black conservatives, his chief concern—like theirs—is moral reform of the poor by their own community-based organizations and social institutions. Moreover, the context of continuing fiscal stringency at all levels of governments dwarfs any call for an oppositional role. Again, Loury is clear about the contribution of grassroots organizations to this new normative discipline:

> Community organizations, churches, public housing resident management associations and the rest can deal with this matter. The point is communities have the ability to establish and enforce norms of behavior which lie beyond the capacity of the state, which, after all, has only the instrument of force, only the threat of incarceration. There are more subtle and more powerful influences over human behavior that communities can invoke. Ostracism, of a sort, is one of them, but it requires an explicit statement of values.[133]

An example of this policing by public shaming is elaborated by Gray:

> The only way you can make a change is through peer pressure. . . . Rules can't be enforced if you have to go through judiciary proceedings. . . . If your momma was a bad housekeeper, and if her stove broke down, we would put the old dirty range out in front of her house, so everybody could see it. Leave it there *all day long*. Go get the brand-new stove, in the carton so everybody could see it, have it brought down, but not to your house. . . . Now when your momma learns to keep the stove clean, she'll get a brand-new one.[134]

Just as Booker T. Washington's call to "cast down your buckets where you are" rested on an obsolete view of economic possibilities in 1895, so the new black privatism advocates black community self-help when global political-economic forces are becoming increasingly elusive. In fact, just as Washington's accommodationist program rationalized a new regime of white supremacy in the industrializing South, self-help supports a contemporary, regressive shift in the entrenchment of racial subordination. In the context of an increased mobility of capital, municipal governments use scarce resources to attract businesses and affluent professionals to their cities.

Subsidizing business development has meant less funds for social services, especially for poor citizens. Increasingly, city governments are contracting with nonprofit and community-based organizations to deliver services. Urban government spends less money this way than by staffing costly human service bureaucracies. In addition to this budget relief, governments are not held directly responsible for the quality of the services. Community-based organizations that deliver shoddy services because of penurious funding will have to confront citizen dissatisfaction. Organizations that once led demonstrations against city hall now work as partners with their former adversaries.[135]

Woodson's NCNE has taken the lead in this trend toward community entrepreneurialism. The organization trains grassroots organizations to instill a normative adjustment to fiscal austerity. Despite a rhetoric of "grassroots" and "empowerment" and a seeming reliance upon "native" experiences, the NCNE program assumes that problems can be solved technically, not politically. The organization seeks to imbue community activists with business values such as "managerialism" and "entrepreneurialism." The NCNE seeks to turn grassroots leaders into "neighborhood executives."[136] Problems can be solved with better organizational and managerial skills, not necessarily through conflict or with more resources. Loury adds that this self-help orientation is "less adversarial in political tone . . . and [that] the welfare state is divisive because of its implication that the poor are entitled to their 'fair share' at the expense of the economically better off."[137] The grassroots leaders who have been trained in business skills will not be making "excessive demands" on the state for redistribution but will instead stretch their threadbare organizational and community resources.

New Black Privatism and Disinvestment

Black conservatives have sought to enhance economic opportunities for the black poor through privatization, deregulation, and tax incentives. Their arguments have valorized privatism and made public action increasingly illegitimate. They argue that public action is illegitimate because it is ineffective and inefficient and creates dependency. They advocate that private individuals and institutions act in the marketplace. Black privatism—exaltation of the interests and actions of black private institutions and the adoption of the familiar bourgeois values of the work ethic, thrift, property acquisition, and sacrifice—emerged during the 1980s in a context of state retrenchment and corporate restructuring. This state retrenchment finds its ideological echo in the early 1970s with the Trilateral Commission's concern that the activism of African Americans and others during the 1960s produced excessive claims on governmental resources: "demand overload" or "excessive democracy." By conservatives deflecting claims on these governmental resources, more funds were available for defense spending, the real U.S. industrial policy.[138] The new right critique of the debilitating effects of state intervention on the individual's liberty and economic livelihood joined libertarian concerns with a corporate agenda for a streamlined state to support capital's global search for cheap labor and lucrative markets.[139]

State retrenchment in domestic policy came in the form of Ronald Reagan's New Federalism. Under New Federalism many categorical grants were concentrated in a few, reduced block grants given to state governments. The Reagan administration boasted that it was reducing the federal government's intrusion into local affairs. Local governments suffered not only from the reduction of federal aid but also from the shift of the control of that aid to often unfriendly state governments. The cumulative impact of budget cuts from 1981 to 1988 was such that the ranking of HUD's budget authority among federal departments fell from fourth to eighth. During the same period, a 69 percent reduction occurred in the total HUD budget (from $33.4 billion to $10.2 billion), including an 89 percent reduction in assisted housing (from $26.7 to $3.9 billion), a 29 percent reduction in the Community Development Block Grant program (from $3.7 to $2.6 billion), and "the elimination of the UDAG's [Urban Development Action Grants]."[140] This trend continued with the Bush administration. Given this public divesting trend, it is not surprising that even former secretary Kemp's "conservative war on poverty" received little verbal or financial backing from the White House.[141]

Cities, forced to pursue economic development with less aid, utilized their dwindling resources to try making themselves more attractive to mobile capital. The poor did not receive the jobs produced by this new economic development. Most metropolitan job growth occurred in mostly white suburban centers. During the 1980s, central cities lost over 30 percent of their job base, while suburban rivals saw employment increase by 25 percent.[142] The proportion of central city per capita income to suburban per capita income decreased from 90 percent in 1980 to 59 percent in 1987.[143] During the 1991–1992 recession, blacks were the only racial group to experience nationally a net job loss, losing 59,479 jobs.[144] Moreover, the quality of their services declined because of revenue lost to downtown property tax relief. The poor were doubly harmed by state retrenchment, which exacerbated a Darwinian struggle among cities, decreeing that those who were not able to adjust to the postindustrial service economy would be on their own. Clearly, blacks, who constitute a significant portion of the central city poor, were not aided by this public disinvestment.[145] Decentralization schemes, whether Richard Nixon's "Black Capitalism" hustle or "community control," have been historically used to deflect demands for redistribution of resources.[146] Black self-help is the latest in "empowerment" schemes that tell desperate black communities to "look within" while governmental assistance and jobs go elsewhere. The populist rhetoric of grassroots control only masks its conservative, disfranchising substance.

To forestall potential black social unrest caused by this massive withdrawal of resources, self-help ideology deflects attention away from the state. Black conservative ideologues and policy entrepreneurs emerged from new right think tanks to push an ideology that borrows from the Protestant ethic and black nationalism.[147] This ideology makes assertive claims on the state seem illegitimate, futile, and unmanly in their dependence on white folks. Thus, a new black privatism was exhumed from the halls of Tuskegee Institute to reestablish traditional private authority in the black community and to delegitimize popular mobilization on behalf of collective grievances.

Whether for philosophical or pragmatic reasons, black privatism—vociferously advocated by black conservatives but also embraced by civil rights organizations and grassroots leaders—shifts the focus on addressing black deprivation inward toward the actions of black individuals and private institutions, such as toward businesses, professional organizations, and nonprofit community-based organizations. This inward shift toward self-help strategies renders public action and popular mobilization illegitimate. Civil rights organizations have tried to accommodate conservative and neoliberal administrations by embracing decentralization and by adding symbolic self-help activities to their bankrupt strategies of lobbying and elite negotiation. Black conservatives and others overstate the effectiveness of black private institutions in addressing black community needs. These private groups have neither the inclination nor the resources to contest adequately real locations of social power. In fact, their self-help ideology and activities obviate the ideological need to engage in such political contests. Corporate culpability in the disinvestment of the black community is obscured by an ideology that uncritically valorizes entrepreneurship and free enterprise. State disinvestment through New Federalism and privatization has drained needed resources from the black community, leaving it defenseless against intractable poverty and its social tragedies. The reemergence of black privatism in the form of a self-help ideology has underwritten the corporate and state disinvestment of inner-city black communities. Ironically, but unsurprisingly, the black poor are worse off for having been granted more "market freedom."

Conclusion

Black self-help ideology fills a normative void of our post–welfare state era. In the 1960s, there was a crisis of black citizens' faith in white-dominated municipal service delivery, punctuated dramatically by urban rebellions. Now that black urban regimes have not delivered the desired goods for a variety of reasons, the legitimacy of public authority itself has been put in question. Self-help ideology, which has its rebirth in the neighborhood decentralization approach of the Carter administration, has been given a tremendous boost by black conservative ideologues supported by the Reagan-Bush administrations and new right think tanks. Black conservative ideologues advance the notion that black self-help organizations have replaced black urban regimes as sources of black legitimacy and can provide the social glue necessary for a minimal semblance of order. Although it is doubtful that black conservatives ever sought or obtained a substantial social base in black communities, the self-help orientation that they helped to launch now dominates discussion of black social problems. The need for a self-help ideology to accompany a contracted state originated before the brutal 1980s and extends to the present neoliberal administration. Transnational capital still demands more social surplus, and the compliant state is forced to do more with less. In this context, there is no other self-help but *conservative* self-help. The emphasis on private over public action, on voluntarism over politics, on decentralization over public investment, and on individual empowerment and moral uplift over black power is an indication that this ideology has successfully redefined black political discourse on strategies and goals. We are likely to continue seeing its appeal throughout the Clinton regime, which is committed to maintaining the political marginality of African Americans.

Black conservative self-help embraces role-model ideology that valorizes individual, voluntarist approaches to systemic social problems. It embraces middle-class leadership uncritically, while proclaiming a phony populism. Also, under the cover of restoring the "entrepreneurial spirit" to the black community, this rhetoric masks a call for black business people to assume community leadership. Middle-class blacks, because of their resources, will benefit disproportionately from whatever new capital is leveraged from the conservative regime. The black conservative approach is worse than past policies that advantaged middle-class blacks and left poor blacks insufficiently unaided. At least with the civil rights organizations' participation in New Deal–Great Society countercyclical policies, some aid did trickle down through black middle-class agencies to the black popular classes. The palpable threat of social disruption leveraged some aid to blacks. Moreover, holding the state and corporate America responsible for their contributions to black misery was a regular feature of black political rhetoric, if not always action. The black conservative approach is worse because, by eliding corporate capital's role, with state support, in black dispossession, black conservatism has left unrecognized and unchecked the private and public disinvestment from black communities.

Conservative, market-based policies have not empowered, nor are they likely to empower, poor black citizens. The self-help/empowerment discourse and punitive policy agenda have been easily extended into the Clinton era. Under the guise of "empowering" the poor and promoting "new social contract" policies such as welfare reform, the Clinton administration expects impoverished blacks to ask less of the state and to do more for themselves with still less. Welfare reform is meant to punish recipients further by forcing them to take low-pay, no-benefit jobs or do "community service" in exchange for their meager checks. As Clinton backs off public investment in the name of deficit reduction, hopes for an arresting of black urban decline recede. Under a black conservative self-help agenda or a Clintonesque neoliberal, social responsibility agenda, the black urban poor will remain poor.

Under the guise of black privatism, new forms of social control have been implemented—to be used when the billions invested in law enforcement cannot protect corporate and suburban property and crime affects more than the random nonblack victim. The one-note response of more police and more prisons, antidrug campaigns, and "stop the violence" moral appeals to a black community in crisis is predictable and woefully misguided. When the possibility of local autonomy and control is severely circumscribed by the mobility of capital and the abdication of the federal government, blacks are repeatedly told to look to themselves for help. The focus on intermediate institutions to serve as moral and spiritual rehabilitation is a cruel hoax for people bereft of basic resources. A new generation of grassroots leaders are being force-fed self-help ideology in order to become more flexible enforcers of black subordination.

Given the historical and structural reasons that I have discussed, self-help initiatives that stress individual, voluntarist, or predominantly market-based solutions cannot empower the black urban poor. Black conservatives have tried to gain political recognition by fashioning an agenda for the black poor. But their phony populism and bankrupt policies are an excuse to withdraw even more resources from the black community, ultimately hurting the very people who are least able to defend themselves.

11

The Crisis of the Black Male: A New Ideology in Black Politics

Willie M. Legette

In the early 1980s, the alleged "crisis of the black male" emerged as a major thesis in public discourse about black life. Journalists, elected officials, scholars, and black spokespersons from various ideological persuasions now focus explicitly on the status of black males as the most significant problem in the black community and have labeled them an endangered species. The perception of a unique crisis among black males has become a standard prop in policymaking elites' discussions of poverty among black Americans. This notion's rapid ascent to consensual understanding is significant, particularly given its inadequacies.

The plight of black men is indeed distressing, and on first impression the present focus may seem justified. However, close examination yields a different conclusion. In this chapter I argue that the crisis-of-the-black-male thesis is an ideology in black politics. It is an interpretation placed on black life that serves the political interests of black men. I conceptualize this ideology as black manhood ideology, which refers not only to the crisis-of-the-black-male thesis, but also to the broader context of black politics and public discourse that rests on patriarchal assumptions. It refers to the emerging consensus that social and economic problems in the black community are the result of black men not being able to perform the roles expected of men in a patriarchal society.

America's beliefs about manhood have played a significant role in the shaping of institutions, symbols, and social and power relations. Manhood is generally understood not only in terms of its social setting, but also in terms of its contrast with womanhood.[1] Thus, the struggle for black equality has been influenced by a traditional understanding of manhood. Black manhood ideology gives political and policy preferences to black men and disregards the needs and equally distressing plight of black women, is sexist and part of an antifeminist backlash that targets black women, approaches gender disparities in the black community as if they were unique or problematic simply because they do not exactly mirror gender disparities in the white community, dovetails with the conservative trend of defining the problems in the black community as culturally induced, and proposes policies to modifying the behavior of black Americans, particularly the black dispossessed.

Public Discourse and Support for the Crisis-of-the-Black-Male Thesis

The issue of black manhood was articulated in the 1960s by Black Power advocates and black nationalists. They incorporated Daniel Patrick Moynihan's contemptuous report, *The Negro Family: A Case for National Action,* into the movement. Moynihan's report was racist and male centered. It attempted to explain racial inequality not within the context of a racist socioeconomic system, but in terms of the behavior of the black poor. He argued that the black community suffered from a "tangle of pathology" and that at the center was "the weakness of family structure."[2] According to Moynihan, the core of the problem was that the black community had "been forced into a matriarchal structure which . . . seriously retards the progress of the group as a whole, and imposes a crushing burden on the Negro male."[3] Thus, the issue of matriarchy shaped the nationalist and Black Power movements. The struggle against racism was equivalent to a struggle for black manhood. Black Power groups in the 1960s asserted the need for black male-dominated leadership and conventional sexual division of labor within black organizations and the family.[4]

The legal equality of women was not a significant issue during the civil rights movement or the early years of the implementation of the 1964 Civil Rights Act. Most black women saw race, not gender, as paramount in determining their life chances. Therefore, they did not devote much time to gender issues. Generally, black women viewed the women's movement with disdain and distrust.[5] Therefore, in the 1960s and 1970s the "woman question" among black activists was limited to the role of women in the civil rights and Black Power movements. Gender became a significant issue among black women activists only when race no longer served as a sufficient explanation for the life chances of black women. In the late 1970s and early 1980s, black women began to organize around race and gender issues. They also experienced social mobility as a result of the civil rights movement and the women's movement.

The crisis-of-the-black-male thesis can be viewed as a response to the entrance of black women into positions denied them before the civil rights and women's rights movements. Thus, it is not by happenstance that the crisis-of-the-black-male thesis emerged in the 1980s. It was a direct response to black feminism. The rise of black feminist consciousness challenged the working assumption that black men would be the major beneficiaries of racial inclusion. It would indeed seem hollow to articulate the crisis-of-the-black-male thesis if black women were not conspicuously present in positions from which they had been excluded during racial segregation. Black male spokespersons now find it necessary to state explicitly their claims and demand that black males have primacy. Floyd Weatherspoon argues in the *Washburn Law Journal* that "the deplorable status of African-American males in the labor market and in the workplace is the result of stereotypical biases and a combination of race plus sex discrimination directed at African-American male applicants and employees."[6] As a legal solution to discrimination against black males, he calls for "a race plus sex model of discrimination."[7]

Proponents of the crisis-of-the-black-male thesis have been able to influence public opinion and policymaking elites regarding the special needs of black males with a number of national reports delineating the status of black males. These reports detail black males' "declining college enrollments; increasing joblessness, even among high school graduates; disproportionate numbers of black male perpetrators and victims of interpersonal violence; excess morbidity and mortality; and escalating rates of substance abuse, homicide, and suicide"[8] These reports, to empirically validate their claims, also contain an array of statistics comparing black and white males. From these reports, one may conclude that black men "have emerged as one of the most troubled segments of American society. By virtually every index, they suffer disproportionately from poverty, academic failure, social and economic isolation, and health-related problems."[9] Clifford Watson and Geneva Smitherman assert that the black male crisis drains the "resources of the nation."[10]

In 1989, at the Black Women's Political Action Forum, Louis Sullivan, then secretary of health and human resources, declared that "more than ever . . . black males urgently require the nurturing and support of the black community." In 1991, John E. Jacob, then of the National Urban League, asserted, "The African American community as a whole must become empowered in the preservation and advancement of the African American male."[11] In 1996, Kweisi Mfume, president and chief executive officer of the National Association for the Advancement of Colored People (NAACP), stated that the organization must address the problem facing black men. According to Mfume, the NAACP must "take the lead in speaking forcefully and meaningfully and arguing in their [black men's] best interest . . . because that is the right thing to do."[12] It is his view that the NAACP can play a role in making the government sensitive to the needs of black males.

Specialists have emerged in the field who conduct workshops in urban areas on the black male crisis. National organizations such as the National Urban League, the Congress of National Black Churches, the Southern Christian Leadership Conference, the Alpha Phi Alpha Fraternity, the NAACP, and the Congressional Black Caucus, as well as scores of local groups, began in the 1980s to emphasize the plight of black males. In 1984, the Urban League Research Department published *Running The Gauntlet: Black Men in America*. The *Black Collegian* dedicated 1991 to those programs that were "actively and positively reclaiming the African American male."[13] The Urban League sponsored several conferences on the status of black males. The black think tank the Joint Center for Political and Economic Studies held a conference in January 1993 entitled "Reclaiming Our Youth: Challenges to Black Male Development." Ronald B. Mincy listed twenty-three national organizations, forty-three community-based organizations, and thirteen school-based or school-linked programs as "programs that serve young black males."[14]

Local, state, and national commissions have been established to address the status of black males. In 1989, Governor Richard F. Celeste established the Governor's Commission on Socially Disadvantaged Black Males in "response to a very real and growing crisis facing African Americans males in Ohio."[15] The Twenty-first Century Commission on African American Males, perhaps the most important and prestigious commission to emerge, was organized in 1991. Chaired by Governor Doug Wilder of Virginia, with Senator Terry Sanford of North Carolina as honorary chairperson, this commission intended to "better the status and destiny of black males in this country."[16] With a prestigious list of elected officials, scholars, corporate, foundation, and civic leaders, the commission claimed to assist Congress in developing a national policy "for addressing the black male crisis."[17]

In 1992, the Kellogg Foundation established the National Task Force on African-American Males. By May 1996, the Kellogg Foundation had awarded more than $11 million in grants for thirty-two projects across the country to improve the opportunities of "black males at risk" and to help "African American men and boys achieve and succeed."[18] Andrew Young, former U.N. ambassador and former Atlanta mayor, served as the task force chairman. In 1996, the task force presented a report on the status of black males entitled *Repairing the Breach: Key Ways to Support Family Life, Reclaim Our Streets, and Rebuild Civil Society in America's Communities.* The report declared that black males were facing "disproportionate risks and challenges . . . from violence, drug use, high rates of HIV infections, joblessness," and alienation.[19] To counter these problems, the task force made recommendations to promote black business development, modify the behavior of black boys, and change the negative images of black males. The task force, guided by black self-help ideology, asserted that blacks must assume "the primary responsibility for leading efforts that will repair the breaches in our social order."[20] The task force report implied that poverty in black communities is separate from the broader context of American political economy. It proposed the development of "a parallel economy within communities" that would "focus on local entrepreneurship, local investment in local businesses, local purchasing of locally-produced goods and services, and local hiring of local workers."[21]

Black churches throughout the country sponsor black manhood training and other programs to address the black male crisis. These churches have intensified efforts to recruit black men and persuade black women to assume a subordinate role in the family.[22] Reverend T. Garrott Benjamin Jr., pastor of Light of the World Christian Church in Indianapolis, stated that "the black male has not only abandoned the church, but he has also left the family as we have traditionally known it. . . . The church has failed because it has presented a female program to men who are basically looking for a way to build and express their manhood."[23]

In November 1995, Trusted Partners, a black Christian men's group, convened its first meeting in Atlanta. Reverend Dr. Henry J. Lyons was the founder of Trusted Partners and president of the National Baptist Convention USA. Trusted Partners wants to change the mind-set and social conditions of the endangered black male. Black men who attended the Trusted Partners conference were asked to go to their local churches and "spread the message of responsibility." Trusted Partners believes that black single mothers are incapable of parenting black boys, which is typical of black manhood ideology. Therefore, each member is required to mentor at least two black male youths who are being raised by single mothers.[24]

Congress embraced the crisis-of-the-black-male thesis. In 1991, "The Plight of African American Men in Urban America" was the topic of a congressional hearing. Testifying before this hearing, Doug Wilder proclaimed that, although black males have "extreme difficulty staying clear of the law and making a future for themselves through honest work, all too many are having no problem whatsoever making babies."[25] Wilder advised black males to establish a life goal "of self-discipline, self-improvement, an abiding spirit of selflessness, and a willingness to work for the common good of family and community alike."[26] It is only then, the former governor suggested, that black men could take "advantage of all opportunities, which do exist, and make full use of the freedoms that are rightly theirs."[27]

At the congressional hearing, Senator Jim Sasson of Tennessee remarked: "Black males need to be prepared for the work force and for participation in society. This means we need to intervene early in the lives of black males to instill the work ethic and family."[28] John Shelby, Republican senator from Alabama, made a similar point, stating:

> I believe we must intervene, early, to keep black males in school by providing strong role models and stressing academic achievement and dis-

> cipline and values. . . . Teachers must develop instructional programs to accommodate the black child who often has very different needs. . . . If we provide this special assistance to the black male child, I believe he will not be . . . in jail or on parole or on probation. . . . Early intervention should improve employment opportunities for black males. . . . Finally, if we provide the role models, discipline and values needed by the black male child, I believe that he will want to be a husband and a father to his children.[29]

The plight of black males has been the focus of a multitude of other conferences and workshops. These black male conferences have in attendance noted political officials, scholars, and black leaders representing the spectrum in black politics. These conferences and workshops are sponsored by many large foundations and public and private institutions.[30] They reveal the underlying ideology with such themes as "Preparing Black Youth for Manhood" and such panel topics as "Responsibility: The Basis of Manhood."[31] In 1990, the National Council of African American Men was formed as an umbrella organization "devoted exclusively to resolving the problems and increasing the life options of young African American men."[32] The first volume of its journal, *Journal of African American Men,* was published in summer 1995.

Many historically black colleges and universities (HBCU) are now sponsoring programs designed to specifically address the social and academic status of black males. Morgan State University has the Center for Educating African American Males. On March 15 and 16, 1990, Morehouse College held the "First National Meeting on the Status of Black Men in America" to inaugurate the Morehouse Research Institute (MRI). The institute receives funding from the Ford and Rockefeller Foundations to conduct research on the status of black males. MRI publishes a journal entitled *Challenge: A Journal of Research on Black Males.*

In 1992, sixteen historically black colleges and universities led by Central State University of Wilberforce, Ohio, created the Consortium for Research and Practicum for Minority Males (MIN-MALES). The Department of Health and Human Services' Office of Minority Health awarded the consortium a $4.34 million grant for the first year of a three-year research project. During the second year of the project, the consortium received $5.9 million to develop "A Series of HBCU Models to Prevent Minority Male Violence." LeMoyne-Owen College developed a research project entitled *The Policy Connection: An Assessment of Public Policies That Impact Youth and Violence and Gang Behavior*. Voohees College has a project called *An Evaluation Study of Strategies to Prevent Violence in Rural Bamberg County*. By improving "the situation of Black males through a series of comprehensive grassroots methods, the MIN-MALES Consortium hopes ultimately to strengthen black family units."[33]

In 1988, Concerned Black Men launched Project 2000 with the objective of providing black male role models for black boys in elementary schools in the Baltimore area. The project encouraged and sometimes trained black men as part-time teacher aides and tutors. Project 2000 expanded to urban centers throughout the country. The 100 Black Men of Detroit launched its Big Brother program to "combat the problems confronting Black male students in the public schools."[34]

Men Against Destruction—Defending Against Drugs and Social Disorder, founded in Omaha in 1989, is one of the most popular community-based organizations providing services for black males. In 1995, there were forty-two chapters in forty-two cities. According to its founder, Eddie Staton, American society needs "fathers everywhere to do a better job of nurturing and caring for our kids."[35] He justifies black role models by stating, "Sometimes as black boys . . . we think we have to be pimps, a hustler or a gang-banger to be somebody. We need models who are respected as well as consistent in their behavior."[36] Furthermore, he states, "we're trying to show black men in our community doing good things."[37]

Henry Louis Gates, director of the African American Studies Institute at Harvard University, wrote in the catalog for the Whitney Museum's "Black Male" exhibit that "every forty-six seconds of the school day, a black child drops out of school, every ninety-six seconds a black boy is born into poverty, and every four hours of every day in the year a black young adult is murdered."[38] Thus, he concluded, "the much discussed crisis of the black male is no idle fiction."[39] A national survey conducted by political scientist Michael Dawson found that 40 percent of black Americans believe that "black men are endangered and their problems deserve special attention."[40] Thus, a number of programs have been initiated to address the needs of black males. These include education and job-training programs that match young black males with black male adult role models, rites-of-passage programs aimed at preparing young black males for manhood, and the creation of all black male schools.

The Call for All Black Male Schools

The call for all black male schools or classes to address exclusively the social and academic needs of black male youths is a concrete public policy consequence of the crisis-of-the-black-male thesis. All black male schools or classes have been proposed and/or implemented in Milwaukee, Miami, Baltimore, San Diego, Philadelphia, Washington, D.C., Chicago, New York City, Detroit, Brooklyn, Norfolk, and smaller cities throughout the country. The all black male schools, according to proponents, grew out of the "survival crisis and endangered status of African-American males."[41] Some of these schools allow any student to apply, but they are geared toward the perceived needs of black males, with an emphasis on black history and culture. Proponents suggest that the schools are necessary to confront American racism and inject an "Afrocentric perspective" or an "Afrocentric cultural ideology" into black male youths.

The Afrocentric perspective rests on the assumption that the problems in the black community are cultural and attitudinal, a view shared by conservative social scientists and many liberals. Thus, the all black male schools with an Afrocentric perspective are designed to rectify the "cultural crisis" in the black community. From this perspective, the all black male academies embrace an ideology similar to that of black female schools of the early 1900s, which sought to assimilate blacks into American society by altering their behavior and personality.[42]

Black male schools, as William Oliver suggests in his argument for Afrocentric institutions, would

> encourage Black Americans to transcend cultural crisis and confusion by reclaiming traditional African values. . . . To facilitate the internalization of an Afro-centric cultural ideology or world view among young black males, blacks must restructure their primary institutions to insure that black males will internalize Afrocentric values. Afrocentric socialization is a much better option than continuing to allow substantial numbers of lower and working class black boys to make the passage from boyhood to manhood under the tutelage of men who define manhood in terms of toughness, sexual conquest, and thrill-seeking.[43]

Those who advocate the all black male schools do not indicate why an Afrocentric perspective or ideology is good for black males but not equally good for black females. A closer examination of the justification for the schools reveals that it is not only the Afrocentric perspective that drives this effort or a concern limited to the academic performance of black boys. These schools are also driven by an antifeminist and black manhood ideology. They want to ensure that black boys represent the bourgeois patriarchal model of manhood. Courtland Lee, professor of counselor education at the University of Virginia and former editor of the *Journal of African American Men*, advocates a secondary school curriculum for black males and relates the impediments to the development of black male adolescents to the crisis of black manhood:

> Historically, manhood has not been a birthright for black males, who have not generally been granted traditionally masculine privilege or power in the United States. Social, cultural, and economic forces manifested in racism and oppression throughout American history have combined to keep black males from assuming traditionally accepted masculine roles. The persistence of such barriers to the achievement and expression of manhood has contributed to black males' failure, in many instance, to master crucial adolescent developmental tasks.[44]

One advocate of black male schools states that "the most obvious psychosocial deficits in the environment of inner-city Black boys is the lack of consistent, positive, literate, Black male role models. . . . I suggest that the creation of all-male kindergarten through third grade classes, taught by male teachers (preferably Black), may overcome many inner-city boys' negative attitudes toward education."[45] The central problems in education, according to the proponents of the black male schools, are a lack of "adequate parenting" and insufficient positive black male role models for black boys.[46] They believe that women suppress the inherent aggressiveness of black males and are too weak to impose discipline on black boys. Na'im Akbar, clinical psychologist at Florida State University and a proponent of the black male crisis, reports in the *Washington Post* that female "teachers overreact to the assertiveness and aggressiveness of young black males. . . . They demand passivity, non-assertiveness, reflectiveness, and non-challenging posture, all the qualities that have been traditionally associated with women."[47] Black boys accordingly "view academic activities as feminine" and thus do not perform well.[48] Psychologists Ivory L. Toldson and Alfred B. Pasteur share this view and find problematic psychological testing that suggests formal education points males toward "stereotypically feminine interests."[49] According to this perspective, the poor academic performance of black males is best viewed as a form of resistance to the "feminization of education." Toldson and Pasteur conclude:

> As a hedge against being turned into women, many black males, who experience schooling as such, resist the educational process. The resistance often reflects the models to which they aspire. The feminization of education with a preponderance of female teachers, particularly during the early years, may well set many males, particularly those who are without adequate male models at home, to treat their female teachers with the same disrespect with which they treat their mothers. The prominence that this holds in the [psyche] of many black males is to no small degree.[50]

Spencer Holland, an educational psychologist and director of the Center for Educating African American Males at Morgan State University, asserts: "We have a stake in educating and socializing our children. But, if we really expect to see a change in the current situation, men have to get involved in this process, because it takes a Black man to prepare a Black boy for whatever he's going to face out there."[51] According to Holland, black boys reject females as "role models, because women cannot provide realistic examples of survival outside of home and school."[52] Robert Holt of Milwaukee claims that black male schools would provide black boys "coping skills necessary to merge into the broader pluralistic society and to deal with racism and some of the things he will confront as a Black man."[53]

Wilder specifically blames black mothers for the poor academic performance of black boys. He remarks: "The responsibilities of being a parent often fall on financially and emotionally deserted mothers. . . . In many of these homes there is a disturbing double standard between what is expected of male and female children. Girls are expected to do household chores, adhere to curfews, and succeed academically. Boys, on the other hand, have little discipline, less responsibility and lenient curfews, if any, imposed upon them."[54] Thus, public schools with mostly female teachers "compound an already calamitous situation" because these schools are "devoid of adult male role models" for black boys.[55]

Insofar as the male schools are intended to compensate for the supposedly debilitating effect of black single mothers, who cannot prepare black males for masculine roles in American society, they are descendants of Daniel Moynihan's report, which blamed black mothers for imposing "a crushing burden on the Negro male." In Moynihan's view, the solution was to remove black males from the black "matriarchal family" and place them in an all-masculine world, the military. Moynihan's proposal came, interestingly, just as the first big expansion of the Vietnam War created a cannon fodder shortage. He and Defense Secretary Robert McNamara devised a joint response to serve their respective concerns, Project 100,000, which sought to funnel young men from inner cities into the armed forces. Moynihan reported: "There is a . . . special quality about military service for Negro men: it is an utterly masculine world. Given the strains of the disorganized and matriarchal family life in which so many Negro youth come of age, the Armed Forces are a dramatic and desperately needed change: a world away from women, a world run by strong men of unquestioned authority."[56] Like Moynihan, proponents of the all black male schools want to give black boys a masculine world away from the supposedly crushing burden of black mothers and female teachers.

The gravity of black manhood ideology that drives proposals for all black male schools prevents advocates from addressing the equally distressing academic performance of black girls with the same force and determination used in addressing the needs of black boys. In this regard, Milwaukee serves as a good example. In January 1990, the Milwaukee Public Schools' (MPS) Board of Directors assembled a task force to study the needs of black male students. The task force reviewed issues relevant to both genders of black students. The problems of black male students were validated, and the task force discovered "the existence of parallel problems for African American females."[57] It concluded that the "educational experiences of female African American students further substantiated the necessity for immediate substantive changes in MPS policies and practices as they affected African American students of both genders."[58]

Nevertheless, Milwaukee school board member Joyce Mallory argued, "When you look at the data, it doesn't take a genius to figure out that the system is failing Black boys."[59] Bell Middle School's principal, Kenneth Holt (who also chaired the committee that proposed all black male schools in Milwaukee), added, "We need to explore a different, more supportive system for African American males to learn in, because in the present system they're being destroyed."[60] Indeed, the Milwaukee school board was one of the first in the country to focus attention on black male students.

Proponents of the black male schools do not call into question the "savage inequality" of the American educational system. This partly explains former President George Bush's endorsement of the schools.[61] According to Rosemary L. Bray, many observers in Detroit believe a proposed male academy "has been helped by a cynical alliance between local black Republicans with a taste for higher political office and white conservatives, who see in the plan an opportunity to push for a voucher program to provide choice for the public schools."[62] The black male schools are certainly compatible with school vouchers advocated by conservative Republicans.

Black male schools and classes have been charged with violating the 1964 Civil Rights Act and at least the sprit, if not the letter, of *Brown* v. *Board of Education* (1954).[63] In Dade County, Florida, after a year of a pilot program called At-Risk All Male Classes, the Department of Education's Office of Civil Rights ruled that the program violated the 1964 Civil Rights Act. The program was disbanded early in its second year. In *Garrett* v. *Board of Education,* a federal district court ruled on the constitutionality of black male academies. The city of Detroit's Board of Education had approved the establishment of three black male academies: Marcus Garvey, Paul Robeson, and Malcolm X. Before these academies were opened in the fall of 1991, the American Civil Liberties Union and the National Organization for Women's Legal Defense and Education Fund filed a sexual discrimination suit on behalf of three black female students; the suit requested an injunction to prevent the schools from opening and a preliminary injunction preventing the Detroit Board of Education from excluding girls from the academies. According to the district court, the exclusion of females from public schools violated the Fourteenth Amendment's equal protection clause unless it could be shown that the sex-based programs served important state objectives and that the discriminatory means used were necessary to achieve those objectives. The plaintiffs insisted that black female students were as badly off as black male students. According to the district court summary, the plaintiffs argued

> that the male academies improperly use gender as a "proxy for other, more germane bases of classification," . . . in this instance, for "at risk" students. Specifically, the gender specific data presented in defense of the Academies ignores the fact that all children in the Detroit public schools face significant obstacles to success. In fact, in its resolution establishing the Academies, the Board acknowledged the "equally urgent and unique crisis facing . . . female students." Urban girls drop out of school, suffer loss of self esteem and become involved in criminal activity. Ignoring the plight of urban females institutionalizes inequality and perpetuates the myth that females are doing well in the current system.[64]

The court ruled that the school district had failed to demonstrate how the exclusion of female students from the academies was necessary to combat the problems facing black males. Furthermore, the court ruled that the school system was failing black females as well. Federal judge George Woods granted the injunction and ordered the Detroit Board of Education to work out a compromise with the American Civil Liberties Union and the National Organization for Women. The board agreed to admit a token number of female students to what were termed "African-centered academies." However, the actions on the part of the federal courts and the Department of Education's Civil Rights Office have not tempered the trend toward providing gender-based education for black male students. In February 1994, at least 90 percent of the students enrolled in the three academies in Detroit were black males.[65]

In addressing the issue of all black male schools, Kenneth Clark sums the matter up best when he states: "I read about these things and I can't believe that we are actually regressing like this. . . . This is contrary to everything that we are fighting against and everything that the research says about the benefits of learning Black and White, male and female together. Even military schools today are coeducational. So why are we talking about segregation and stigmatizing?"[66] In another context he observes, "For adults to impose this nonsense on children is academic child abuse."[67] One study found that black male students' grades in single-sex classes classroom were no better than the grades of students in regular classes. The author concludes this may be a "reflection of the economic and sociopolitical conditions that exist in America's cities."[68]

Race, Gender, and Academic Performance

The conservative and antifeminist posture underpinning the schools is clear, but is there legitimate empirical basis for a particular emphasis on black male students? How does their status compare with that of black females and with other racial/gender groups? Gender disparities with respect to students below the modal grade, performance on standardized tests, and high school dropout rate are roughly similar across racial groups. However, the most troubling disparity is clearly between blacks and whites, not between black males and black females.

Male students are more likely to fall below the modal grade than are female students of their respective race or ethnic group. Black students are more likely to be below the modal grade than are white students. As students get older, a higher percentage fall below the modal grade. However, the disparity between black males and white males is about the same in each age group, as is the disparity between black females and white females. For instance the percentage of fifteen- to seventeen-year-old black females and black males below the modal grade was 10 and 11 percentage points higher than that of their white gender counterparts, respectively. The noted exception is the twelve to fourteen age group. The same pattern exists for Hispanics as well. (See Table 11.1.)

TABLE 11.1 Percent of Students One or More Years Below Modal Grade, by Race/Ethnicity and Gender, 1995

	Black		*White*		*Hispanic*	
Age	*Male*	*Female*	*Male*	*Female*	*Male*	*Female*
6–8	18.8	14.8	20.5	14.7	11.4	17.5
9–11	31.2	23.6	28	21.6	31.1	20.6
12–14	45	30.9	33.4	24.8	42.4	34.5
15–17	47.5	34.6	36.5	25	47.6	39.5

SOURCE: Bureau of the Census, *Current Population Survey,* Internet Release, June 1997.

Males perform better than females on many standardized tests; similarly, black males perform better than black females. A two-year study of SAT scores found that the SAT was biased against females and hampered the educational opportunities for black women.[69] In 1992, black males scored 19 points higher than black females on the SAT, while males in general scored 52 points higher than did females. However, white students scored 196 points higher than did black students. Students' performance on national reading and mathematics examinations reveals a similar pattern. Female students perform better than males on reading examinations, and generally black and white male students perform better than females on math examinations. Hispanic females outperform males on math examinations. However, for math and reading for each grade level black students score significantly lower than white students (see Tables 11.2 and 11.3).

TABLE 11.2 1994 National Reading Assessments Proficiency Means

	Black		*White*		*Hispanic*	
Grade	*Male*	*Female*	*Male*	*Female*	*Male*	*Female*
12	258	269	286	301	262	276
8	229	243	260	274	233	247
4	180	194	219	228	185	196

NOTE: The scores are based on a scale from 0 to 500.

SOURCE: U.S. Department of Education, National Center for Education Statistics, Office of Educational Research and Improvement (Washington, D.C.: U.S. Department of Education, September 1996).

TABLE 11.3 1992 National Math Assessments Proficiency Means

	Black		*White*		*Hispanic*	
Grade	*Male*	*Female*	*Male*	*Female*	*Male*	*Female*
12	276	273	307	298	200	201
8	236	236	277	277	245	247
4	191	189	228	219	280	284

NOTE: The scores are based on a scale from 0 to 500.

SOURCE: U.S. Department of Education, National Center for Education Statistics, Office of Educational Research and Improvement (Washington, D.C.: U.S. Department of Education, September 1996).

Studies by the National Center for Education Statistics have found that across racial groups, girls have better academic records than boys and boys are generally less willing to submit to classroom discipline than are girls.[70] Myra Sadker and David Sadker summarize the differences between boys' and girls' performance in this way:

> Labeled as problems in need of special control or assistance, boys are more likely to fail a course, miss promotion, or drop out of school. Prone to take risks, they jeopardize not only their academic future but their lives as they dominate accident, suicide, and homicide statistics. In fact, because the educational failures of boys are so visible and public, schools invest extra resources on their behalf, and yet the catastrophic results continue. Girls suffer silent losses, but boys' problems are loud enough to he heard throughout the school.[71]

Studies also demonstrate that black female students indeed "suffer silent losses." The Sadkers find that the students "most likely to receive teacher attention were white males; followed by minority males, white females and then minority females."[72] Jacqueline Jordan Irvine finds that black girls in the higher elementary grades receive less academic feedback from teachers than do black boys.[73]

On national tests administered in 1990, only 48.7 percent of black thirteen-year-olds had mastered basic problem solving in mathematics, compared with 82 percent of white students and 55 percent of Hispanics. Moreover, only 3.9 percent of black thirteen-year-olds had mastered moderately complex procedures and reasoning in mathematics, compared with 21 percent of white students and 6.4 percent of Hispanics.[74] There is also about a four-year gap in reading abilities between blacks and whites with the same number of years of education. The major point is that blacks, both male and female, earn lower grades, score below the national average on standardized tests, and are much more likely to be suspended or expelled from school because of discipline problems than are white students.[75]

These studies and test scores indicate that the gender disparities among black students are common to all groups in American society and that black males do not suffer from problems that uniquely set them apart from black females. Disparity between black male and female academic performance is insignificant when both groups are doing poorly and their constraints are the same: racism, economic deprivation, and class inequalities. The American educational system reproduces these constraints. Public schools have failed to educate black and poor children. The focus on black male students and on efforts to create black male schools obscures this basic reality by centering attention on the allegedly peculiar gender characteristics of a segment of the larger population that is ill-served by the educational system.

Race, Gender, and Educational Attainment

The relatively low educational attainment of black men is constantly cited as an indication of the black male crisis. The Census Bureau publishes two statistics on high school dropout rates: the proportion of twenty-five- to twenty-nine-year-olds who have dropped out of high school and the proportion of sixteen- to twenty-four-year-olds who have dropped out of high school. My evaluation concentrates on the latter group because it represents current trends and is the main focal population of the crisis-of-the-black-male thesis regarding educational attainment.

Since 1970, the dropout rates among black males and black females have been declining at a faster rate than those of white males and white females. From 1970 to 1996, the dropout rates declined from 29.4 to 13.5 percent and from 26.6 to 12.5 percent for black males and black females, respectively. During this period, white females' and white males' dropout rates declined by 6.8 and 4.9 percent, respectively. Hispanics had comparatively high dropout rates and smaller declines, of 3.4 and 6.6 percent for Hispanic males and females, respectively. It is worth noting, given the emphasis placed on black males, that black females were the only female group for whom decline in dropout rates over this period was lower than that for the males within their race/ethnic group.

The data show that there are race and gender patterns in dropout rates. Whites are less likely to drop out than blacks or Hispanics. Males are more likely to drop out than are females. Nevertheless, the differences between male and female dropout rates within race/ethnic groups are insignificant. Thus, like all other groups, black male and female dropout rates—except in 1982—have been about the same. Therefore, the response of black males to the school systems seems not to be different from that of black females (see Figure 11.1). Comparison of high school dropout rates by race/ethnicity and gender

FIGURE 11.1 Percent of High School Dropouts Among Persons Sixteen to Twenty-four, by Gender and Race/Ethnicity, 1970–1996, Selected Years

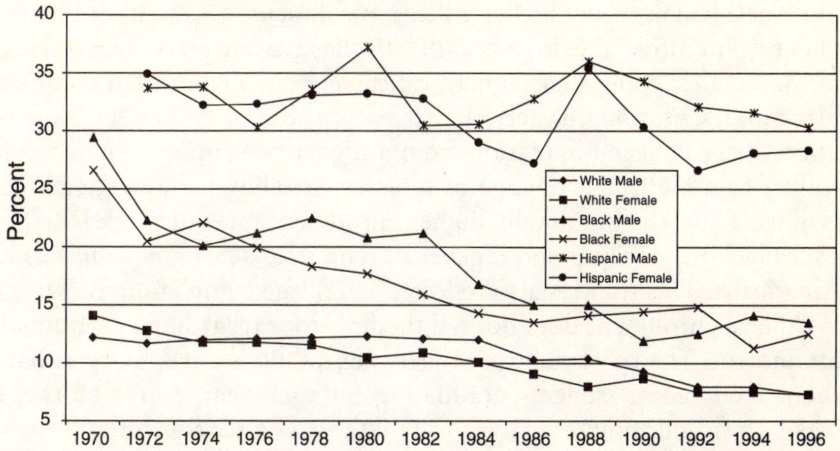

SOURCE: U.S. Department of Education, National Center for Education Statistics, *Digest of Education Statistics 1997* (Washington, D.C.: U.S. Department of Education, 1997).

shows substantial differences between race and ethnic groups but not between gender within groups.

The declining college enrollment rates of black males during the late 1970s and 1980s are frequently cited in delineations of the black male crisis.[76] This focus on black males gives the impression that the college enrollment rates of black males are significantly lower than the enrollment rates of black females, thus implying that black males need special attention. Is the disparity between the college enrollment rates of black males and black females sufficient to justify the attention given to black male college enrollment? To answer this question I focus on the college enrollment rates of eighteen- to twenty-four-year-olds. This is generally the focal population of the proponents of the crisis-of-the-black-male thesis and reflects current trends. Because of annual fluctuations in black college enrollment, the issue of gender disparity is best comprehended by looking at college enrollment over several years. The gender disparity then proves to be marginal.

From 1976 to 1988, black male college enrollment rates declined by 10 percent, whereas black female enrollment declined by only

2 percent. Yet black female college enrollment rates remained lower than those of black males for all but three years during this period (see Figure 11.2). In only eight of the twenty-six years from 1970 to 1995 did black females have higher college enrollment rates than did black males. Not until the last decade of these twenty-six years were black females' college enrollment rates generally higher than those of black males. During this period, there was a shift in the gender distribution of the college population from a higher percentage of males enrolling to a higher percentage of females enrolling for all race/ethnic groups. Thus, the marginally higher enrollment rates of black females over black males represents a general trend that is not unique to black Americans. This trend is also reflected in college completion rates.

College enrollment does not tell the full story regarding educational attainment. The percentage of students enrolling is always larger than the percentage of students graduating for each year. Although there was significant annual fluctuation in college completion rates in each

FIGURE 11.2 Percent of High School Graduates Eighteen to Twenty-four Years Enrolled in College, by Gender and Race/Ethnicity, 1970–1995, Selected Years

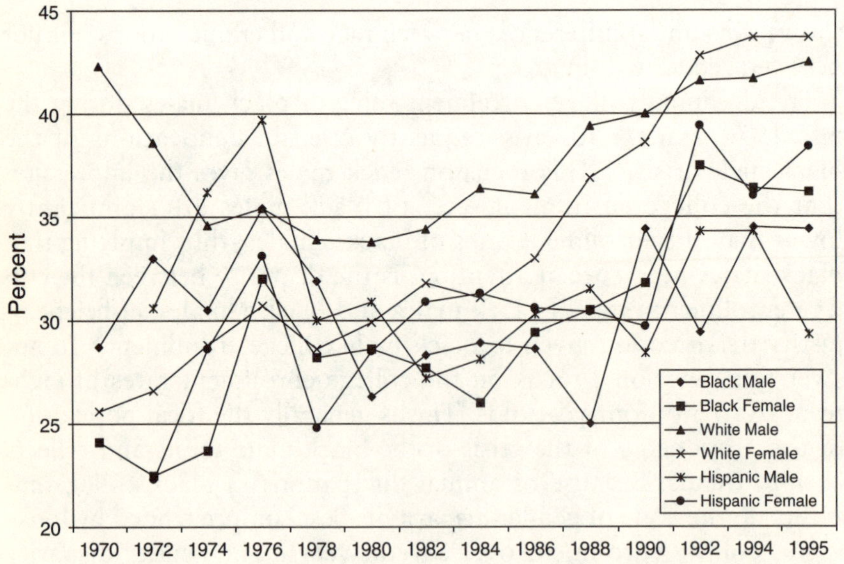

SOURCE: Bureau of the Census, *Current Population Survey,* Internet release http://www.census.gov/population/socdemo/education/tablea-02.txt. April 8, 1998.

group, from 1970 to 1996 there were marginal differences in the percentage of black males and black females completing four years of college or more. In fourteen of these years, black females had higher completion rates than did black males. However, there were only three years in which black female completion rates were between 3 and 4 percent above the completion rates of black males.

A similar gender gap in educational attainment is reflected in the Hispanic population. Among the racial/ethnic groups, only white males' college completion rates were consistently above those of their racial gender counterpart. However, this trend began to change in 1990. Beginning then, younger white women demonstrated higher levels of college attainment than did younger white men. Therefore, as with college enrollment rates, the gender disparities among blacks began to show among whites (see Figure 11.3). Thus, as opportunities

FIGURE 11.3 Percent of Persons Twenty-five to Twenty-nine Years Completing Four Years of College or More, by Gender and Race/Ethnicity, 1970–1996, Selected Years

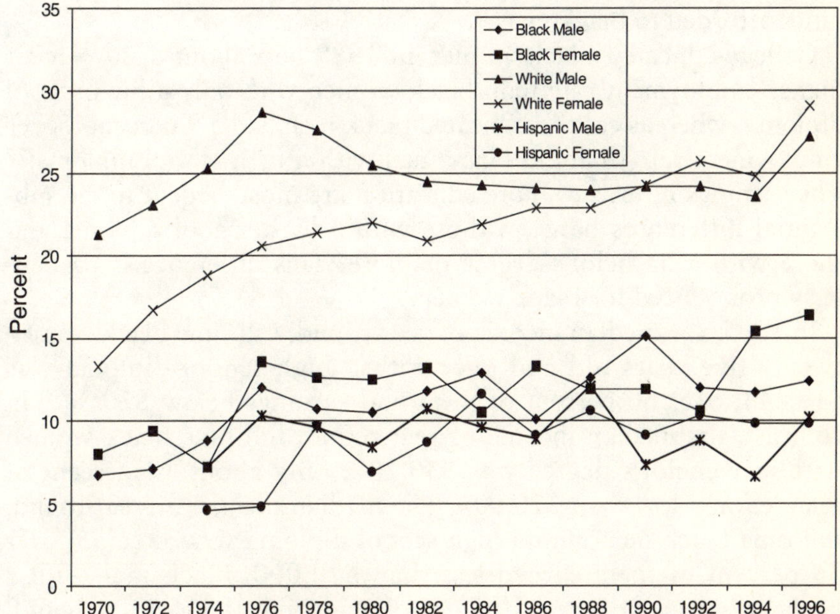

SOURCE: Bureau of the Census, *Current Population Survey,* Internet release http://www.census.gov/population/socdemo/education/tablea-02.txt. April 8, 1998.

open up for women, the black male status seems similar to that of other male groups relative to racial gender counterpart. The problem is not the gender disparity in the black community in educational attainment but the large gap between blacks and whites. The attention to gender detracts from the larger role of racism and economic inequality as factors that circumscribe educational opportunities for all blacks.

Educational Attainment and Income

Two economic incentives for pursuing a college degree are enhanced employment opportunities and higher income possibilities. Based on these incentives, black women have a greater motivation to attain a college education than do black men because of the low status accorded to them with a high school diploma. So their greater educational attainment relative to black men, especially as compared to white females' educational attainment relative to that of white men, is more a function of the limited options available to black women without a college degree than of more limited educational opportunities afforded to black men.

College-educated black women in 1989 had about a 20 percent higher employment rate than black women with only a high school diploma, whereas college-educated black men had a 9 percent higher employment rate than did black men with a high school diploma.[77] The earnings returns to more education are most evident in the substantial differences between those with a high school diploma and those with a bachelor's degree or more. This difference is particularly pronounced for black women.

In 1995, the median income of year-round, full-time black women twenty-five years old and over with a high school diploma was $17,643; over 60 percent of them had earnings below $20,000. In contrast, the median income of year-round, full-time black women with a bachelor's degree was $30,287; only about 19 percent of them earned less than $20,000. The median income of year-round, full-time black men with a high school diploma was $22,555; over 36 percent of them earned less than $20,000. Black men with a bachelor's degree or more had a median income of $36,920; about 8 percent of them earned less than $20,000. The median income of year-round, full-time white women with a high school diploma was

$20,175; about 49 percent of them earned less than $20,000. White women with a bachelor's degree or more had a median income of $34,252; about 13 percent of them earned less than $20,000. In 1995, the median income of year-round, full-time white men twenty-five years old and over with a high school diploma was $30,544; about 22 percent of them had earnings below $20,000. In contrast, the median income of year-round, full-time white men with a bachelor's degree was $50,244; only about 7 percent of them earned less than $20,000. Thus, year-round, full-time working black women make less than black men, white women, and white men with similar educational attainment.[78]

The earnings returns to more education by race and gender groups show not only that black women have a greater incentive to pursue additional education compared to other groups but also that significant race and gender inequality exists between groups with the same level of education. These returns further show that black women suffer from income inequality more than black men do.

Gender and Affirmative Action

The special focus on black males is sometimes justified by the claim that they have achieved less from affirmative action than black women. At a congressional hearing, Senator Carol Moseley-Braun argued that black men had "benefited the least of any group from affirmative action" and that black men are "the segment of the population that has faced the most persistent discrimination, that has encountered the toughest problems, and has had the longest road to travel."[79] Black women are said to have the "double advantage" of being "double counted" as minority and female.

Another explanation given is that white men feel threatened by black men, either because they are more likely to resist racism or because their "demeanor" is less white. A definition of white demeanor is never provided in such explanations, however. Andrew Hacker asserts that black women are hired before black men because they are better able to adapt to white organizations and white authority than can black men. Black men are viewed by white employers as rebels with a "chip on the shoulder."[80] In another context, Hacker writes: "When organizations feel compelled to hire more black workers, they prefer to take on black women rather than black men. Black women are perceived as being less assertive and more accommodating. They hope that black women will show less resentment or hostility, and will be less apt to present themselves as 'black' in demeanor and appearance."[81]

Black males, according to Oliver, "represent the greatest threat to the continued political economic subjugation of blacks."[82] Derrick Bell sees the advantage of black women in terms of both the double count and white fears. He writes: "Affirmative action policy enables institutions to engage in 'double count.' African American women are symbolically less threatening than black males, whose very maleness itself triggers subliminal images of physical retaliation and rage against whites for the historical injury inflicted upon the African American community."[83]

Essence subtitled its 1992 issue on black men *Why White Men Fear Black Men*. Thus, it is white fear of black males that accounts for black women's alleged receipt of the greatest benefits of affirmative action. This implies that black women are more accommodating to racial discrimination than are black men. Not only is this an insult to black women, but it also totally disregards the role of black women in the Afro-American liberation struggle. The notion that the black male is the greatest threat to white domination is nothing more than male machismo or a version of the stereotype of the angry buck. Nevertheless, the argument that black women have benefited from affirmative action more than black men serves the interest of black men. Thus, Weatherspoon maintains that employers should "design recruitment plans that are directed specifically at recruiting African-American males."[84]

Karen Fullbright noted in 1986 that the notion that black women are doubly advantaged is not based on theoretical work or empirical studies because black women have been overlooked in most of these works.[85] However, there is now sufficient empirical work to refute the assertion that black women have benefited more from affirmative action than have black men. A detailed analysis of the transformation of black women, white women, and black men in professional occupations reveals two important facts. One, black women's representation in professional occupations since 1960 has increased at a higher rate than black men's or white women's. Two, black women have not achieved parity in professional occupations with white males, black males, or white females.

Natalie J. Sokoloff conducted a detailed study examining the progress of black women, black men, and white women as they entered the professional ranks between 1960 and 1980. She divided professional occupations into three categories to assess the gains of each group: male dominated, female dominated, and gender neutral. Sokoloff found that black men increased their share from 1.5 to 2.7 percent of male-dominated professions. White women increased their representation in male-dominated professions from 6.2 to 18.1 percent. And black women increased their representation from 0.2 to 1.4 percent.[86]

David A. Cotter et al. studied occupational segregation by gender and the earnings gap in the 1980s. They found that black women had lower relative earnings compared to white men than to white women. They also found that all women improved their occupational position relative to white men, but that black women improved less than white women, reversing the trends of the 1970s. Thus, black women are more segregated from white men in traditional white male-dominated occupations than are white women.[87]

Curlew Thomas and Barbara Thomas investigated occupational segregation to delineate the extent to which black females and black males have achieved occupational parity with white men. They concluded that "a larger proportion of black women than black men would have to change occupational categories to achieve occupational parity with white men."[88] Therefore, black women have gained less than black men or white women in the most desired, white male–dominated professions.

In addition, black women are not doing as well as black men or white women in the gender-neutral professions. For instance, among college professors black women tend to be relegated to the lower and less secure rungs of the faculty ladder. In 1989, only 9.2 percent of black female and 19.3 percent of black male faculty enjoyed the job security and higher pay associated with full and associate professorial ranks in American college and universities. By contrast, 28.2 percent and 59.6 percent of white female and white male faculty held these ranks, respectively.[89] Mary-Christine Phillip reports that black women are more likely than their white women counterparts to earn less money. Black women earned a median $38,712 on eleven-to-twelve-month contracts, compared with $40,254 for white women of similar status.[90]

Black Female-Headed Households and the Status of Black Males

The progress of black women in white-collar occupations in the 1970s and 1980s reflects not the fears of white men, but the changing structure of the American economy. Most jobs created during this period were in services and trades that are dominated by women.[91] Among college-educated women, 19 percent of black women and only 13 percent of white women work in the lower ranks of administrative support and clerical jobs.[92] As victims of a race/gender segregated workforce that is manifested in white-collar occupations, black women are overly represented as dietitians, prekindergarten teachers, social workers, registered nurses, lab technicians, file clerks, typists, keypunch operators, and calculating machine operators.[93] There is evidence that black women are now filling positions left behind by white women as the latter move up the professional occupational hierarchy.[94] According to Julianne Malveaux, black women have less success than white women in moving out of traditional female jobs. She points out that, even though the "quality of work among black women changed, it changed because black women moved from one set of stratified jobs to another, not because they left 'typically' female jobs."[95] The conclusion that Delores P. Aldridge made about a decade ago rings true today: "The need continues to exist for increased stress on providing equal employment and training opportunities for African-American women who cannot afford to get caught up in issues centering around being background figures in deference to African-American men in the world of work. African-American women continue to be plagued by their sex and race, with lines often being blurred as to which is the more damnable."[96]

Emphasis on the status of black males is often linked to the high incidence of poverty among black female-headed households. This perspective supports a view that the solution to poverty among black Americans lies in increasing husband-wife families in the black community. The focus thereby returns to black males. William Julius Wilson has argued that low income and high unemployment rates among black males decrease their marriage potential, thus fueling formation of female-headed households, which are likely to be impoverished.[97] Therefore, his prescription is to increase the employment status of black males as a means to increase their marriageability. William Darity Jr. and Samuel Myers Jr., in the Urban League report of 1992, call for "salvaging" black males to eradicate poverty in the black community.

> As long as young men continue to be marginalized, . . . the prospects for increasing the share of black families with male heads seems remote. . . . Since the culprit in this link remains the deteriorating position of young black males with little training or education beyond high school, the solution must lie in salvaging what otherwise could be a lost generation of men. Failure to reverse the neglect of these disadvantaged members of our communities will only mean that future inequality will be more difficult to eradicate.[98]

The issue for Darity and Myers is the need to create not only two-parent families but also families with black male heads. On the thirtieth anniversary of Martin Luther King's assassination, Jesse Jackson described the contemporary black predicament by stating, "Our men are unemployed and our women husbandless."[99]

The primacy given to men was shown in a reactionary piece in the *New York Times* by Sylvia Ann Hewlett and Cornel West. They argue that a war is being waged against parents by big businesses, government policies, and mass media, with fathers as the main victims. "Fatherhood in particular has been left twisting in the wind by a society intent on other agendas."[100] They assert, without noting the context of gendered wage disparity and discrimination, that men's incomes have been declining at a rate faster than women's. According to these authors, "African-Americans are still living in the shadows of slavery, which demolished the male parental role and dignity and strength that came with it."[101]

What is the male parental role? We can only assume that the role the authors have in mind is the role defined for males in a patriarchal society. Are we to believe that the conditions in which the dispossessed black population lives do not affect the ability of females to parent their children? I suspect that the writers understand that it does. But the real problem for these authors is the fact that poor black women cannot find marriageable black males. They note that the "extraordinary rate of joblessness has led to a drastic fall in the number of black men who can reasonably expect to be married and support their children. There are now only 40 employed black men for every 100 black women."[102] The high unemployment rate of poor black women is not a problem because the presumption is that only men need to work and support their families.

This focus on the marriageability of black males clearly rests on patriarchal assumptions and ensures black males primacy for employment, training, and education. Furthermore, this focus attempts to impose a norm of black women's dependency on black men. The increased independence that middle-class women now derive from increased employment opportunities, which is one result of the women's movement, is not viewed as an appropriate goal for poor black women.

On a practical level, improving the employment status of black men and reconstituting two-parent families do not offer a meaningful solution to the problem of black poverty and inequality, and the former hardly guarantees the latter. Hacker concludes, "Emulating the white family structure would close only about half of the income gap" between black and white families.[103] And Robert Mare and Christopher Winship find that changes in the employment status of black men explain only 20 percent of the decline in their marriage rates since 1960.[104] Moreover, men's "flight from commitment" despite race or class strongly suggests there is little assurance that black men with decent jobs would remain committed to the family. Black women, like white women, have a difficult time actually getting child support when it is awarded, and black women are less likely to be awarded child support than white women. In 1989, only 34.5 percent of black women eligible for child support were awarded it, as compared to 67.5 percent of eligible white women. This is a reflection of the unequal access women have to the necessary resources and knowledge required to successfully pursue child support awards.[105] Focusing on black single female-headed households as a cause of poverty and marriage as a solution helps to maintain a race- and gender-segregated workforce in which black females and black males remain available as cheap labor supply in a market-driven economy. Instead of demanding higher wages for poor working people, the advocates of two-parent families are suggesting that poor people pool their resources through marriage. This serves the interests of those who exploit the poor and does not reduce inequalities.

The issue here is not whether public policy should be geared toward improving the marriageability of black men or whether two-parent families are better than single-parent families. Rather, the issue is whether black poor women are entitled to the fundamental claims of liberal democracy, namely, the means for self-development and human dignity. The well-being of black women and their children should not be dependent upon the goodwill of black men when appropriate public policy could provide black women the opportunity to support themselves and their children.

Largely because the concern is with males, the question of a gender-segregated workforce and its impact on black female poverty never enters the discussion. In 1991, 17.7 percent of black single female householders worked and remained below poverty. The focus on black males diverts attention from feminist agendas that are urgently needed in the black community, such as education and training, equal pay for comparable work, paid maternity leave, and child care. In the 1980s when comparable worth had a high status on the feminist agenda, Malveaux explained why it was important not only for black women but also for the black community as a whole:

> The black community, as well as black women, will accrue gains when comparable worth is implemented. The first gain is an obvious one—the gain from higher black family wages when black women earn equitable pay. Given the large number of black women heading households, the need for black women to earn equitable pay cannot be overstated. But even where there is another household earner, black women's contribution to black family income frequently makes the difference between black family poverty and black family survival.[106]

Gender and Crime

The high percentage of black males who are incarcerated or victims of violent crimes or deaths is the most obvious circumstance of the life of black males that distinguishes their plight from that of black females and the rest of the American population. The American public is constantly reminded that about one-third of young black males are under criminal justice control. The fact is that men are more likely to be victims of violent crime, die of murder, or be incarcerated than are women. However, when black women are compared to white women, the disparities are similar to the disparities between black men and white men. Black men are 5.9 times more likely to be killed than white men, whereas black women are 3.7 times more likely than white women.[107] An important aspect of the crime victimization issue is selection of the salient indicators. Taking homicide as the major indicator, the male crisis advocates stack the deck for their position. If they include rape and domestic violence, then black women look more victimized by crime.

Even though the criminal justice control rates for young black males are high and increasing, from 1989 to 1994 young black females experienced the greatest increase in criminal justice control of the groups studied by Marc Mauer and Tracy Huling. According to their study, black men under criminal justice control increased by 31 percent, whereas black women increased by 78 percent. In contrast, the percentage of white males under criminal justice control increased by 8 percent, whereas the percentage of white females increased by 40 percent. In 1994, 30 percent of black males, 7 percent of white males, 5 percent of black females, and 1.4 percent of white females were under criminal justice control.

Between 1980 and 1992, the number of black females in state or federal prisons increased by 278 percent, whereas the number of black males increased by 186 percent. From 1986 to 1991, the number of black women in state prisons for crimes related to drug offenses increased by 828 percent, from 667 in 1986 to 6,193 in 1991. Black males increased by 429 percent, from 13,974 to 73,932.[108] The problem is that too many black men and women are under criminal justice control; to focus on black males ignores underlying conditions that encourage dispossessed populations to engage in criminal activity.

The disproportionate number of blacks in prison is not simply a matter of blacks committing more crime. It also reflects the race and class bias of the criminal justice system. A plausible explanation for the disparities between blacks and whites under criminal justice control lies within the social, economic, and political circumstances in which the dispossessed black population lives. These disparities are not a reflection of a different value or culture system in the black community. More often, they are the internalization of conventional commodified goals. The difference is that a disproportionate number of blacks are denied the legitimate means of attaining these goals. Crime becomes a means of compensating for denied opportunities. The specific behavior of poor black males may represent their version of masculinity compensating for the humiliations attendant on their dispossessed social status. This behavior does not suggest that black men suffer under constraints that black women do not.

The Million Man March

The Million Man March, called by Louis Farrakhan, was an outgrowth of the crisis of the male thesis and black manhood ideology. Indeed, Louis Farrakhan is the personification of black manhood ideology. The march reflected his agenda for black America. He is an advocate of the principles of black self-help. Fundamentally, black self-help implies that black people are not full citizens with the corollary rights to make demands on the American state. He advocates a patriarchal model for black life. And he largely blames black people for the material conditions in black communities. He feels that black men have not assumed their role as head of the household or public life. The march was "an opportunity for Black men to stand up, assume responsibility and take their rightful place as head of the household" and black public life.[109] In this regard, the march was fueled by two seemingly contradictory motives. On the one hand, it was to counter the racial stereotypes of black men as irresponsible and not fulfilling traditional male roles; on the other hand, black men were to atone for not being responsible and not fulfilling traditional male roles. Adolph Reed Jr. explains this contradiction this way, "A bunch of 'I's gathered to pat themselves on the back for being 'responsible' and to provide a model for those benighted bloods—the 'we' who are really 'they'—who need moral tutelage."[110]

Farrakhan's view regarding the irresponsibility of black men has been documented in his speeches and writings. His Saviours' Day address in April 1995 articulated his views of black men and why the march was called:

> America is troubled today because you [black man] are asleep in the bottom of America. . . . And you have to repent for being so slow in accepting your duty and your responsibility. You have to repent for being the fool, the clown, the buffoon, the pimp, the punk, the hustler. . . . That's why I'm calling on the Black man all over America to stand up like a man and be a man, and let's go to Washington on behalf of our suffering people and say to America: we demand justice. Justice for the poor, justice for the locked out, justice for the weak of the nation. But first we have to atone; we have to repent. So on October 16, 1995

> we are going to call it A Day of Atonement. . . . Atoning for putting our women and children on the front line to fight, bleed and die for our advancement, while we as men stayed at home. Atoning for what we have done to one another to make our communities what they have become, and then accepting our responsibility to do something for self.[111]

This statement is consistent with Farrakhan's view that black people are largely responsible for their own deprivation and that it is not the responsibility of government to reduce racial inequalities and to address the problems in the black community. Farrakhan also believes that black people must atone before making demands on the government. That the rationale for the Million Man March—atonement, responsibility, reconciliation, black male leadership—and Farrakhan's agenda for black people have not been contentious issues in black public discourse is indicative of the victim-blaming consensus that has emerged in black politics and the power of black manhood ideology. The march received popular support because of the growing view among political elites and black intellectuals that the problems in the black community are cultural and behavioral. Fundamentally, the support for the march was the result of the view that the black community suffers from a crisis of manhood.

Olando Patterson explains why the march was needed:

> [There are a] growing number of children born to female children with little or no social or economic support from the biological fathers or any other man, for that matter. The resulting abusive, mal-socialization of children by mothers who were themselves abused and mal-socialized is at the heart of the social and moral chaos in what is called the underclass. The situation is one of complete social anarchy and moral nihilism, reflected in the casual devaluation of human life. . . . Linked to this social and moral catastrophe are the other well-known pathologies. . . . Although government action is needed, solving these problems will take considerably more than changes in government policy. Clearly, the message of the Million Man March was long overdue.[112]

Reverend Joseph Lowery justified his participation by claiming: "Black America is like a house on fire. The crisis is that great. Here's someone I often disagree with, someone I may not even like. But, if the guy says let's put water on the fire, I'm going to help."[113] Peter Grier, writing in the *Christian Science Monitor,* points out that the march was not a drive for political power but a response to a social crisis characterized by a "large majority of African-American households . . . headed by women; deprived of strong male role models."[114] In a similar vein, Richard Majors sees the march as an effort to bring black men together to "reaffirm their commitment to valuing the family and black community" and to debunk the argument made by "Republicans and others saying directly or indirectly that 'black men are shiftless; they won't do anything for themselves.'"[115]

The latter statement by Majors reveals what influenced the high number of middle-class black men to attend the march. They wanted to counter the popular stereotypes of black men as irresponsible. This concern influenced Michael Eric Dyson, director of the Institute of African American Studies at the University of North Carolina: "The peaceful march succeeded in countering various stereotypes of black men—that they are violent, that they are bereft of mainstream values, that they have no interest in spiritual or moral matters, that they blame social structures or blind forces for their problems."[116] The statements by Majors and Dyson reflect the inordinate attention and energy the black petite bourgeoisie invest to counter racial stereotypes rather than developing tough-minded political strategies to improve the material conditions in the black community.

The notion that black people are responsible for the problems in the black community as well as American racism was repeated at the march as Farrakhan told his audience that the "degenerate mind of white supremacy" will come to a "natural death" when black people refrain from criminal and "anti-social behavior" and stop producing "culturally degenerate films and tapes." The objective of the march came through when Farrakhan stated, "Black man clean up . . . and the world will respect and honor you."[117]

The march was more than a day of atonement. Black men did not have to come to the nation's capital to atone or to claim responsibility for the problems in the black community. The march's purpose was to send a powerful political message: The American state is not the appropriate institution to reduce racial inequality, black people are America's problem, and America needs a new black leader who will not burden the state with demands from its black citizens.

Conclusion

The issues addressed in this chapter—the crisis-of-the-black-male thesis, the call for all black male schools, black role models, black male marriageability, the notion that black women benefit more from affirmative action than do black men, and the Million Man March—are all driven and held together by black manhood ideology. These concepts have evolved in a political context defined most of all by governmental rejection of downwardly redistributive policy as a legitimate response to poverty and inequality. This environment favors variants of the view that the constraints surrounding the black community are not lack of opportunity, racial discrimination, and structured economic inequality, but the values and behavior of the black dispossessed. This view is a regurgitation of the "culture-of-poverty" ideology.

The call for black role models is simply another way to give preferences to black middle-class males and to assert the class interests of the black petite bourgeoisie. It is the self-aggrandizement of the black petite bourgeoisie in its worst form. This call not only inflates this group's social status but also diverts attention from the operations of American political economy that produce and reproduce these problems in the first place. The crisis-of-the-black-male thesis attempts to justify a black antifeminist backlash. The critiques proffered by proponents of this thesis regarding the implementation of affirmative action and their policy for eliminating poverty reflect their generally antifeminist posture.

The focus on the behavior and attributes of black males reinforces racist stereotypes and feeds popular misconceptions about poor people. The argument perpetuates the myth that the poor are different from the rest of us. It implies that the alleviation of poverty requires personal transformation, such as the acquisition of skills, the work ethic, and, according to some, an Afrocentric worldview. This approach conflicts with few vested interests in American society. It is apolitical and does not address the systemic forces responsible for poverty and those who benefit from the basic inequalities in American society. Its prescriptions avoid the fundamental questions of joblessness, powerlessness, and the unequal distribution of wealth and resources. More importantly, this approach does not address the need to politicize the black dispossessed.

PART FIVE
Conclusions

12

Toward a More Perfect Union: Beyond Old Liberalism and Neoliberalism

Rogers M. Smith

THE FINEST ACHIEVEMENTS of the Great Society were the monumental legislative acts that created, for the first time in the nation's history, legal equality for all Americans regardless of race. The 1964 Civil Rights Act and the 1965 Voting Rights Act, read expansively by the Supreme Court, finally terminated the systems of legal apartheid that had survived the end of slavery and grown like virulent weeds through the first half of the twentieth century. But legal equality is only a start, a formality that cannot itself generate a matching social reality. It can be nullified or reversed if hostile social, economic, and political forces are not successfully combated.

After winning those great legislative victories, American liberals had to turn to even more difficult but more crucial battles for broader social transformations that would make equal legal rights secure. Here their vision failed them. They chose paths to reform that were too often wrongheaded or halfhearted; and they suffered dispiriting losses. Today, many of the neoliberals who flocked to Bill Clinton have concluded that these larger battles for racial equality should be given up or pursued only via drearily familiar devices of private assistance and black self-help that, time and time again, have actually helped to rebuild racial hierarchies.[1]

As Alexis de Tocqueville noted long ago, Americans tend to cast all their debates over principles and policies as constitutional issues.[2] Thus, controversies over whether and how to transform the nation's racial inequalities are often pitched as disputes over constitutional requirements of liberty and equality. That tendency can be costly. The nation's constitutional traditions contain some tropes that are easily exploitable by those ill-disposed toward real racial progress. These hypnotizingly familiar slogans give pause to many who, in at least part of their hearts, are willing to support change. Consequently, this chapter attacks those tropes of American political rhetoric and sketches an alternative way of understanding constitutional government. It does so to suggest, first, how ill-conceived, if not hypocritical, many past and current objections to racial progress have been and, second, how liberal rhetoric and liberal thought can more successfully address the tasks that remain.

Opposition to Racial Progress, Past and Present

Social, economic, and political arrangements provide people with material goods, political and social status, and discourses and practices that convey some sense of why their lives have meaning and worth. All past and present social, economic, and political systems have done so in unequal ways. Through merit, good fortune, or, most often, greater power, some people have controlled vastly more material resources and benefits, enjoyed higher status, and been especially commended in the prevailing social narratives about the character and value of different human lives. Throughout U.S. history, the dominant economic structures, political hierarchies, and narratives of human worth have placed most white men above most people of color.

These home truths are numbingly familiar, but just for that reason they are worth recalling. They should lead us to expect that, even after most whites have supported or at least acquiesced in the elimination of explicit legal mandates for black subordination, many will still be strongly tempted to seek ways to maintain or even enhance their long-standing superior position in the nation's most powerful political, social, economic, and cultural institutions. That is where Americans are in the 1990s. Ever since the great moral fervor of the 1960s civil rights movement subsided, forces working to reestablish such superiority have been reappearing, but in modified forms that can recapture respectability.

The pattern has occurred before, in ways that ought to make us sensitive to the dangers of our own time. The first major instance came after "the first emancipation," the gradual elimination of slavery in the northern states from the 1770s through the 1790s, which was accompanied by expanded legal and political rights for free blacks. Frightened by subsequent growth in the numbers of African American freemen, whites eventually passed reactionary new laws, federal and state, North and South, limiting free blacks' rights and enhancing the legal powers of slave owners.[3]

Even more striking are the parallels between the 1960s and the 1860s, between the modern civil rights movements and the reforms embodied in the Reconstruction era statutes, amendments, and programs. The post–Civil War enactments made all native-born African Americans citizens and guaranteed them basic rights. The nation further eroded the racial basis of its citizenship by making Africans eligible for naturalization and promising to shield all who expatriated themselves to join the United States. The Reconstruction measures also began to do much more than simply mandate legal equality. They started to transform the subjugating racial stratifications in the nation's economic and cultural arrangements. The Freedmen's Bureau, the Freedmen's Bank, and new black colleges such as Howard University all represented forms of special economic, medical, legal, and educational assistance to blacks long denied virtually all governmental benefits.[4]

That dawn soon clouded over. Northern whites were happy to end slavery, but few wanted to accept blacks as equal citizens, much less to assist them to become so. The Republicans began to lose white votes to the Democrats without gaining enough black votes to compensate. They responded by gutting all programs assisting African Americans, either eliminating them or ensuring, as in the case of black education, that they were aimed not at achieving racial equality but at preparing African Americans for subordinate economic statuses, for unskilled or semiskilled manual labor.[5]

The Supreme Court, dominated by business-minded Republican appointees, played a critical role in these retreats from Reconstruction. Increasingly, its justices held that constitutional equality forbade all forms of governmental aid targeted to blacks, especially when such aid involved restrictions on owners and employers. In the 1883 *Civil Rights Cases,* Justice Joseph Bradley struck down Congress's 1875 ban on racial discrimination in all places of public accommodation, explaining that the time had finally come for the pampered black man to cease to be "the special favorite of the laws."[6] He must have his rights "protected in the ordinary modes by which other men's rights are protected."[7] After the Court thus declared open season for whites to discriminate against blacks, they did so zealously. But, occasionally deterred by profit motives, businesses did not do so persistently enough for white supremacists, who soon sought governmental support for their preferred arrangements. In 1896, the Supreme Court, in *Plessy* v. *Ferguson,* buttressed by new Darwinian "scientific" accounts naturalizing racial aversion and proclaiming blacks inferior, eagerly embraced thinly veiled new forms of governmental discrimination against blacks, the "separate but equal" Jim Crow laws.[8]

For good measure, the United States in these years sanctioned massive disfranchisement of African Americans, strove to end the existence of Native American nations by redistributing their collectively held lands to (mostly white) individuals, banned Chinese immigration on racial grounds, and became an imperial power over Filipino and Puerto Rican "races" held to be unfit for full citizenship.[9] Overall, by 1910 doctrines and practices of racial supremacy were riding higher than they had in 1860.

Today, it is the accomplishments of the 1960s civil rights movement and the antipoverty Great Society that have been progressively discredited. The monumental measures of the mid-1960s included not only the 1964 Civil Rights Act and the Voting Rights Act but also even more broadly transformative efforts: school desegregation; "War on Poverty" social assistance programs such as Head Start, food stamps, and Medicaid; job and housing programs designed to benefit racial minorities, among many others. The most shrill opposition to these policies has centered on welfare, especially Aid to Families with Dependent Children, unemployment benefits, and food stamps, and on various forms of affirmative action, especially preferential treatment for racial and ethnic groups in hiring, contracting, admissions to universities and professional schools, and the design of electoral systems. Both welfare and affirmative action are painted as chiefly means to penalize hard-working whites on behalf of undeserving blacks. Chicago law professor Richard Epstein, openly linking arms with Justice Bradley, has extended these arguments to attack the 1964 Civil Rights Act. It bans racial discrimination by businesses just as did the 1875 law that Bradley struck down and is therefore, Epstein says, an inefficient and unjust form of "affirmative action." By requiring employers to hire and serve racial minorities when they may not wish to do so, the law commits the ultimate sin of hindering market forces in order to promote equality.[10] And though civil rights measures have often been adopted by legislatures, executive officials, educators, and even businesses, critics harp most on their promotion by allegedly Constitution-deforming judges.

The evils attributed to civil rights rulings are legion. This chapter focuses on three criticisms of judicial activism on behalf of minorities that have become particularly popular among American elite opinion-shapers, academics, and journalists: the *balkanization, democratic,* and *competence* criticisms. Some offering these critiques are proudly conservative or neoconservative. Some may be called neoliberal. Others plausibly see themselves as on the left. Most of these otherwise varied critics agree that these inadequacies of the judiciary in promoting minority rights stem from the root problems of the liberalism of the 1960s and early 1970s, both as a political movement and as a political philosophy.

We should be honest: There is something to each of these criticisms. But those somethings should not persuade us to abandon either the progressive aspirations of the 1960s or the judiciary as one forum for achieving them. Reform via the judiciary and other governmental institutions can be pursued more successfully if certain errors in the way liberal courts have tried to remedy the burdens of the disadvantaged are corrected. These errors penetrate to the most basic ways that contemporary liberals have conceived of what they are trying to remedy and reform. Rethinking them suggests how liberal reforms might signal long-overdue inclusion of blacks in the basic goods the political system is supposed to promote for all, rather than special group privileges, and how judicial remedies might set principled boundaries to democratic politics without micromanaging outcomes.[11]

The Three Criticisms

These three critiques of judicial activism on behalf of minorities are so common that they need little documentation.[12] The *balkanization* charge holds that modern judicial decisions are fostering senses of group identity and group entitlements that reject all emphases on common national membership and genuinely shared values. This contention is standard among critics of affirmative action for minorities in hiring and educational admissions programs. The indictment usually extends also to other governmental measures, including mandatory school desegregation, revisions of electoral systems under the Voting Rights Act, and educational curricula redesigned to include more cultures and languages. These arguments have been advanced by neoconservative academics such as Nathan Glazer and Abigail Thernstrom, by Reagan-Bush administration spokespersons, and by black intellectuals such as Thomas Sowell, Shelby Steele, and Stephen Carter.[13] Neoliberals such as Paul Starr and Theda Skocpol have chimed in, arguing that "affirmative action policies have helped to perpetuate racism" and that social programs should be aimed not at blacks or even the poor, but at "all Americans."[14]

In one of the best books of this sort, Thernstrom draws the common conclusion. Showing no great feel for adjectives, she writes that "the dark side to affirmative action" in voting, as in other areas, is that it produces a "heightened sense of group membership."[15] This sense "works against that of common citizenship" and may thus "threaten democratic institutions."[16] Reagan-Bush appointed judges, like the Reagan-Bush Justice Departments, have vehemently endorsed similar views. In *Richmond* v. *Croson* (1989),[17] for example, the Supreme Court struck down a municipal affirmative action system for construction grants that was modeled on a previously upheld congressional statute. The plurality thought that, in the absence of showings of specific racist harms, such programs threatened to ignite a fractious "politics of racial hostility." Justice Antonin Scalia made the same point more vehemently: "Racial preferences appear to 'even the score' (in some small degree) only if one embraces the proposition that our society is appropriately viewed as divided into races, making it right that an injustice rendered in the past to a black man should be compensated for by discriminating against a white. Nothing is worth that embrace."[18]

Conservatives, neoconservatives, and neoliberals are not the only ones who raise the specter of incendiary balkanization of the political community resulting from judicially endorsed racial classifications. Social democrats such as Michael Walzer have long derogated arrangements that treat the United States as a "federation of groups rather than a community of citizens" as "deeply and bitterly divisive."[19] And it is true that some supporters of race- and gender-conscious governmental measures, and racial and gender politics, argue for them out of an embrace of the primacy of racial and gender identities and differences and explicit support for certain kinds of racial nationalism and gender separatism.[20] Many such adherents see themselves as on the left. They are undisturbed by charges that they are rejecting any unifying quest for consensual community values because they regard such a quest as at best naive and illusory, at worst a cynical invitation to experience further repression. So the contention that at least some contemporary advocacy of racial and gender claims threatens to balkanize American political life is not confined to conservatives, nor is it simply a straw man.[21]

The second, *democratic* argument maintains that judicial activism unjustly and imprudently displaces and demoralizes active engagement in democratic politics. This position has a long lineage in American law, dating back at least to nineteenth-century Harvard law professor (and champion of imperialism) James Bradley Thayer. It was a chief motif of progressive critics of early-twentieth-century procorporate judicial activism, including Louis Brandeis and Oliver Wendell Holmes (who joined in judicial acquiescence to Jim Crow). It then became an explicitly conservative position in the hands of their intellectual progeny, Felix Frankfurter, his clerk Alexander Bickel, and Bickel's close friend, Robert Bork, whose calls for judicial deference always stress the evils of preempting democracy.[22] This is also a frequent theme of Justice Scalia's.[23]

But this democratic argument is even more visible further left. Neoliberals often stress that democratic coalitions supportive of progressive social policies cannot be forged without an abandonment of both race-targeted policies and heavy reliance on the judiciary.[24] Like the Republicans after Reconstruction, these professedly progressive Democrats believe that public measures to aid African Americans are not "politically sustainable."[25] Although Clinton quietly endorsed minority set-asides in public construction programs during his first presidential campaign, he largely steered clear of race-based affirmative action in both his presidential runs. Hence, his electoral success is said to vindicate this contention.

Arguing more in terms of democratic principles, Walzer identifies himself with this view. In "Philosophy and Democracy," Walzer argues that, though the dangers of judicial activism on behalf of civil rights were easily exaggerated, nonetheless such actions meant that "citizens have, to whatever degree, lost control over their own lives. And then they have no reason, no democratic reason, for obeying the decrees of the judges."[26] Walzer's theme is shared by most other communitarian-minded academic advocates of democracy, such as Benjamin Barber and Michael Sandel.

It can be argued to the contrary that controversial judicial decisions do more to stimulate democratic political activity than to inhibit it and that most judicial decisions have little effect on democratic activity either way.[27] Yet it is true that the types of activism favored by many legal academics seem to approach an ideal of government by judiciary, however much reality falls short of it. Moreover, the empirical effect of judicializing political disputes can be to cast them wholly as matters of legal rights and to inflate the influence of lawyers in ways that work against the authority of other citizens. So this second argument is also not merely a disingenuous ploy by opponents of modern judicial decisions.

The third challenge, to judicial *competence*, has been even more extensively elaborated in recent years. Tales have been widely recounted of how lower courts and their appointed "special masters" have at times taken over the running of schools, prisons, and hospitals; mandated taxes to pay for busing or imposed crushing fines on public officials who refused to desegregate; and overturned sitting city governments while redesigning apportionment and electoral systems to be more racially representative.[28] Each particular judicial intervention has its defenders and detractors. The judiciary's critics stress that judicial involvements have often been protracted, highly controversial, and without many apparent achievements. Those histories are said to prove that interventionist courts have repeatedly botched their jobs both technically and politically, generating popular resentments that have undermined liberal causes. Hard struggles to win genuinely widespread democratic support for meaningful change are held to be necessary if changes are instead to be made effectively and securely. The point the critics minimize is that the courts have frequently acted only when confronted by long-term, severe, and deteriorating situations, making it difficult to decide whether their role has amounted to a net plus or minus over what might have occurred with more deferential benches.

Yet the judiciary's shortcomings do not need exaggerating to make the point that unelected officials in the judicial branches have assumed much work traditionally performed by elected legislative and executive officers. To some degree, this third criticism is thus a variant of the second, a complaint that judges are doing what more democratically accountable officials should do.[29]

But the argument of incompetence has some independent force. Even when judges and their expert assistants may technically be no worse, and in some cases better, than those who had been making the governing decisions prior to judicial involvement, it still remains true that in a fully efficient political system, many of these matters would not be so extensively decided by persons with the limited and specialized types of professional skills, training, and experience that judges possess.

The fact that all these criticisms have some credibility does not, however, support the hasty neocon conclusion that judicial and legislative efforts to help racial and ethnic minorities should be surrendered. Significant progress may well be possible if changes are made in contemporary liberal precepts and prescriptions. The remainder of this chapter argues for the transformation of five counterproductive features of the remedial approaches that have predominated in race (and gender) judicial decisions, in the academic literature calling for decisions favorable to minorities, and in the more general statements of contemporary liberal political theory on which they have drawn. Three are errors most characteristic of equal protection analysis, and two are problems of modern judicial and political liberalism more broadly. These counterproductive features are (1) reliance on fuzzy claims of moral equality; (2) an undue focus on moral motivations; (3) advocacy of symbolic, restorationist remedies; (4) depiction of the constitutional system as a neutral umpire of disputes; and (5) excessive investment in judicial solutions to the problems progressives must address.

The Errors of Equal Protection Remedies

In modern constitutional jargon, the requirements of the equal protection clause are often said to express an "antidiscrimination principle." It forbids, at a minimum, official actions motivated by beliefs that "members of one race are less worthy than other people."[30] This formulation is quite defensible; but to many legal liberals, it seems too weak. Hence, they frequently argue that the "core value" at stake in equal protection is "that all people have equal worth."[31] This moral equality requires that all persons be treated with, in Ronald Dworkin's famous formulation, "equal concern and respect," though there is much disagreement about what that implies.[32] Most legal writers concur that the antidiscrimination principle is an "anti-dissing" principle. It requires courts to decide whether legislation is motivated by disrespect for certain persons or groups. And it points to judicial remedies that, in the view of the court, will succeed in placing each mistreated group, race, or gender in the position it would have been in had immoral official motives and actions never occurred.

Constitutional Equality. Attractive as this notion sounds, it is foolish to view the equal protection clause and liberal constitutionalism more broadly as committed to vindicating the equal moral worth of all persons. Judgments of moral worth usually have something to do with assessing what people believe and how they act—and rightly so. It is far from self-evident that morally David Duke and Rosa Parks are identically worthy despite their contrasting beliefs and conduct. Views that require us to presume they have equal worth often come across as the sort of standardless, leveling egalitarianism that critics of the left love to deride. More importantly, they enfeeble courts and others from making distinctions about which programs are adequately egalitarian and which are not and about what role the judiciary should have in reform. These are distinctions that effective progressive judicial and political measures cannot do without.

The widespread deference given to claims for moral equality in American mass opinion, at least in the form of lip service, probably stems from the cultural influence of Christianity and its assertion that all persons are morally equal in the eyes of God. For less pious intellectuals, Christian influences have been augmented by the writings of Immanuel Kant, who rested moral equality on all persons' noumenal identities as rational beings. Both these moral traditions are impressive, but they are not identical. To be led by faith to treat all as beloved of the Christian God is not the same as to be led by reason to treat all as rational self-legislators. Few legal writers, moreover, dare to invoke either of the controversial metaphysical and epistemological views the Christian and Kantian moral positions entail or to adhere to the most demanding political implications of these outlooks.

As a result, most legal writers say little about the basis of their assertions of equal worth, occasionally contending simply that this moral principle is uncontroversial in our culture.[33] That is a weak answer. Even if true, it would not help us distinguish among the different versions of moral equality that prevail. To do so, we must abandon flabby talk of absolutely equal worth and recognize a more minimal sense of moral equality as our guide to the meaning of government's obligation to treat all with equal concern and respect.[34] Dworkin is right to trace the moral respect we owe persons to their possession of the cognitive, self-comprehending, and self-guiding capacities that make them moral agents.[35] But their possession of these capacities only supports the mild egalitarian claim that all persons deserve some *minimum* of moral respect. Since they do not all possess or exercise these capacities to the same degree, and especially since they do not all value these moral capacities in others, their moral agency does not support the stronger claim that they are all *precisely* equal in moral worth. Racists are not morally worthless; but, ceteris paribus, they *are* worth less than nonracists because of their racism.

In liberal constitutionalism historically, the political implication of this weaker notion of minimal moral desert has generally been that all persons (*including* racists) are equally entitled to basic rights and liberties. That position forbids unjust subjugation of all persons, even as it still allows us ultimately to judge some people to be more morally estimable than others and to treat some beliefs as properly subject to public repudiation. If we take this view, then we flesh out the meaning of equal concern and respect as "respect" for the basic rights and liberties of all and "concern" that all persons have meaningful access to resources and opportunities, so that their possession of those basic rights is not merely a deceptive formality. Once we elaborate a theory of what those rights and liberties are, this approach enables us to define the basic goods a liberal constitutional order should attempt to secure for everyone and to demand action when the system is failing. At the same time, this view indicates which egalitarian claims go too far, at least as guides for court-ordered remedies.

The Focus on Immoral Motivations. For many liberal scholars, the antidiscrimination principle's call for equal respect implies that courts adjudicating equal protection claims should chiefly focus on whether disturbing social conditions can be traced to immoral official motivations and actions. That focus is a mistake.[36] It requires courts to uphold any program, no matter how devastating to blacks or any other Americans, if judges cannot telepathically divine what was really in the legislators' hearts and minds when they created it.

Judges are still better advised to follow Sir William Blackstone, with all his limitations, than Harry Blackstone. They should ask whether under existing conditions, whatever their source, there are individuals, groups, races, or a gender that is effectively and corrigibly deficient in the legal, social, and material resources and opportunities the system aims to promote for everyone.[37] If so, then some citizens do not possess the basic rights and liberties promised by a liberal constitutional order. Insofar as some do not possess those rights meaningfully, the constitutional system has failed. Whenever the constitutional system has failed, or not yet succeeded, courts ought to promote greater success insofar as they can. Whether inadequate conditions result from good or ill official intentions, from dissing or blundering, or from any official intentions and actions at all should not matter much.

Certainly, motives of racial bigotry are evil, and liberal regimes should be committed to their repudiation. It is perfectly appropriate for government to deny tax exemptions to racist religious schools, to punish overt "hate crimes" more severely than similar acts that do not contribute to racial antagonisms, to feature arguments against racism prominently in public education, and so forth. But illicit motives are hard for courts to ascertain; and it is dangerously Orwellian for governments to attempt to alter inner motivations directly. I also suggest that the greatest evil of past racial injustices is not that whites hated blacks. It is that whites hurt blacks in ways that prevented blacks from obtaining, even to some minimal extent, the basic goods the system promotes. Inadequate access to decent jobs, housing, schooling, transportation, and the political offices that might be used to realize change or at least to ward off further harms are the great evils of racial injustice that government should be most concerned with, if for no other reason than they are the things government *can* do something about directly. And even though social affirmations of respect are indeed vital to all of us, those messages can be sent most powerfully by policies that genuinely strive to remedy such concrete evils. As social signs, actions speak louder than words.

The Limits of Symbolic Restorationist Remedies. That point leads to the problems with the particular remedies the courts have preferred to impose. Partly as a result of the prevalence of motivation-centered equal protection analyses, the judiciary's remedial task is often conceived as a quest to create the conditions that victims of injustice would have experienced had immoral official motives been absent. I say "partly" because courts have also been influenced by standard legal models of compensatory justice, in which the function of courts is to place victims of injustice in roughly the condition they would be in had a specific legal violation never occurred. For example, if I bash the fender of your car, compensatory models say I must pay to have the fender repaired, leaving you just as you presumably would have been had I never damaged your property (although I am worse off, which is the price of my negligence or malice).[38]

Conservatives on and off the bench have long noted that from this traditional compensatory viewpoint many race-conscious "remedies" seem inappropriate (see, again, Scalia's opinion in the *Richmond* case). Affirmative action programs are frequently and plausibly held to provide positions to persons who cannot credibly claim that they would have occupied those spots but for past discrimination. And these programs deny positions to people who never engaged in the discrimination the programs are meant to remedy and therefore often resent these measures bitterly. Similarly, mandatory school integration now often involves minority students who never experienced de jure segregation, as well as white students who are not responsible for the past discrimination that occurred almost everywhere, though they benefit from it. Courts have also restructured electoral systems in ways that aided blacks who were not in politics, and so not directly burdened, when the previous systems were in effect, to the detriment of other candidates who were not the architects or the immediate beneficiaries of the earlier systems. From traditional compensatory perspectives, these actions do not put those harmed where they would have been without the harm or apportion the costs of change on those who inflicted the harm; so they just do not look like compensatory remedies. They look like disguised claims of group entitlements.[39]

But it is viewing these measures through "remedial" lenses that makes them seem novel and suspect. The truth is that most of these forms of governmental aid are neither historically unusual nor inappropriate. American governments have always provided special assistance to specific groups whenever the nation could efficiently further its basic goals by doing so, often with few recriminations. Indeed, the Supreme Court has frequently ruled that such "legislation special in character" is entirely appropriate if it serves the general good.[40] These facts are blurred when courts and commentators perversely try to conceive of these means as strictly compensatory remedies. No one can actually know what America would be like if white bigotry had not been massively expressed in laws and social practices. The focus on undoing bigoted motives thus produces a tendency to design remedies that simply supply visible symbols showing that governmental motives are pure now. If the badge of past official prejudice has been, for example, segregated schools, the task is to ensure that schools are visibly integrated—and that is all the task is taken to be. Remedies are not specifically concerned with whether the integrated schools will end the further harms, arguably the more important harms, of inadequate education that blacks have suffered.[41] If we accept instead that the harms of past discrimination in schooling should at least include the denial of adequate schooling to blacks, we have to take a broader view of what counts as a remedy for such failures. That view was endorsed by W.E.B. Du Bois in 1935:

> The Negro needs neither segregated schools nor mixed schools. What he needs is education. What he must remember is that there is no magic, either in mixed schools or in segregated schools. A mixed school, with poor and unsympathetic teachers, with hostile public opinion, and no teaching of truth concerning black folks, is bad. A segregated school with ignorant placeholders, inadequate equipment, poor salaries, and wretched housing, is equally bad. Other things being equal, the mixed school is the broader, more natural basis for the education of all youth. But other things seldom are equal.

A more adequate remedial approach, then, must be concerned with the wide range of elements—physical equipment, qualified teachers, honest and effective curriculum—that are necessary for minimally decent education. Contemporary research largely confirms Du Bois's judgment that such education is most successfully provided in mixed schools, but schools whose racial mixing is part of a larger "comprehensive and rapid program of change in the schools" that includes other efforts to improve school facilities, teaching, morale, and student performance.[42] Thus, as desegregation scholar Charles V. Willie argues, those "who suggest that school desegregation should limit concern to formulas for race mixing only are clearly wrong."[43] Although more judges are realizing this, many judicially ordered remedial plans still focus simply on achieving integrated student and, at most, faculty and administrative populations. In some cities, such as Atlanta, visible integration of administrative and faculty positions has taken precedence over any real reform in the classroom experiences of students.[44]

The General Errors of Liberal Judicial Activism

The problems of equal protection remedies are compounded by views of liberal constitutionalism that are compatible with the legal doctrines just criticized but not dependent on them. Two views are especially problematic: the notion that the constitutional system should operate as a neutral umpire of civic life and the notion that constitutional goals are chiefly to be pursued by courts.

The Constitution as Neutral Umpire. Liberals have frequently but wrongly portrayed a just constitutional system as a fair umpire that intrudes on citizens' lives only to restore the balance when some persons, public or private, have wrongfully harmed others. That hallowed view is deeply deceptive. It misdescribes what most Americans have wanted, and should want, from their political system. In practice, it permits American governments to maintain innumerable affirmative actions that chiefly benefit already-favored citizens, especially white men, such as aid to big businesses and biased subsidies of housing and education. Meanwhile, the United States continues to neglect those traditionally subordinated groups that were long denied most of these benefits and still receive meager shares.

Opposed to the piously misleading "umpire" view is another way of depicting the U.S. constitutional system, one less rhetorically familiar but more accurate. In this view, constitutional governance is conceived as a collective, goal-oriented political enterprise designed to make certain human goods, the aforementioned basic rights, liberties, and opportunities, available to all citizens. Government exists fundamentally not to adjudicate but to help generate the material resources and social arrangements people need to have meaningful possession of these goods. In practice, most citizens and both major parties have wanted their government to be run as this sort of "achievement enterprise."[45] As presidents have learned during economic downturns, voters may initially support umpire rhetoric, but they toss out officials who do not help most people obtain basic goods—and rightly so. In evaluating governmental performance, we should take as our constitutional touchstone the question of whether public officials and institutions are advancing those goals as much as they can.

The pervasiveness of the umpire image traces back at least to John Locke's *Second Treatise,* which defines the task of government as "to be Umpire, by settled standing Rules, indifferent, and the same to all Parties."[46] But Locke and other liberal writers also portray constitutional institutions as human creations designed to help people achieve substantive benefits. That portrait is in the end more historically, sociologically, and philosophically plausible.

The American Constitution similarly is best seen not simply as a referee of preexisting rights. Its construction was a collective human endeavor to achieve public goods of peace, prosperity, national community, and the advancement of certain forms of liberty that were not being realized under the Articles of Confederation.[47] The Constitution's culminating aim, to "secure the Blessings of Liberty" to its founders and their posterity, is most plausibly understood not as merely promising protection for what Americans already had. They sought to expand their still-quite-limited enjoyment of those blessings, and with varying degrees of energy and skill the officials of their national government have tried to do so. In this century, it has been commonly accepted by American voters and politicians that these "blessings" should include public education at all levels; national defense, including protection for U.S. economic expansion abroad; and economic growth via fiscal policy, aid to transportation systems, and innumerable forms of help for developers, entrepreneurs, and established industries.

In addition to quarreling with Republicans over ways and means of doing those things, Democrats since the New Deal have insisted that seriously trying to provide such goods for *all* requires extra aid to those most in need, including children of poverty, the unemployed, the elderly, the sick, and the disabled. Republicans have generally opposed extra assistance, except for those who are already well off. If the cups of the affluent overflow, so they say, all will be able to lick at the trickles. Both parties' positions, however, implicitly support a view of American constitutional government as basically an enterprise for helping people acquire the goods they need. Both have also thought that government could and should give special benefits to some groups in order to advance the good of all.

But for over 80 percent of America's history, most of the measures government took to promote economic and political opportunities, material prosperity, education, transportation, housing, and other goods were of direct avail primarily to white male citizens or some subset thereof. That is what the civil rights movement and the resulting Great Society programs began to change. Sometimes the constraints they addressed had been explicitly imposed by discriminatory laws, sometimes by pervasive discrimination by private institutions and individuals, sometimes by the disadvantaging social and economic systems in which minorities and women were forced to dwell. The pertinent fact, however, is simply that governmental endeavors that should have benefited everyone had never reached everyone. A similar lack of resources continues to plague many members of minority groups and women now, even though formal rights are more generally extended. Thus, today the nation's long-standing constitutional goals require comparable measures to secure these basic opportunities for every American. Because group-based policies both assisted some and disadvantaged others, group-based policies will often be the most efficient way to provide comparable aid to those thus far held down. Those measures should not be seen as fulfilling any novel or special entitlements, nor need they be depicted chiefly as remedies for past bigotry. They are historically well-precedented efforts to complete the constitutional enterprise that is supposed to aid all citizens but as yet does not.

To be sure, finding policies that can better generate material resources and systems of social, economic, and political opportunity for all is difficult. Courts should be wary of demanding too much. But history should also make judges wary of demanding too little. It should be their special task to insist that the nation's basic constitutional ends must be pursued prudently, conscientiously, but continuously, and for all citizens.

Toward More Effective and More Democratic Remedies. This notion of the constitutional obligations of liberal governments may seem demanding, in many ways beyond the scope of judicial competence. It is. Modern liberal judicial activism erroneously assumes that every failure of the system affecting minorities, women, or anyone else must be remedied by the judiciary. Achieving the system's goals is instead the constitutional responsibility of all of government, and each branch should do only what it competently can. That includes courts, but not only or ultimately courts. Undue reliance on the judiciary tends to pressure judges into defining a "remedy" as simply whatever things they can do, such as requiring schools to be integrated, instead of things they cannot do, such as making schools minimally good. Yet integration alone may well not be enough to remedy past failures, in schooling and in other areas, that burden minorities and most women.

The answer is not to shrink the notion of a remedy. The proper response is for the judiciary to signal to more suitable elements of government, in ways that can push those agencies to undertake corrective measures, why current conditions represent failure in terms of the constitutional system's objectives. That task requires more explicit judicial accounts of basic constitutional objectives. But usually corrective measures will then be best achieved by democratic deliberation among elected officials, experts, and the citizenry—thus easing the tension between judicial activism and democratic ideals and, more importantly, making for more successful constitutional self-governance.

Encouragingly, in the late 1980s some leading legal voices began sounding similar themes. The nation's most prominent constitutional advocate, Laurence Tribe, advocates replacing the antidiscrimination principle with an "antisubjugation principle" that "aims to break down legally created or legally reenforced systems of subordination that treat some people as second class citizens."[48] Catherine

MacKinnon has similarly argued for replacing the antidiscrimination approach (which she terms the "difference" approach) with an (anti-) "dominance" approach. It calls for changes that go beyond correcting particular gender injustices to transforming settled systems of female subordination.[49] Others have sketched related "antisubordination" or "nonsubordination" positions.[50]

On the bench, Justice John Paul Stevens has increasingly stressed that "the Constitution requires us to evaluate" all decisions, including those concerning race- and gender-conscious measures, "primarily by studying their impact on the future," on the "forward-looking" constitutional goals they may accomplish, not simply as means of compensating past specific injuries.[51] All these positions represent the sort of shift away from attending to bad motives in the past and toward bad effects in the present and good results in the future that I am urging.

But there are problems with the moves in this direction thus far. First, this turn requires us to have some account of the Constitution's fundamental goals, the basic goods it aims to promote, and what counts as their meaningful possession. Without some notion of the liberties, opportunities, and interests the Constitution should be read as most concerned with, we cannot decide what constitute improper forms of subjugation or dominance or what sorts of future arrangements should be sought. Judicial intervention in the name of promoting constitutional goals then becomes a potential loose cannon, even if one that is likely to fire futilely into the air. But so far none of the scholars advocating these approaches has provided any substantial definition of what we should treat as unacceptable subjugation, subordination, or domination.

It makes sense to explicate what counts as subjugation in terms of an account of the basic liberties that persons should have—what is subjugation but the deprivation of fundamental freedoms? That is one reason various legal and political theorists, myself included, have sketched theories of constitutional liberty of this sort in recent years.[52] Most of us revisionist liberals accept that people deserve at least some minimal moral respect because of their capacities for moral agency, their socially and biologically constituted capabilities to reflect critically on their identities, values, and pursuits and to decide on ways of life that seem to them, for the time being at least, fulfilling and worthwhile. But whereas Dworkin and others have seen respect for such agency as calling for governmental "neutrality" on questions of the good life, many believe it suggests certain elements that any morally defensible view of human goods must contain and thus certain standards for what count as morally responsible decisions and conduct. My view is that if we assign moral importance to human agency, to persons' capacities for reflective self-governance (or, as I have termed it, "rational liberty"), then a liberal political society must be one united "by a shared political and social purpose: to promote ways of life that advance liberty for all."[53] These standards present human freedom not as something simply given by nature or as a purely individual achievement, but as resulting in significant measure from social and political institutions. Hence, they prescribe the basic tasks of a liberal constitutional system. Insofar as possible, liberal governments must work to ensure that neither public officials nor private individuals harm persons' capacities to live freely, except when necessary to prevent similar but more extensive harms. Thus, governments must maintain the police functions of protection for basic rights and liberties stressed by traditional theories of umpire liberalism.

But governments should also do more. They should seek to establish or encourage political, economic, educational, and social institutions that *empower* people by expanding their opportunities and their mental and material resources. Governments admittedly must be wary of adopting policies that coerce some excessively in order to assist others, but their focus should be on actively enhancing, not merely preserving, all citizens' abilities to pursue free and fulfilling lives.[54]

On this view of liberal constitutionalism, what rights and liberties should be deemed basic in any specific constitutional system? The answer must, in part, be relative to the condition of each particular society. As Amartya Sen has argued, because the cares and aspirations of a community's members are bound up with its current forms of life, rational freedom for them will involve courses of conduct unavailable to or unvalued by many people in other times and places.[55] The person too ill-educated to be employable in Tokyo may be much better educated than an illiterate but self-supporting peasant in Nepal. Yet that person will still find it hard to function in his or her society. He or she needs more formal education to have a minimal education. In terms of each of the rights and liberties deemed basic to freedom in American society, then, courts should rely on varied sources of governmental and private expertise presented by adversarial parties to judge what conditions constitute adequate minimal possession of the right in question.[56]

But many of the cognitive capacities and material resources that equip people for reflective self-governance are recognizable enough across societies. With sufficient information, we can make reasonable judgments about what job-seekers in Tokyo, peasant farmers in Nepal, and black teenagers in Detroit need in order to take advantage of the options available to them and about what changes would *expand* their powers and opportunities. Accordingly, the general liberal admonition should be that governments must strive to secure for all those rights, liberties, and mental and material resources that will enable people to lead free lives within the sorts of societies they actually inhabit, while always seeking to favor those existing and emergent institutions that appear to contribute most to that end.

In modern America, some endeavors are so commonly thought to be basic to freedom that courts should automatically treat them as fundamental, protected by strict judicial scrutiny, unless it can be shown that they are peripheral in the case of a person advancing an equal protection claim. These basics include

- a right to live with one's family, inclusively defined
- a right to an education that prepares a person for meaningful participation in the national economy and society
- a right to pursue one's preferred line of work, subject to attaining suitable qualifications, and to participate in the economy as an equal bearer of legally established property rights
- a right to the freedoms of conscience and expression
- a right to vote and to participate generally in political self-governance, along with a right to expatriate oneself physically or politically if one cannot accept the principles of American political society
- a right to marry among consenting adults, regardless of gender
- a right to travel and reside where one wishes within the nation
- rights to be presumed innocent and treated fairly by the criminal justice system[57]

This list provides more specific content to the broad category of unconstitutional subjugation.

For the most part, these are rights and interests American courts have already given constitutional status under the "fundamental rights" strands of equal protection and due process doctrine.[58] That fact is significant. It indicates that many judges hearing clashing arguments in many contexts over long periods of time have concluded that these liberties are indeed experienced as basic to the ways of life most American citizens actually follow. Admittedly, some items on the list, such as the rights of education, expatriation, and same-sex adult marriage, have not been so designated by the federal courts. But many state constitutions treat education as a fundamental governmental duty.[59] Since 1870, U.S. statutes have proclaimed a more constricted form of expatriation to be a "natural right."[60] And same-sex couples are gaining increasing legal recognition. Strong arguments can be made that all these rights are practical prerequisites of freedom in a society like the United States. With them, most Americans would have what they require to live freely and meaningfully.

Even so, this list is far from definitive or final. Rather than justify it further, however, I will add only three points. First, staples such as food, clothing, and shelter are much more necessary to genuine freedom. Why do they not lead the list of basic rights?[61] I wish they could. But provision of basic goods is a matter of production as much as of distribution; and production is hard. The history of this century raises profound doubt about whether modern economies can legally guarantee such basics to all citizens without stifling productive activities in ways that prevent states from providing many citizens with these staples in actuality. Rights to nonexistent commodities do no one any good. Thus, at present there is not a compelling case for constitutionally guaranteeing able-bodied citizens more than opportunities to earn income via productive labor, as well as rights to purchase and sell goods. But legislators and executive officials should place the highest priority on finding ways to ensure that all citizens have such opportunities in actuality and can gain the capacities to take advantage of them. As Gordon Lafer argues,[62] these imperatives mean officials must promote not just job training but also job creation, public and private.

Second, since the system's task is to secure these basic goods for all to a minimally meaningful extent, governmental provision of formal access to, for example, schools or jobs that are atrocious by the standards of that society should not suffice.[63] In addition to correcting total deprivations of these rights, governments should be concerned with relative inequalities in the forms of these rights that people possess. The size of the gap between a less advantaged person's access to a public good and a richly endowed person's access to it is part of the question of whether everyone has sufficient access to that good. A grammar school education may be ample when few have much more, but it is generally not adequate for success within communities in which the vast majority have high school degrees and some college, rendering these credential prerequisites for virtually all jobs. And in an advanced market economy, full-time jobs may still not pay enough to lift workers above widely accepted poverty lines. Thus, judicial estimates of the concrete demands posed by life in a given society must include concern for the degree of disadvantage imposed by great inequalities in the distribution of resources that make particular rights effective.

The difficulties of this task make it unreasonable for judges to insist on very precise requirements. But in regard to education, American courts have often not found it too difficult to reach consensus on whether pupils are receiving a minimally adequate schooling.[64] They might reasonably also entertain equal protection challenges to public programs that created additional jobs for already marketable professionals without addressing the needs of those for whom adequately paying jobs do not exist. In regard to these and other goods, courts should recognize that relative deprivations can become decisive deprivations.

Third, when an official action is *not* itself a deprivation of one of these basic constitutional liberties or interests, but is so widely perceived as endorsing race or gender prejudice that it plainly serves to encourage further invidious discriminations, the courts should find the harm it wreaks on constitutional goals sufficient to outweigh almost any benefits that might be claimed for it. An example here is *Palmer* v. *Thompson*,[65] in which the Court wrongly upheld a decision by Jackson, Mississippi, to close its public swimming pools rather than integrate them. The majority refused to recognize that this governmental choice plainly signaled that integration, even if constitutionally mandated, was undesirable and segregation perfectly reasonable. In many such cases, the state's explicit or implicit reliance on a "suspect classification" will be important evidence that it is encouraging bias, and so such classifications can properly be grounds for increased judicial scrutiny. Nonetheless, courts can do so without engaging in subtle examinations of motives. Judges should instead look to the consequences of legislative actions, including whether officials are so widely perceived as biased that they effectively legitimate current racist inequalities and future harmful conduct. This sort of inquiry should not involve the problems of current motive analyses.[66]

The type of "antideprivation" approach I am suggesting jettisons two important currently existing constraints on constitutionally based judicial interventions. It abandons requirements that litigants prove these interests were harmed by invidiously motivated official actions, and it counts great relative as well as absolute deprivations of these interests as constitutional violations. Critics of judicial guardianship may understandably be alarmed by these recommendations.

Their concerns have force. Once we recognize that meaningful remedies for the system's failures must go beyond symbolic affirmations of untainted state motives, it should be particularly clear that courts will often be able to play, at most, an instigating role in achieving such remedies. They should invalidate or suspend existing policies and programs that perpetuate absolute or excessively inegalitarian relative deprivations of basic constitutional interests and indicate the broad performance parameters that constitutionally acceptable alternatives must meet. But then courts should leave it largely to elected officials and administrative agencies to choose among the range of programs that fall within these parameters. Judges should be much more reluctant than they have been about appointing expert special masters to design and then administer specific reforms. Instead, the involvement of elected officials in these choices should at least provide opportunities for democratic debates and deliberation about the available options and for development of significant political support that can help the selected alternative succeed. Thus, the changes I am proposing make it advisable for courts to engage in the sort of "colloquy" with other branches of government and the people that Alexander Bickel has called for—a colloquy in which the courts strive to inject into democratic debates more conscious concern with the unfinished tasks of fulfilling basic constitutional goals.[67]

Examples of the type of ruling I am recommending may be found in the decisions of the numerous state courts, including New Jersey, Kentucky, Montana, and Texas, that have invalidated highly inegalitarian systems of school financing.[68] In part because the Supreme Court has rejected any federal equal protection basis for strong educational rights, these rulings are based on various state constitutional provisions and are not identical in their content or their desirability. They have also met with quite mixed political responses. But at their best, as in Kentucky, the state courts' interventions seem clearly valuable. There the State Supreme Court did not empower its own experts to dictate a school financing system. Instead, it forged from materials provided by all the parties concerned a general but substantive set of criteria for an adequate education. And it focused not on achieving precise equality via redistribution but on ensuring that the basic good of a right to education was at last minimally supplied to all. Thus prodded, the long-deadlocked Kentucky legislature was able rather rapidly to come up with what appears to be a satisfactory plan. If the plan works, this fairly limited judicial involvement should be at an end for the foreseeable future.

In some other circumstances, such as the controversial Yonkers public housing litigation, the ongoing commitment to unconstitutional segregation policies of a community's majority and its elected officials may require much more extensive judicial displacement of normal decisionmaking processes, a possibility even the Rehnquist Court has acknowledged.[69] More often, it may well be that the judiciary will feel compelled to intervene on several occasions over a period of years, criticizing different aspects of the ongoing legislative and executive development of constitutionally effective institutions and policies. But as long as such a recurring role is not so constant as to amount to judicial governance, it should not always be interpreted as judicial failure or inefficiency. It will often be an appropriate part of the ongoing dialogue and cooperation that should characterize a constitutional system of separated powers, in which each branch bears responsibility to help ensure that the system as a whole pursues its goals as well as possible. That approach could go far toward easing the tensions between judicial activism and democratic politics and toward promoting more competent governance.

It is harder to claim that the approach recommended here would end all charges of balkanization when race-conscious measures are adopted. But most Americans are proud of the good things their political system has accomplished, and they will support further public efforts if they promise similar achievements. Most also know, or can be brought to see through arguments such as that laid out in Michael K. Brown's chapter in this volume, that government assistance programs have always involved group classifications of some sort, normally justified in terms of the public goals the programs served. Thus, progressives should not present aid to minorities chiefly as juridical "remedies." They should be portrayed as what they should be: further steps in the historic American political enterprise of including all citizens in the system's benefits while trying to expand those benefits for all. Only a government that strives to help people instead of just umpiring them, and that takes on the challenge of helping even those the system has heretofore held back, can enable Americans to fulfill their hopes for a society in which genuine rights and opportunities are secure for all. Shifting legal and political discourse in this direction is certainly not easy, even though Clinton's presence in the White House may lead to many more receptive federal judges over time. But if even a Gerald Ford appointee such as Justice Stevens, who initially opposed affirmative action, can come to embrace a more positive view of American constitutionalism, then it should be possible to build sufficient support to replace divisive controversies with shared efforts by all branches of government to extend to all citizens the blessings that a free political system is supposed to provide.

Notes

Chapter 1

1. Francis X. Clines, "Clinton Hails F.D.R. at Memorial's Opening," *New York Times,* May 3, 1997.

2. Robert Greenstein, "Looking at the Details of the New Budget Legislation: Social Program Initiatives Decline over Time While Upper Income Tax Cuts Grow" (Washington, D.C.: Center on Budget and Policy Priorities, August 12, 1997).

3. Eric Pianin and John F. Harris, "President, GOP Agree on Balanced Budget Plan," *Washington Post,* May 3, 1998.

4. Andrew Kopkind, "The Manufactured Candidate," *The Nation,* February 3, 1993, 116; Marshall Frady, "Death in Arkansas," *New Yorker*, February 22, 1993, 107–108; David Maraniss, *First in His Class: A Biography of Bill Clinton* (New York: Simon and Schuster, 1995).

5. James R. Dickenson, "Democrats Seek Identity After Loss," *Washington Post*, December 17, 1984.

6. For more on the creation of the DLC, see Philip A. Klinkner, *The Losing Parties: Out-Party National Committees, 1956–1993* (New Haven: Yale University Press, 1994), 179–188; and John F. Hale, "A Different Kind of Democrat: Bill Clinton, the DLC, and the Construction of a New Party Identity" (Paper presented at the annual meeting of the American Political Science Association, Washington, D.C., September 2–5, 1993).

7. John F. Hale, "The Democratic Leadership Council: Institutionalizing a Party Faction" (Paper presented at The State of the Parties: 1992 and Beyond conference, Ray C. Bliss Institute of Applied Politics, University of Akron, Akron, Ohio, September 1993), 10.

8. William Galston and Elaine C. Kamarck, "The Politics of Evasion: Democrats and the Presidency" (Washington, D.C.: Progressive Policy Institute, 1989), 3–4.

9. Hale, "A Different Kind of Democrat," 14–16.

10. Gwen Ifill, "Democratic Group Argues over Goals," *New York Times*, May 7, 1991.

11. Dan Balz and David S. Broder, "Democrats Argue over Quota Clause," *Washington Post,* May 7, 1991.

12. Hale, "The Democratic Leadership Council," 15–16.

13. Stanley B. Greenberg, *Middle Class Dreams: The Politics and Power of the New American Majority* (New York: Times Books, 1995), 205–206.

14. Tom Rosenstiel, *Strange Bedfellows: How Television and the Presidential Candidates Changed American Politics, 1992* (New York: Hyperion, 1993), 50; Kopkind, 116.

15. E. J. Dionne Jr., *Why Americans Hate Politics* (New York: Touchstone, 1991); and Thomas Byrne Edsall and Mary D. Edsall, *Chain Reaction: The Impact of Race, Rights, and Taxes on American Politics* (New York: Norton, 1991, 1992).

16. Rosenstiel, 51; Jack W. Germond and Jules Witcover, *Mad as Hell: Revolt at the Ballot Box, 1992* (New York: Warner Books, 1993), 202.

17. Brown's portrayal of Larry Holman is typical of this analysis. Peter Brown, *Minority Party: Why the Democrats Face Defeat in 1992 and Beyond* (Washington, D.C.: Regnery Gateway, 1991), 143–144, relates sympathetically how Holman, a recent migrant from Iowa to South Carolina, did not get a particular job because of racial preferences, even though Brown admits that there is no way of knowing Holman's score on the employment test or whether the job eventually went to a minority. Brown then quotes Holman as saying, "I blame the Democrats for these kinds of programs." Moreover, Brown fails to note that Holman's move from Iowa stemmed from the disastrous impact of Republican policies on that state's economy in the 1980s. Thus, Brown substitutes the imagined sins of affirmative action and the Democrats for the real ones of the Republicans.

18. Michael Kramer, "The Brains Behind Clinton," *Time,* May 4, 1992, 45.

19. Frady, 132. See also Christopher Hitchens, "Minority Report," *The Nation,* March 2, 1992, 258.

20. Mickey Kaus, "RFK Envy," *New Republic,* June 29, 1992, 13.

21. Sidney Blumenthal, "Firebell," *New Republic,* May 25, 1992, 14.

22. Chuck Philips, "'I Do Not Advocate . . . Murdering,'" *Los Angeles Times,* June 17, 1992. See also *Washington Post,* June 16, 1993; and Sheila Rule, "Rapper Chided by Clinton Calls Him a Hypocrite," *New York Times,* June 17, 1992.

23. Bob Woodward, *The Agenda: Inside the Clinton White House* (New York: Simon and Schuster, 1994), 41.

24. Germond and Witcover, 303; David S. Broder and Thomas B. Edsall, "Clinton Finds Biracial Support for Criticism of Rap Singer," *Washington Post,* June 16, 1993; David S. Broder, "Clinton's Gamble with Jesse Jackson," *Washington Post,* June 17, 1993.

25. Thomas B. Edsall, "Black Leaders View Clinton Strategy with Mix of Pragmatism, Optimism," *Washington Post,* October 28, 1992.

26. Germond and Witcover, 304.

27. Tom B. Edsall, "Clinton Stuns Rainbow Coalition," *Washington Post,* June 14, 1992.

28. Gwen Ifill, "Clinton at Jackson Meeting: Warmth, and Some Friction," *New York Times,* June 14, 1992.

29. Michael Kramer, "The Green-Eyed Monsters," *Time*, June 29, 1993, 49; Richard Cohen, "Sister Souljah: Clinton's Gumption," *Washington Post,* June 16, 1992; Broder and Edsall; Joe Klein, "The Jesse Primary," *Newsweek,* June 22, 1992, 28.

30. Rosenstiel, 51.

31. Ibid., 53.

32. Andrew Hacker, "The Blacks and Clinton," *New York Review of Books,* August 28, 1993, 14.

33. Bill Clinton and Al Gore, *Putting People First: How We Can All Change America* (New York: Times Books, 1992), 64.

34. Hacker, 14.

35. Thomas B. Edsall, "The Special Interest Gambit," *Washington Post,* January 3, 1993; Rosenstiel, 281.

36. Paul J. Quirk and Jon K. Dalager, "The Election: A 'New Democrat' and a New Kind of Presidential Campaign," in Michael Nelson, ed., *The Elections of 1992* (Washington, D.C.: Congressional Quarterly Press, 1993), 78; Harold W. Stanley and Richard G. Niemi, *Vital Statistics on American Politics* (Washington, D.C.: Congressional Quarterly Press, 1990), 100.

37. Richard E. Cohen, *Changing Course in Washington: Clinton and the New Congress* (New York: Macmillan, 1993), 53; Edsall, "The Special Interest Gambit."

38. Kenneth O'Reilly, *Nixon's Piano: Presidents and Racial Politics from Washington to Clinton* (New York: Free Press, 1995), 420.

39. Elizabeth Drew, *On the Edge: The Clinton Presidency* (New York: Simon and Schuster, 1994), 343.

40. Jann S. Wenner and William Greider, "The Rolling Stone Interview: President Clinton," *Rolling Stone,* December 9, 1993, 81.

41. *Public Papers of the Presidents of the United States: William J. Clinton, 1993, Volume II* (Washington, D.C.: GPO, 1994), 1981–1991; Gwen Ifill, "After Clinton's Sermon Blacks Are Looking for Action, Not Amens," *New York Times,* November 21, 1993.

42. *Public Papers of the Presidents of the United States: William J. Clinton, 1994, Volume II* (Washington, D.C.: GPO, 1995), 1468–1470.

43. Ibid., 1470.

44. Philip A. Klinkner, *Midterm: The Elections of 1994* (Boulder: Westview Press, 1996).

45. Mickey Kaus, "They Blew It," *New Republic,* December 5, 1994, 14.

46. Joe Klein, "Wither Liberalism?" *Newsweek,* November 21, 1994, 56.

47. Press release from the Center on Budget and Policy Priorities, December 4, 1996.

48. In the final House vote on welfare reform, Democrats divided evenly, 98–98. In the Senate, 25 Democrats voted in favor, with only 21 opposed to the bill.

49. Noah Isackson, "Demand Grows for Basic Needs," *Chicago Tribune,* December 11, 1997; Dennis O'Brien, "City's 30 Shelters Filled to Capacity," *Baltimore Sun,* December 5, 1997; Laura Griffin, "News Charities Put Focus on Emergency Aid Agencies," *Dallas Morning News,* November 27, 1997. For more extensive discussion of this legislation and its consequences, see chapter 6 in this volume.

50. Holly Idelson, "Clinton Comes to Defense of Affirmative Action," *Congressional Quarterly Weekly Report,* July 22, 1995, 2194.

51. Bill Clinton, *Between Hope and History: Meeting America's Challenges for the Twenty-first Century* (New York: Times Books, 1996), 132–133.

52. "Transcript of Second Presidential Debate," *New York Times,* October 17, 1996.

53. Ruy Teixeira, *Who Joined the Democrats?: Understanding the 1996 Election Results* (Washington, D.C.: Economic Policy Institute, 1996, http://epn.org/epi/epevnc.html]).

54. Steven A. Holmes, "Clinton Panel on Race Urges Variety of Modest Measures," *New York Times,* September 18, 1998.

55. "Remarks by the President at University of California at San Diego Commencement," White House Press Release, June 27, 1997.

56. Kenneth T. Walsh, "Learning from Big Jumbo: Why Clinton Scrutinizes Presidents Obscure and Legendary," *U.S. News and World Report,* January 26, 1998, 33.

Chapter 2

1. Frances Fitzgerald, *Cities on a Hill* (New York: Simon and Schuster, 1986).

2. Allan Bloom, *The Closing of the American Mind* (New York: Simon and Schuster, 1987).

3. Russell Jacoby, *The Last Intellectuals: American Culture in the Age of Academe* (New York: Basic Books, 1987).

4. Robert N. Bellah, Richard Madsen, William M. Sullivan, Ann Swidler, and Steve Tipton, *Habits of the Heart: Individualism and Commitment in American Life* (New York: Harper and Row, 1985); Robert N. Bellah,

Richard Madsen, William M. Sullivan, Ann Swidler, and Steven M. Tipton, *The Good Society* (New York: Random House, 1991).

5. Individualism, of course, is a major strand in the history of western political and social theory. See C. B. MacPherson, *The Political Theory of Possessive Individualism* (New York: Oxford University Press, 1962).

6. William Foote Whyte, *Streetcorner Society: The Social Structure of an Italian Slum* (Chicago: University of Chicago Press, 1943); Herbert Gans, *The Urban Villagers: Group and Class in the Life of Italian-Americans* (New York: Anchor Books, 1962).

7. John Higham, *Strangers in the Land: Patterns of American Nativism, 1860–1925,* 2d ed. (New York: Atheneum, 1981), 67.

8. Salvatore La Gumina, *WOP! A Documentary History of Anti-Italian Discrimination in the United States* (San Francisco: Straight Arrow Books, 1973), 233.

9. William P. Dillingham, *Reports of the Immigration Commission: Dictionary of Races or Peoples* (Washington, D.C.: GPO, 1911), 82, 129.

10. Edward Alsworth Ross, *The Old World in the New* (New York: Century Company, 1914), 155.

11. Ibid., 156–157.

12. Ibid.

13. Ibid., 36.

14. Ibid., 44.

15. David Hollinger, "How Wide the Circle of the 'We'? American Intellectuals and the Problem of the Ethnos Since World War II," *American Historical Review* (April 1993):317–333.

16. Susan Okin, *Women in Western Political Thought* (Princeton: Princeton University Press, 1979), 10.

17. Higham.

18. Madison Grant and Charles Stewart Davison, *The Alien in Our Midst, or, Selling Our Birthright for a Mess of Industrial Pottage* (New York: Galton, 1930).

19. John Bodnar, Rober Simon, and Michael P. Weber, *Lives of Their Own: Blacks, Italians, and Poles in Pittsburgh, 1900–1960* (Champaign: University of Illinois Press, 1982), 240.

20. Rosalind Rosenberg, *Beyond Separate Spheres: Intellectual Roots of Modern Feminism* (New Haven: Yale University Press, 1982), 194.

21. See Micaela di Leonardo, *The Varieties of Ethnic Experience: Kinship, Class, and Gender Among California Italian-Americans* (Ithaca: Cornell University Press 1984), 129–135, for a more extensive critique of the community myth. See also Stow Persons, *Ethnic Studies at Chicago, 1905–45* (Urbana: University of Illinois Press, 1987); Higham; and Oscar Handlin, *The Uprooted* (Boston: Little, Brown, 1951).

22. Robert Park and Herbert Miller, *Old World Traits Transplanted* (New York: Harper and Brothers, 1921), 61.

23. Ibid.

24. Ibid., 62, 237.

25. Ibid., 71.

26. Ibid.

27. Ibid., 269.

28. Ibid., 264.

29. Ibid., 269–270.

30. Ibid., 270.

31. Herbert Gans, *The Levittowners: Ways of life and Politics in a New Suburban Community* (New York: Vintage Books, 1967); David Riesman, *The Lonely Crowd: A Study of the Changing American Character* (New Haven: Yale University Press, 1950); William H. Whyte, *The Organization Man* (New York: Simon and Schuster, 1956); Lee Rainwater et al., *Workingman's Wife* (Dobbs Ferry, N.Y.: Oceana Publications, 1959); Mirra Komarovsky, *Blue-Collar Marriage* (New York: Random House, 1964).

32. Milton Gordon, *Assimilation in American Life: The Role of Race, Religion, and National Origins* (New York: Oxford University Press, 1964).

33. Nathan Glazer and Daniel Patrick Moynihan, *Beyond the Melting Pot: The Negroes, Puerto Ricans, Jews, Italians, and Irish of New York City*, 2d ed. (Cambridge, Mass.: MIT Press, 1970); Michael Novak, *The Rise of the Unmeltable Ethnics: Politics and Culture in the Seventies* (New York: Macmillan, 1971); Andrew Greeley, *Why Can't They Be like Us? America's White Ethnic Groups* (New York: Dutton, 1971); Richard Gambino, *Blood of My Blood: The Dilemma of the Italian-Americans* (New York: Anchor Books, 1974).

34. Werner Sollors, *Beyond Ethnicity: Consent and Descent in American Culture* (New York: Oxford University Press, 1987), 21.

35. Novak, 136.

36. Nancy Seifer, *Absent from the Majority: Working Class Women in America* (New York: National Project on Ethnic America, American Jewish Committee, 1973), 8.

37. Gambino, 343.

38. Deanna Paoli Gumina, *The Italians of San Francisco, 1850–1930* (New York: Center of Migration Studies, 1978), 37.

39. Irving Howe, *World of Our Fathers: The Journey of the East European Jews to America and the Life They Found and Made* (New York: Simon and Schuster, 1976), 170–171.

40. Stephen Steinberg, *The Ethnic Myth: Race, Ethnicity, and Class in America*, 2d ed. (Boston: Beacon Press, 1981), 218ff.; di Leonardo, 47–151.

41. Douglas S. Massey and Nancy A. Denton, *American Apartheid: Segregation and the Making of the Underclass* (Cambridge: Harvard University Press, 1992), 33ff.; di Leonardo, 129.

42. The following discussion relies on Sara Evans, *Personal Politics: The Roots of Women's Liberation in the Civil Rights Movement and the New Left* (New York: Random House, 1979); Adolph Reed Jr., ed., *Race, Politics, and Culture: Critical Essays on the Radicalism of the 1960's* (Westport, Conn.: Greenwood Press, 1986); James Miller, *Democracy Is in the Streets: From Port Huron to the Siege of Chicago* (New York: Simon and Schuster, 1987); John R. Logan and Harvey L. Molotch, *Urban Fortunes: The Political Economy of Place* (Berkeley and Los Angeles: University of California Press, 1987); and Barbara Bergmann, *The Economic Emergence of Women* (New York: Basic Books, 1986).

43. See Adolph Reed Jr., *The Jesse Jackson Phenomenon* (New Haven: Yale University Press, 1986); Martin Shefter, *Political Crisis/Fiscal Crisis: The Collapse and Revival of New York City* (New York: Basic Books, 1985); Norman Fainstein, "The Underclass/Mismatch Hypothesis as an Explanation for Black Economic Deprivation," *Politics and Society* 4 (1987):1–29; Stanley Lieberson, *A Piece of the Pie: Blacks and White Immigrants Since 1880* (Berkeley and Los Angeles: University of California Press, 1980); Michael Brown, "The Segmented Welfare System: Distributive Conflict and Retrenchment in the United States, 1968–84," in Michael Brown, ed., *Remaking the Welfare State: Retrenchment and Social Policy in America and Europe* (Philadelphia: Temple University Press, 1988); and Frances Piven and Richard Cloward, *The Breaking of the Social Compact* (New York: New Press, 1998). See also chapter 4 in this volume.

44. Massey and Denton, 49.

45. Chapter 4.

46. Sollors, 17.

47. Carol B. Stack, *All Our Kin: Strategies for Survival in a Black Community* (New York: Harper and Row, 1974); Herbert Gutman, *Work, Culture, and Society in Industrializing America: Essays in American Working-Class and Social History* (New York: Random House, 1976); Lawrence Levine, *Black Culture and Black Consciousness: Afro-American Folk Thought from Slavery to Freedom* (New York: Norton, 1977).

48. Greeley, 18.

49. Linda Gordon, *Heroes of Their Own Lives: The Politics and History of Family Violence, Boston, 1880–1960* (New York: Penguin, 1988). Gordon is concerned in this study to delineate the racist and sexist ideology of the social welfare establishment and its hypocrisy in denying the presence of male violence and child abuse among its own kind.

50. Novak, 35.

51. di Leonardo, 96–128.

52. Steinberg, 219.

53. di Leonardo, 222.

54. Ibid., 37.

55. Ibid., 181.

56. Susan Estabrook Kennedy, *If All We Did Was Weep at Home: A History of White Working-Class Women in America* (Bloomington: Indiana University Press, 1979), 241–242.

57. Gutman; Judith E. Smith, "Our Own Kind: Family and Community Networks," *Radical History Review* 17 (1978):99–120; Judith Smith, *Family Connections: A History of Italian and Jewish Immigrant Lives in Providence, Rhode Island, 1900–1940* (Albany: State University of New York Press, 1985).

58. Alice Echols, *Daring to Be Bad: Radical Feminism in America, 1967–75* (Minneapolis: University of Minnesota Press, 1989).

59. See also Micaela di Leonardo, "Women's Culture and Its Discontents," in Brett Williams, ed., *The Politics of Culture* (Washington, D.C.: Smithsonian Institution Press, 1991), 219–242; and Micaela di Leonardo, *Exotics at Home: Anthropologies, Others, American Modernity* (Chicago: University of Chicago Press, 1998), chap. 2.

60. Elaine Showalter, "Feminist Criticism in the Wilderness," in Elizabeth Abel, ed., *Writing and Sexual Difference* (Chicago: University of Chicago Press, 1982), 27.

61. Judith Moschkovich, "–But I Know You, American Woman," in Cherrie Moraga and Gloria Anzaldúa, eds., *This Bridge Called My Back: Writings by Radical Women of Color* (Watertown, Mass.: Persephone Press, 1981), 82.

62. Temma Kaplan, "Female Consciousness and Collective Action: The Case of Barcelona, 1910–1918," *Signs* 7(3) (1982):543.

63. Gerda Lerner, "Politics and Culture in Women's History: A Symposium," *Feminist Studies* 6(1) (1980):53.

64. Carol Gilligan, *In a Different Voice: Psychological Theory and Women's Development* (Cambridge, Mass.: Harvard University Press, 1982), 17.

65. Nancy Cott, "Feminist Theory and Feminist Movements: The Past Before Us," in Juliet Mitchell and Ann Oakley, eds., *What Is Feminism? A Re-Examination* (New York: Pantheon Books, 1986), 49–62.

66. Kaplan, 543.

67. Two of the more obvious examples are Riane Eisler, *The Chalice and the Blade* (New York: Harper and Row, 1987), which asserts "those dimly lit Neolithic and Paleolithic Ages when Goddess religions flourished" (cover

blurb); and Jean Shinoda Bolen, *Goddesses in Everywoman* (New York, Harper and Row, 1984), which offers a pre–"running with the wolves" Jungian trip through Greek mythology. See also Marija Gimbutas, *The Language of the Goddess* (London: Thames and Hudson, 1989), xxi.

68. Merlin Stone, *When God Was a Woman* (New York: Dial Press, 1976); Elizabeth Gould Davis, *The First Sex* (New York: Putnam's, 1971).

69. Sally Gearheart, *The Wanderground: Stories of the Hill Women* (Watertown, Mass.: Persephone Press, 1978); Charlotte Perkins Gilman, *Herland* (New York: Pantheon Books, 1979).

70. Adolph Reed Jr., "The 'Black Revolution' and the Reconstitution of Domination," in Reed, ed., *Race, Politics, and Culture,* 78.

71. See, for example, Linda K. Kerber, Catherine C. Greeno and Eleanor Maccoby, Zella Luria, Carol B. Stack, and Carol Gilligan, "Viewpoint: On *In a Different Voice:* An Interdisciplinary Forum," *Signs* 11(2) (1986):304–333.

72. Jill McLean Taylor, Carol Gilligan, and Amy Sullivan, *Between Voice and Silence: Women and Girls, Race and Relationship* (Cambridge, Mass.: Harvard University Press, 1995).

73. di Leonardo, 210.

74. Marianne Williamson, *A Woman's Worth* (New York: Random House, 1993), 6.

75. Ibid., 15, 120, 137.

76. See Clarissa Pinkola Estes, *Women Who Run with the Wolves: Myths and Stories of the Wild Woman Archetype* (New York: Ballantine Books, 1992); and John Gray, *Men Are from Mars, Women Are from Venus: A Practical Guide for Improving Communication and Getting What You Want in Your Relationship* (New York: HarperCollins, 1992).

77. Katha Pollitt, "Are Women Morally Superior to Men? Marooned on Gilligan's Island," *The Nation,* December 28, 1992. This article was also published in *Utne Reader,* no. 59 (September-October 1993):101–109, with an angry response by Deborah Tannen, who was criticized in the article.

78. Ibid., 806–807.

79. Janet Sayers, *Biological Politics: Feminist and Antifeminist Perspectives* (New York: Tavistock, 1982). See also Verta Taylor and Leila Rupp, "Women's Culture and Lesbian Feminist Activism: A Reconsideration of Women's Culture," *Signs* 19(3) (1993):32–61, which, in its zeal to defend the women's culture construct, implies that only lesbians are feminist activists in the American present and claims feminist political status for drug abuse and religious groups.

80. Stephan Thernstrom, *The Other Bostonians: Poverty and Progress in the American Metropolis, 1880–1970* (Cambridge, Mass.: Harvard University Press, 1973), 169.

81. Debora Silverman, *Selling Culture: Bloomingdale's, Diana Vreeland, and the New Aristocracy of Taste in Reagan's America* (New York: Pantheon Books, 1986).

82. "The Glamour Word on . . . *Tony 'n' Tina's Wedding,*" *Glamour* (October 1988):175.

83. Frank Levy, *Dollars and Dreams: The Changing American Income Distribution* (New York: Norton, 1988); Doug Henwood, "US: #1 in Poor, #3 in Rich, #8 in Middle Class," *Left Business Observer*, December 13, 1993, 5.

84. Michael Katz, *In the Shadow of the Poorhouse: A Social History of Welfare in America* (New York: Basic Books, 1986).

85. William Ryan, *Blaming the Victim,* 2d ed. (New York: Random House, 1976).

86. Frances Fox Piven and Richard Cloward, *Regulating the Poor* (New York: Pantheon Books, 1971), 281.

87. George Russell, "Minority Within a Minority: The Underclass," *Time,* August 29, 1977, 15; Ken Auletta, *The Underclass* (New York: Vintage Books, 1983); Chicago Tribune Staff, *The American Millstone: An Examination of the Nation's Permanent Underclass* (Chicago: Contemporary Books, 1986); William Julius Wilson, *The Truly Disadvantaged: The Inner City, the Underclass, and Public Policy* (Chicago: University of Chicago Press, 1987), 151.

88. Russell, 15.

89. Wilson, 151.

90. Philip Kasinitz, "Facing Up to the Underclass," *Telos* (Summer 1988): 178.

91. Mike Royko, "Don't Shed a Tear for Maxwell Street," *Chicago Tribune,* November 2, 1993.

92. Francis X. Clines, "As Pizza Maker Knows, Sinatra Still Delivers," *New York Times,* October 10, 1993.

93. Sam Roberts, "Fighting the Tide of Bloodshed on Streets Resembling a War Zone," *New York Times,* November 15, 1993.

94. Steinberg, 272.

95. Claire Jean Kim, "The Racial Triangulation of Asian Americans," *Politics and Society* (forthcoming); Ashley Dunn, "Southeast Asians Highly Dependent on Welfare in the U.S.," *New York Times*, May 19, 1994.

96. Suzanne Model, "The Ethnic Niche and the Structure of Opportunity: Immigrants and Minorities in New York City," in Michael Katz, ed., *The "Underclass" Debate: Views from History* (Princeton: Princeton University Press, 1993), 161–193.

97. Steinberg, 275.

98. di Leonardo, *The Varieties*, 177.

99. Jim Sleeper, *The Closest of Strangers: Liberalism and the Politics of Race in New York* (New York: Norton, 1990), 208.

100. See Gerald Marzorati, Benjamin Barber, Mary Ann Glendon, Dan Kemmis, Christopher Lasch, and Christopher Stone, "Who Owes What to Whom?" *Harper's* (February 1991):43–54.

101. Amitai Etzioni, *The Responsive Community: Rights, Responsibilities, and the Communitarian Agenda* (New York: Crown, 1993), 253–267.

Chapter 3

1. Quoted in Donna Minkowitz, "Wrong Side of the Rainbow," *The Nation,* June 28, 1993, 892.

2. Ruth Marcus, "Clinton Makes Emotional Appeal Against Crime," *Washington Post,* November 14, 1993.

3. Althea Knight, "Strategies to End the Carnage," *Washington Post,* October 27, 1993.

4. Lance Morrow, "The U.S. Campaign," *Time,* August 31, 1992, 24–27.

5. "Children of the Shadows," *New York Times,* 1993.

6. Barbara Whitehead, "Dan Quayle Was Right," *Atlantic Monthly* (April 1993):66. Judith Stacey, "The Neo-Family-Values Campaign," in Roger Lancaster and Micaela di Leonardo, eds., *The Gender/Sexuality Reader* (New York: Routledge, 1997), 453–470, writes persuasively of a network of scholars, policy institutions, and think tanks characterizing themselves as on the liberal left that carried the family values debate into the 1990s.

7. Whitehead.

8. Cornel West, *Race Matters* (Boston: Beacon Press, 1993), 5.

9. David Ellwood, *Poor Support* (New York: Basic Books, 1988), 134.

10. Stephanie Coontz, *The Way We Never Were* (New York: Basic Books, 1992), 202–204, 236; Arline Geronimus, "Teenage Childbearing and Social and Reproductive Disadvantage: The Evolution of Complex Questions and the Demise of Simple Answers," *Family Relations* 40(4) (1991):463–471.

11. Kenneth Jackson, *Crabgrass Frontier* (New York: Oxford University Press, 1985); Coontz; David Bartelt, "Housing the 'Underclass,'" in Michael Katz, ed., *The "Underclass" Debate: Views from History* (Princeton: Princeton University Press, 1993), 118–157.

12. Robert F. Drinan, "The Crisis in Family Law," *Vital Speeches of the Day* 26(20), May 20, 1958, 638, 640.

13. James Gilbert, *A Cycle of Outrage* (New York: Oxford University Press, 1986); Lynn Spigel, *Make Room for TV* (Chicago: University of Chicago Press, 1993); Jacob Panken, "Psychotherapeutic Value of Books in the Treatment and Prevention of Juvenile Delinquency," *American Journal of Psychotherapy* 1(1) (1947):71–86.

14. According to Whitehead, 50: "These [the 1950s] were the years when the nation confidently boarded up orphanages and closed foundling hospitals, certain that such institutions would never again be needed. In movie theaters across the country parents and children could watch the drama of parental separation and death in the great Disney classics, secure in the knowledge that such nightmare visions . . . were only make-believe."

15. Rickie Solinger, *Wake Up Little Susie* (New York: Routledge, 1992), examines the ways in which these experiences were raced. Social workers argued that black teen mothers suffered from hypersexuality, pathological selfishness, and dependency, nurtured by family and cultural disorganization. Some social workers recommended benign neglect, for nobody wanted to adopt the babies anyway and their grandmothers could care for them. Others joined lawmakers in urging a punitive welfare policy, especially in the face of increasing civil rights agitation. For example, "suitable home laws" enacted in many states deprived young mothers of benefits. In 1960, twenty-three thousand teen mothers were removed from the Aid to Families with Dependent Children rolls in Louisiana alone. In many states, teen mothers were excluded or evicted from public housing, and several legislatures discussed making teen motherhood a criminal offense.

I do not intend to portray teen mothers, or the other people described here, as mere victims. Many organized their own lives against great obstacles and fought for social change. I am interested in misogyny, homophobia, and discrimination, but others have described with great success the experiences, agony, and agency of those discriminated against. As examples, see Lancaster and di Leonardo; John D'Emilio, "Homosexual Menace," and Elizabeth Kennedy and Madeline Davis, "The Reproduction of Butch-Fem Roles," both in Kathy Peiss and Christina Simmons, eds., *Passion and Power* (Philadelphia: Temple University Press, 1989), 226–240, 241–258; Lillian Faderman, *Odd Girls and Twilight Lovers* (New York: Columbia University Press, 1991); Erving Goffman, *Asylums* (Garden City, N.Y.: Anchor Books, 1961); and Carol Warren, *Madwives* (New Brunswick: Rutgers University Press, 1987).

16. Freeman and Grayson, 244–245.

17. Cited in John Neill, "Whatever Became of the Schizophrenogenic Mother?" *American Journal of Psychotherapy* 44 (1990):501.

18. Edward Kempf, "Bisexual Factors in Curable Schizophrenia," *American Journal of Psychiatry* (1948): 414–419; Franklin S. Klaf and Charles A. Davis, "Homosexuality and Paranoid Schizophrenia: A Survey of 150 Cases and Controls," *American Journal of Psychiatry* (June 1960):1070–1075; Theodore Lidz, Beulah Parker, and Alice Cornelison, "The Role of the Father in the Family Environment of the Schizophrenic Patient," *American Journal of Psychiatry* (August 1956):126–132; Theodore Lidz, Alice Cornelison, Stephen Fleck, and Dorothy Terry, "The Intrafamilial Environment

of Schizophrenic Patients: Marital Schism and Marital Skew," *American Journal of Psychiatry* (September 1957):241–248; Freeman and Grayson, "Maternal Attitudes in Schizophrenia," *American Journal of Psychiatry* (June 1960):45–52; Freida Fromm-Reichmann, "Psychotherapy of Schizophrenia," *American Journal of Psychiatry* (December 1954): 410–419; S. Jibson Weinberg, "A Sociological Analysis of a Schizophrenic Type," *American Sociological Review* 15(5) (1950):600–610; Gregory Bateson et al., "Toward a Theory of Schizophrenia," *Behavioral Science* 1 (1956):4. Hilde L. Mosse, "The Misuse of the Diagnosis Childhood Schizophrenia," *American Journal of Psychiatry* (March 1958):791–794, writes that children were often misdiagnosed as schizophrenics (although the disease was believed to set in at adolescence) and sent to hospitals or schools for the mentally defective, where they received electroconvulsive shock therapy and became very disoriented. Some also received lobotomies. See also Charles. W. Wahl, "Some Antecedent Factors in the Family Histories of 568 Male Schizophrenics of the United States Navy," *American Journal of Psychiatry* (September 1956):201–210; Bertram Roberts and Jerome Myers, "Schizophrenia in the Youngest Male Child of the Lower Middle Class," *American Journal of Psychiatry* (August 1955):129–134; and Neill.

Black Americans were invisible in discussions of the schizophrenogenic mother, with schizophrenia in black neighborhoods studied epidemiologically, like tuberculosis, illegitimacy, and juvenile delinquency, linked to social disorganization, congestion, and blight. See Robert Faris, *Mental Disorders in Urban Areas* (Reprint, New York: Hafner, 1960).

Blacks rarely had access to private therapists, and therapists worried that it would be impossible to communicate with them openly anyway. See, especially, Ralph W. Heine, "The Negro Patient in Psychotherapy," *American Journal of Psychiatry,* 373–376.

19. Louis West, William Dodge, and Robert Williams, "An Approach to the Problem of Homosexuality in the Military Service," *American Journal of Psychiatry* (November 1958):392–396.

20. Ibid., 392.

21. Manfred Guttmacher, "The Homosexual in Court," *Journal of the American Psychiatric Association* (February 1956):594–595.

22. Guttmacher, 594–595. Most sodomy laws forbid "carnal copulation by human beings with each other against nature . . . or with animals, fowl, or corpses." Karl M. Bowman and Bernice Engle, "A Psychiatric Evaluation of Laws of Homosexuality," *American Journal of Psychiatry* (February 1956):577. See also Edith Balassa, "Rehabilitation of Delinquent Girls," *American Journal of Psychotherapy* 1(3) (1947); and West, Dodge, and Williams. Except for a few large-scale studies in state hospitals and prisons, gay black men were ignored. Even in these studies, they appear only in the contexts of electroshock and criminal sentencing.

23. William Julius Wilson, *The Truly Disadvantaged* (Chicago: University of Chicago Press, 1987), 7.

For an argument that takes a slightly different approach but rails equally against our nostalgia for a golden age, see Michael Katz, "Reframing the Debate," in Katz, ed., 440–447.

24. Several excellent social histories document this diversity. See, as examples, Kenneth Kusmer, *A Ghetto Takes Shape* (Urbana: University of Illinois Press, 1976); Kenneth Kusmer, "Ghettos Real and Imagined," *International Journal of Urban and Regional Research* (December 1997):706–711; Kenneth Kusmer, "African Americans in the City Since World War II," *Journal of Urban History* 21 (May 1995):4; Kenneth Kusmer, "The Black Urban Experience in American History," in Darlene Clark Hine, ed., *The State of Afro-American History* (Baton Rouge, La.: LSU Press, 1986):89–123; James Grossman, *Land of Hope* (Chicago: University of Chicago Press, 1989); Thomas Sugrue, *The Origins of the Urban Crisis* (Princeton: Princeton University Press, 1996); Arnold Hirsch, *Making the Second Ghetto* (Cambridge: Cambridge University Press, 1983); and Arnold Hirsch and Raymond Mohl, *Urban Policy in Twentieth-Century America* (New Brunswick: Rutgers University Press, 1993).

While attempting to distance himself from Wilson's vision by arguing that the ghetto *is* organized (by the dog-eat-dog law of the jungle), Loic Waquant makes this mistake again in the widely acclaimed "Three Pernicious Myths About the Ghetto," *International Journal of Urban and Regional Research* 21(2) (1997):341–353. He, too, refuses to consider the qualities that made ghettos different versions of class and race on the ground: patterns of migration; where people went when; the gender, ethnic, and class mix of what they found; the conditions of the labor market and the union movement; processes of ecological growth and change; the availability of schools and teachers; the energy and success of social movements. Put simply, there was and is no *ghetto*.

25. St. Clair Drake and Horace Cayton, *Black Metropolis* (New York: Harcourt, Brace, 1945).

26. Ibid.

27. Ibid., 565, 566, 567.

28. All quotes in this paragraph are from ibid., 559–563.

29. Karen Olson, "Old West Baltimore: Segregation, African-American Culture, and the Struggle for Equality," in Elizabeth Fee, Linda Shopes, and Linda Zeidman, eds., *The Baltimore Book* (Philadelphia: Temple University Press, 1991), 57–78.

30. Steven Gregory, "The Changing Significance of Race and Class in an African-American Community," *American Ethnologist* 19(2) (1992):259.

31. Drake and Cayton, 572.

32. Shirlee Taylor Hazlip, *The Sweeter the Juice* (New York: Simon and Schuster, 1994), 78–80. See also Kusmer, "Ghettos Real and Imagined." Steven Gregory, *Black Corona* (Princeton: Princeton University Press, 1998), offers a detailed critique and exposition of the actual class complexity in a black community. See also Norman Fainstein and Susan Nesbitt, "Did the Black Ghetto Have a Golden Age? Class Structure and Class Segregation in New York City, 1949–1970, with Initial Evidence for 1990," *Journal of Urban History* 23 (November 1996):1.

33. Joseph Jordan, . . . *You'll Never See Those Days Anymore* (Washington, D.C.: Institute for the Preservation and Study of African-American Writing and the D.C. Community Humanities Council, 1990), 35–36; Theresa Trainor, "I'm a Native Southwest Person . . . That's Where My Heart Is," (Washington, D.C.: American University, Department of Anthropology, 1992, nonthesis option paper); Theresa Trainor, "We Are Not Weeping Willow Trees: A Story of 20th Century African American Men Growing Up in Southwest" (Washington, D.C.: American University, Department of Anthropology, 1993); Essie Olds, personal communication to the author, 1997, on the use of "slaughterhouses" to refer to segregated hospitals.

34. Green.

35. Quoted in Kenesaw Landis, *Segregation in Washington* (Chicago: University of Chicago Press, 1948).

36. S. L. Fishbein, "Washington's Wickedest, the Second Precinct," *Washington Post* series, March 14–March 21, 1954.

37. Drake and Cayton, 564–599.

38. Landis; Brett Williams, "There Goes the Neighborhood," in Anna Lou deHavenon, ed., *There's No Place Like Home* (Westport, Conn.: Bergin and Garvey Press, 1997):145–164; Brett Williams, with Tanya Ramos et al., *Park Users and Neighbors: Rapid Ethnographic Assessment of the Civil War Defenses of Washington and Anacostia Park* (Denver: National Park Service, 1997). For a compelling discussion of these processes on the national level, see chapter 5 in this volume.

39. Trainor, 31.

40. Ibid.,71.

41. Drake and Cayton, 201.

42. Records of the NAACP, National Archives of the United States, Washington, D.C.

43. Records of the NAACP, Redevelopment Land Authority, the District Commissioners' General Files, and the Washington, D.C. Housing Authority, National Archives of the United States, Washington, D.C.

44. Alfred Lewis and Harry Gabbett, "Juveniles Harass 'Baby' Precinct," *Washington Post*, 1958 (no further date given), newspaper clipping on file, Historical Society of Washington, D.C.

45. David Reisman, "Recreation and the Recreationist," *Marriage and Family Living* 16(1) (February 1954):23; Spigel; Leo Bogart, *The Age of Television* (New York: Frederick Ungar, 1956). Warren claims that for the hospitalized schizophrenic women of the Bay Area, life revolved around television, in part because they were isolated from social contacts with relatives and friends and expected to center their lives in the family home.

46. Olson. See also Elsa Barkley Brown and Gregg D. Kimball, "Mapping the Terrain of Black Richmond," *Journal of Urban History* 21 (March 1995):296–346; Kathryn Schneider Smith, *Washington at Home* (Northbridge, Calif.: Windsor, 1988); and National Capital Planning Commission, "Extending the Legacy" (Washington, D.C.: National Capital Planning Commission, 1996).

47. Cited in Coontz, 107.

48. Whitehead, 82.

49. See, for example, Louise Lamphere and Patricia Zavella, *Situated Lives* (Ithaca: Cornell University Press, 1997); Lancaster and di Leonardo; Gilbert Herdt, ed., *Gay and Lesbian Youth* (New York: Harrington Park Press, 1989); Elliot Liebow, *Tell Them Who I Am* (New York: Free Press, 1993); E. Anthony Rotundo, *American Manhood* (New York: Basic Books, 1993); Holly Sklar, *Chaos or Community?* (Boston: South End Press, 1995); Kath Weston, *Families We Choose* (New York: Columbia University Press, 1992); Brett Williams, *Upscaling Downtown* (Ithaca: Cornell University Press, 1988); Brett Williams, "Poverty Among African Americans in the Urban United States," *Human Organization* 51(2) (1992):164–173; Terry Williams and William Kornblum, *Growing Up Poor* (Lexington, Mass.: Heath, 1985); Patricia Zavella, *Women's Work and Chicano Families* (Ithaca: Cornell University Press, 1987); and Patricia Zavella, "*Mujeres* in Factories," in Micaela di Leonardo, ed., *Gender at the Crossroads of Knowledge* (Berkeley and Los Angeles: University of California Press, 1991), 312–338.

Chapter 4

1. William P. Barr, speaking on *This Week with David Brinkley,* April 26, 1992, quoted in Daniel Patrick Moynihan, "How the Great Society 'Destroyed the American Family,'" *The Public Interest* (Summer 1992):53. Barr was attorney general for President George Bush at the time.

2. See Charles Murray, *Losing Ground: American Social Policy, 1950–1980* (New York: Basic Books, 1984); Lawrence Mead, *The New Politics of Poverty* (New York: Basic Books, 1992); and Mickey Kaus, *The End of Equality* (New York: Basic Books, 1992). Murray's argument does not depend on assumptions about the culture of poverty.

3. A glossy brochure entitled "The Welfare Mess" and mailed to many California voters by the state Republican committee during the 1994 elections is

a striking illustration of this. Crime, drugs, black women, and welfare are portrayed as sordidly related and leading to innumerable social ills, from teen pregnancy to declining SAT scores. The brochure was certainly inflammatory; it also appealed to contemporary racial animosities. For an analysis of the use of such stereotypes in the 1980 election, see J. David Greenstone, "The Decline and Revival of the American Welfare State: Moral Criteria and Instrumental Reasoning in Critical Elections," in Michael K. Brown, ed., *Remaking the Welfare State: Retrenchment and Social Policy in America and Europe* (Philadelphia: Temple University Press, 1988), 165–181. See also Donald R. Kinder and Lynn M. Sanders, *Divided by Color: Racial Politics and Democratic Ideals* (Chicago: University of Chicago Press, 1996), chap. 9.

4. Thomas B. Edsall, "What Clinton Won," *New York Review of Books,* December 3, 1992, 43. Mickey Kaus, "They Blew It," *New Republic,* December 5, 1994, 1, argues, "If President Clinton had pushed for welfare reform rather than health care reform, we would now be talking about a great Democratic realignment, rather than a great Republican realignment." See also Thomas Byrne Edsall and Mary Edsall, *Chain Reaction: The Impact of Race, Rights, and Taxes on American Politics* (New York: Norton, 1992).

5. Michael Lind, *The Next American Nation: The New Nationalism and the Fourth American Revolution* (New York: Free Press, 1995); Jim Sleeper, *The Closest of Strangers* (New York: Norton, 1990), 158–164.

6. Theda Skocpol, *Social Policy in the United States* (Princeton: Princeton University Press, 1995), 250–274; William Julius Wilson, *When Work Disappears: The World of the New Urban Poor* (New York: Vintage Books, 1996), 235–238; Paul M. Sniderman and Edward G. Carmines, *Reaching Beyond Race* (Cambridge, Mass.: Harvard University Press, 1997).

7. Walter Korpi, "Social Policy and Distributional Conflict in the Capitalist Democracies: A Preliminary Comparative Framework," *West European Politics* 3 (1980):304–307.

8. Early European social policies that were inclusive but means-tested were understood to be universalistic and were the precursors to the solidaristic policies of both Sweden and Great Britain that emerged after 1945. See Peter Baldwin, *The Politics of Social Solidarity* (New York: Cambridge University Press, 1991), 89, 100, 113–114.

9. Michael K. Brown, "Remaking the Welfare State: A Comparative Perspective," in Brown, ed., *Remaking the Welfare State,* 12–14; Robert Greenstein, "Universal and Targeted Approaches to Relieving Poverty: An Alternative View," in Christopher Jencks and Paul Peterson, eds., *The Urban Underclass* (Washington, D.C.: Brookings Institution, 1991), 440–442. Means-tested entitlements were protected by the 1993 budget decisions as well, but not of Republican budget policies beginning in 1995.

10. William Julius Wilson, "Another Look at the Truly Disadvantaged," *Political Science Quarterly* 106 (1991–1992):656.

11. Jill Quadagno, *The Color of Welfare: How Racism Undermined the War on Poverty* (New York: Oxford University Press, 1994), 172–173.

12. Sniderman and Carmines, *Reaching Beyond Race,* 105–109, 115–218, 153–254. See also Kinder and Sanders, *Divided by Color,* 188–192.

13. In *Pasadena City Board of Education* v. *Spangler,* 427 U.S. 424 (1976), the Supreme Court overturned a desegregation plan requiring annual adjustment of school boundaries. Justice William Rehnquist argued that the Court could not accept remedies to overcome voluntary housing preferences. But, of course, the existence of de facto segregation has very little to do with voluntary housing preferences and very much to do with public housing policies for the poor and middle class, among other things. I am indebted to Francis Fox Piven for suggesting the example of education.

14. For a disturbing portrayal of the racial stratification in public education, see Jonathan Kozol, *Savage Inequalities* (New York: Crown, 1991).

15. Ferebee/Martz to Rufus Miles, July 7, 1950, 5, RG 51, Series 39.3, Box 125, Folder 831, National Archives (hereafter cited as NA), Washington, D.C.

16. Martha Ozawa, "The Fading Issue of the Stigma Attached to Income Support Programs for the Elderly: A Study," *Journal of Gerontological Social Work* 3 (1981):51–63; Martin Gilens, "'Race Coding' and White Opposition to Welfare," *American Political Science Review* 90 (1996):593–604. David O. Sears and Jack Citrin, *Tax Revolt: Something for Nothing in California* (Cambridge: Harvard University Press, 1985), 49, found that citizen's evaluations of social policy during the tax revolt of the late 1970s had a specific racial component: "Services whose clienteles are most widely thought to be racial minorities tend to be favored least. Welfare, public housing, food stamps, and unemployment compensation are the obvious examples."

17. Judith N. Shklar, *American Citizenship: The Quest for Inclusion* (Cambridge, Mass.: Harvard University Press, 1991), 85–86; see also 63–65, 91–94.

18. U.S. Bureau of the Census, *Measuring the Effect of Benefits and Taxes on Income and Poverty: 1986,* Series P–60, no. 164-RD–1 (Washington, D.C.: GPO, 1988), 11–12. Obviously, far more whites than blacks receive means-tested transfers, but that is not the point; the question is whether specific groups are more likely to be the beneficiary of one type of policy rather than another.

19. Wilson, *The Truly Disadvantaged,* 119. See also Richard M. Titmuss, *The Philosophy of Welfare* (London: Allen and Unwin, 1987), 129.

20. Skocpol, *Social Policy,* 221; cf. Quadagno, *The Color of Welfare,* who emphasizes the role of white racism in the failures of the Great Society.

21. Federal audits of the program revealed that the money benefited all children rather than just poor children and was being used as a substitute for

local education funding. The program functioned more as a universal entitlement than a categorical aid program for poor children. Jerome T. Murphy, "The Education Bureaucracies Implement Novel Policy: The Politics of Title I of ESEA, 1965–1972," in Allan P. Sindler, ed., *Politics and Policy in America* (Boston: Little, Brown, 1973), 170–171, 174; Allan J. Matusow, *The Unraveling of Liberalism* (New York: Harper and Row, 1985), 223–224.

22. Wilson relies on a *New York Times* article as his source: Toby Cohen, "Reagan's New Deal," *New York Times,* August 19, 1981. This view of the New Deal is mistaken; aside from social insurance, which provided few benefits in the 1930s, most New Deal social policies, including significantly the WPA public employment programs, were means-tested.

23. St. Clair Drake and Horace Cayton, *Black Metropolis: A Study of Negro Life in a Northern City* (New York: Harcourt, Brace, 1945), 101, define the color line as segregating blacks from whites and subordinating blacks by "denying them the right to compete, as individuals, on equal terms with white people for economic and political power." Drake and Cayton argue that the color line persisted because of racial prejudices—"folk-beliefs," as they call them; economic interests that served to rationalize discriminatory behavior; and the fear of losing one's social status by associating with African Americans. I am arguing that relief institutionalized, as well as expressed, the subordinate status of African Americans.

24. U.S. Congress, Senate, *Unemployment and Relief Hearings,* 75th Cong., 2d sess., 1351; *New York Times,* July 2, 1938. Hopkins was head of the Works Progress Administration, and Williams was his chief deputy.

25. Lisabeth Cohen, *Making a New Deal* (New York: Cambridge University Press, 1991), 287.

26. John Kirby, *Black Americans in the Roosevelt Era: Liberalism and Race* (Knoxville: University of Tennessee Press, 1980), 32–35. Gunnar Myrdal's theory of the vicious circle—an apt metaphor for the New Deal's racial liberalism—purported to explain why social reform would diminish white racism. Racial prejudice, he argues, in *An American Dilemma* (New York: Harper and Row, 1944), 75, was propelled by a cumulative cycle of causation in which white racism led to the degradation of African Americans and then in turn confirmed to whites their superiority and justified their racial privileges. "White prejudice and Negro standards thus mutually 'cause' each other," as Myrdal put it.

27. Peter Kellogg, "Northern Liberals and Black America: A History of White Attitudes, 1936–1952" (Ph.D. diss., Northwestern University, 1971), 3, 8–9.

28. Nancy J. Weiss, *Farewell to the Party of Lincoln* (Princeton: Princeton University Press, 1983), 209–235.

29. Accounts of the shift of black political organizations to a class perspective include Charles R. Lawrence, "Negro Organizations in Crisis" (Ph.D.

diss., Columbia University, 1953) chap. 5; Raymond Wolters, *Negroes and the Great Depression* (Westport, Conn.: Greenwood Press, 1970), chaps. 12–13; Dona Cooper Hamilton, "The National Urban League During the Depression, 1930–1939" (Ph.D. diss., Columbia University, 1982), esp. chap. 4; and Cicero Alvin Hughes, "Toward A Black United Front: The National Negro Congress Movement" (Ph.D. diss., Ohio University, 1982), chaps. 2–4.

30. Alice Kessler-Harris, *A Woman's Wage: Historical Meanings and Social Consequences* (Lexington: University Press of Kentucky, 1990), 70–72, 76–77.

31. Of uninsured workers in covered industries, black women were most severely affected: 55 percent of black women were uninsured, compared to 40 percent of black men, 30 percent of white women, and 17 percent of white men. Wayne F. Caskey to Jacob Perlman, September 27, 1940, RG 47, Social Security Board Files, Box 41, 050.01, NA.

32. Richard Sterner, *The Negro's Share: A Study of Income, Consumption, Housing, and Public Assistance* (New York: Harper and Row, 1943), 241. The data in Figures 4.1 and 4.2 are based on all cities over 250,000 population in which at least 5 percent of the population is African American. The 1940 census apparently underestimated the number of workers on WPA rolls as a result of enumerator error. There was a discrepancy between the census count and WPA payrolls. There is no way to estimate what difference, if any, this would make in the figures. U.S. Bureau of the Census, *Population,* Vol. 3, *The Labor Force,* Sixteenth Census of the United States (Washington, D.C.: GPO, 1943), Part 1, 3. But the census data are consistent with other studies of the number of black workers on WPA rolls in the early 1940s. Sterner, *The Negro's Share,* 239–244, for example, reports a similar trend based on WPA data.

33. Sterner, *The Negro's Share,* 214. *Report of the New Jersey State Temporary Commission on the Condition of the Urban Colored Population* (Trenton: 1939), 16, hereafter cited as *New Jersey State Commission;* Cheryl Lynn Greenberg, *Or Does It Explode? Black Harlem in the Great Depression* (New York: Oxford University Press, 1991), 158; Commonwealth of Pennsylvania, *Employability of Pennsylvania's General Assistance Case Load, April 1941* (Harrisburg, Penn.: Department of Public Assistance, June 1941), 13; U.S. Bureau of the Census, *Characteristics of the Population: United States Summary—Divisions and States,* Sixteenth Census of the United States (Washington, D.C.: GPO, 1943), vol. 1, Tables 37, 40. See also National Resources Planning Board, *Security, Work, and Relief Policies* (Washington, D.C.: GPO, 1942), 117. I am indebted to Woody Sanders for uncovering the reference to the New Jersey state commission.

34. National Urban League, "The Negro Working Population and Na-

tional Recovery," a special memorandum submitted to Franklin Delano Roosevelt, January 4, 1937, 3, NUL Papers, Series 1, Box 1, Library of Congress, Washington, D.C.; Arthur M. Ross, "Race, Cultural Groups, Social Differentiation," *Social Forces* 18 (1940):551; Forrester B. Washington, "The Negro and Relief," in *Proceedings of the National Conference of Social Work, 1934* (Chicago: University of Chicago Press, 1934), 183.

35. Orley Ashenfelter, "Changes in Labor Market Discrimination over Time," *Journal of Human Resources* 4 (1970):406–408; Myrdal, *An American Dilemma,* 298–299, 301; William A. Sundstrom, "Last Hired, First Fired? Unemployment and Urban Black Workers During the Great Depression," *Journal of Economic History* 52 (1992):415–429; Hamilton, "The National Urban League," 83–91.

36. Alfred Edgar Smith, "Negro Clients on Federal Unemployment Relief," December 31, 1935, 3, FERA, General Subject Series, Box 31, 060, NA.

37. Hamilton, "The National Urban League," 104–105, 142–144; Greenberg, *Or Does It Explode?* 156–157.

38. National Urban League, The Negro Worker's Councils, Bulletin no. 11, June 11, 1936, 5, NUL Papers, Series 1, Box 9, Library of Congress.

39. Christopher G. Wye, "The New Deal and the Negro Community: Toward A Broader Conceptualization," *Journal of American History* 59 (1972):636–637. Wye's study of Cleveland revealed that 16.7 percent of black WPA workers had held skilled jobs prior to the Depression but less than 1 percent held skilled jobs on emergency work projects. The discrepancy for black women was even higher.

40. Sterner, *The Negro's Share,* 229.

41. Greenberg, *Or Does It Explode?* 158; *New Jersey State Commission,* 16–17, 85–86; Irene E. Murphy, "Social Effects of Prolonged Unemployment on Negro Family Life," in *Michigan State Conference on Employment Problems of the Negro* (Detroit: October 8, 1940), 38, RG 183, Lawrence A. Oxley Files, Box 1398, NA.

42. Donald Howard, *The WPA and Federal Relief Policy* (New York: Russell Sage Foundation, 1943), 291–293; Sterner, *The Negro's Share,* 245–246.

43. Washington, "The Negro and Relief," 184; Hamilton, "The National Urban League," 326.

44. *New Jersey State Commission,* 18; *Second Report of the New Jersey Temporary Commission on the Condition of the Urban Colored Population* (Trenton: June 1940), section on relief.

45. Alfred Edgar Smith, Report of May 1938, 4, RG 69, WPA Central Files, Box 92, NA.

46. Quoted in Richard J. Jensen, "The Causes and Cures of Unemployment in the Great Depression," *Journal of Interdisciplinary History* 19

(1989):578. Public opinion data demonstrate that many people thought work relief was charity and that people could find work if they wanted to. In August 1937, 55 percent of people surveyed in a public opinion poll thought WPA workers could find work if they wanted to; by April 1939 the proportion had increased to 69 percent. See Hadley Cantril, ed., *Public Opinion, 1935–1946* (Princeton: Princeton University Press, 1951), 895, Tables 17, 18; 896, Table 35.

47. William Brock, *Welfare, Democracy, and the New Deal* (New York: Cambridge University Press, 1988), 333.

48. Jo Ann Argersinger, *Toward a New Deal in Baltimore* (Chapel Hill: University of North Carolina Press, 1988), 53; Brock, *Welfare, Democracy, and the New Deal,* 334.

49. *Chicago Defender,* August 5, 1939, WPA, Division of Information, Negro Press Digest and Related Clippings, 1936–1940, Box 4, NA.

50. *Atlanta World,* June 24, 1939, RG 69/70.71, WPA, Negro Press Digest, 1936–1940, Box 4, NA.

51. J. Douglas Brown, *An American Philosophy of Social Security* (Princeton: Princeton University Press, 1972), 132.

52. U.S. Advisory Council on Social Security, *Final Report of the Advisory Council on Social Security, 1938* (Washington, D.C.: GPO, 1938), 17–18.

53. Brown, *An American Philosophy,* 143–144; Michael Fooner, "Some Child Welfare Problems in Social Insurance," *Social Service Review* 16 (1942):652–653; Alice Kessler-Harris, "Designing Women and Old Fools: The Construction of the Social Security Amendments of 1939," in Linda K. Kerber, Alice Kessler-Harris, and Kathryn Kish Sklar, eds., *U.S. History as Women's History* (Chapel Hill: University of North Carolina Press, 1995), 87–106.

54. Oscar C. Pogge, "Family Relationships and Old-Age and Survivor's Insurance," *Social Security Bulletin* (July 1945):8.

55. Fooner, "Some Child Welfare Problems," 652–653. Fooner says that there is no record in either congressional hearings or debates of this provision, and thus it is unclear why the law was written this way.

56. Martha Derthick, *The Influence of Federal Grants* (Cambridge, Mass.: Harvard University Press, 1970), 61–63.

57. Winifred Bell, *Aid to Dependent Children* (New York: Columbia University Press, 1965), 9; Myrdal, *An American Dilemma,* 359.

58. E. Franklin Frazier, "Some Effects of the Depression on the Negro in Northern Cities," *Science and Society* 2 (1938):494. Frazier's data were derived from FERA reports.

59. Nancy J. Weiss, *The National Urban League, 1910–1940* (New York: Oxford University Press, 1974), 253.

60. Murphy, "Social Effects of Prolonged Unemployment," 33–34. Mur-

phy's report is all too prescient and reads as if it were written yesterday. There is some recent evidence that the proportion of female-headed families in the 1930s may have been higher than believed because the Census Bureau did not classify female-headed families living with in-laws or parents separately until very recently. See Hamilton, "The National Urban League," 326. See also Frances Fox Piven and Richard Cloward, *The Mean Season* (New York: Pantheon Books, 1987), 55–56; and David Ellwood and Mary Jo Bane, "The Impact of AFDC on Family Structure and Living Arrangements," *Research in Labor Economics* 7 (1986):137–207.

61. U.S. Bureau of the Census, *U.S. Census of Population: 1960,* Subject Reports: Industrial Characteristics, PC(2)-7F (Washington, D.C.: GPO, 1963), Table 3; U.S. Bureau of Labor Statistics, *Handbook of Labor Statistics: 197,* BLS Bulletin 1666 (Washington, D.C.: GPO, 1971), Tables 68, 71.

62. Elizabeth Alling and Agnes Leisy, "Aid to Dependent Children in a Postwar Year," Public Assistance Report no. 7, Federal Security Agency, Social Security Administration (Washington D.C.: Social Security Administration, 1950), 6–8.

63. Lora S. Collins, "Public Assistance Expenditures in the United States," in Otto Eckstein, ed., *Studies in the Economics of Income Maintenance* (Washington, D.C.: Brookings Institution, 1967), 132–133. Collins found a negative correlation between percent nonwhite in a state's population and the recipient rate, the number of children receiving ADC per 1,000 children when controlling for dependency. But her results are skewed by the pattern in West Virginia, which had few blacks but a very high recipient rate. Nevertheless, her study makes clear that blacks, largely in the South, received less than they either needed or were entitled to. For recent evidence on discrimination in the AFDC program in the South, see Robert Lieberman, "Race and the Administration of Social Policy, 1935–1965" (Paper presented at the annual meeting of the Social Sciences History Association, Baltimore, Maryland, November 4–7, 1993).

64. Dorothy K. Newman et al., *Protest, Politics, and Prosperity: Black Americans and White Institutions, 1940–75* (New York: Pantheon Books, 1978), 281, Table 7–16. See also Frances Fox Piven and Richard Cloward, *Regulating the Poor: The Functions of Public Welfare* (New York: Pantheon Books, 1971), chaps. 4–5, who document the use of work requirements to exclude people, mainly African Americans in the South, from the welfare rolls in the 1950s.

65. Carol Goldstein, "Some Eligibility Problems in the Illinois Aid to Dependent Children Program," *Social Service Review* 18 (1944):213–214.

66. Grace Marcus, "Reappraising Aid to Dependent Children as a Category," *Social Security Bulletin* (February 1945):3.

67. All the quotations are taken from Donald S. Howard, "Public Assistance Returns to Page One—I," *Social Work Journal* (April 1948):49, 51.

68. Paul Molloy, "The Relief Chiselers Are Stealing Us Blind," *Saturday Evening Post,* September 8, 1951, 32 ff.

69. Benjamin H. Lyndon, "Relief Probes: A Study of Public Welfare Investigations in Baltimore, New York, Detroit, 1947–1949" (Ph.D. diss., University of Chicago, 1953), 137–138.

70. Rickie Solinger, *Wake Up Little Susie: Single Pregnancy and Race Before* Roe *v.* Wade (New York: Routledge, 1992), 29, quoting Jimmie H. Davis, then governor of Louisiana, who was leading the charge to use "suitable home" laws to expel black families from ADC.

71. Ibid., 42.

72. National Urban League, "The Newburgh Plan," 3–4, NUL Papers, Series I, 1960–1966, Box 47, Folder: 1962 Public Welfare Situation, Library of Congress.

73. Solinger, *Wake Up Little Susie,* 42, 45–46, 49, 58–59, 192–193; Melissa J. Miller, "Effects of Stereotype Thinking on the American Welfare System" (Senior thesis, American Studies, University of California, Santa Cruz, 1987). See also Wahneema Lubiano, "Black Ladies, Welfare Queens, and State Minstrels," in Toni Morrison, ed., *Race-ing Justice, En-gendering Power: Essays on Anita Hill, Clarence Thomas, and the Construction of Social Reality* (New York: Pantheon Books, 1992), 323–363. The classic account of the welfare purges of the 1950s is Bell, *Aid to Dependent Children.*

74. Barbara Boland, "Participation in the Aid to Families with Dependent Children Program (AFDC)," in *Studies in Public Welfare,* Subcommittee on Fiscal Policy, Joint Economic Committee, Congress of the United States, Paper no. 12, Part 1 (Washington, D.C.: GPO, 1973), 153, Table 3.

75. U.S. Bureau of the Census, *Statistical Abstract of the United States, 1961* (Washington, D.C.: GPO, 1962), 43, Table 41; U.S. Bureau of the Census, *Statistical Abstract of the United States, 1977* (Washington, D.C.: GPO, 1978), 46, Table 60.

76. Quadagno, *The Color of Welfare,* 160–162, 171–173.

77. Kaus, *The End of Equality,* 125–129.

78. Donald C. Baumer and Carl E. Van Horn, *The Politics of Unemployment* (Washington, D.C.: Congressional Quarterly, 1985), 115–116, 159–165.

79. *Regents of University of California* v. *Bakke,* 438 U.S. 265 (1978), quoted in Gertrude Ezorsky, *Racism and Justice* (Ithaca: Cornell University Press, 1991), 133.

Chapter 5

1. U.S. Bureau of the Census, *Negroes in the United States, 1920–1932* (Washington, D.C.: GPO, 1935), 55.

2. "President Truman's Message to Congress, February 2, 1948," in Albert P. Blaustein and Robert L. Zangrando, eds., *Civil Rights and the American Negro: A Documentary History* (New York: Trident Press, 1968), 380–384. The bill was not subsequently passed, but Truman did issue executive orders to prohibit discrimination in the federal civil service and segregation in the armed forces.

3. Murray Edelman, *Constructing the Political Spectacle* (Chicago: University of Chicago Press, 1988).

4. I have borrowed the concept "deep politics" from Peter Dale Scott, who, in *Deep Politics: The Assassination of JFK* (Berkeley and Los Angeles: University of California Press, 1993), uses it to describe an entirely different subject, the assassination of John F. Kennedy. As applied by Scott, deep politics refers to the hidden, complex relationships among government officials, the intelligence agencies, the FBI, and organized crime figures at the time Kennedy was assassinated. I employ it in a similar manner to refer to the close, continuing relationships between government officials involved in regulating housing and the institutions that make up the industry.

5. William S. Worley, *J. C. Nichols and the Shaping of Kansas City: Innovation in Planned Residential Communities* (Columbia: University of Missouri Press, 1990).

6. Mark H. Rose, "There Is Less Smoke in the District: J. C. Nichols, Urban Change, and Technological Systems," *Journal of the West* (January 1986):48.

7. National Association of Real Estate Boards, *Code of Ethics* (1924), art. 34, published in Harry Grant Atkinson and L. E. Frailey, *Fundamentals of Real Estate Practice* (New York: Prentice-Hall, 1946), 428–429.

8. Ibid.

9. Bureau of National Affairs, *The Housing and Development Reporter* (Washington, D.C.: Bureau of National Affairs, 1976).

10. Ibid.

11. Department of Housing and Urban Development, *1974 Statistical Yearbook of the Department of Housing and Urban Development* (Washington, D.C.: GPO, 1976), 116–117.

12. Federal Housing Administration, *Underwriting Manual* (Washington, D.C.: GPO, February 1938), quoted in Brian J.L. Berry, *The Open Housing Question: Race and Housing in Chicago, 1966–1976* (Cambridge, Mass.: Ballinger, 1979), 9.

13. Quoted in ibid., 9, 11.

14. Luigi M. Laurenti, "Theories of Race and Property Value," in Alfred N. Page and Warren R. Seyfried, eds., *Urban Analysis: Readings in Housing and Urban Development* (Glenview, Ill.: Scott, Foresman, 1970), 274.

15. Mark Gelfand, *A Nation of Cities: The Federal Government and Urban America, 1933–1965* (New York: Oxford University Press, 1975), 221.

16. Nathan Glazer and David McEntire, eds., *Housing and Minority Groups* (Berkeley and Los Angeles: University of California Press, 1960), 140.

17. *Shelly* v. *Kraemer,* 334 U.S. 1 (1948).

18. Herbert Gans, *The Levittowners: Ways of Life and Politics in a Suburban Community* (New York: Pantheon Books, 1967), 372.

19. Kenneth T. Jackson, *Crabgrass Frontier: The Suburbanization of the United States* (New York: Oxford University Press, 1985), 241.

20. Public Law 90-284, 90th Congress (1968).

21. D.C. Public Interest Research Group, Institute for Local Self-Reliance, and Institute for Policy Studies, *Redlining: Mortgage Disinvestment in the District of Columbia* (Washington, D.C.: D.C. Public Interest Research Group, Institute for Local Self-Reliance, and Institute for Policy Studies, 1975).

22. Public Law 93-495, 93d Cong., Title V, and amendments (1974), and Public Law 94-200 (1975).

23. Martin Anderson, *The Federal Bulldozer: A Critical Analysis of Urban Renewal, 1949–1962* (Cambridge, Mass.: MIT Press, 1964).

24. Nathaniel S. Keith, *Politics and the Housing Crisis Since 1930* (New York: Universe Books, 1973).

25. John Mollenkopf, "The Post-War Politics of Urban Development," in William K. Tabb and Larry Sawers, eds., *Marxism and the Metropolis: New Perspectives on Urban Political Economy* (New York: Oxford University Press, 1978), 140.

26. Ibid., 138.

27. Anderson, 65.

28. Chester Hartman, "The Housing of Relocated Families," in James Q. Wilson, ed., *Urban Renewal: The Record and the Controversy* (Cambridge, Mass.: MIT Press, 1966), 322, reprinted from *Journal of the American Institute of Planners* 30 (November 1964):266–286.

29. Susan S. Fainstein, Norman I. Fainstein, Richard Child Hill, Dennis Judd, and Michael Peter Smith, *Restructuring the City: The Political Economy of Urban Redevelopment,* rev. ed. (New York: Longman, 1986).

30. Chester Hartman, *Yerba Buena: Land Grab and Community Resistance in San Francisco* (San Francisco: Glide Publications, 1974), 19.

31. Ibid., 190.

32. Clarence Stone, *Economic Growth and Neighborhood Discontent: System Bias in the Urban Renewal Program of Atlanta* (Chapel Hill: University of North Carolina Press, 1976), 186.

33. Anderson, 65–66.

34. In my analysis of the urban policies of the post–civil rights era, I focus upon those policies that were meant to directly influence patterns of racial segregation. These policies can, in effect, be regarded as the best candidates for reversing the effects of the pre–civil rights policies that reinforced the practices of the real estate and housing market. I do not discuss in this chapter the vast range of urban policies meant to treat the problems of the ghetto or to improve the education, employment prospects, etc., of African Americans.

35. Reynolds Farley and William H. Frey, "Changes in the Segregation of Whites from Blacks During the 1980s: Small Steps Toward a More Integrated Society," *American Sociological Review* 59 (February 1994):23–45.

36. Douglas S. Massey and Andrew B. Gross, "Explaining Trends in Racial Segregation, 1970–1980," *Urban Affairs Quarterly* 27(1) (September 1991):13–35; Douglas S. Massey and Mitchell L. Eggers, "The Spatial Concentration of Affluence and Poverty During the 1970s," *Urban Affairs Quarterly* 29(2) (December 1993):299–315; Sam Roberts, "Shifts in 80's Failed to Ease Segregation," *New York Times,* July 15, 1992; Norman Fainstein, "Race, Class, and Segregation: Discourses About African Americans," *International Journal of Urban and Regional Research* 17(3) (September 1993):390–392.

37. John E. Farley, "Race Still Matters: The Minimal Role of Income and Housing Cost as Causes of Housing Segregation in St. Louis, 1990," *Urban Affairs Review* 31(2) (November 1995):11.

38. Dennis R. Judd, *The Politics of American Cities: Private Power and Public Policy,* 3d ed. (New York: HarperCollins, 1988), 188.

39. *St. Louis Post-Dispatch,* June 3, 1971.

40. Quoted in Charles M. Lamb, "Fair Housing Implementation from Nixon to Reagan," Working Paper no. 11 (Madison, Wisc.: Robert M. La Follette Institute of Public Affairs, June 1992), 5.

41. Ibid., 5–6.

42. Ibid., 10–15.

43. William E. Nelson Jr. and Michael S. Bailey, "The Weakening of State Participation in Civil Rights Enforcement," in Dennis R. Judd, ed., *Public Policy Across States and Communities* (Greenwich, Conn.: JAI Press, 1985), 155–167.

44. Paul George Lewis, "Housing and American Privatism: The Origins and Evolution of Subsidized Home-Ownership Policy," *Journal of Policy History* 5(1) (1993):37.

45. Ibid.

46. R. Allen Hays, *The Federal Government and Urban Housing* (Albany: State University of New York Press, 1985), 112.

47. Lewis, 39.

48. Ibid.

49. Ibid.

50. Andrew Cuomo, "Testimony of Secretary Andrew Cuomo Before the Senate Appropriations Subcommittee on VA, HUD, and Independent Agencies" (March 12, 1998) (http://www.hud.gov/tst31298.html).

51. Quoted in James T. Campen, "The Struggle for Community Investment in Boston, 1989–1991," in Gregory D. Squires, ed., *From Redlining to Reinvestment: Community Responses to Urban Disinvestment* (Philadelphia: Temple University Press, 1992), 69.

52. Gregory D. Squires, "Community Reinvestment: An Emerging Social Movement," in Squires, ed., 2.

53. Mitchell Zuckoff, "Study Shows Racial Bias in Lending," *Boston Globe,* October 9, 1992.

54. Squires, 71–75.

55. Joint Center for Housing Studies of Harvard University, *The State of the Nation's Housing* (Cambridge, Mass.: Joint Center for Housing Studies, Harvard University, 1998), 8–9.

56. National Low Income Housing Coalition, *Housing at a Snail's Pace* (Washington, D.C.: National Low Income Housing Coalition, 1998), 5.

57. Ibid., 75.

58. Adam Bickford and Douglas Massey, "Segregation in the Second Ghetto: Racial and Ethnic Segregation in American Public Housing, 1977," *Social Forces* 69 (June 1991):1035.

59. Douglas S. Massey and Shawn M. Kanaiaupuni, "Public Housing and the Concentration of Poverty," *Social Science Quarterly* 74(1) (March 1993):109–122.

60. John Goering, Ali Kamely, and Todd Richardson, *The Location and Racial Composition of Public Housing in the United States* (Washington, D.C.: Office of Policy Development and Research, HUD, December 1994), 22.

61. John Goering, Helene Stebbins, and Michael Siewert, *Report to Congress: Promoting Housing Choice in HUD's Rental Assistance Programs* (Washington, D.C.: Office of Policy Development and Research, HUD, April 1995), 6.

62. Ibid.

63. Dennis R. Judd, "The Role of Governmental Policies in Promoting Residential Segregation in the St. Louis Metropolitan Area," *Journal of Negro Education* (June 1998):214–240.

64. The decision was handed down in *Gatreaux* v. *Chicago Housing Authority,* 296 F. Supp. 907 (N.D. IL, 1969). For a history of the case, see Mary David, "The Gatreaux Assisted Housing Program," in G. Thomas Kingsley

and Margery Austin Turner, eds., *Housing Markets and Residential Mobility* (Washington, D.C.: Urban Institute Press, 1993). See also Goering et al., 47.

65. Goering et al., 43–78.

66. Ibid., 45.

67. Joint Center for Housing Studies.

68. Ibid.

69. Ibid., 9.

70. Dennis R. Judd and Todd Swanstrom, *City Politics: Private Power and Public Policy,* 2d ed. (New York: Longman, 1998), 314–315. In a legal action that began in the mid-1970s, the U.S. Department of Housing and Urban Development and the local chapter of the National Association for the Advancement of Colored People sued the City of Yonkers, alleging that the city had used zoning to intentionally segregate the city by race. After years of bitter controversy, in 1988 Yonkers finally agreed to allow the construction of eight hundred units of public housing.

71. Judd, "The Role of Governmental Policies."

72. Thomas A. Clark, "The Suburbanization Process and Residential Segregation," in Gary A. Tobin, ed., *Divided Neighborhoods: Changing Patterns of Racial Segregation* (Newbury Park, Calif.: Sage, 1987), 114.

73. Ibid., 115.

74. Jackson, 205.

75. John R. Logan and Harvey L. Molotch, *Urban Fortunes: The Political Economy of Place* (Berkeley and Los Angeles: University of California Press, 1987), 195.

76. Clark, 135.

77. Logan and Molotch, 194.

78. John E. Farley, "Metropolitan Housing Segregation in 1980: The St. Louis Case," *Urban Affairs Quarterly* 18(3) (March 1983):351.

79. Thomas F. Pettigrew, "Attitudes on Race and Housing: A Social Psychological View," in Amos H. Hawley and Vincent P. Rock, eds., *Segregation in Residential Areas: Papers on Racial and Socioeconomic Factors in Choice of Housing* (Washington, D.C.: National Academy of Sciences, 1973).

80. Douglas S. Massey and Nancy A. Denton, "Suburbanization and Segregation in U.S. Metropolitan Areas," *American Journal of Sociology* 94(3) (November 1988):605.

81. Massey and Eggers; Roberts.

82. John F. Kain, "Housing Market Discrimination and Black Suburbanization in the 1980's," in Tobin, ed., 68.

83. Farley, "Metropolitan Housing Segregation," 16; Farley, "Race Still Matters."

84. Richard P. Nathan and Charles F. Adams Jr., "Four Perspectives on Urban Hardship," *Political Science Quarterly* 104(3) (Fall 1989):483–508.

85. Massey and Denton, 595–596.

86. John Kasarda, "Inner-City Concentrated Poverty and Neighborhood Distress: 1970 to 1990," *Housing Policy Debate* 4(3) (1993):253–302.

87. See Judd, "The Role of Governmental Policies."

Chapter 6

1. This last phrase is from Theda Skocpol, Peter Evans, and Dietrich Rueschemeyer, eds., *Bringing the State Back In* (Cambridge: Cambridge University Press, 1985). Although there is no evidence that Skocpol is a Clinton insider, she was asked to dine at the White House, and her work clearly justifies the type of approach to social policy taken by the first Clinton administration, at least.

2. The major initial protests were around the cuts in benefits to immigrants, which, although a serious nativist attack, were also the most easily "fixable" in the short run. Over the long haul, the abdication of federal responsibility for ensuring basic economic security and for protecting all poor people from the most punitive behavioral controls at the state level is the most chilling aspect of the PRWORA.

3. In 1974, Aid to the Aged, Aid to the Blind, and Aid to the Permanently and Totally Disabled (enacted in 1956) were consolidated in a new program called Supplementary Security Income. In 1962, Aid to Dependent Children was renamed Aid to Families with Dependent Children. In 1998, the program became Temporary Aid to Needy Families.

4. This and other arguments found throughout this chapter are developed more fully in Mimi Abramovitz, *Regulating the Lives of Women: Social Welfare Policy from Colonial Times to the Present,* 2d ed. (Boston: South End Press, 1996); and Mimi Abramovitz, *Under Attack, Fighting Back: Women and Welfare in the United States* (New York: Monthly Review Press, 1996). See also chapter 4 in this volume.

5. During the 1960s and 1970s, Congress enacted formal work programs, such as the Community Work Program and the Work Incentive Program. Like the earlier informal work requirements that stemmed from strict and meager provisions, formal work programs channeled poor women into the low-paid labor market. Indeed, the Work Incentive Program appeared during the economic boom of the late 1960s when low unemployment rates created shortages of cheap labor. It was made more restrictive and punitive in 1971, after various exemptions had severely lowered participation rates. See Nancy Rose, *Workfare or Fair Work: Women, Welfare, and Government Work Programs* (New Brunswick, N.J.: Rutgers University Press, 1995).

6. U.S. Congress, House Committee on Ways and Means, *Overview of Entitlement Programs: 1993 Green Book Background Material and Data on Programs Within the Jurisdiction of the Committee on Ways and Means* (Washington, D.C.: GPO, May 15, 1993).

7. Much of the argument for this approach is best articulated in Lawrence Mead, *The New Politics of Poverty: The Non-Working Poor in America* (New York: Basic Books, 1992).

8. For examples of these studies, see Government Accounting Office, *Work and Welfare: Current AFDC Work Programs and Implications for Federal Policy* (Washington, D.C.: Government Accounting Office, April 1987); Government Accounting Office, *Welfare to Work: States Begin JOBS but Fiscal and Other Problems May Impede Their Progress* (Washington, D.C.: Government Accounting Office, 1991); Jan L. Hagen and Irene Lurie, *Implementing JOBS: Initial State Choices,* Summary Report (Albany: Nelson A. Rockefeller Institute of Government, State University of New York, 1992); Katherine Porter, *Making JOBS Work* (Washington, D.C.: Center on Budget and Policy Priorities, 1990); and James Riccio and Daniel Friedlander, *GAIN: Program Strategies, Participation Patterns, and First-Year Impacts in Six Counties* (New York: Manpower Demonstration Research, May 1992).

9. The extent of this rise is documented in Congressional Budget Office, *A Preliminary Analysis of Growing Caseloads in AFDC,* Staff Memorandum (Washington, D.C.: Congressional Budget Office, December 1991).

10. See Robert Moffitt, *Incentive Effects of the U.S. Welfare System: A Review Institute for Research on Poverty,* Special Report no. 48 (Madison: Institute for Research on Poverty, University of Wisconsin, 1991); and Isaac Shapiro, Steven S. Gold, Mark Sheft, Julie Strawn, Lanna Summer, and Robert Greenstein, *The States and the Poor: How Budget Decisions in 1991 Affected Low-Income People* (Washington, D.C., and Albany: Center on Budget and Policy Priorities and Center for the Study of the States). See William J. Wilson and K. M. Neckerman, "Poverty and Family Structure: The Widening Gap Between Evidence and Public Policy Issues," in S. Danziger and D. H. Weinberg, eds., *Fighting Poverty: What Works and What Doesn't* (Cambridge, Mass.: Harvard University Press, 1986), 232–259, for a discussion of the meaning and uses of this kind of data.

11. Quoted in the *Boston Globe,* April 2, 1995.

12. Cited in Ann Withorn, "Why Do They Hate Us So Much?" *American Journal of Orthopsychiatry* 30(6) (1996).

13. Department of Health, Education, and Welfare, *"Having the Power, We Have the Duty,"* HEW Report on Social Services and Poverty (Washington, D.C.: GPO, 1962).

14. There is so much literature on the underclass. We share Adolph Reed's critique of the literature as expressed in "The Underclass as Myth and

Symbol," *Radical America Magazine* 24(1), reprinted in Reed, *Stirrings in the Jug: Black Politics in the Post–Segregation Era* (Minneapolis: University of Minnesota Press, 1999). Also of note here are Christopher Jencks and Paul Peterson, eds., *The Urban Underclass* (Washington, D.C.: Brookings Institution, 1991); R. Mincy, Isabel V. Sawhill, and D. A. Wolff, "The Underclass: Definition and Measurement," *Science* 248 (1990):450–453; E. R. Ricketts and Isabel V. Sawhill, "Defining and Measuring the Underclass," *Journal of Policy Analysis and Management* 7(2) (1988):316–325; and William J. Wilson, *The Truly Disadvantaged: The Inner City, the Underclass, and Public Policy* (Chicago: University of Chicago Press, 1987).

15. In addition to Mead, it is probably enough to refer here to the conservatism of Charles Murray, *Losing Ground: American Social Policy, 1950–1980* (New York: Basic Books, 1984). The underclass, named or unnamed, is a staple of conservative social theory.

16. In addition to Christopher Jencks, *Rethinking Social Policy: Race, Poverty, and the Urban Underclass* (New York: Basic Books, 1992), Mickey Kaus, *The End of Equality* (New York: Basic Books, 1992) is a good example here, as are Sarah McLanahan and Irwin Garfinkel, "Single Mothers, the Underclass, and Social Policy," *Annals of the American Academy of Political and Social Science* 509 (January 1989):92–105; John D. Kasarda, "Urban Industrial Transition and the Underclass," *Annals of the American Academy of Political and Social Science* 509 (January 1989):1, 26–48; William J. Wilson, "The Underclass: Issues, Perspectives, and Public Policy," *Annals of the American Academy of Political and Social* Science 509 (January 1989):183–193; and William J. Wilson "Cycles of Deprivation and the Underclass Debate," *Social Service Review* 56(4) (1985):541–559. Of course, these books harken back to once-reviled and now-exonerated Daniel Patrick Moynihan, *The Negro Family: The Case For National Action* (Washington, D.C.: GPO, 1965).

17. Christopher Jencks, "What Is the Underclass—and Is It Growing?" *Focus* 12(1) (Spring–Summer 1989):14–26.

18. David Ellwood, *Poor Support: Poverty in the American Family* (New York: Basic Books, 1988); Daniel Patrick Moynihan, *Family and Nation: The Godkin Lectures, Harvard University* (New York: Harcourt Brace Jovanovich, 1986); Murray; Lawrence Mead, *Beyond Entitlement* (New York: Basic Books, 1986; Lawrence Mead, *New Politics of Poverty* (New York: Basic Books, 1994). For an interesting update on Mead's thinking, see his edited *The New Paternalism: Supervisory Approaches to Poverty* (Washington, D.C.: Brookings Institution Press, 1997).

19. A useful argument here was made by Diana Pearce that we could see welfare programs as a "half-full" glass that needed filling, rather than a "half-empty" glass not worth keeping. Conference on Women, Poverty, and Welfare, Dartmouth College, Dartmouth, New Hampshire, April 1995.

20. For classic statements of this ideology, see Seymour Martin Lipset, ed., *Class Citizenship and Social Development: Essays by T. H. Marshall* (Chicago: University of Chicago Press, 1965); Richard M. Titmuss, *Commitment to Welfare* (New York: Pantheon Books, 1968); and Harold L. Wilensky and Charles N. Lebeaux, *Industrial Society and Social Welfare* (New York: Free Press, 1965).

21. A notable exception is the current priority that the National Organization for Women Legal Defense Fund has been giving to fighting the effects of welfare reform at all levels. See also chapter 3 of this volume.

22. For examples of such arguments, see any issue of *Survival News*, the national welfare rights newspaper, published in Boston.

23. William J. Wilson, *The Declining Significance of Race* (Chicago: University of Chicago Press, 1980).

24. An obvious example of how this dynamic works are provisions in the new welfare reform that make it impossible for women convicted of a drug felony to receive TANF—a rule to "protect" families that will disproportionately affect black and Latina mothers under the rubric of changing the behavior of the underclass.

25. Clinton-Gore Transition Team, "Clinton-Gore on American Families" (December 1992).

26. Most guilty of this logic in general are Thomas Byrne Edsall and Mary D. Edsall, *Chain Reaction* (New York: Norton, 1991); and David Ellwood, whose earlier work is more explicitly tied to welfare. Also, the entire "communitarian" tendency falls victim to this same error. Reed does a fine job of exposing the fallacy of the "values" argument.

27. Ellwood, 44.

28. Here Edsall and Edsall; and Kaus were the most clear in their arguments for realism.

29. Jencks, *Rethinking Social Policy*, 233–234.

30. See Kaus; and almost any issue of the *New Republic* during the early years of the Clinton administration.

31. Theda Skocpol, "Targetting Within Universalism," in Jencks and Peterson, eds., 433–434.

32. Cited in Diane Dujon and Ann Withorn, *For Crying Out Loud: Women's Poverty in the United States* (Boston: South End Press, 1996), 183.

33. Jencks, *Rethinking Social Policy*, 235.

34. For a recent statement of this view, see Richard Cloward and Frances Fox Piven, "A Class Analysis of Welfare," *Monthly Review* 44 (1993):25–31.

35. Abramovitz, *Under Attack*.

36. Of course, the practice of making AFDC a race card is not new. Winifred Bell, *Aid to Dependent Children* (New York: Columbia University Press, 1965), noted that early postwar attacks on AFDC represented a "last

stand" against advances for black Americans. She noted then that "certainly, the attack seemed to derive some of its virulence from the struggle over civil rights" (58).

37. For one good example of this, see Robert Rector, "Combatting Family Disintegration, Crime, and Dependence: Welfare Reform and Beyond," (Heritage Foundation) *Backgrounder,* no. 983 (April 1994).

38. See Allan Payne, "Absence of Judgement: What Social Workers Believe About the Poor Will Hamper Welfare Reform," *Policy Review* (November–December 1996):50.

39. Lockheed Martin is one of the companies in the forefront of this transformation.

40. See Payne.

41. In the 1993 fight over the North American Free Trade Agreement, the Clinton administration avoided making any compromises with the left and chose instead to make deals with the very congressional forces, led by Newt Gingrich, who are most abusive toward AFDC. The potential implications of such alliances are chilling.

42. Cited in Timothy Smeeding, "Cross-National Perspectives on Income Security Programs," in *The War on Poverty: What Worked?* Testimony before the Congress of the United States Joint Economic Committee, September 25, 1991.

43. See Betty Reid Mandell and Ann Withorn, "Keep on Keeping On: Welfare Rights Organizing in Massachusetts," in Robert Fisher and Joel Kling, eds., *Mobilizing for Change* (Newbury Park, Calif.: Sage, 1993).

Chapter 7

1. Devereux Bowly Jr., *The Poorhouse: Subsidized Housing in Chicago, 1895–1976* (Carbondale: Southern Illinois University Press, 1978), 116–119.

2. Harvey W. Zorbaugh, *The Gold Coast and the Slum* (Chicago: University of Chicago Press, 1976).

3. Thomas Lee Philpott, *The Slum and the Ghetto: Neighborhood Deterioration and Middle-Class Reform, Chicago 1880–1930* (New York: Oxford University Press, 1978), 267.

4. Steve Bogira, "Prisoners of the War Zone," *The Reader,* October 3, 1986.

5. Paul Kleppner, *Chicago Divided: The Making of a Black Mayor* (DeKalb: Northern Illinois University Press, 1983), 139.

6. Larry Bennett, "Postwar Redevelopment in Chicago: The Declining Politics of Party and the Rise of Neighborhood Politics," in Gregory Squires, ed., *Unequal Partnerships* (New Brunswick: Rutgers University Press, 1989), 167–171.

7. Ed Marciniak, *Reclaiming the Inner City: Chicago's Near North Revitalization Confronts Cabrini-Green* (Washington, D.C.: National Center for Urban Ethnic Affairs, 1986), 158.

8. Woodstock Institute, *Focusing In: Indicators of Economic Change in Chicago's Neighborhoods* (Chicago: Woodstock Institute, May 1994), 16–17, 56–59, 64–65.

9. Chicago Fact Book Consortium, eds., *Local Community Fact Book: Chicago Metropolitan Area, 1990* (Chicago: Academy Chicago, 1995), 57.

10. Arnold R. Hirsch, *Making the Second Ghetto: Race and Housing in Chicago, 1940–1960* (New York: Cambridge University Press, 1983), 122–124.

11. Martin Meyerson and Edward C. Banfield, *Politics, Planning, and the Public Interest* (New York: Free Press, 1964); Hirsch, *Making the Second Ghetto,* 212–258.

12. Roger Biles, *Richard J. Daley: Politics, Race, and the Governing of Chicago* (DeKalb: Northern Illinois University Press, 1995), 171–173.

13. Hirsch, *Making the Second Ghetto,* 243, 265.

14. Metropolitan Planning Council, "Changing the Paradigm: A Call for New Approaches to Public Housing in the Chicago Metropolitan Area" (Chicago: Metropolitan Planning Council, October 1996); Nicholas Lemann, *The Promised Land* (New York: Vintage Books, 1992), 304; Alex Kotlowitz, *There Are No Children Here* (New York: Doubleday, 1991), 259–260.

15. John Schmidt, "Bold Plans for Curing Sick Housing," *New York Times,* October 11, 1988.

16. Michael H. Schill, "Chicago's Mixed-Income New Communities Strategy: The Future Face of Public Housing," in Willem Van Vliet, ed., *Affordable Housing and Urban Redevelopment in the United States* (Thousand Oaks, Calif.: Sage, 1997), 135–157.

17. Sandy Banisky, "Chicago Housing Authority Watches Its Best Efforts Fail," *Baltimore Sun,* June 18, 1996.

18. Larry Bennett, "Do We Really Wish to Live in a Communitarian City?: Communitarian Thinking and the Redevelopment of Chicago's Cabrini-Green Public Housing Complex," *Journal of Urban Affairs* 20(2) (1998): 99–116.

19. Phat X. Chiem and Flynn McRoberts, "Cabrini Tenants File Suit to Halt Razing More of Their High-Rises," *Chicago Tribune*, October 25, 1996. In the summer of 1997, we were invited to provide expert testimony in support of the Cabrini-Green LAC lawsuit. This chapter is adapted from the report that we completed in December 1997. In July 1998, the LAC, CHA, and city of Chicago reached a tentative out-of-court settlement. For details, see Flynn McRoberts and J. Lin Allen, "When Two Worlds Collide at Cabrini," *Chicago Tribune,* July 30, 1998.

20. Chicago Housing Authority, "The Urban Revitalization Demonstration Program" (Chicago: Chicago Housing Authority, May 5, 1993), 10.

21. Ibid., 19.

22. Vince Lane, "Public Housing: Into the Future," *Chicago Sun-Times,* March 14, 1995.

23. Chicago Housing Authority, "Hope VI Revitalization Plan: Cabrini-Green Extension" (Chicago: Chicago Housing Authority, June 30, 1997), 1.2.

24. North Town Community Partnership, "Project Hope: Commitment to Community Change" (Chicago: North Town Community Partnership, December 1995), iv–v.

25. Ibid., 1.

26. Ibid., 3.

27. Draper and Kramer Realty Advisors, "Market Analysis of Market Rate Units in Cabrini-Green Revitalization Project—Phase 1" (Chicago: Draper and Kramer Realty Advisors, June 1995), 7, 9.

28. Tracy Cross and Associates, "An Analysis of the Potential for Market Rate Residential Development, Cabrini–Hope VI Urban Revitalization Program, Chicago, Illinois" (Chicago: Tracy Cross and Associates, February 1997), II.1.

29. Ibid., II.22.

30. Chicago Housing Authority, "The Urban Revitalization Demonstration Program," 20.

31. Ibid.

32. Ibid.

33. William Julius Wilson, *The Truly Disadvantaged: The Inner City, the Underclass, and Public Policy* (Chicago: University of Chicago Press, 1987); William Julius Wilson, *When Work Disappears: The World of the New Urban Poor* (New York: Knopf, 1996).

34. Wilson, *The Truly Disadvantaged,* 49, 56.

35. Wilson, *When Work Disappears,* 20.

36. Ibid., 62.

37. Wilson, *The Truly Disadvantaged,* 138.

38. Bernard C. Watson, *Stupidity, Sloth, and Public Policy: Social Darwinism Rides Again* (Washington, D.C.: National Urban Coalition, n.d.), 9; Michael Katz, *The Undeserving Poor: From the War on Poverty to the War on Welfare* (New York: Pantheon Books, 1989), 11–22.

39. Stephen Steinberg, *Turning Back: The Retreat from Racial Justice in American Thought and Policy* (Boston: Beacon Press, 1995), 137–155; Katz, *The Undeserving Poor,* 16–35, 195–223; Charles Valentine, *Culture and Poverty: Critique and Counterproposals* (Chicago: University of Chicago Press, 1968), 13–17, 67–77; Oscar Lewis, *Anthropological Essays* (New York: Random House, 1970), 67–80; Adolph Reed Jr., "The 'Underclass' as Myth and Symbol: The Poverty of Discourse About Poverty," *Radical Amer-*

ica 24 (Winter 1992):22–24, reprinted in Reed, *Stirrings in the Jug: Black Politics in the Post–Segregation Era* (Minneapolis: University of Minnesota Press, 1999).

40. Stow Persons, *Ethnic Studies at Chicago, 1905–45* (Champaign: University of Illinois Press, 1987), 33, 40–41.

41. Wilson, *When Work Disappears,* 17.

42. Persons, *Ethnic Studies at Chicago,* 41, 49; Valentine, *Culture and Poverty,* 24; Brett Williams, "Black Urban Poverty in the United States," *Human Organization* 51 (Summer 1992):164–174.

43. Howard Chudacoff, "Introduction, 1976" to Zorbaugh, *The Gold Coast and the Slum,* ix–xiii; Valentine, *Culture and Poverty,* 24, 27, 35.

44. Chudacoff, "Introduction," x–xii; Reed, "The 'Underclass' as Myth and Symbol," 30.

45. David C. Ranney, "Class, Race, Gender, and Poverty: A Critique of Some Contemporary Theory and Practice" (Chicago: Great Cities Institute, College of Urban and Public Affairs, University of Illinois–Chicago, 1997); Adolph Reed Jr., "The Liberal Technocrat," *The Nation,* February 6, 1988, 167–170; Reed, "The 'Underclass' as Myth and Symbol"; Valentine, *Culture and Poverty,* 17; Williams, "Black Urban Poverty."

46. See Oscar Lewis, *Five Families: Mexican Case Studies in the Culture of Poverty* (New York: Random House, 1959); Oscar Lewis, *La Vida: A Puerto Rican Family in the Culture of Poverty—San Juan and New York* (New York: Random House, 1966); and Lewis, *Anthropological Essays.*

47. Lewis, *Anthropological Essays;* Valentine, *Culture and Poverty,* 47–77; Katz, *The Undeserving Poor,* 16–23.

48. Wilson, *The Truly Disadvantaged,* 28; Sanford F. Schram, *Words of Welfare: The Poverty of Social Science and the Social Science of Poverty* (Minneapolis: University of Minnesota Press, 1995), 150–151; Reed, "The 'Underclass' as Myth and Symbol," 34–35; Arline Geronimus, "Teenage Childbearing and Personal Responsibility: An Alternative View," *Political Science Quarterly* 112 (Fall 1997):405–430.

49. Geronimus, "Teenage Childbearing"; Kristin Luker, *Dubious Conceptions: The Politics of Teenage Pregnancy* (Cambridge, Mass.: Harvard University Press, 1996), 127–128.

50. Watson, *Stupidity, Sloth, and Public Policy;* Katz, *The Undeserving Poor,* 3–10.

51. Katz, *The Undeserving Poor,* 11–16; Jill Quadagno, *The Color of Welfare: How Racism Undermined the War on Poverty* (New York: Oxford University Press, 1994).

52. Lewis, *Anthropological Essays;* Valentine, *Culture and Poverty,* 47–77.

53. Daniel P. Moynihan, *The Negro Family: A Case for National Action* (Washington, D.C.: GPO, 1965).

54. E. Franklin Frazier, *The Negro Family in the United States* (Chicago: University of Chicago Press, 1939); Moynihan, *The Negro Family,* 64;

Valentine, *Culture and Poverty,* 20–43, 67–69; Katz, *The Undeserving Poor,* 23–35.

55. Wilson, *The Truly Disadvantaged.*

56. Chicago Housing Authority, "Hope VI Revitalization Plan," 4.11–12.

57. Ibid., 4.3.

58. Karl E. Taeuber and Alma F. Taeuber, *Negroes in Cities* (Chicago: Aldine, 1965), 100; John Yinger, *Closed Doors, Opportunities Lost: The Continuing Cost of Housing Discrimination* (New York: Russell Sage Foundation, 1995), 117.

59. Douglas S. Massey and Nancy A. Denton, *American Apartheid* (Cambridge, Mass.: Harvard University Press, 1993), 92–96; Anthony Downs, *Neighborhoods and Urban Development* (Washington, D.C.: Brookings Institution, 1981), 94–95.

60. Cross, "An Analysis of the Potential for Market Rate Development," II.22.

61. Yinger, *Closed Doors, Opportunities Lost,* 132.

62. Ibid., 119.

63. Ibid., 119–120.

64. Philip Langdon, *A Better Place to Live* (New York: Harper Perennial, 1995); Herbert Muschamp, "Can New Urbanism Find Room for the Old?" *New York Times,* June 2, 1996.

65. Blair Kamin, "Neighborhood Project," *Chicago Tribune,* August 6, 1997.

66. Michael Pollan, "Town-Building Is No Mickey Mouse Operation," *New York Times Magazine,* December 14, 1997, 58.

67. James Q. Wilson, "Planning and Politics: Citizen Participation in Urban Renewal," in James Q. Wilson, ed., *Urban Renewal: The Record and the Controversy* (Cambridge, Mass.: MIT Press, 1973), 407–421.

68. Cabrini-Green Local Advisory Council and the Empowerment Network Foundation, *"Vision 2000": Cabrini-Green Master Plan* (Chicago: Cabrini-Green Local Advisory Council and the Empowerment Network Foundation, February 1994), 8–9.

69. Patrick Reardon, "Cuts Imperil CHA Plans for Cabrini," *Chicago Tribune,* February 10, 1994.

70. Chicago Housing Authority, "The Urban Revitalization Demonstration Program," 19.

71. Kevin Coyle, *Hardball: A Season in the Projects* (New York: Putnam's, 1993), 23.

72. Margaret Smith, "A Mother's Prayer," *Voices of Cabrini,* April 24, 1994.

73. Gloria Corkrell, "Untitled," *Voices of Cabrini,* December 19, 1993.

74. This quotation, as well as subsequent quotations from Cabrini-Green

residents, are drawn from interviews that we conducted between July and December 1997.

75. Wim Wiewel, "Industries, Jobs, and Economic Development Policy in Metropolitan Chicago: An Overview of the Decade," in Lawrence B. Joseph, ed., *Creating Jobs, Creating Workers: Economic Development and Employment in Metropolitan Chicago* (Champaign: University of Illinois Press, 1990), 27–59; Nikolas C. Theodore and D. Garth Taylor, "The Geography of Opportunity: The Status of African Americans in the Chicago Area Economy" (Chicago: Chicago Urban League, March 1991).

76. Chicago Housing Authority, "Hope VI Revitalization Plan," 9.3.

77. Fox Butterfield, "Crime Fighting's About-Face," *New York Times,* January 19, 1997.

78. Department of Research and Program Development, Chicago Housing Authority, "Crime Incidence in Chicago Housing Authority Developments, 1993" (Chicago: Department of Research and Program Development, Chicago Housing Authority, March 1994).

79. George Papajohn and Colin McMahon, "Gangs Truce Opens Window of Peace," *Chicago Tribune,* April 28, 1993.

80. Andrew Martin, "City Records Minor Drop in Major Crimes," *Chicago Tribune,* January 16, 1995.

81. Digital City Chicago, Web site URL: http://www.chicago.digitalcity.com/community/crime.

82. Suhir Alladi Venkatesh, "The Gang in the Community," in C. Ronald Huff, ed., *Gangs in America* (Thousand Oaks, Calif.: Sage, 1996), 241–255.

83. Bogira, "Prisoners of the War Zone."

84. Sheryl Kennedy, "Parents Win Battle; Jenner Won't Close," *Chicago Tribune,* November 20, 1997.

85. Angela Williams, Letter to CHA chief of police Leroy O'shields, n.d.

86. We want to thank Mark Pratt, *Voices of Cabrini* coeditor, who supplied us with a nearly complete set of *VOC* issues.

87. Metropolitan Tenants Organization, "Children+Female-Headed Households+African American/Latino: Nowhere to Live in Chicago" (Chicago: Metropolitan Tenants Organization, March 1994), 2.

88. Nathalie P. Voorhees Center for Neighborhood and Community Development, "The Plan to Voucher Out Public Housing: An Analysis of the Chicago Experience and a Case Study of the Proposal to Redevelop the Cabrini-Green Public Housing Area" (Chicago: Nathalie P. Voorhees Center for Neighborhood and Community Development, University of Illinois–Chicago, May 1997), 9.

89. Paul B. Fischer, "A Racial Perspective on Subsidized Housing in the Chicago Suburbs" (Chicago: South Suburban Housing Center, 1992).

90. Voorhees Center, "The Plan to Voucher Out Public Housing," 14.

91. Ibid., 20–23.

92. Carol B. Stack, *All Our Kin: Strategies for Survival in a Black Community* (New York: Harper Collophon, 1975); Kathryn Edin and Laura Lein, *Making Ends Meet: How Single Mothers Survive Welfare and Low-Wage Work* (New York: Russell Sage Foundation, 1997), 149–167.

93. R. Allen Hays, *The Federal Government and Urban Housing* (Albany: State University of New York Press, 1985), 174–191; John C. Teaford, *The Rough Road to Renaissance* (Baltimore: Johns Hopkins University Press, 1990), 145–162.

94. Letter to Andrew Cuomo, Secretary, U.S. Department of Housing and Urban Development, June 27, 1997.

Chapter 8

1. For an excellent analysis of the historical relationship between race and occupational structures, see Harold M. Baron, "The Demand for Black Labor," *Radical America* 5 (March–April 1971):1–46; and Harold M. Baron, "The Web of Urban Racism," in Louis Knowles and Kenneth Prewitt, eds., *Institutional Racism in America* (Englewood Cliffs, N.J.: Prentice-Hall, 1969), 134–176.

2. The tendency even among labor historians to gloss over union racism has come under challenge, most notably in the work of Herbert Hill. For two recent articles, see Herbert Hill, "Black Workers, Organized Labor, and Title VII of the 1964 Civil Rights Act: Legislative History and Litigation," in Herbert Hill and James E. Jones, *Race in America* (Madison: University of Wisconsin Press, 1993), 263–341; and Herbert Hill, "Meany, Reuther, and the 1964 Civil Rights Act," *New Politics* 25 (Summer 1998):82–107.

3. See Lawrence H. Fuchs, "The Reactions of Black Americans to Immigration," in Virginia Yans-McLaughlin, ed., *Immigration Reconsidered* (New York: Oxford University Press, 1990), 295–297; and David. J. Hellwig, "Patterns of Black Nativism," *American Studies* 23 (Spring 1982):85–98.

4. Thomas Muller, *Immigrants and the American City* (New York: New York University Press, 1993), 91. Scholars over several decades have puzzled over why more blacks did not gravitate to northern labor markets during the half century after slavery. The answer to this conundrum is found in a 1944 book: John G. Van Deusen, *The Black Man in White America* (Washington, D.C.: Associated Publishers, 1944), 30, wrote: "Regardless of qualifications, most Northern Negroes at this time found themselves forced into domestic and personal service or restricted to odd jobs at unskilled labor. History does not show many peoples who have migrated because of persecution alone. The Negro is not dissimilar to others, and where no economic base was assured, he preferred to endure those ills he had rather than fly to others he

knew not of." See also Stephen Steinberg, *The Ethnic Myth* (Boston: Beacon Press, 1989), chap. 7.

5. This was noted by Gunnar Myrdal, *An American Dilemma* (New York: Harper and Row, 1964), 1005.

6. U.S. Bureau of the Census, *Historical Statistics of the United States* (Washington, D.C.: GPO, 1975), 500; Gerald David Jaynes and Robin M. Williams Jr., *A Common Destiny* (Washington, D.C.: National Academy Press, 1989), 273.

7. See Frances Fox Piven and Richard A. Cloward, *Poor People's Movements* (New York: Vintage Books, 1979), chap. 4.

8. In a paper written for the National Advisory Commission on Civil Disorders in 1968, "Escaping from Poverty: A Comparison of the Immigrant and Black Experience," in *People, Plans, and Policies* (New York: Columbia University Press, 1991), chap. 18, Herbert Gans debunks the notion that blacks arriving in northern cities were following in the footsteps of earlier immigrants and therefore could anticipate the same beneficial outcomes.

9. William Julius Wilson, *The Truly Disadvantaged* (Chicago: University of Chicago Press, 1987).

10. Karen Gerard, "New York City's Economy: A Decade of Change," *New York Affairs* 8(2) (1984):7.

11. Richard Levine, "New York Lost 34,000 Jobs over Summer," *New York Times,* October 19, 1990.

12. Norman Fainstein, "The Underclass/Mismatch Hypothesis as an Explanation for Black Economic Deprivation," *Politics and Society* 15(4) (1986–1987):403–451.

13. Ibid., 439. According to data on New York City compiled by Roger Waldinger, "Ladders and Musical Chairs: Ethnicity and Opportunity in Post-Industrial New York," *Politics and Society* 15 (1986–1987):379–380, 17 percent of whites in 1970 were employed in manufacturing, as compared to 13 percent of blacks. By 1980, there were 38 percent fewer whites employed in manufacturing, whereas the decline for blacks was only 13 percent. In absolute numbers, 115,180 whites lost their jobs, as compared to 7,980 blacks. See also Walter W. Stafford, *Closed Labor Markets: Underrepresentation of Blacks, Hispanics, and Women in New York City's Core Industries* (New York: Community Service Society of New York, 1985).

14. Wilson, *The Truly Disadvantaged,* 12.

15. Joleen Kirschenman and Kathryn M. Neckerman, "'We'd Love to Hire Them, but . . . ': The Meaning of Race for Employers," in Christopher Jencks and Paul E. Peterson, eds., *The Urban Underclass* (Washington, D.C.: Brookings Institution, 1991), 104. Jaynes and Williams, *A Common Destiny,* 146, comment, "The extent of discrimination against blacks

in the workplace has apparently not been extensively investigated by direct tests similar in design to the audits of residential housing markets."

16. Margery Austin Turner, Michael Fix, and Raymond J. Struyk, "Opportunities Denied, Opportunities Diminished: Discrimination in Hiring" (Washington, D.C.: Urban Institute, 1991), 1.

17. Leonard Buder, "Employment Agency Accused of Bias," *New York Times*, February 21, 1990. Two years later, the agency settled the lawsuit brought by the State Attorney General's Office by paying more than $1.75 million to the aggrieved parties. However, the counsel for the employment agency "denied the company ever used code words on applications and said that it plans to continue using the placement practices instituted before the lawsuits were filed." Calvin Sims, "Job Discrimination Case Settled for $1.7 Million," *New York Times*, December 26, 1991.

18. Reported in Turner et al., "Opportunities Denied, Opportunities Diminished." A similar gap in black and white perceptions of job discrimination has turned up in public opinions polls over the years. For example, in 1991 the percentage saying that compared with whites, blacks have equal or greater job opportunity was 33 percent for blacks and 60 percent for whites. See Jennifer L. Hochschild, *Facing Up to the American Dream* (Princeton: Princeton University Press, 1995), 63.

19. Quoted in Charles E. Silberman, *Crisis in Black and White* (New York: Vintage Books, 1964), 4.

20. Charles W. Mills, *The Racial Contract* (Ithaca: Cornell University Press, 1997), 130.

21. Dinesh D'Souza, *The End of Racism* (New York: Free Press, 1995), 289, 336.

22. Stephan Thernstrom and Abigail Thernstrom, *America in Black and White* (New York: Simon and Schuster, 1997).

23. See, for example, Herbert R. Northrup and John A. Larson, *The Impact of the AT&T-EEO Consent Decrees*, Labor Relations and Public Policy Series no. 20 (Philadelphia: University of Pennsylvania, 1979); and Hill, "Black Workers," 263–341.

24. See, for example, Jonathan S. Leonard, "The Impact of Affirmative Action on Employment," *Journal of Labor Economics* 2 (1984):439–463; Cedric Herring and Sharon M. Collins, "Retreat from Equal Opportunity," in Michael Peter Smith and Joe R. Feagin, eds., *The Bubbling Cauldron* (Minneapolis: University of Minnesota Press, 1995), 163–181; and M. V. Lee Badgett and Heidi Hartmann, "The Effectiveness of Equal Employment Opportunity Policies," in Margaret C. Simms, ed., *Economic Perspectives on Affirmative Action* (Washington, D.C.: Joint Center for Political and Economic Studies, 1995), 55–97.

25. William Julius Wilson, *When Work Disappears* (New York: Knopf, 1996), 112.

26. The reservation wage for jobless black men in Wilson's sample was $6.00 per hour, compared to $6.20 for jobless Mexican men and $7.20 for jobless Puerto Rican men. The figure for white men was over $9.00 per hour.

27. Wilson, *When Work Disappears,* 132.

28. Ibid., 129.

29. Ibid., 111.

30. Ibid., 127.

31. Gordon W. Allport, *The Nature of Prejudice* (Garden City, N.Y.: Anchor Books, 1958), 8.

32. Ibid., 9.

33. Mills, *The Racial Contract,* 18.

34. For example, in a history of Jim Crow in Mississippi, Neil McMillan, *Dark Journey* (Urbana: University of Illinois Press, 1990), 117, writes: "Nearly every plantation county in Mississippi could claim at least one substantial black farmer who through a combination of ownership and rental cultivated several hundred and sometimes even a thousand or more acres, employed numerous sharecroppers, and otherwise operated on a scale normally thought to be limited only to the more successful whites. These 'Negro Success Stories,' as they were called in the reports of the United States Department of Agriculture, were objects of pride and envy to both races. Officials in the regional offices of the USDA found in them evidence of 'the steady progress of Negro farmers throughout the . . . deep South.' They were proof, as their more sympathetic white neighbors believed, that the crop-lien system was the 'poor man's opportunity,' that only the black sharecroppers' profligacy, their penchant for excursions, crap games, and whiskey, kept them down."

35. For a case study of racist obstacles confronting black students graduating from a technical high school, see Deirdre Royster, *Troubling Passage: A Case Study of the School-Work Transition of Young Black and White Men in Baltimore City* (Ann Arbor, Mich.: UMI Dissertation Services, 1997).

36. In *The Declining Significance of Race* (University of Chicago Press, 1978), 151, William Julius Wilson acknowledges that "the improved job situation for the more privileged blacks in the corporate and government sectors is related both to the expansion of salaried white-collar positions and to the pressures of state affirmative action programs." But instead of seeing that the good fortune of the black middle class did not necessarily signify the deracialization of labor markets, he draws the opposite inference: "In view of these developments, it would be difficult to argue that the

plight of the black underclass is solely a consequence of racial oppression, that is, the explicit and overt efforts of whites to keep blacks subjugated."

37. The racial stratification within white-collar corporations has been extensively documented in studies conducted by Sharon Collins. See Sharon Collins, "The Making of the Black Middle Class," *Social Problems* 30 (April 1983):369–382; Sharon Collins, "The Marginalization of Black Executives," *Social Problems* 36 (October 1989):317–329; Sharon Collins, "Blacks on the Bubble: The Vulnerability of Black Executives in White Corporations," *Sociological Quarterly* 34 (August 1993):429–447; and Sharon Collins, *Black Corporate Executives: The Making and Breaking of a Black Middle Class* (Philadelphia: Temple University Press, 1997).

38. Collins, "The Making of the Black Middle Class," 377.

39. Ibid., 379.

40. Also to be considered are the varied and subtle ways in which old-fashioned racism afflicts even the black middle class. For two recent works, see Joe E. Feagin and Melvin P. Sikes, *Living with Racism* (Boston: Beacon Press, 1994); and David Wellman, *Portraits of White Racism* (Cambridge: Cambridge University Press, 1993).

41. Michael K. Brown and Steven P. Erie, "Blacks and the Legacy of the Great Society: The Economic and Political Impact of Federal Social Policy," *Public Policy* 29 (Summer 1981):301.

42. Collins, "The Making of the Black Middle Class," 379.

43. John Bound and Richard B. Freeman, "Black Economic Progress: Erosion of the Post–1965 Gains in the 1980s," in Steven Shulman and William Darity Jr., eds., *The Question of Discrimination* (Middletown, Conn.: Wesleyan University Press, 1989), 47.

44. Michael deCourcey Hinds, "Minority Business Set Back Sharply by Courts' Rulings," *New York Times,* December 23, 1991.

45. For example, when the Reagan administration reduced social spending between 1980 and 1981, 76 percent of the 400 employees laid off in Chicago's Department of Human Services were black, as were 40 percent of the 186 workers laid off in the Department of Health. In contrast, the federal cutbacks barely affected the predominantly white workforce in Chicago's Streets and Sanitation Department, which is funded with local revenues. See Collins, "The Making of the Black Middle Class," 377.

46. Kirk Johnson, "Black Workers Bear Big Burden as Jobs in Government Dwindle," *New York Times,* February 2, 1996.

47. Melvin L. Oliver and Thomas M. Shapiro, *Black Wealth/White Wealth* (New York: Routledge, 1995), 86.

48. Ibid., 88, 94.

49. Young, *To Be Equal,* 54. This was to become a common refrain among civil rights leaders. Bayard Rustin, "From Protest to Politics: The Future of

the Civil Rights Movement," *Commentary* 39 (February 1964):25, wrote, "What is the value of winning access to public accommodations for those who lack money to use them?" Martin Luther King Jr., "Showdown for Non-Violence," *Look,* April 16, 1968, 28, wrote, "What good is it to be allowed to eat in a restaurant if you can't afford a hamburger?"

50. In October 1963, the issue of compensation was debated in no less public a forum than the *New York Times Magazine*. Already on the defensive, Whitney Young, "Compensation—Yes," *New York Times Magazine,* October 6, 1963, 129, wrote: "The Urban League is asking for a special effort, not for special privileges. This effort has been described as 'preferential treatment,' 'indemnification,' 'special consideration,' 'compensatory activity.' These are 'scare' phrases that obscure the meaning of the proposal and go against the grain of our native sense of fair play. . . . What we ask now is for a brief period there be a deliberate and massive effort to include the Negro citizen in the mainstream of American life."

Kyle Haselden, who was an editor at *Christian Century* and author of a book entitled *The Racial Problems in Christian Perspective* (New York: Harper, 1959), argued in "Compensation–No," *New York Times Magazine,* October 6, 1963, 128, that "our goal should be parity, not preferment," and he struck the chord that would pervade the anti–affirmative action discourse: that "compensation for Negroes is a subtle but pernicious form of racism."

51. For more detailed examination of the crisis in liberalism, see Stephen Steinberg, *Turning Back* (Boston: Beacon Press, 1995), chap. 4.

52. For a detailed account, see John David Skrentny, *The Ironies of Affirmative Action* (Chicago: University of Chicago Press, 1996), chaps. 4, 7.

53. Hugh Davis Graham, *The Civil Rights Era* (New York: Oxford University Press, 1990), 325.

54. Hugh Davis Graham, "Race, History, and Policy: African Americans and Civil Rights Since 1964," *Journal of Policy History* 6(1) (1994):23.

55. In *The Civil Rights Era,* 334–335, Graham provides this account of the job protests during the summer of 1969: "In Chicago, job protests launched by a coalition of black neighborhood organizations shut down twenty-three South Side construction projects involving $85 million in contracts. . . . The demonstrations in Pittsburgh were more violent than in Chicago, but were similarly organized and focused on job discrimination in construction. One clash in Pittsburgh in late August left 50 black protestors and 12 policemen injured. . . . Racial violence over jobs also occurred in Seattle, and black coalitions announced job protest drives for New York, Cleveland, Detroit, Milwaukee, and Boston."

56. In *The Ironies of Affirmative Action,* chap. 4, Skrentny suggests that crisis management provided the principal rationale behind the Nixon administration's vigorous support of the Philadelphia Plan.

57. Perhaps the most germane account comes from Arthur Fletcher, *The Silent Sell-Out* (New York: Third Press, 1974), 65: "I decided to go ahead with the Philadelphia Plan of putting specifications of minority employment goals in all contracts. I did this because my study and experience had convinced me that such targets were essential if we are to measure results in terms of minority employment. Without such targets, the paper compliance, and the indeterminable ineffectiveness of the government programs would go on. I had not come to Washington to preside over the continuation of the ineffective programs of the past."

58. Graham, *The Civil Rights Era,* 446–447.

59. See Jean Stefancic and Richard Delgado, *No Mercy: How Conservative Think Tanks and Foundations Changed America's Social Agenda* (Philadelphia: University of Pennsylvania Press, 1996), chap. 4. See also Amy Elizabeth Ansell, *New Right, New Racism* (New York: New York University Press, 1997), chap. 3.

60. See, for example, Paul Starr, "Civic Reconstruction: What to Do Without Affirmative Action," *American Prospect* 8 (Winter 1992):7–14; and Jeffrey Klein, "The Race Course," *Mother Jones* 22 (September 1997):3–5.

61. See Joe Klein, "The End of Affirmative Action," *Newsweek,* February 13, 1995, 36–37.

Chapter 9

1. *Baker* v. *Carr,* 369 U.S. 186 (1962).

2. But single-member districting systems may discriminate as well, and, indeed, the new freedom was itself a temptation to mischief. Gerrymandered lines may result in vote dilution. Furthermore, a number of difficult options are posed once a legitimate minority district is created. Is justice served by the creation of the first district? What number of minority citizens is sufficient to give effect to their preferences? When does the elimination of one, or more, minority district(s) represent impermissible retrogression? To what extent does an "influence" district compensate? These questions are encompassed in the separate notions of "vote dilution" and "retrogression" and came to make up the main contention over voter discrimination now firmly connected to calculations about the impact of at-large (or multimember) elections or racially gerrymandered district lines.

3. *Yolanda Garza et al.* v. *County of Los Angeles, California, et al.,* 756 F. Supp. 1298 (1989).

4. Abigail M. Thernstrom, *Whose Votes Count? Affirmative Action and Minority Voting Rights* (Cambridge, Mass.: Harvard University Press, 1987).

5. See, e.g., Carol Swain, "Black Majority Districts: A Bad Idea," *New*

York Times, June 3, 1993, and Swain, *Black Interests: The Representation of African Americans in Congress* (Cambridge and London: Harvard University Press, 1995).

6. Stuart Taylor Jr., "Electing by Race," *The American Lawyer* (June 1991); and Thomas Edsall and Mary Edsall, *Chain Reaction: The Impact of Race, Rights, and Taxes on American Politics* (New York: Norton, 1991).

7. *Shaw* v. *Reno,* 509 U.S. 125 (1993).

8. Lani Guinier, "The Triumph of Tokenism: The Voting Rights Act and the Theory of Black Electoral Success," *Michigan Law Review* 89 (1991): 1077–1154.

9. For additional sources of this chapter not already cited, see U.S. Constitution, Article 1, Section 2 and Amendments 14, 15, 17, 19, 22, 23, 24, 26; *Colgrove* v. *Green,* 328 U.S. 549 (1945); *Gomillion* v. *Lightfoot,* 364 U.S. 339 (1960); *Mobile* v. *Bolden,* U.S. 446 U.S. 55 (1980); *Thornburg* v. *Gingles,* 478 U.S. 30 (1986); Charles Fager, *Selma 1965: The March That Changed the South* (Boston: Beacon Press, 1975); David Garrow, *Protest at Selma: Martin Luther King, Jr. and the Voting Rights Act of 1965* (New Haven: Yale University Press, 1978); Edward Still, "Alternatives to Single-Member Districts," in Chandler Davidson, ed., *Minority Voting Dilution* (Washington, D.C.: Howard University Press, 1984), 249–267; Aryeh Neier, *Neier Only Judgement: The Limits of Litigation in Social Change* (Middletown, Conn.: Wesleyan University Press, 1982), 80–94; Margaret Edds, *Free at Last: What Really Happened When Civil Rights Came to Southern Politics* (Bethesda, Md.: Adler and Adler, 1987); Frances Fox Piven and Richard A. Cloward, *Why Americans Don't Vote* (New York: Pantheon Books, 1988); John Zimmerman, "Electoral Systems: Many Ways to Elect Officials," *Current Municipal Problems* 14 (1988):514–525; Laughlin McDonald, "The Quiet Revolution in Minority Voting Rights," *Vanderbilt Law Review* 42 (May 1989):1249–1297; Douglas Massey and Nancy Denton, "Hypersegregation in U.S. Metropolitan Areas: Black and Hispanic Segregation Along Five Dimensions," *Demography* 26 (August 1989):373 ff.; Frank Parker, *Black Votes Count: Political Empowerment in Mississippi After 1965* (Chapel Hill: University of North Carolina Press, 1990); Center for Constitutional Rights, *And Before I'll Be a Slave: A Guide to Community-Based Voting Rights Litigation* (New York: Center for Constitutional Rights, 1990); Alex Willingham, "Voting Rights and Community Empowerment: Political Struggle in the Georgia Black Belt," in John Gaventa, Barbara Ellen Smith, and Alex Willingham, eds., *Communities in Crisis: Appalachia and the South* (Philadelphia: Temple University Press, 1990), 123–137; Bernard Grofman and Chandler Davidson, eds., *Controversies in Minority Voting: The Voting Rights Act in Perspective* (Washington, D.C.: Brookings Institution, 1992); "The Supreme Court, Racial Politics, and the Right to Vote: *Shaw* v. *Reno*

and the Future of the Voting Rights Act," *American University Law Review* 44 (October 1994); Edward Still and Robert Richie, "Alternative Electoral Systems as Voting Rights Remedies" (Washington, D.C.: Center for Voting and Democracy, 1995).

Chapter 10

1. See Efrain Hernandez Jr., "Solutions in the Self: Minister Pushes Private Responsibility," *Boston Globe,* May 18, 1992; Don Aucoin and Peter S. Canellos, "A Community Takes Responsibility: Black Manifesto Urges a New Social Contract," *Boston Globe,* May 8, 1992; Michael Renzendes, "Wilkerson Touts Black Self-Reliance: Says Government Must Act as Well," *Boston Globe*, June 22, 1992; Evan Thomas with Howard Fineman, Ann McDaniel, Eleanor Clift, and Carolyn Friday, "The Economic Crisis of Urban America," *Business Week,* May 18, 1992, 43; "Where Does He Stand? Bush's Court Nominee Confounds the Critics and Presents a Quandary for Black Leaders," *Newsweek,* July 15, 1991, 16–17; Robbie Morganfield, "Nation of Islam Spreads Self-Help Message: Celebration of Family Day Features Talk by Farrakhan," *Houston Chronicle,* September 11, 1994; Frederick D. Robinson, "Self-Help Can Chip Away at Mountain of Despair," *Atlanta Constitution,* July 26, 1990; Wendell Anthony, "Self-Help, Self-Respect: A Good Message for the Black Men of Detroit," *Detroit News,* July 7, 1994; Angelo B. Henderson, "Sharpton Says Self-Help Is the Road to Salvation," *Detroit News,* November 11, 1991; K. I. Pedizisai, "Brown Promotes Black Self-Help: Columnist Brings 'Buy Black' Campaign to Cleveland Expo," *Call and Post,* June 18, 1992; and Jerry M. Guess, "NAACP Stays True to Self-Help Principle," *Wall Street Journal,* May 14, 1992.

Predictably, the self-help message has been taken up by government leaders, journalists, civic organizations, and conservative intellectuals as something African Americans should embrace. See Dinesh D'Souza, "Up from Dependency," *Wall Street Journal,* March 25, 1992; "It Was Self-Help, Not Politics, That Helped Blacks in the 1980s," *Atlanta Journal,* August 13, 1991; Karen M. Thomas, "African-Americans and the GOP: Republicans' Self-Help Message Helps Attract Blacks," *Chicago Tribune,* August 19, 1992; "Democrats Pass a Self-Help Platform," *Chicago Tribune,* July 13, 1992; Clarence Page, "Clinton's Message: Self-Help, Without Civil Rights Rhetoric," *Chicago Tribune,* December 29, 1993; Iver Peterson, "Whitman's Urban Agenda Outlines Self-Help Program," *New York Times,* March 7, 1995; Darryl Fears, "Neighborhood Self-Help Envisioned: Civic Experts Urge Citizens to Organize and Urban and Suburban Areas to Cooperate," *Atlanta Journal Constitution,* November 13, 1993; and David Holmstrom,

"Inner Cities Being Redone American Way—Self-Help," *Christian Science Monitor,* April 22, 1994.

For articles criticizing or tempering the enthusiasm for self-help, see Derrick Z. Jackson, "Self-Help for Whom?" *Boston Sunday Globe,* September 22, 1991; "Self-Help and the Urban League," *St. Louis Post-Dispatch,* August 19, 1994; and "Black Self-Help Is Only Part of the Answer," *St. Louis Post-Dispatch,* January 29, 1994.

2. Of course, I see black conservatives as the vanguard of trends that will further impoverish and debilitate the black community. Quite a different view appears in a recent hagiography of this group. See Joseph G. Conti and Brad Stetson, *Challenging the Civil Rights Establishment: Profiles of a New Black Vanguard* (Westport, Conn.: Praeger, 1993).

3. Charles Lane and Howard Fineman, "Defying the Stereotypes: The New Clout of 'Black Conservatives,'" *Newsweek,* July 15, 1991, 18–19; John Hope Franklin, "Booker T. Washington, Revisited," *New York Times,* August 1, 1991; August Meier, *Negro Thought in America, 1880–1915: Racial Ideologies in the Age of Booker T. Washington* (Ann Arbor, Mich.: Ann Arbor Paperbacks, 1966).

4. Preston H. Smith II, "The Limitations of Racial Democracy: The Politics of the Chicago Urban League, 1916–1940" (Ph.D. diss., University of Massachusetts at Amherst, 1989).

5. Ann Withorn, "Helping Ourselves: The Limits and Potential of Self-Help," *Social Policy* 11(3) (November–December 1980):21.

6. Franklin, "Booker T. Washington, Revisited."

7. Withorn, "Helping Ourselves," 21.

8. U.S. Bureau of the Census, *Statistical Abstract of the United States, 1993* (Washington, D.C.: GPO, 1993), 469.

9. Robert L. Woodson Sr., "Is the Black Community a Casualty of the War on Poverty?" *Heritage Lectures* 45 (1990):3; Playthell Benjamin, "GOP Goes the Weasel: Tony Brown Stands Up for Republicans," *Village Voice,* August 20, 1991, 41.

10. Robert L. Woodson, "Self-Help, Not Big Daddy, Must Rescue the Black Underclass," *Washington Post,* May 12, 1985.

11. Lane and Fineman, "Defying the Stereotypes"; Lena Williams, "Growing Black Debate on Racism: When Is It Real, When an Excuse?" *New York Times,* April 5, 1992.

12. Woodson, "Self-Help, Not Big Daddy."

13. See the fictional black conservative Gleason Golightly, who becomes Derrick Bell's alter ego in *Faces at the Bottom of the Well: The Permanence of Racism* (New York: HarperCollins, 1992), 158–194.

14. John Jacob, "An Overview of Black America in 1984," in James D. Williams, ed., *The State of Black America 1985* (New York: National Urban

League, 1985), v. Black conservative journalist Joseph Perkins, "Urban League Emphasizes an Agenda of Self-Help," *Wall Street Journal,* August 6, 1986, writes approvingly of the 1986 NUL convention featuring conservative speakers, commenting that "Mr. Jacob and other black leaders are anxious about the black conservatives getting credit, perhaps wary that some of their constituency will be wooed away."

15. Glenn C. Loury, "The Moral Quandary of the Black Community," *Public Interest* 79 (Spring 1985):11.

16. Glenn C. Loury, "Internally Directed Action for Black Community Development: The Next Frontier for 'The Movement,'" *Review of Black Political Economy* 13(1–2) (Summer–Fall 1984):38.

17. Ibid., 38.

18. See Bernadette Chachere, "Comments on the Glenn C. Loury Article," *Review of Black Political Economy* 13(1–2) (Summer–Fall 1984): 47–49.

19. Dorothy Height, "Self-Help—a Black Tradition," *The Nation,* July 24–31, 1989, 136–138.

20. Ibid.

21. "Has the New Generation Changed the Civil Rights Agenda?" *Ebony* 47(10) (August 1990):62.

22. Roy L. Brooks, *Rethinking the American Race Problem* (Berkeley and Los Angeles: University of California Press, 1990).

23. Smith, "The Limitations of Racial Democracy."

24. Clarence Page, "Toward a New Black Agenda," *Chicago Tribune,* April 17, 1985.

25. Loury, "Internally Directed Action," 39. See also Loury, "The Moral Quandary," 16.

26. Gordon Lafer, "Minority Unemployment, Labor Market Segmentation, and the Failure of Job-Training Policy in New York City," *Urban Affairs Quarterly* 28(2) (December 1992):206–235.

27. Brooks, *Rethinking the American Race Problem.*

28. Adolph Reed, "The Underclass as Myth and Symbol: The Poverty of Discourse About Poverty," *Radical America* 24 (January 1992):21–40, reprinted in Reed, *Stirrings in the Jug: Black Politics in the Post–Segregation Era* (Minneapolis: University of Minnesota Press, 1999). Apparently, values and habits are not the only things the masses are supposed to emulate. Tony Brown declares that now that he has decided to join the Republican Party, the black masses will follow. "Now that they see me doing it, the little guy will know it's all right for them to do it." Quoted in Benjamin, "GOP Goes the Weasel," 42.

29. William J. Wilson, *The Truly Disadvantaged: The Inner City, the Underclass, and Public Policy* (Chicago: University of Chicago Press, 1987).

30. Loury, "The Moral Quandary," 14, 15, 16.

31. Ibid., 15.

32. Cited in Clara Germant, "A Black Journalist Looks at Civil Rights Today," *Christian Science Monitor,* January 15, 1993.

33. See "What Price Self-Reliance?" *The Progressive* (March 1985):11.

34. Billy J. Tidwell, *Playing to Win: A Marshall Plan for America* (Washington, D.C.: National Urban League, 1991). See also John E. Jacob, "A Marshall Plan for America: A Land of Diverse People Living and Working Together," *Vital Speeches* 58(1) (October 15, 1991):58–63; and John E. Jacob, "Black America, 1990: An Overview," in Janet Dewart, ed., *The State of Black America 1991* (New York: National Urban League, 1991), 7. Whitney Young Jr., *To Be Equal* (New York: McGraw-Hill, 1964), 26, was first to call for a "domestic Marshall Plan."

35. Woodson, "Self-Help, Not Big Daddy."

36. Ibid. Doug Henwood, *Left Business Observer* 67 (1994):7, points out that 90 percent of poverty funds go to the poor.

37. Woodson, "Self-Help, Not Big Daddy." See also Woodson, "Is the Black Community a Casualty?"

38. Pamela Roby, ed., *The Poverty Establishment* (Englewood Cliffs, N.J.: Prentice-Hall, 1974); Betty Reid Mandell, ed., *Welfare in America: Controlling the "Dangerous Classes"* (Englewood Cliffs, N.J.: Prentice-Hall, 1975); Frances Fox Piven and Richard A. Cloward, *Regulating the Poor: The Functions of Public Welfare* (New York: Random House, 1972); Frances Fox Piven, "Ideology and the State: Women, Power, and the Welfare State," in Linda Gordon, ed., *Women, the State, and Welfare* (Madison: University of Wisconsin Press, 1990), 250–264. See also Ray Forrest, "The Privatization of Collective Consumption," in Mark Gottdiener and Chris G. Pickvance, eds., *Urban Life in Transition* (Newbury Park, Calif.: Sage, 1991), 177.

39. "Black America Under the Reagan Administration: A Symposium of Black Conservatives," *Policy Review* (Fall 1985):39.

40. Ibid., 40.

41. Ibid., 39.

42. Ibid.

43. Ibid.

44. Woodson, "Self-Help, Not Big Daddy."

45. Glenn Loury, "Freeing the Inner-City Poor," in Marc Lipsitz, ed., *Revitalizing Our Cities: New Approaches to Solving Urban Problems* (Washington, D.C.: Fund for an American Renaissance and National Center for Neighborhood Enterprise, 1986), 113.

46. Barbara Ransby and Tracye Matthews, "Black Popular Culture and the Transcendence of Patriarchal Illusions," *Race and Class* 35(1) (1993): 60; Reed, "The Underclass as Myth and Symbol."

47. Frances Fox Piven and Richard A. Cloward, "The Contemporary Relief Debate," in Fred Block, Richard A. Cloward, Barbara Ehrenreich, and

Frances Fox Piven, *The Mean Season: The Attack on the Welfare State* (New York: Pantheon Books, 1987), 64–65.

48. Teresa L. Amott, "Black Women and AFDC: Making Entitlement Out of Necessity," in Gordon, ed., *Women, the State, and Welfare*, 281.

49. Diana Pearce, "Welfare Is Not *for* Women: Why the War on Poverty Cannot Conquer the Feminization of Poverty," in Gordon, ed., *Women, the State, and Welfare,* 275.

50. Piven and Cloward, "The Contemporary Relief Debate," 94–98.

51. Julianne Malveaux, "The Political Economy of Black Women," in Mike Davis, Manning Marable, Fred Pfeil, and Michael Sprinker, eds., *The Year Left 2: Toward a Rainbow Socialism* (London: Verso Books, 1987), 52–73. See also Margaret C. Simms and Julianne Malveaux, eds., *Slipping Through the Cracks: The Status of Black Women* (New Brunswick: Transaction Books, 1986).

52. Robert Greenstein, Kathryn Porter, Isaac Shapiro, Paul Leonard, and Scott Barancik, *Still Far from the Dream: Recent Developments in Black Income, Employment, and Poverty* (Washington, D.C.: Center on Budget and Policy Priorities, 1988), 35.

53. Piven, "Ideology and the State," 254–255.

54. Woodson, "The Poor and Conservatives," 5.

55. Greenstein et al., *Still Far from the Dream,* x: "The earnings of the typical full-time black worker were $315 a week in 1987, virtually the same as in 1980 and lower than in any year from 1972 to 1979, after adjusting for inflation."

56. Saskia Sassen, *The Mobility of Labor and Capital: A Study in International Investment and Labor Flow* (Cambridge: Cambridge University Press, 1988), 150.

57. Frances Fox Piven and Richard A. Cloward, "Explaining the Politics of the Welfare State or Marching Back Toward Pluralism?" in Roger Friedland and A. F. Robertson, eds., *Beyond the Marketplace: Rethinking Economy and Society* (New York: Aldine de Gruyter, 1990), 260; Fred Block, "Rethinking the Political Economy of the Welfare State," in Block et al., *The Mean Season,* 128–134.

58. Woodson describes himself, in Lee A. Daniels, "New Black Conservatives," *New York Times Magazine,* October 4, 1991, 23, as "a pragmatist because I'm more concerned with concrete prescriptions than labels. My views contain elements of liberalism, conservatism, black nationalism and American patriotism." For a good look at the intersection of nationalism, sexism, and conservatism in new cultural forms, see Ransby and Matthews, "Black Popular Culture." See also E. Frances White, "Africa on My Mind: Gender Counter Discourse and African American Nationalism," *Journal of Women's History* 2(1) (Spring 1990):73–97.

59. Loury, "The Moral Quandary," 11.

60. Glenn C. Loury, "Making It All Happen," in Robert L. Woodson, ed., *On the Road to Economic Freedom: An Agenda for Black Progress* (Washington, D.C.: Regnery Gateway, 1987), 111.

61. Quoted in Benjamin, "GOP Goes the Weasel," 41.

62. See Ransby and Matthews, "Black Popular Culture," 63.

63. Attorney Larry Thompson is quoted in Lane and Fineman, "Defying the Stereotypes," 18, as saying about Clarence Thomas's admiration for Malcolm X: "I think the core of [Thomas's] beliefs is we can't simply preach on and on that all we have to do is get more assistance from the government. It may be a nationalistic argument more than anything else."

64. See Jerry G. Watts, "Racial Discourse in an Age of Social Darwinism," *Democratic Left* 18(4) (July–August 1990):3–5.

65. Woodson, "Self-Help, Not Big Daddy."

66. Michael McQueen, "Robert Woodson May Have White House Access, but the Conservative Infuriates Black Leaders," *Wall Street Journal,* June 2, 1987. See also "Where Does He Stand?" 16.

67. Julianne Malveaux, "Why Are the Black Conservatives All Men?" *Ms.* (March–April 1991):60–61, first noticed the masculinist cast of the publicly visible black conservatives. Although she mainly focuses on Shelby Steele and the issue of affirmative action, the sports metaphors of "leveling the playing field" and "rules of the game" imply that special privileges are unmanly. She points out that they miss how the notion of playing by the rules of the game is already racially and sexually rigged because of a concern with appearances.

68. Lisa Jones, "The Invisible Ones: The Emma Mae Martin Story, the One Thomas Didn't Tell," *Village Voice,* November 12, 1991, 27–28; Joel F. Handler, "The Judge and His Sister: Growing Up Black," *New York Times,* July 23, 1991.

69. Steven P. Erie, Martin Rein, and Barbara Wiget, "Women and the Reagan Revolution: Thermidor for the Social Welfare Economy," in Irene Diamond, ed., *Families, Politics, and Public Policy* (New York: Longman, 1983), 103. Corporations and real estate developers who have profited from the poverty industry are not criticized or even mentioned by Woodson. Yet corporate largesse at the expense of the poor has been a regular feature of social programs. For a recent example of corporate pimping of programs designed for the poor, see Jason DeParle, "Private Interests Are Said to Benefit from U.S. Plan for Needy," *New York Times,* March 18, 1992.

70. Kevin Phillips, *The Politics of Rich and Poor: Wealth and the American Electorate in the Reagan Aftermath* (New York: Harper Perennial, 1991), 67.

71. Woodson, "Is the Black Community a Casualty?" 9.

72. Ibid.

73. "Black America Under the Reagan Administration," 41.

74. Woodson, "Is the Black Community a Casualty?" 9.

75. *From the Center* (Summer 1992). This is the NCNE newsletter.

76. John Sibley Butler, *Entrepreneurship and Self-Help Among Black Americans: A Reconsideration of Race and Economics.* (Albany: State University of New York Press, 1991), 319.

77. E. Franklin Frazier, *Black Bourgeoisie: The Rise of a New Middle Class* (New York: Free Press, 1957).

78. Butler, *Entrepreneurship and Self-Help,* 327–328. He writes, "One of the fallacies evolving from research on the nature of the inner-city Afro-American community is that the people are not capable of creating or re-creating organizations which can help to bring a sense of stability to their community." This populist belief in the ability of poor people alone to solve their own problems is one of the main appeals of this ideology to grassroots activists in the inner city. Perhaps a deeper reading will reveal instead that this faith in the "capacity" of the poor is based on their re-creating themselves in the image of the black bourgeoisie.

79. Robert L. Woodson, "A Legacy of Entrepreneurship," in Woodson, ed., *On the Road to Economic Freedom,* 19, laments that "small black firms, the backbone of the racially localized black economy, could not compete with the newly integrated, low-priced, large volume department stores, supermarkets, fast food chains, and shopping centers."

80. Butler, *Entrepreneurship and Self-Help,* 326.

81. Ibid.

82. Ibid., 329.

83. Ibid., 330.

84. Ibid., 278.

85. Ibid., 330.

86. Robert L. Woodson, ed., *Black Perspectives on Crime and the Criminal Justice System* (Boston: Hall, 1977), 170. See also Robert L. Woodson, ed., *Youth Crime and Urban Policy: A View from the Inner City* (Washington, D.C.: American Enterprise Institute for Public Policy Research, 1981).

87. Robert L. Woodson, "Founder's Letter," in National Center for Neighborhood Enterprise, *Programs and Activities* (Washington, D.C.: National Center for Neighborhood Enterprise, 1993), 1.

88. Frank Riessman, "Self-Help Ethos," *Social Policy* (Summer 1982): 42–43.

89. Woodson, *Youth Crime and Urban Policy,* 117.

90. It is here that civil rights groups' countercharge to Woodson—namely, that he is not doing anything different from themselves—rings true. See McQueen, "Robert Woodson May Have White House Access."

91. NCNE, *Programs and Activities,* 1–3.

92. Woodson, *Youth Crime and Urban Policy,* 5.

93. NCNE, *Programs and Activities,* 17.

94. Ibid., 32–34.

95. McQueen, "Robert Woodson May Have White House Access."

96. Jack Kemp, "Tackling Poverty: Market-Based Policies to Empower the Poor," *Policy Review* 51 (Winter 1990):2–5.

97. Hilary Silver, "Privatization, Self-Help, and Public Housing Home Ownership in the United States," in Willem van Vliet and Jan van Weesep, eds., *Government and Housing: Developments in Seven Countries* (Newbury Park, Calif.: Sage, 1990), 124.

98. NCNE, *Programs and Activities,* 5–6.

99. Loury, "Freeing the Inner-City Poor," 107–113.

100. Ibid., 109.

101. "Second Thoughts," *Wall Street Journal,* February 3, 1988.

102. Robert L. Woodson, *Private Sector Alternatives to the Welfare State: A New Agenda for Black Americans,* Policy Report no. 131 (Dallas: National Center for Policy Analysis, November 1987). See also Woodson, "A Legacy of Entrepreneurship."

103. Quoted in "Black America Under the Reagan Administration," 32.

104. Public housing authorities contract with a tenant management corporation; the public housing tenants manage the complex. The management corporation is responsible for "policy formation, developing rules and regulations governing project residency, and ensuring that tenants at large have the opportunity to participate in policy making and operations." See Manpower Demonstration Research Corporation, *Tenant Management: Findings from a Three-Year Experiment in Public Housing* (Cambridge, Mass.: Ballinger, 1981), 22.

105. NCNE, *Programs and Activities,* 6.

106. According to an independent audit in 1986 by the accounting firm Coopers and Lybrand, rent collection increased 77 percent, which was "seven times the increase at public housing citywide." See David Osborne, "They Can't Stop Us Now," *Washington Post Magazine,* July 30, 1989, 14. Osborne, 19, reports that repairs are more timely because the maintenance people are residents living on the premises. More generally, however, Manpower Demonstration Research, *Tenant Management,* 5, reports that in public housing projects under tenant management "average rent collections, vacancy rates, or speed of response to maintenance requests . . . was not significantly better than housing authority management."

107. Osborne, "They Can't Stop Us Now," 19. Gradually, the RMC stopped contracting services from external companies and began providing the services itself through businesses run by residents, or if it did contract with an outside company, the contractor had to hire residents. One of the

created businesses was a catering service. The first contract for the catering service was the Heritage Foundation. Kimi Gray, "A Model for Privatizing Public Housing," in Lipsitz, ed., *Revitalizing Our Cities,* 65, reports, "The Heritage Foundation people, accustomed to eating salads, became accustomed to eating spare ribs, collard greens, and cornbread. They liked it at board meetings." I guess we could call this right-wing multicultural sharing or perhaps a modern version of the plantation "service" tradition.

108. Michael A. Stegman, *More Housing, More Fairly: Report of the Twentieth Century Fund Task Force on Affordable Housing—Background Paper on the Limits of Privatization* (New York: Twentieth Century Fund Press, 1991), 117.

109. Cited in Osborne, "They Can't Stop Us Now," 15. Gray stresses the importance of money as power, and she alludes to misguided debates over what "politics" or "economics" will lead to black advancement. The problem is the artificial separation of politics from economics. Gray's point is well taken—perhaps more than she intends. Her ability to garner resources for Kenilworth-Parkside derives largely from her *political* anointment as a showpiece for the "success of self-help."

110. Robert Kolodny, "Self-Help Can Be an Effective Tool in Housing the Urban Poor," *Journal of Housing* 38 (March 1981):137. See also George Lipsitz, *A Life in the Struggle: Ivory Perry and the Culture of Opposition* (Philadelphia: Temple University Press, 1988), esp. 145–172.

111. Kolodny, "Self-Help Can Be an Effective Tool," 139.

112. Stegman, *More Housing,* 16.

113. Silver, "Privatization," 129–131. See also General Accounting Office (GAO), *Public Housing: Planned Kenilworth-Parkside Sale Raises Issues for Future Transactions* (Washington, D.C.: General Accounting Office, December 1989), 4.

114. Quoted in Osborne, "They Can't Stop Us Now," 16.

115. Woodson, "Self-Help, Not Big Daddy." Woodson reports that "teenage pregnancies have declined, in the District of Columbia's Kenilworth/Parkside development they are down 50 percent since 1982; in the same project, the percentage of welfare recipients has declined 46 percent in the same three year period; the number of female-headed households has decreased in the resident-managed projects in all of these cities. . . . These successes can be ascribed to the residents assuming responsibility for their own lives." According to Osborne, "They Can't Stop Us Now," 29, although "all sources agree that teenage pregnancy—once the norm—has dropped significantly . . . accurate numbers are hard to come by at Kenilworth (when asked how much welfare dependency had been reduced, for instance, Kimi Gray and her top managers gave wildly different figures)."

116. Quoted in Osborne, "They Can't Stop Us Now," 29–30.

117. Woodson, *Private Sector Alternatives,* 11, 31, claims that these benefits have occurred in other tenant-managed public housing projects. He substantiates his claim that these projects "cost less" with a study that the National Center for Neighborhood Enterprise submitted to the U.S. Department of Housing and Urban Development in 1984 entitled "The Grass Is Greener in Public Housing: From Tenant to Resident to Homeowner." See also Stegman, *More Housing,* 85.

118. Stegman, *More Housing.*

119. Silver, "Privatization"; Stegman, *More Housing.*

120. Stegman, *More Housing,* 16. See also GAO, *Planned Kenilworth-Parkside Sale.*

121. Jason DeParle, "H.U.D. Choice Wary of Selling Public Housing: Cisneros Fears Creating a Burden for Tenants," *New York Times,* January 13, 1993.

122. "Black America Under the Reagan Administration," 40.

123. Ibid.

124. Woodson, "Is the Black Community a Casualty?" 6.

125. William Raspberry, "Kemp at HUD Paving Path Out of Dependency," *News and Observer* (Raleigh, N.C.), May 15, 1990.

126. Brooks, *Rethinking the American Race Problem.* Emmett D. Carson, "The Black Underclass Concept: Self-Help Versus Government Intervention," *American Economic Association Papers and Proceedings* (May 1986):348, says, "There is no question that community-based self-help programs aimed at improving the attitudes of those in the underclass are desirable and should be encouraged." Although Floyd W. Hayes, "Governmental Retreat and the Politics of African-American Self-Reliant Development: Public Discourse and Social Policy," *Journal of Black Studies* 22(3) (March 1992):341, finds black conservatives a throwback to an outmoded form of capitalism, he sees that their "insistence on moral uplift and economic self-help strategies was admirable but limited."

127. Cornel West, "Nihilism in Black America: A Danger That Corrodes from Within," *Dissent* (Spring 1991): 224–225. West declares: "The nihilistic threat is now more powerful than ever before because the armor to ward against it is weaker. . . . Like alcoholism and drug addiction, nihilism is a disease of the soul. It can never be completely cured and there is always the possibility of relapse. . . . Nihilism is not overcome by arguments or analyses; it is tamed by love and care."

128. Cornel West, *Race Matters* (Boston: Beacon Press, 1993), 58.

129. For a similar critique of how progressives provide unintended support for a social pathology position in a different domain, see Tricia Rose, "'Fear of a Black Planet': Rap Music and Black Cultural Politics in the 1990s," *Journal of Negro Education* 60(3) (1991):288–289.

130. West, "Nihilism in Black America," 223. On the same page, he claims this enemy "has been and is neither oppression nor exploitation but rather the nihilistic threat—that is, loss of hope and absence of meaning."

131. West, *Race Matters,* 58.

132. Ibid.

133. Loury, "Freeing the Inner-City Poor," 112–113.

134. Quoted in Osborne, "They Can't Stop Us Now," 19. Peer pressure is widely used by these public housing RMCs. See Kolodny, "Self-Help Can Be an Effective Tool," 140.

135. Kolodny, "Self-Help Can Be an Effective Tool," 141, 140, points out that "self-help and user control does create . . . greater tolerance for existing conditions." See Steven Katz and Margit Mayer, "Gimme Shelter: Self-Help Housing Struggles Within and Against the State in New York City and West Berlin," *International Journal of Urban and Regional Research* 9(1) (1985):17; and Nancy A. Naples, "Contradictions in the Gender Subtext of the War on Poverty: The Community Work and Resistance of Women from Low Income Communities," *Social Problems* 38(3) (August 1991):316–332.

Those who see the potential of "progressive self-help" think that the experience of "going it alone" will make groups more critical of the state. They will then use their self-help experience to protest the distribution of a social surplus to private companies and affluent households. See Withorn, "Helping Ourselves," 26. For an argument that emphasizes the political leverage that community-based organizations have by delivering contracted services, see Margit Mayer, "Politics in a Post-Fordist Society," *Socialist Review* 21(1) (1991):105–124.

136. NCNE, *Programs and Activities.*

137. Loury, "Making It All Happen," 111.

138. See Samuel Bowles, David Gordon, and Thomas E. Weisskopf, *Beyond the Wasteland: A Democratic Alternative to Economic Decline* (Garden City, N.Y.: Anchor Press, 1983).

139. See M. Patricia Marchak, *The Integrated Circus: The New Right and the Restructuring of Global Markets* (Montreal: McGill-Queen's University Press, 1991).

140. Timothy Barkenov, Robin Boyle, and Daniel Rich, *Privatism and Urban Policy in Britain and the United States* (Oxford: Oxford University Press, 1989), 134.

141. See Paula Dwyer, "The Poverty Thing," *New Republic,* January 30, 1989, 13–15; and Peter Hong, "How Kemp Built a Housing Bill That May Stand Up in Congress," *Business Week,* July 2, 1990, 43.

142. Mike Davis, "Who Killed LA? A Political Autopsy," *New Left Review* 198 (January–February 1993):24.

143. Christopher Farrell, Michael Mandel, and Michael Schroeder, "The Economic Crisis of Urban America," *Business Week,* May 18, 1992, 42.

144. Rochelle Sharpe, "Losing Ground: In Latest Recession, Only Blacks Suffered Net Employment Loss," *Wall Street Journal,* September 14, 1993.

145. "The Economic Crisis of Urban America," 38.

146. Arthur I. Blaustein and Geoffrey Faux, *Star Spangled Banner Hustle: The Story of a Nixon Promise* (Garden City, N.Y.: Anchor Books, 1972).

147. James Jennings, "The 'New' Black Neo-conservatism: A Critique," *Trotter Review* (Fall 1987):16. See also Robert Gooding-Williams, "Black Neoconservatism: A Critical Introduction," *Praxis International* 7(2) (July 1987):133–142.

Chapter 11

1. E. Anthony Rotundo, *American Manhood: Transformations in Masculinity from the Revolution to the Modern Era* (New York: Basic Books, 1993), 3–7.

2. Daniel Patrick Moynihan, "The Negro Family: The Case for National Action," in Lee Rainwater and William L. Yancey, eds., *The Moynihan Report and the Politics of Controversy* (Cambridge, Mass.: MIT Press, 1967), 76.

3. Ibid., 75.

4. See Paula Giddings, *When and Where I Enter: The Impact of Black Women on Race and Sex in America* (New York: William Morrow, 1984), 261–336; Sara Evans, *Personal Politics: The Roots of Women's Liberation in the Civil Rights Movement and the New Left* (New York: Vintage Books, 1980), 263–285; Flora Davis, *Moving the Mountain: The Women's Movement in America Since 1960* (New York: Simon and Schuster, 1991), 356–385; Nigel Young, *An Infantile Disorder? The Crisis and Decline of the New Left* (Boulder: Westview Press, 1977), 114–126; Blanche Linden-Ward and Carol Hurd Green, *American Women in the 1960s: Changing the Future* (New York: Twayne, 1993), 28–66.

5. Giddings, *When and Where I Enter,* 307.

6. Floyd D. Weatherspoon, "African American Males: Stereotypical Biases Engender a Case of Race Plus Sex Discrimination," *Washburn Law Journal* 36(1) (1996):26.

7. Ibid.

8. I. Mukenge Rousseau, Foreword to *Challenge: A Journal of Research on Black Men* 1(1) (July 1990):1.

9. Richard Majors, "An Infrastructure for African American Males," *Urban Institute: Policy and Research Report* (Summer–Fall 1992):32.

10. Clifford Watson and Geneva Smitherman, *Educating African American Males: Detroit's Malcolm X Academy Solution* (Chicago: Third World Press, 1996), 47.

11. U.S. Congress, Senate, Committee on Banking, Housing, and Urban Affairs, *The Plight of African-American Men in Urban America*, 102d Cong., 1st sess., March 19, 1991, May 21, 1991, 129.

12. Lorrie Grant, "NAACP to Tackle Problems Facing Black Males," Reuters, NewsBank NewsFile, July 8, 1996.

13. Jawanza Kunjufu, "The Male Academy: In Whose Interest?" *Black Collegian* 22 (November–December 1991):46.

14. Ronald B. Mincy, ed., *Nurturing Young Black Males: Challenges to Agencies, Programs, and Social Policy* (Washington, D.C.: Urban Institute Press, 1994), App. B.

15. Kunjufu, "The Male Academy," 46. Ohio, California, North Carolina, and Maryland, as well as Indianapolis, have established commissions to focus on the status of black males.

16. Millicent Lawton, "National Crusade to Improve Destiny of Black Males Launched," *Education Week,* May 29, 1991, 5.

17. Members of the Twenty-first Century Commission on African-American Males include former Governor Thomas H. Kean of New Jersey; Mayor Kurt Schmoke of Baltimore; David A. Hamburg, president of the Carnegie Corporation of New York; Benjamin L. Hooks, executive director of the NAACP; and Franklin Jenifer, president of Howard University. The commission's honorary board includes seven members of Congress and former President Jimmy Carter. The commission's cochairpersons were Mayor David N. Dinkins of New York; Arthur A. Fletcher, chairperson of the U.S. Commission on Civil Rights; Dorothy Height, president of the National Council of Negro Women; John Jacob, of the National Urban League; and U.S. representative Edolphus Towns, Democrat from New York. See Peter Schmidt, "Movement Grows to Rescue Black Males 'in Crisis,'" *Education Week* 10 (September 26, 1990): 9.

18. Gerda Gallop, "Repairing Breach," *Battle Creek* (Michigan) *Enquirer,* NewsBank, NewsFile, May 14, 1996.

19. Bobby William Austin, ed., *Repairing the Breach: Key Ways to Support Family Life, Reclaim Our Streets, and Rebuild Civil Society in America's Communities, Executive Summary* (Dillon, Colo.: Alpine Guild, 1996), 6.

20. Ibid., 8.

21. Ibid., 7–8.

22. Tucker Carlson, "That Old-Time Religion: Why Black Men Are Returning to Church," *Policy Review* (Summer 1992):13–17.

23. Scott L. Miley, "And Church Wins Young Men?" *Indianapolis Star,* May 28, 1994.

24. Mike Wilson, "Winning the Hearts, Minds of Black Men," *St. Petersburg Times,* November 9, 1995.

25. Senate Committee on Banking, Housing, and Urban Affairs, *The Plight of African-American Men,* 24.

26. Douglas L. Wilder, "Straight Talk on Black Families," *Readers Digest* (July 1991):99.

27. Ibid.

28. Senate Committee on Banking, Housing, and Urban Affairs, *The Plight of African-American Men,* 86.

29. Ibid.

30. For instance, the Twenty-first Century Commission on African-American Males conference in May 1991 was sponsored by the Carnegie Foundation, the Kellogg Foundation, and Xerox Corporation. Howard University and the National Association for Equal Opportunity in Higher Education provided financial support as well. See Lawton, "National Crusade," 5.

31. The University of North Carolina–Charlotte, held a conference on March 14, 1998, entitled "Preparing Black Youth for Manhood Conference." Benedict College, Columbia, South Carolina, held a conference April 10–12, 1997, entitled "The Black Male Conference: Eagles Taking Flight." Both conferences had a panel addressing the responsibility of manhood.

32. Majors, "An Infrastructure," 33.

33. Regina Jingles, "Taking a Stand," *Black Collegian* 26 (April 1996): 24.

34. David J. Dent, "Survival Lessons," *Essence* 21 (April 1991):88.

35. Linda Fullerton, "Mad Dads Groups Seek to Save African-American Children," *St. Paul Pioneer Press,* October 12, 1995.

36. Ibid.

37. Ibid.

38. Quoted in Ellis Cose, *A Man's World: How Real Is Male Privilege—and How High Is Its Price?* (New York: HarperCollins, 1995), 53.

39. Ibid.

40. Ibid., 56.

41. Clifford Watson and Geneva Smitherman, "Educational Equity and Detroit's Male Academy," *Equity and Excellence* 25 (1992):90.

42. Audrey T. McCluskey, "The Historical Context of the Single-Sex Schooling Debate Among African Americans," *Western Journal of Black Studies* 17(4) (1993):199.

43. William Oliver, "Black Males and Social Problems: Prevention Through Afrocentric Socialization," *Journal of Black Studies* 20 (September 1989):38.

44. Courtland C. Lee, "Adolescent Development," in Mincy, ed., *Nurturing Young Black Males,* 35.

45. Spencer Holland, "Positive Role Models for Primary-Grade Black Inner-City Males," *Equity and Excellence* 25 (1992):40.

46. Ibid.

47. Na'im Akbar, "Young, Black, Male, and Trapped," *Washington Post,* September 24, 1989.

48. Holland, "Positive Role Models," 41.

49. Ivory L. Toldson and Alfred B. Pasteur, "The Black Male Mystique: At Once Admired and Feared—an Exposition of What It Means to Be Black and Male in America," *Journal of African-American Male Studies* 1(2) (1994):76.

50. Ibid.

51. Quoted in Charles Whitaker, "Do Black Males Need Special Schools?" *Ebony* (March 1991):20.

52. Holland, "Positive Role Models," 42.

53. Quoted in Dent, "Survival Lessons," 90.

54. Wilder, "Straight Talk on Black Families," 99.

55. Holland, "Positive Role Models," 40.

56. Moynihan, "The Negro Family," 88. See also Lisa Hsiao, "Project 100,000," *Vietnam Generation* 2 (1990).

57. Christine J. Faltz and Donald O. Leake, "The All-Black School: Inherently Unequal or a Culture-Based Alternative," in Mwalimu J. Shujaa, ed., *Beyond Desegregation: The Politics of Quality in African American Schooling* (Thousand Oaks, Calif.: Corwin Press, 1996), 245.

58. Ibid.

59. Whitaker, "Do Black Males Need Special Schools?" 18.

60. Quoted in ibid., 17.

61. Julie A. Miller, "Bush Endorses Civil-Rights Revisions to Permit Academies for Black Males," *Education Week,* September 11, 1991, 24.

62. Rosemary L. Bray, "Are Black Male Schools the Answer?" *Emerge* (October 1991):50.

63. *Brown* v. *Board of Education of Topeka,* 347 U.S. 483 (1954). For legal arguments supporting all black male schools or all black schools, see Pamela J. Smith, "All-Male Black Schools and the Equal Protection Clause: A Step Forward Toward Education," *Tulane Law Review* 66 (1992): 2003–2055; Christopher Steskal, "Creating Space for Racial Difference: The Case for African-American Schools," *Harvard Civil Rights–Civil Liberties Law Review* 27 (1992):187–218; and Sonia R. Jarvis, "Brown and the Afrocentric Curriculum," *Yale Law Journal* 101(6) (1992):1285–1304. For an argument delineating the legal problems with these schools, see Kevin D. Brown, "The Dilemma of Legal Discourse for Public Educational Responses to the 'Crisis' Facing African-American Males," *Capital University Law Review* 23(1) (1994):63–130.

64. *Garrett* v. *Board of Education,* 775 F. Supp. 1004, 1006 (E.D. Mich. 1991), 125.

65. "Detroit's African-Centered Academics: Disarm Skeptics, Empower Boys," *Black Issues in Higher Education* 18 (February 1994):18–21.

66. Whitaker, "Do Black Males Need Special Schools?" 18.

67. Sam Roberts, "Separate Schools for Male Blacks Igniting Debate," *New York Times,* November 12, 1990.

68. Cynthia Hudley, "Assessing the Impact of Separate Schooling for African American Male Adolescents," *Journal of Early Adolescence* (December 12, 1995), http:/www2.elibrary.com. January 13, 1996.

69. Valora Washington and Joanna Newman, "Setting Our Own Agenda: Exploring the Meaning of Gender Disparities Among Blacks in Higher Education," *Journal of Negro Education* 60(1) (1991):20.

70. Andrew Hacker, *Two Nations: Black and White, Separate, Hostile, Unequal* (New York: Scribner's, 1992), 177.

71. Myra Sadker and David Sadker, *Failing at Fairness: How America's Schools Cheat Girls* (New York: Scribner's, 1994), 197.

72. Ibid., 50.

73. Jacqueline Jordan Irvine, "Teacher-Student Interactions: Effects of Student, Sex, and Grade Level," *Journal of Educational Psychology* 78(1) (1986):18.

74. U.S. Department of Education, *Digest of Education Statistics, 1992* (Washington, D.C.: U.S. Department of Education, 1992).

75. William P. O'Hare, Kevin M. Pollard, Taynia L. Mann, and Mary M. Kent, "African Americans in the 1990s," *Population Bulletin* 46 (July 1991): 20.

76. Washington and Newman, "Setting Our Own Agenda," 19.

77. Joseph R. Meisenheimer II, "Black College Graduates in the Labor Market," *Monthly Labor Review* 113 (November 1990):19–20.

78. U.S. Bureau of the Census, *Total Money Earnings in 1995 of Persons 25 Years Old and Over, by Educational Attainment, Sex, and Race,* Internet release, June 26, 1997.

79. Weatherspoon, "African American Males," n. 333.

80. Joel Dreyfuss, "Roundtable: White Men on Black Power," *Essence* (November 1992):66.

81. Hacker, *Two Nations,* 115. See also Christopher Jencks, *Rethinking Social Policy: Race, Poverty, and the Underclass* (Cambridge, Mass.: Harvard University Press, 1992), 36–49.

82. Oliver, "Black Males and Social Problems," 38.

83. Derrick Bell, "The Effects of Affirmative Action on Male-Female Relationships Among African Americans," *Sex Roles* 21 (1989):14.

84. Weatherspoon, "African American Males," 85.

85. Karen Fullbright, "The Myth of the Double-Advantage: Black Female Managers," *Review of Black Political Economy* 14(2–3) (Fall–Winter 1986):33–45.

86. Natalie J. Sokoloff, *Black Women and White Women in the Professions: Occupational Segregation by Race and Gender, 1960–1980* (New York: Routledge, 1992), 46.

87. David Cotter et al., "Occupational Gender Segregation and the Earnings Gap: Changes in the 1980s," *Social Science Research* 24(4) (1995): 450.

88. Curlew O. Thomas and Barbara B. Thomas, "Occupational Segregation and Isolation Between Black Men and Black Women, 1970–1988," *Free Inquiry in Creative Sociology* 21(2) (1993):215.

89. Carrell Peterson Horton and Jessie Carney Smith, eds., *Statistical Record of Black America* (Detroit: Gale Research, 1990), 132.

90. Mary-Christine Phillip, "Despite Gains, Sexism and Racism Present Unique Hurdle for Black Women in Academia," *Black Issues in Higher Education,* March 11, 1993, 12.

91. Bette Woody, "Black Women in the Emerging Services Economy," *Sex Roles* 21 (1989):49.

92. Meisenheimer, "Black College Graduates."

93. Nadja J. Zalokar, *The Economic Status of Black Women: An Exploratory Investigation,* U.S. Commission on Civil Rights Staff Report (Washington, D.C.: GPO, 1990); Woody, "Black Women in the Emerging Services Economy"; and Julianne Malveaux and Phyllis Wallace, "Minority Women in the Workplace," in Karen Shallcross Koziara, Michael H. Moskow, and Lucretia Dewey Tannereds, eds., *Working Women: Past, Present, Future* (Washington, D.C.: Bureau of National Affairs, 1987), 265–298.

94. Sokoloff, *Black Women and White Women,* 121.

95. Julianne Malveaux, "The Economic Interests of Black and White Women: Are They Similar?" *Review of Black Political Economy* 14 (Summer 1985):16.

96. Delores P Aldridge, "African-American Women in the Economic Marketplace: A Continuing Struggle," *Journal of Black Studies* 20 (December 1985):153.

97. William Julius Wilson, *The Truly Disadvantaged: The Inner City, the Underclass, and Public Policy* (Chicago: University of Chicago Press, 1987), 145.

98. William Darity Jr. and Samuel Myers Jr., "Racial Earnings Inequality into the 21st Century," in Janet Dewart, ed., *The State of Black America 1992* (New York: Urban League, 1992), 138.

99. Shepard Paul, "30 Years Late: King's Dream of Colorblind Society Still Unrealized," *Times and Democrat* (Orangeburg, S.C.), April 5, 1998.

100. Sylvia Ann Hewlett and Cornel West, "A Parents' Bill of Rights Would End a 30-Year War," *New York Times*, April 12, 1998.

101. Ibid.

102. Ibid.

103. Hacker, *Two Nations,* 95.

104. Robert D. Mare and Christopher Winship, "Socioeconomic Change and the Decline of Marriage for Blacks and Whites," in Christopher Jencks and Paul E. Peterson, eds., *The Urban Underclass* (Washington, D.C.: Brookings Institution, 1991), 194.

105. Paula Ries and Anne J. Stone, eds., *The American Woman, 1992–93: A Status Report* (New York: Norton, 1992), 270–271.

106. Julianne Malveaux, "Comparable Worth and Its Impact on Black Women," *Review of Black Political Economy* 14 (Fall–Winter 1985–1986): 54.

107. U.S. Department of Justice, *Criminal Victimization in the United States, 1990* (Washington, D.C.: U.S. Department of Justice, 1992), 18.

108. Marc Mauer and Tracy Huling, *Young Black Americans and the Criminal Justice System: Five Years Later* (Washington, D.C.: Sentencing Project, 1995).

109. Ron Daniels, "The Million Man March: From Patriarch to Partnership," in Haki R. Madhubuti and Maulana Karenga, eds., *Million Man March/Day of Absence: A Commemorative Anthology* (Chicago: Third World Press, 1996), 108.

110. Reed Adolph Jr., "Triumph of the Tuskegee Will," *Village Voice,* October 21, 1995, 36.

111. Louis Farrakhan, "Saviours' Day address delivered at the International Amphitheater in Chicago," February 26, 1995, http://www.noi.org/finalcall/savs96_2.html. January 26, 1997.

112. Olando Patterson, "Why Whites and Blacks Seem so Divided: The Paradox of Integration," *New Republic* 6 (November 1995), http://www.enews.con/magazine/thr/archieve/1995/11/110695.4.html. January 26, 1997.

113. John Corry, "Presswatch: Loony Tunes," *American Spectator* (December 1995), http://www.amspec.org/archieves/95–12_toc.thml. January 26, 1997.

114. Peter Grier, "Motives of the Million Man Marchers: Some March as Role Models, Others to End the Cycle of Violence," *Christian Science Monitor,* October 16, 1995.

115. Robbie Morganfield, "Building the Million Man March/Christians Split on Supporting Farrakhan Event," *Houston Chronicle,* October 8, 1995.

116. Michael Eric Dyson, "Words Unsaid," *Christian Century,* November 22–29, 1995, 1100.

117. Louis Farrakhan, "Day of Atonement," in Madhubuti and Karenga, eds., *Million Man March,* 23.

Chapter 12

1. Paul Starr, "Civil Reconstruction: What to Do Without Affirmative Action," *American Prospect* 8 (1992):7–14; Jim Sleeper, *Liberal Racism* (New York: Viking, 1997).

2. Alexis de Tocqueville, *Democracy in America* (Garden City, N.Y.: Anchor Books, 1969), 270.

3. Arthur Zilversmit, *The First Emancipation* (Chicago: University of Chicago Press, 1967), 85–222; Ira Berlin, *Slaves Without Masters: The Free Negro in the Antebellum South* (New York: Pantheon Books, 1974), 10–35, 50–58; Philip S. Foner, *History of Black Americans: From Africa to the Emergence of the Cotton Kingdom* (Westport, Conn.: Greenwood Press, 1975), 345–387, 508–518.

4. Eric Foner, *Reconstruction: America's Unfinished Revolution, 1863–1877* (New York: Harper and Row, 1988), 153–175, 346–411.

5. Ibid., 412–459, 512–601.

6. *Civil Rights Cases,* 109 U.S. 3 (1883), 25.

7. Ibid.

8. *Plessy* v. *Ferguson,* 163 U.S. 537 (1896); Charles A. Lofgren, *The* Plessy *Case: A Legal-Historical Interpretation* (New York: Oxford University Press, 1987). The Court was entering an era when its rulings are usually characterized as overwhelmingly probusiness; but that was not the case here. Many businesses objected to the ways segregation laws denied them the freedom *not* to discriminate against blacks when they found that financially advantageous.

9. Rogers M. Smith, *Civic Ideals: Conflicting Visions of Citizenship in U.S. History* (New Haven: Yale University Press, 1997), 347–469.

10. Richard A. Epstein, *Forbidden Grounds: The Case Against Employment Discrimination Laws* (Cambridge, Mass.: Harvard University Press, 1992). Charles Murray and Richard Herrnstein, *The Bell Curve: Intelligence and Class Structure in American Life* (New York: Free Press, 1994), gave Epstein's program a pseudobiologistic foundation. They contend that affirmative action has meant that blacks, whom they believe are on average significantly lower in cognitive abilities than whites, are currently overrepresented in skilled professions in the United States and performing poorly, as black officeholders were said to do during Reconstruction.

11. This chapter focuses on the federal judiciary and modern liberalism in relation to civil rights for African Americans. But both in the 1860s and the 1960s, struggles for African American rights were intimately bound up

with struggles for women's rights, and my arguments are also pertinent to the judiciary's treatment of gender issues.

12. Much of what follows draws on Rogers M. Smith, "The Errors of Liberal Ways and Means: Problems of Equal Protection Remedies," *Journal of Political Philosophy* 1 (1993):185–212.

13. Nathan Glazer, *Affirmative Discrimination: Ethnic Inequality and Public Policy* (Cambridge, Mass.: Harvard University Press, 1975); Abigail Thernstrom, *Whose Votes Count? Affirmative Action and Minority Voting Rights* (Cambridge, Mass.: Harvard University Press, 1987); Thomas Sowell, *Civil Rights: Rhetoric or Reality?* (New York: William Morrow, 1984); Shelby Steele, *The Content of Our Character: A New Vision of Race in America* (New York: St. Martin's Press, 1996); Stephen Carter, *Reflections of an Affirmative Action Baby* (New York: Basic Books, 1991).

14. Starr, 9; Theda Skocpol, "Sustainable Social Policy: Fighting Poverty Without Poverty Programs," *American Prospect* 2 (1990):67.

15. Thernstrom, 242–244.

16. Ibid. Former Great Society advocate Theodore H. White put the argument more pungently in his best-selling *America in Search of Itself: The Making of the President, 1956–1980* (New York: Warner Books, 1982), 101, 129, 136. White decried the influence on the judiciary and other officials of the idea of group entitlements, which he termed "a monster whose shadow hangs over all American politics today." It "led to the definition of groups, by age and sex, by color and race . . . splintering the country instead of opening it" and creating "a nation of dependents."

17. *Richmond* v. *Croson,* 488 U.S. 469 (1989). See also *Adarand Constructors Inc.* v. *Pena,* 115 S.Ct. 2097 (1995).

18. *Richmond* v. *Croson,* 527.

19. Michael Walzer, *Spheres of Justice: A Defense of Pluralism and Equality* (New York: Basic Books, 1983), 148–154.

20. Harold Cruse, *Plural but Equal* (New York: William Morrow, 1987), 378–382; Gerald D. Jaynes and Robin M. Williams, eds., *A Common Destiny: Blacks and American Society* (Washington, D.C.: National Academy Press, 1989), 184–186.

21. The legitimacy granted to black nationalist Louis Farrakhan by left black leaders such as Jesse Jackson, conservatives such as Clarence Thomas, and the media underlines this point. Farrakhan's potential for racial and ethnic divisiveness is indisputable.

22. Robert H. Bork, *The Tempting of America: The Political Seduction of the Law* (New York: Free Press, 1990).

23. For example, in dissenting from the Court's invalidation of a Louisiana requirement of "balanced" treatment for "Creation Science," *Edwards* v. *Aguillard,* 482 U.S. 578 (1987), Scalia scolds that striking down "a law

approved by the democratically elected representatives of the people is no minor matter."

24. William J. Wilson, "Race-Neutral Programs and the Democratic Coalition," *American Prospect* 1 (1990):81.

25. Skocpol, 67; Starr, 14.

26. Michael Walzer, "Philosophy and Democracy," *Political Theory* 9 (1981):395.

27. But see Philip Klinkner, "Dwarfing the Political Capacity of the People? The Relationship Between Judicial Activism and Voter Turnout, 1840–1988," *Polity* 25 (1993):633–646, arguing that periods of high judicial activism tend to be periods of lower voter turnout.

28. See, e.g., R. Shep Melnick, *Regulation and the Courts: The Case of the Clean Air Act* (Washington, D.C.: Brookings Institution, 1983); Thernstrom; and Jeremy Rabkin, *Judicial Compulsions: How Public Law Distorts Public Policy* (New York: Basic Books, 1989).

29. Rabkin, xii, 6.

30. Paul Brest, "Foreword: In Defense of the Antidiscrimination Principle," *Harvard Law Review* 90 (1976):6–7, 48.

31. Laurence H. Tribe, *American Constitutional Law,* 2d ed. (Minneola, N.Y.: Foundation Press, 1988), 1515.

32. Ronald Dworkin, *Taking Rights Seriously* (Cambridge, Mass.: Harvard University Press, 1978), 180. See, e.g., Kenneth L. Karst, "Foreword: Equal Citizenship Under the Fourteenth Amendment," *Harvard Law Review* 91 (1977):6; and John Hart Ely, *Democracy and Distrust: A Theory of Judicial Review* (Cambridge, Mass.: Harvard University Press, 1980), 82, for other seminal statements of this view.

33. Dworkin, 158–159. For further critical discussion of Dworkin's 1978 position, see Smith, "The Errors of Liberal Ways and Means."

34. Rogers M. Smith, *Liberalism and American Constitutional Law* (Cambridge, Mass.: Harvard University Press, 1990), 185–197.

35. Ronald Dworkin, "Foundations of Liberal Equality," in *The Tanner Lectures on Human Values* (Salt Lake City: University of Utah, 1990), 9:7, 22, 40–41, 66–71, 102–104. In these Tanner Lectures Dworkin retracts his earlier view that "neutrality among theories of the good" is "the heart of liberalism" in favor of a view holding that liberalism rests on a "single political vision" in which liberty, equality, and community are complementary features. This change represents progress in the general direction I endorse here; but Dworkin still claims to preserve neutrality on the good life as a "theorem" of liberalism in a way I find misleading, since his own account shows the neutrality to be sharply limited. He also is still committed to a principle of equal moral worth, although this principle is now more prop-

erly presented as recognition of the agency of all persons, without any strong assertion of absolutely equal ultimate worth.

36. For further discussion, see Smith, "The Errors of Liberal Ways and Means." Cf. Ruth Colker, "Anti-subordination Above All: Sex, Race, and Equal Protection," *New York University Law Review* 61 (1986):1005–1011, offering a similar diagnosis in support of a somewhat different approach.

37. Ultimately, this inquiry resolves into the question of whether there are individuals who lack requisite resources and opportunities. But for three reasons, it is appropriate in the making of that judgment to attend to the status of groups, races, or genders to which individuals are conventionally assigned and may well assign themselves. First, histories of public and private discrimination have often systematically denied meaningful possession of basic rights and opportunities to persons on the basis of these identities. It will therefore sometimes be more efficient, and may indeed be necessary, for governments to address those deprivations on a group basis. Even when the general pattern is undeniable, fine-grained individual assessments of the severity of such deprivations may be extraordinarily costly and cumbersome, if not impossible.

Second, decisions on whether individuals are in fact significantly deprived of the basic goods the system is seeking to promote often cannot be made without attention to their group affiliations. For those in gray areas, it may be their membership in a traditionally subjugated and still disadvantaged group that provides the decisive evidence showing that the obstacles they face in possessing basic goods are unduly severe.

Third, the communal flourishing of a particular group may be fundamental to the free lives its members wish to pursue. That flourishing may not involve any significant denial of any other basic rights or opportunities to anyone. In that case, concern that the individuals possess meaningful freedoms dictates concern that their group be able to pursue its collective aspirations. That collective capacity cannot be discerned without the group being the focus of analysis.

38. For a similar critical analysis of compensatory justice models, see Cass R. Sunstein, "The Limits of Compensatory Justice," in John W. Chapman, ed., *Nomos XXXIII: Compensatory Justice* (New York: New York University Press, 1991), 281–310.

39. These now-familiar difficulties of current approaches are elaborated in Alan D. Freeman, "Legitimizing Racial Discrimination Through Antidiscrimination Law: A Critical Review of Supreme Court Doctrine," *Minnesota Law Review* 62 (1978):1055–1057.

40. See, e.g., *Central Lumber Co.* v. *South Dakota,* 226 U.S. 157, 158 (1912), cited in Stanford Lyman, "The Race Question and Liberalism:

Casuistries in American Constitutional Law," *International Journal of Politics, Culture, and Society* 5 (1991):197–198, which defends affirmative action much as I do here.

41. Correspondingly, studies of the "success" of desegregation efforts often focus solely on how far "racial balance" is achieved. See, e.g., Robert E. England and David R. Morgan, *Desegregating Big City Schools: Strategies, Outcomes, and Impacts* (New York: Associated Faculty Press, 1986), 119–120.

42. Cited in Jennifer Hochschild, *The New American Dilemma: Liberal Democracy and School Desegregation* (New Haven: Yale University Press, 1984), 190. See also Jaynes and Williams, eds., 80–81, 358–361, 373–379. Rita E. Mahard and Robert L. Crain, "Research in Minority Achievement in Desegregated Schools," in Christine H. Russell and Willis D. Hawley, eds., *The Consequences of School Desegregation* (Philadelphia: Temple University Press, 1983), 122–123, argue that, although other factors are necessary, racial mixing does in itself enhance educational achievement because it signals opportunities to minorities that reinforce their sense of efficacy. Charles V. Willie, "The Intended and Unintended Benefits of School Desegregation," in Willy DeMarcell Smith and Eva Wells Chunn, eds., *Black Education: A Quest for Equity and Excellence* (New Brunswick: Transaction Books, 1989), 131–132, argues that whites, too, experience an educationally beneficial enhancement of their "social self-concept" in integrated settings.

43. Charles V. Willie, *School Desegregation Plans That Work* (Westport, Conn.: Greenwood Press, 1984), 199.

44. Ibid., 197; Clarence N. Stone, *Regime Politics: Governing Atlanta, 1946–1988* (Lawrence: University of Kansas Press, 1989), 103–106.

45. Michael Oakeshott, *On Human Conduct* (Oxford: Clarendon Press, 1975), 111–122, has explicitly decried the "enterprise association" view of the liberal state I am advancing in favor of a "civil association" position that sees the state simply as establishing organizing rules for the civil pursuit of self-chosen ends by members of the society. I think his belief that these rules can be somehow nonpurposive, nondeterminative of the types of ways of life citizens end up choosing is simply illusory. But his failing is shared by many versions of neo-Kantian liberalism, such as the works of Rawls and Dworkin in the 1970s.

46. John Locke, "An Essay Concerning the True Original, Extent, and End of Civil Government," in *Locke's Two Treatises of Government*, ed. Peter Laslett (New York: New American Library, 1965), 367, 409.

47. For other, in some ways contrasting, efforts to view the Constitution in terms of its "aspirations," the ideals or goals it is trying to realize, see Sotorios A. Barber, *On What the Constitution Means* (Baltimore: Johns Hop-

kins University Press, 1984); and Gary J. Jacobsohn, *The Supreme Court and the Decline of Constitutional Aspiration* (Totowa, N.J.: Rowman and Littlefield, 1986).

48. Tribe, 1515.

49. Catherine A. MacKinnon, *Feminism Unmodified: Discourses on Life and Law* (Cambridge, Mass.: Harvard University, 1987), 32–45.

50. Colker; Cass R. Sunstein, "The Anticaste Principle," *Michigan Law Review* 92 (1996):2410–2455. Iris Marion Young, *Justice and the Politics of Difference* (Princeton: Princeton University Press, 1990), argues for a "politics of difference" based on assistance to oppressed groups in a manner much like that proposed here. She defines oppression by specifying five forms of domination, not basic legal rights. Though plausible enough, her approach must still be further specified into such rights to be legally workable; and when she provides those specifications, Young advocates too rigid a system of representation according to ascribed group identities. Though broadly consonant with the analysis here, she thus unduly hinders recognition that governmental efforts to combat oppression are not forms of special privilege but rather inclusion of all in the same benefits the system promises to promote for all.

51. See, e.g., his opinions in *Wygant* v. *Jackson Board of Education,* 476 U.S. 267 (1986); *Johnson* v. *Transportation Agency,* 480 U.S. 616 (1987); and *Richmond* v. *Croson.*

52. Notable are William A. Galston, *Liberal Purposes: Goods, Virtues, and Diversity in the Liberal State* (New York: Cambridge University Press, 1991), collecting and expanding arguments to which I am especially indebted; Joseph Raz, *The Morality of Freedom* (Oxford: Clarendon Press, 1986); Will Kymlicka, *Liberalism, Community, and Culture* (Oxford: Clarendon Press, 1989); Thomas A. Spragens Jr., *Reason and Democracy* (Durham, N.C.: Duke University Press, 1990); and Stephen Macedo, *Liberal Virtues: Citizenship, Virtue, and Community in Liberal Constitutionalism* (Oxford: Clarendon Press, 1990).

53. Rogers M. Smith, "'One United People': Second-Class Female Citizenship and the American Quest for Community," *Yale Journal of Law and the Humanities* 1 (1989):290; Smith, *Liberalism and American Constitutional Law,* 217. The position thus requires judgments of what count as human capacities or capabilities for rational freedom, which are inevitably controversial. But every moral theory that gives any place to human rational agency at all makes similar demands. See, e.g., Dworkin; and cf. Amartya Sen, "Well-Being, Agency, and Freedom: The Dewey Lectures, 1984," *Journal of Philosophy* 82 (1985):186–245.

No proof that we must take these moral commitments as compelling or required by nature or some higher power can be provided; but there are powerful reasons for embracing them. Enhancement of our personal and collective capacities to understand ourselves and our environments and to govern our conduct provides some relief against the feelings of uncertainty and vulnerability that are endemic to the human condition. We also gain increased abilities to pursue whatever activities seem, on reflection, most conducive to our happiness and prosperity. Thus, these capacities serve as preconditions for the attainment of a wide variety of more specific goods. (The view of reflective freedom advanced here thus encompasses both the dimensions of "well-being freedom" and "agency freedom" delineated by Sen, 202–204.) This position also commits us to realizing, insofar as we can, a vision of human beings as capable of responsible moral judgments. Although disputable, that vision seems to me a compelling one that can sustain belief in human moral worth and dignity. See Smith, *Liberalism and American Constitutional Law,* ix, 205–207.

54. To use another of Sen's (208–209) distinctions, governments should thus be concerned to find arrangements that increase persons' "procedural control" over their ways of life as well as their "effective power" to achieve their ends. In large, complex modern societies, such powers often have to be provided by governmental institutions making many decisions in their constituents' interest but without their direct participation.

55. Ibid., 199, contends that "resource requirements" for basic "functionings," such as "being acceptably well informed," can "vary a great deal with the nature of the community in which one lives and with other contingent circumstances."

56. As these arguments imply, I do not believe that persuasive judgments of the minimal conditions necessary for persons to possess particular basic rights in a particular society can be simply derived from any general liberal constitutional theory of the sort I am sketching here.

57. Smith, *Liberalism and American Constitutional Law,* 237. Sunstein, "The Anticaste Principle," 2429, briefly suggests a similar account.

58. My argument can thus properly be described as inverting the dominant "antidiscrimination" approach to equal protection by placing primary reliance on the now-lesser fundamental rights strand of modern equal protection activism, instead of the currently featured suspect classifications strand. The suspect classifications strand says courts should scrutinize much more suspiciously laws that use a dangerous classification, such as race; the fundamental rights strand says courts should impose such demanding scrutiny on laws that infringe on basic constitutional liberties. Again, logically a fundamental rights approach centers ultimately on personal, not group, rights. As Freeman, 1061, notes, there is "no necessary relation between the fundamental right concept and racial discrimination, since the doctrine is principally concerned with the fundamentality" of rights, a "concern that is ostensibly neutral with respect to the race of the claimants." But as he also observes,

"Since racial minorities bear so disproportionately the burdens of economic class in the United States," such rights activism can be "in fact" a major initiative "on behalf of those minorities." And as previously suggested, use of group classifications such as race may frequently be necessary both to judge how far individuals are denied basic rights and to design programs that can be effective in providing to individuals resources needed to make their formal rights meaningful. The suspect classifications approach sets the legal presumption too heavily against affirmative action, against the use of group categories for these purposes.

Minimizing reliance on suspect classifications may still seem risky, but I do not think much really would be lost. Such classifications are supposed to be suspect and to trigger heightened scrutiny because they are rarely plausible reasons for limiting personal freedoms. As noted, these classifications have been thought to have the additional advantage of sparing judges the controversial task of defining which liberties are constitutionally most basic. But judges have had to do that anyway, often as strained and vulnerable readings of what "equality" requires. And as noted in the text, some attention to suspect classifications is still warranted to curb measures that signal state support for racial or gender bigotry but that do not directly invade any fundamental rights. Otherwise, however, the benefits promised by suspect classifications can be better attained by attention to whether they harm citizens' fundamental rights or assist them.

59. Mark Jaffe and Kenneth Kersch, "Guaranteeing a State Right to Quality Education: The Judicial-Political Dialogue in New Jersey," *Journal of Law and Education* 20 (1991):276.

60. I-mien Tsiang, *The Question of Expatriation in America Prior to 1907* (Baltimore: Johns Hopkins University Press, 1942).

61. Cf. Henry Shue, *Basic Rights: Subsistence, Affluence, and U.S. Foreign Policy* (Princeton: Princeton University Press, 1980).

62. Gordon Lafer, "The Politics of Job Training: Urban Poverty and the False Promise of JTPA," *Politics and Society* 22 (September 1994):349–388.

63. For example, in *San Antonio School District* v. *Rodriguez,* 411 U.S. 1 (1973), the Supreme Court upheld a system of financing public schools via local property taxes that was so unequal as to render poorer districts unable to meet what most persons in the state educational system regarded as minimally adequate educational standards. The Court's ruling reflects an unduly formalistic and unrealistic sense of what meaningful possession of this constitutional interest requires.

64. State courts have indicated that inequalities in educational resources are unacceptable when they leave some districts below levels necessary for a minimally adequate education, as defined by the preponderance of opinion among a state's educational authorities, taking national performance levels into account. Although the finding of such a preponderance may

seem improbable, disputes in these cases have rarely centered on whether the education provided in the poorest districts was actually "adequate." Few have claimed this. The debates have been over the extent and manner of increased funding for them (see A. Thomas Stubbs, "After *Rodriguez:* Recent Developments in School Finance Reform," *Tax Lawyer* 44 [1990]: 67–99). Similarly, even conservative policy analysts are willing to define income levels that place some full-time workers below the poverty line, making those jobs clearly inadequate.

65. *Palmer* v. *Thompson,* 403 U.S. 217 (1971).

66. Charles R. Lawrence III, "The Id, the Ego, and Equal Protection: Reckoning with Unconscious Racism," *Stanford Law Review* 39 (1987): 356, has similarly suggested that courts examine the symbolic message that legal classifications convey by looking at the "preponderance of the evidence" regarding a classification's "historical and social context" to determine if "a significant portion of the population thinks of the governmental action" in invidious racial (or gender) terms. I differ only in that I would have courts make these inquiries to decide whether a legal measure is imposing stigma that will encourage further harm to minority rights. Lawrence is looking for evidence of "unconscious," invidious racial motives.

67. Alexander M. Bickel, *The Least Dangerous Branch* (Indianapolis: Bobbs-Merrill, 1962).

68. *Abbott et al.* v. *Burke,* 1990 N.J. Lexis 64 (1990); *Rose and Blandford* v. *Council for Better Education,* 1989 Ky. Lexis 55 (1989); *Helena Elementary School District* v. *State,* 769 P.2d 684 (Mont. 1989); *Edgwood Independent School District* v. *Kirby,* 777 S.W.2d 3912 (Tex. 1989), discussed also in Stubbs.

69. *Spallone* v. *United States,* 58 L.W. 4103, 4108 (1990).

About the Editor and Contributors

Editor

Adolph Reed Jr. is professor of political science on the graduate faculty of the New School for Social Research. His most recent books are *W.E.B. Du Bois and American Political Thought: Fabianism and the Color Line* (Oxford University Press, 1997); *Stirrings in the Jug: Black American Politics in the Post-Segregation Era* (University of Minnesota Press, forthcoming); and *Class Notes* (New Press, forthcoming). He serves on the Interim National Council of the Labor Party and the boards of the Public Citizen and the Public Health Institute.

Contributors

Mimi Abramovitz is professor of social work, Hunter College School of Social Work and the Graduate Center, City University of New York. She is author of *Regulating the Lives of Women: Social Welfare Policy from Colonial Times to the Present* (South End Press, 2d rev. ed., 1996); and *Under Attack, Fighting Back: Women and Welfare in the United States* (Monthly Review Press, 1996). She is current researching a book on the history of activism of poor and working-class women in the twentieth-century United States, and she is working on a social welfare policy textbook. She is actively involved in the fight against welfare reform.

Larry Bennett teaches in the Political Science Department at DePaul University. He is the author of *Neighborhood Politics: Chicago and Sheffield* (Garland, 1997). Currently, he is working on a study of sports stadium projects and their neighborhood impacts.

Michael K. Brown is professor in the Board of Study in Politics at the University of California–Santa Cruz. He is a contributor to and the editor of *Remaking the Welfare State: Retrenchment and Social Policy in America and Europe* (Temple University Press, 1988), and author of *Race, Money, and the American Welfare State* (Cornell University Press, 1999).

Micaela di Leonardo has written *The Varieties of Ethnic Experience* (Cornell University Press); and *Exotics at Home: Anthropologies, Others, American Modernity* (University of Chicago Press). She is editor of *Gender at the Crossroads of Knowledge* (University of California Press); and coeditor of *The Gender/Sexuality Reader* (Routledge). She teaches anthropology and women's studies at Northwestern University.

Dennis R. Judd is professor in the Department of Political Science, University of Missouri–St. Louis. He is editor of the *Urban Affairs Review* and of the Globalization and Community book series for the University of Minnesota Press. He has published extensively about urban politics, urban redevelopment, and related subjects and is coauthor, most recently, of *City Politics* (Addison-Wesley, 2d ed., 1998); *The Politics of Urban America* (Allyn and Bacon, 2d ed., 1998); and *Places to Play: The Remaking of Cities for Tourists* (Yale University Press, forthcoming).

Philip A. Klinkner is associate professor of government and director of the Arthur Levitt Public Affairs Center at Hamilton College. He is the coauthor, with Rogers Smith, of *The Unsteady March: The Rise and Decline of America's Commitment to Racial Equality* (University of Chicago Press).

Willie M. Legette teaches political science at South Carolina State University. His current research is on black political development in South Carolina since World War II.

Preston H. Smith is an associate professor of politics at Mount Holyoke College, where he teaches black politics, African American studies, and urban political economy. He writes on black self-help ideology, black interest-group organizations, community development, and housing policies. He was a Ford Foundation Postdoctoral Fellow for Minorities in 1995, and he serves on the board of the Housing Discrimination Project and works with community groups in Holyoke and Springfield, Massachusetts. He is currently working on a book tentatively titled *The Quest for Racial Democracy.*

Rogers M. Smith is professor of political science at Yale University, where he is codirector of the Center for the Study of Race, Inequality, and Politics. He is the author of *Liberalism and American Constitutional Law* (Harvard University Press, 1985); and *Civic Ideals: Conflicting Visions of Citizenship in U.S. History* (Yale University Press, 1997), among other works.

Stephen Steinberg is a professor in the Department of Urban Studies at Queens College and the Ph.D. Program in Sociology at the Graduate School of the City University of New York. His recent book *Turning Back: The Retreat from Racial Justice in American Thought and Policy* (Beacon Press) received the Oliver Cromwell Cox Award for Distinguished Anti-Racist Scholarship. His other books include *The Ethnic Myth: Race, Ethnicity, and Class* *in America* (Beacon Press). In addition to his scholarly publications, he has written in *The Nation, Reconstruction,* and *New Politics.*

Brett Williams teaches anthropology and American studies at American University. For the last twenty-one years, she has lived and worked in Washington, D.C., where she has been active in a number of community organizations concerned with such issues as gentrification and displacement, the state of the public schools, the gutting of public housing, and environmental justice. She has also participated in many public anthropology programs, producing museum exhibits, films, festivals, community plays, and seminars on topics ranging from urban fishing, gardening, and soccer, to teenage parenting. She is the author of a book on the labor hero John Henry and of *Upscaling Downtown: Stalled Gentrification in Washington, D.C.* (Cornell University Press, 1988), as well as many articles on migrant farm labor, urban poverty, and the culture of debt. She is currently completing a book on debt and beginning a project on the history of Washington.

Alex Willingham teaches in the Political Science Department at Williams College. He has been active in research, analysis, and trial testimony on the application of the Voting Rights Act in a range of lawsuits, including the *Shaw* v. *Reno* case.

Ann Withorn is professor of social policy at the College of Public and Community Service, University of Massachusetts–Boston. She is an activist and writer about welfare rights, feminist issues, and left issues and is coeditor, with Diane Dujon, of *For Crying Out Loud: Women's Poverty in the United States* (South End Press); and author of *Serving the People: Social Services and Social Change* (Columbia University Press).

Index